Beethoven

String Quartets
The Galitzin Quartets
Op. 127, Op. 132 and Op. 130

Their Creation, Origins and Reception History
Incorporating
Contextual Accounts of Beethoven and His Contemporaries

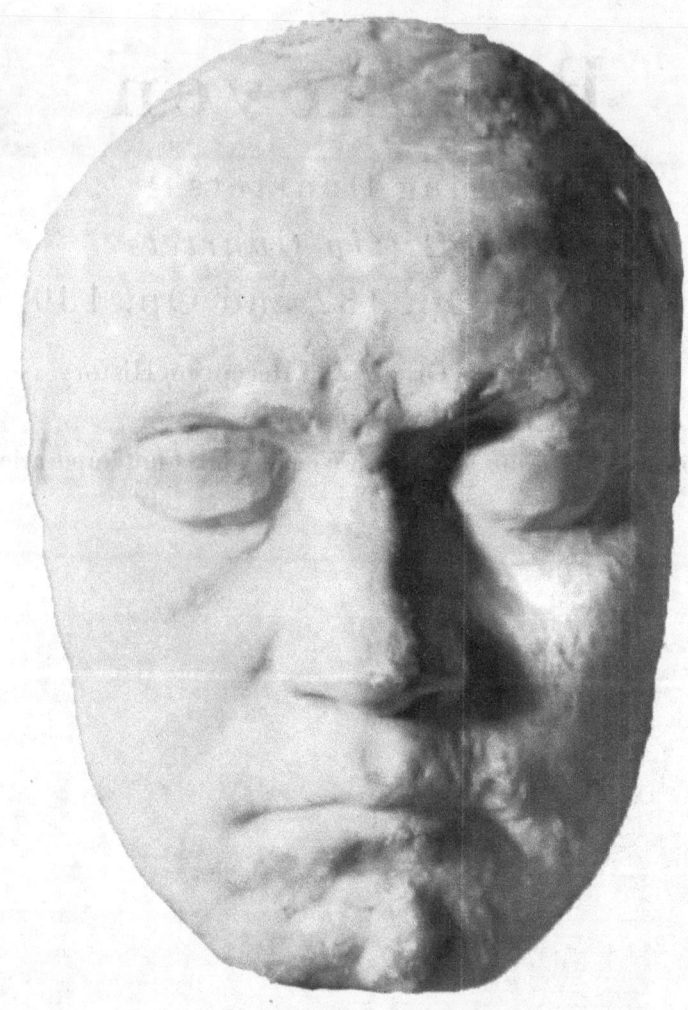

BEETHOVEN
As depicted by the life mask taken by Franz Klein in 1812
(derived from a copy in the author's possession)

BEETHOVEN
STRING QUARTETS
THE GALITZIN QUARTETS
OP. 127, OP. 132, AND OP. 130

THEIR CREATION ORIGINS AND RECEPTION HISTORY

Incorporating contextual accounts of
Beethoven and his contemporaries

Terence M. Russell

Jelly Bean Books

The right of Terence Russell to be identified as the
Author of the Work has been asserted by him in accordance
with the Copyright, Designs and Patents Act 1988.

Copyright © Terence M. Russell 2022

Published by
Jelly Bean Books
136 Newport Road
Cardiff
CF24 1DJ

ISBN: 978-1-915439-14-7

www.candyjarbooks.co.uk

All rights reserved.
No part of this publication may be reproduced, stored in a
retrieval system, or transmitted at any time or by any means,
electronic, mechanical, photocopying, recording or otherwise
without the prior permission of the copyright holder. This book is
sold subject to the condition that it shall not by way of trade or
otherwise be circulated without the publisher's prior consent in any
form of binding or cover other than that in which it is published.

CONTENTS

Author's Note	I
Introduction	IX
Editorial Principles	XIX
Beethoven's Financial Transactions	XXI
Beethoven String Quartets	
The Galitzin Quartets	1
String Quartet in E-flat major, Op. 127	65
String Quartet in A minor, Op. 132	154
String Quartet in B-flat major, Op. 130	224
Bibliography	290
Index	324
About the Author	328

AUTHOR'S NOTE

I have cherished the idea of making a study of the life and work of Beethoven for many years. This statement requires a few words of personal reflection. I first encountered Beethoven in my early piano lessons — Minuet in G major, WoO 10, No. 2. At the same time I became acquainted with his piano pupil Carl Czerny — *Book One, Piano Studies*. My heart sank when I discovered the rear cover advertised a further *99* books in the same series — scales, arpeggios studies for the left hand, studies for the right hand — all the way to his Op. 824! By coincidence, my *Czerny Book One* was edited by Alec Rowley — who had the same surname as my music teacher. In my childish innocence, I often wondered why *he himself* never appeared to give me a lesson!

In my teenage years I found myself drawn ever closer to Beethoven's music in the manner that ferromagnetic materials are ineluctably held captive in the sway of a magnetic field. The impulse to which I yielded is well described in words the conductor Bruno Walter gave in one of his rare public addresses: 'It is my belief that young people at that age are more easily impressed by what is heroic and grandiose; that they more easily understand works of art in which passionate feelings are violently uttered in raised accents, and that the lighter sounds of cheerfulness are less impressive to them.' I do indeed recall the stirring effect made on me on first hearing the Overture *Egmont*, the unfolding drama of the Fifth Symphony and the declamatory opening chords of the *Emperor* Piano Concerto.

I resolved to read everything I could about Beethoven, starting with Marion Scott's pioneering English-language study of the composer in the *Master Musicians series*. My father took out a subscription for me for *The Gramophone* magazine, enabling me to read reviews of the new 'LP' recordings – none of which though I could afford! The LP was then – 1950s – beginning to supplant the 78 rpm shellac records, stacks of which could be purchased for as little as six pence each in 'old' money. At this same time I had the privilege of hearing Beethoven's music performed by the *Hallé Orchestra* under the baton of Sir John Barbirolli, and experienced the *Carl Rosa Opera Company* perform the composer's only opera *Fidelio*, I borrowed the piano-reduction score from the City Library to become better acquainted with this moving work – only to find the score's fists full of notes were well beyond my capabilities. Nonetheless, since then *Fidelio's* every note has been woven into my DNA. I also recall the period when the *London Promenade Concerts* were designated 'Friday night is Beethoven night'.

Through these influences I resolved to visit Vienna to see where Beethoven had lived and worked. But how? The support for such travel was beyond the means of my family. Fortunately in my final year at school (1959) an opportunity presented itself. I saw a poster that stated *WUS – World University Service* – required volunteers to work in the Austrian town of Linz to help relocate refugees who were living there in improvised wooden shacks – displaced and dispossessed victims of the Second World War. To those participating all expenses would be paid together with free accommodation – in one of the crumbling wooden shacks! From Linz, I planned to make my way to Vienna.

I applied to *WUS* and, despite being a mere school-leaver, I was accepted. The *WUS* authorities doubtless reasoned the building-trade skills I had acquired during my secondary education in the building department of a technical school would be useful. This proved to be the case. At the refugee camp I dug trenches and was allowed to assist as a bricklayer. All about me were wide-eyed children eager to help but mostly getting in the way. I recall one afternoon when a reporter from *The Observer* newspaper paid a visit to our construction site to gather material for an article he was writing on European post-war recovery – he generously admired my trenches and brickwork!

Of lasting significance was another visit, this time from a Belgian priest. He took a group of us to the nearby *Mauthausen* Concentration Camp, recently opened as a silent and solemn memorial to those who had perished there. It was a deeply moving experience. Years later I learned of the views of the ardent Beethovenian Sir Michael Tippet. After the horrors of the *Holocaust*, he posed the question for mankind: 'What price Beethoven now?' He posited: 'Could we any longer find solace in Beethoven's setting of Schiller's *Ode to Joy* and its utopian vision – "Be embraced you Millions"?'

My refugee contribution duly came to end and Vienna beckoned. On arrival there I found scenes reminiscent of *The Third Man* and *Harry Lime*. I recall, for example, encountering cobblestones piled high in the streets waiting to be replaced after having been disturbed by the heavy armoured vehicles that had so recently passed over them. But Vienna was welcoming. I visited the houses where Beethoven had lived and worked and paused outside others associated with him that were identified by a commemorative plaque and the Austrian flag. A particularly memorable occasion was attending a recital in the great salon within the palace of Beethoven's noble patron Prince Lobkowitz – the very one where the *Eroica* Symphony had been premiered. Ultimately, my steps led me to the composer's first resting place in the *Währinger Ortsfriedhof.* I paid silent homage to the great man and, as I did so, discovered nearby the resting place of Franz Schubert to whom Beethoven was an endless source of admiration and inspiration.

I felt a youthful impulse to discover yet more about Beethoven and his music. But absorption in musicology would have to take second place. My chosen career beckoned in the guise of architecture – 'the mother of the arts' and 'the handmaid of society'. There was room though for Beethoven's music and from that time on it has been my constant companion through attendance at recitals, in concerts and music-making in the home. And at home a reproduction of Franz Kline's 1812 study of the composer has greeted me each day for more than half a century.

On my retirement from a career in architectural practice, research and university teaching, the opportunity finally presented itself for me to devote time to researching Beethoven musicology. Having attained my eightieth year also emboldened me to make progress with my good intentions!

With these autobiographical remarks outlined I will say a few remarks about my working method – see also the comments made in *Editorial Principles*.

As a member of staff of The University of Edinburgh, I had the good fortune to have access to the *Reid Music Library*, formed from a nucleus of books bequeathed by General John Reid and augmented over the years by such custodians as Sir Donald Francis Tovey, sometime *Reid Professor of Music* and renowned Beethoven scholar. Over a period of three years, I made a survey of the many works in the Reid collection. I consulted each item in turn making records on paper slips — many hundreds — that I deemed to be relevant for my researches. I confined my searches to book-publications, as reflected in my accompanying bibliography. All of this was quite some years ago, the cut-off date for my researches being 2007. Beyond this date I have not surveyed any further works. I am mindful though that Beethoven musicology and related publication continue to be a major field of endeavour in the manner of the proverbial 'ever rolling stream'.

In the intervening years since completing my archival researches, personal tribulations associated with family illness and bereavement slowed my progress in giving expression to my projected intentions. Latterly, however, with renewed energy, and more time at my disposal, I have been able to make progress. My studies take the form of a set of monographs. These trace the creation origins and reception history of each of Beethoven's piano sonatas and string quartets. The resulting texts also incorporate contextual accounts of Beethoven and his contemporaries. Also included in my musicological surveys are two related Beethoven anthologies. The set of monographs in question, identified by short title, are:

Beethoven: An anthology of selected writings.
Beethoven: The piano sonatas: An anthology of selected writings.

The Piano Sonatas:
Op. 2–Op. 28
Op. 31–Op. 81A
Op. 90–Op. 111

The String Quartets:
Op. 18, Nos. 1–6
Op. 59, Nos. 1–3 (Razumovsky); Op. 74 (The Harp);
Op. 95 (Quartetto Serioso)
Op. 127, Op. 132 and Op. 130 (Galitzin)
Op. 131, Op. 135; Grosse Fuge, Op. 133 and Op. 134 (Fugue transcription)

I provide further information about these studies in the introduction to each individual monograph. Suffice it for me to state here the basic premise upon which my work is founded. I believe it is rewarding, concerning the life of a great artist, to find connections between who he *was* and what he *did*; in Martin Cooper's words 'between his personality, as expressed on the one hand in human relationships, and on the other in artistic creation'. (*Beethoven, The Last Decade*) That is not to say I consider it essential to the enjoyment of Beethoven's music to know this or that fact about it. His music can be enjoyed, as millions do, with — in Robert Simpson's apt phrase —'an innocent ear', for what it is and how it reaches out to us in purely musical terms without any prejudging of its merits based upon extra-musicological facts.

I must make a further point. I am mindful that a scholar who ventures into a field of study that is not rightly his may be regarded with some suspicion. In this regard I can but ask the reader to place his or her trust in me in the following way. I have attempted to bring to my work the care which publishers and their desk editors have required of me in my book writings relating to architecture — listed elsewhere.

As inferred, it is now more than sixty years since I paid homage to Beethoven in Vienna's *Währinger Ortsfriedhof* and my warmth of feeling towards the composer and his music have grown with the passing of the years. My studies are not intended to be propaedeutic — that would be pretentious. However, if in sharing with others what I have to say contributes to their knowledge and understanding of the composer, and thereby increases their own feelings towards him and his works, my own pleasure in bringing my work to completion will be all the more enhanced.

It is perhaps fitting that my studies should appear in Beethoven's 250th Anniversary Year — I must confess more by chance than design!

When Beethoven arrived in Vienna, he was unknown. He was armed though with a note of encouragement from his youthful friend and benefactor Count Ferdinand Waldstein. It contained the often-quoted words: 'Receive Mozart's spirit from Haydn's hands.' Some forty years later Beethoven passed away in the House of the black-robed Spaniards at 200 *Alservorstädter*, the *Glacis* where he had lived since the autumn of 1825. Soldiers had to be called to secure the doors to the inner courtyard of the house from the pressure of onlookers. His body was blessed in the *Alservorsttädt Parish Church*, schools were closed and perhaps as many as 10,000 people formed a funeral procession — an honour ordinarily reserved for monarchs. The *Marcia Funebre* from the composer's Op. 26 Piano Sonata was performed at the funeral ceremony. Franz Grillparzer read the funeral oration. Franz Schubert, who, as remarked in life so admired Beethoven, was one of the pallbearers. The composer's mortal remains were lowered into a simple vault. Beethoven now belonged to history.

Dr Terence M. Russell
Edinburgh 2020

INTRODUCTION

The subjects of this study are the creation origins and reception history of Beethoven's string quartets. It is one of four that broadly correspond with the generally accepted periods into which the composer's compositions are held to conform and which have been described as 'early', 'middle', and 'late' and their counterparts, 'imitative', 'heroic' and 'introspective'. In our first study the string quartets Op. 18, Nos. 1–6 are considered alongside the transcription for string quartet of the Piano Sonata in E major, Op. 14. In the second part are the string quartets Op. 59, Nos. 1–3 (*Razumowsky*), Op. 74 in E-flat major, (*The Harp*) and Op. 95 in F minor (*Quartetto serioso*). In the third part are the string quartets Op. 127, Op. 132, and Op. 130 – the Galitzin Quartets. The fourth part of our study concludes with the string quartets Op. 131, Op. 135 and the *Great Fugue*, Op. 133 together with Beethoven's four-hand keyboard transcription Op. 134.

The collection of writings presented here derives from the string quartet compositions of Beethoven's so-called third period. They take the form of extended essays that may serve the reader as a source of reference — in the manner of programme notes to a recital. Accordingly, the remarks relating to each string quartet are 'free standing' and can be read independently. That said they are also interlinked by the events unfolding in the composer's life. An attempt has been made, therefore, to interrelate the individual essays so that they may be read as a continuous narrative — in typical book fashion. A summary outline of this narrative is provided in the Index for each individual string quartet. Thereby, the reader is provided not only with a guide to the contents discussed in each quartet-text but also has an over-arching time-line of the principal events bearing on Beethoven's life and work. By way of an introduction to the individual essays in this part of our survey, we provide the following summary-outline bearing upon the compositions to which we make reference.

Beethoven returned to the genre of writing for the string quartet in the spring of 1824. His last essay in the medium had been the String Quartet, Op. 95 that was composed over the period 1810–11 but which was not premiered until 1814. In his remaining years Beethoven devoted his energies exclusively to writing string quartets. They stand alone, distant from the *Choral* Symphony and the *Missa Solemnis*. His renewed interest in the medium may be seen in response to the inner promptings of his developing and changing artistic and emotional outlook. Beethoven, however, was no 'desk' composer. Throughout his career he had composed in response to an external stimulus. Concerning the so-called 'late' quartets we see him creatively stirred primarily by a commission from Prince Galitzin of St.

Petersburg for three string quartets. Additionally, circumstances in Vienna in the 1820s favoured the string quartet in public music-making with the advent of the professional string quartet. In this context the return to Vienna of Beethoven's long-term friend the violinist Ignaz Schuppanzigh – and the establishment of the Quartet bearing his name – provided an added incentive to Beethoven to compose quartets. Moreover, Beethoven always composed with performance in mind, even in the case of his most challenging compositions. Last, and by no means least, in an era when composers did not receive performance royalties, Beethoven needed the income for which his compositions were an essential source.

Beethoven worked solely on string-quartet composition from the spring of 1824 until the end of end of 1826 when mortal illness compelled him to lay down his pen. Five quartets were the outcome as identified in our opening remarks. Their numbering, in relation to their chronological sequence, requires a few words of explanation. The Quartets in E-flat major, Op. 127, A minor, Op. 132 and B-flat major, Op. 130 form a group – a triptych – and were composed in response to a commission from the Russian Prince Galitzin – from which they derive their soubriquet *The Russian Quartets*.

The Quartet in E-flat major, Op. 127, was largely composed during the second half of 1824, and was completed around February the following year. From then to the midsummer of 1825 Beethoven composed the A-minor Quartet, Op. 132. He worked on the first version of the Quartet in B-flat major, Op. 130 – including the *Grosse Fuge*, Op. 133 – completing it in November 1825. Composition of the C-sharp minor Quartet, Op. 131 was commenced towards the end of 1825 and was completed in the summer 1826. The string Quartet in F major, Op. 135 and the four-hand piano transcription of the Great Fugue, Op, 134 occupied Beethoven throughout the autumn of 1826 during which period he also wrote an alternative finale for the Quartet Op. 130.

Notwithstanding this extraordinary flow of compositions, Beethoven's was 'the unhappiest of mortals' — his own words. Not only was he experiencing ill health and the distress occasioned by his nephew's attempted suicide but he also felt neglected. We discern this from the recollections of the German playwright and musicologist Johann Friedrich Rochlitz. He relates a meeting with the composer in Vienna in the summer of 1822. He gives the following account. Beethoven lamented: 'You will hear nothing of me here.' He acknowledged his Opera *Fidelio* received occasional performance but as for his symphonies — 'They have no time for them — likewise the concertos'. As for the piano sonatas: 'They went out of fashion here long ago, and fashion here is everything.' It is a remarkable fact that only one of Beethoven's piano sonatas received public performance in his lifetime — the Piano Sonata in A-flat major, Op. 26.

Beethoven's return to the medium of the string quartet in the last years and months of his life has been described as testifying to the centrality of the medium to his musical and personal identity. Notwithstanding, as we have remarked, Beethoven composed in order to earn a living. In this context, Barry Cooper's cautionary words have relevance: '[The] romantic notion of the aging master turning his back on the world of public music in 1824 in order to devote himself to the string quartet as the loftiest and most esoteric genre of the day, without concern for immediate profit but purely for art's sake and perhaps for a small circle of admirers in an increasingly hostile world must be laid aside.' Early in his career Beethoven had composed his chamber music for wealthy patrons. By the 1820s this had changed. Publishers vied for his works. They agreed a flat fee with him for a composition and were then at liberty to publish the work without conferring additional royalties. For his part Beethoven new the value of his work and always struck a hard bargain.

In the late quartets, Beethoven progressively increases the number of movements creating a new formal conception quite unlike anything preceding it. The E-flat major Quartet retains the four-movement sonata form but thereafter the style of musical conception and the number of movements are increased. The A minor Quartet possesses five, the B-flat major Quartet six, and the C-sharp minor has seven movements. Only in the F major Quartet, Op. 135 does he elect to return to the four-movement design. Moreover, in this quartet he reverts to shorter and less discursive movements – a harbinger, perhaps, of new things to come and the onset of a 'fourth' period?

Discussing some of the characteristics of Beethoven's late works Maynard Solomon observes: '[Struggle] is sublimated into ecstasy, as in the *Arietta* of the Piano Sonata, Op. 111; chaos strives for lucid formation, as in the transition to the fugue of the *Hammerklavier* Sonata and in the opening of the finale of the Ninth Symphony; victorious conclusions are incessantly sought after and discovered, as in the *Grosse Fuge*, the Piano Sonata Op. 110, and the finale of the Quartet in C-sharp minor, Op. 131.' In support of his contention he quotes from the writings of that pillar of the English musical establishment Sir Charles Hubert Hastings Parry: 'Beethoven had by now found the accepted scheme of organisation which he himself had brought to perfection too constraining and restrictive to the impulse of his thought, and therefore endeavoured to find new types of form to revive sundry earlier types of organisation and combine them in various ways which departed from the essential principles upon which composers had been working for generations.'

Gestated within a few years — in some cases within only a few months — of each other, it is not surprising that the late quartets share thematic and other resemblances — for example a four-note configuration. For many authorities these imply the late quartets share an underlying unity — 'a unified corpus'. Others consider the five last quartets and the Great Fugue to be 'drenched in evocations of the human voice' that are meant to 'sing or to speak instantly to the heart' (Joseph Kerman). By way of illustration, we recall Beethoven's 'wordless recitative' at the beginning of the finale to the Ninth Symphony — where the cellos and bases recall themes heard in the previous movements. The implied meaning is then made evident when the baritone member of the vocal quartet proclaims: 'O friends, not these sounds; let us rather strike up something more seemly, more joyful.'

To audiences whose ears were tuned to the sounds of a Mozart or Haydn string quartet, Beethoven's new soundworld was perplexing. As one reviewer of his latest compositions complained: 'You could never know where you were with Beethoven.' That said, both Mozart and Haydn challenged their own audiences. Gerald Abraham remarks how Beethoven's 'inner ear' came to accept a degree of dissonance painful to most ears for more than half a century after his death. An entry in the contemporaneous *Allgemeine musikalische Zeitung* supports the foregoing. The *AmZ* gives an account of the first *Edinburgh Music Festival* — the precursor, by a century-and-a-half, of the present-day *Edinburgh International Festival*. Beethoven is initially compared with Haydn and Mozart. The reviewer acknowledges: '[The] admirable qualities [of] these three famous men are so utterly different in their style and manner.' He continues: 'The first appeared to be more distinguished because of his broad manner and knowledge of effect; the second because of his noble feeling and cultured expression.' Next it is Beethoven's turn: 'With an imagination less ordered and mature than Haydn's and Mozart's, Beethoven seems to posses as much fire and vigour as both.' The reviewer elaborates: 'There is a certain wildness and Herculean capturing of imagination that is characteristic of this excellent musician. It is his pleasure to wander about in the regions of darkness and magic and to make the heart shudder with sounds that appear to resound from the inhabitants of an undiscovered land and from whose borders no traveller returns!' Writing in the contemporary *Berliner Allgemeine musikalische Zeitung*, the reviewer maintained, more sedately, that Beethoven's most recent quartets required repeated hearings in order to be understood. 'Only after careful study of the score', he encouraged, 'will the unfamiliar harmonies seem like the streaks of the Milky Way'.

Critics of the day clearly found it difficult to come to terms with the late quartets' long movements, unorthodox forms, organic textures, cross-referencing themes — sometimes woven in complex variation form — and, as remarked, a new level of dissonance. If that were not enough, to cite Maynard Solomon once more, 'Beethoven ... provided puzzles, jokes, and challenges to his listeners, deflating expectations of easy comprehension with respect to parallels between music and the assignment of meaning in the imagination.'

Assimilation of the late quartets throughout the nineteenth century was slow and protracted. As remarked, neither Op.131 nor Op.135 were performed in Beethoven's lifetime and for several years the companion quartets received only a handful of performances in the composer's native Vienna. They were received more favourably in other musical centres, notably Berlin, Leipzig and Paris. *The Beethoven Quartet Society* was founded in London in 1845 with the express aim of 'honouring Beethoven'. Its founder was Thomas Alsager, a pioneering music critic to *The Times*. One of the aims of the Society was to encourage an understanding of Beethoven's quartets from a study of their scores. The Society has the distinction of being the first in England to perform the complete cycle of Beethoven's string quartets during the music season of 1845. In Zurich, in 1854, Richard Wagner organised and coached a rehearsal of the C-sharp minor Quartet and contributed analytical notes to the work. More generally, his Centennial Essay of 1870 is recognised for having nurtured a more positive attitude towards, and reception of, Beethoven's late chamber music. William Kinderman remarks: 'Beethoven's deafness, which was previously regarded as the handicap that explained the eccentricities of these works, was seen by Wagner as an enabling factor that had shielded Beethoven from the turmoil of the outer world and enhanced his ability to dwell in the inner-world of the imagination. For Wagner, Beethoven was a deaf "seer" who led the way to new artistic perspectives.

By the 1870s Beethoven was becoming deified. He was perceived as a near mythic figure, a revolutionary genius without equal and the embodiment of qualities of freedom, inspiration and creativity. His image was reproduced in painting and sculpture with a scowling countenance as if defying fate and adversity. Notwithstanding this celebrity, in 1885 the prominent Viennese music critic Theodore Helm had occasion to write: 'Still today, among all the creations of Beethoven [the late quartets] are the least understood and most in need of a psychological and musical commentary.'

He maintained: 'Unlike their predecessors, they were entirely individual, extremely personal, subjective, and wholly divorced from the outside world.' Harold Truscott summarizes the nineteenth century conception — or misconception — of the late quartets: '[They] were regarded reverently as a sort of last will and testament, separate from the rest of his work, regarded awesomely as utterances almost in an unknown tongue, scarcely meant for human ears.'

The dilemma posed by the works in question persisted into the early years of the twentieth century. For example, the English composer and writer on music Thomas Frederick Dunhill remarked the late quartets 'were little more than imperfectly realized sketches' (*Chamber Music: A Treatise for students*, 1913). In his *Les Quatuors de Beethoven* (Paris, 1925) the French musicologist Joseph de Marliave introduced the late quartets by explaining: 'Lack of comprehension of Beethoven's motive force in the composition of these quartets is the chief reason they are so often thought obscure. The attitude of mind in which people listen to chamber music must undergo a radical change before the listener can understand them.' He elaborates: 'As a rule, the concert-goer is accustomed to notice, especially at the first hearing of a piece, mainly that aspect of it which appeals to the ear — *Aria* and *cantilena* passages, for example, and technical details of theme and melody. The rest he considers an elaborate development of the thematic material, which it is unnecessary to follow with the same close attention as the theme itself, and the ear may rest for a space in order to pick up the return of the subject with revived interest.' De Marliave considered such an attitude to be impossible with the last quartets where, he believed, this type of development to be non-existent — 'Beethoven's thought is linked, bar by bar, from start to finish, into a continuous organic whole, in which all must be grasped or nothing.'

De Marliave's near contemporary, the American musician-musicologist Arthur Shepherd, reflected: 'By reason of their many unique features; their apparent departure from classical procedure; their daring instrumentation; and their generally "problematic" character, much conjectural theorising had grown up around these last quartets. They were long regarded as baffling, experimental, if not indicative of a mental decline on the part of the composer. It became almost axiomatic among musicians, that they were, in many respects, unplayable.' (*The string quartets of Ludwig van Beethoven*, 1935).

Prince Galitzin's words of assurance to Beethoven have proved to be prophetic: 'One might say that your genius is centuries before its time and that there is no listener sufficiently enlightened to appreciate the full beauty of this music. But future generations will honour you and bless your memory more than your contemporaries are able.' (Galitzin to Beethoven, St. Petersburg, 8 April 1824.)

TMR

EDITORIAL PRINCIPLES

By its very nature a study of this kind draws extensively on the work of others. Every effort has been made to acknowledge this in the text by indicating words quoted or adapted with single quotation marks. Wherever possible, for the sake of consistency, I have retained the orthography of quoted texts making only occasional silent changes of spelling and capitalization. Deleted words are identified by means of three ellipsis points ... and interpolations are encompassed within square brackets [ ]. Quoted words, phrases and longer cited passages of text remain the intellectual property of their copyright holders.

I address the reader in the second person notwithstanding that the work is my own. It follows that I must bear the responsibility for any errors of misunderstanding or misinterpretation for which I ask the reader's forbearance. A collaboration I must acknowledge is the help I received from the librarians of the Reid Music Library at the University of Edinburgh. Over the three-year period it took me to compile my reference sources, they served me with unfailing courtesy, often supplying me with twenty or more books at a time. In converting my manuscript into book format, I wish to thank my editorial coordinator, William Rees, for his support and painstaking care. I would also like to thank Shaun Russell for his work designing the cover for each of the twelve volumes.

My admiration for Beethoven provided the initial impulse to commence this undertaking and has sustained me over the several years it has taken to bring my enterprise to completion. That said, I am no Beethoven idolater. I am mindful of the danger that awaits one who ventures to chronicle the work of a great artist. I believe it was Sigmund Freud who suggested that biographers may become so disposed to their subject, and their emotional involvement with their hero, that their work becomes an exercise in idealisation. In response to such a charge let me say. First, I am no biographer. I do however make occasional reference to Beethoven's personal life and his relationships with his contemporaries. Second, I acknowledge Beethoven has his detractors. Accordingly, I have not shrunk from allowing dissentient voices, critical of Beethoven and his work, to be heard. These, however, are few and are silenced amidst the adulation that awaits the reader in support of the endeavours of one of humanity's great creators and one who courageously showed the way in overcoming personal adversity.

TMR

BEETHOVEN'S FINANCIAL TRANSACTIONS

Beethoven's negotiations with his music publishers make many references to his compositions. Today they are recognised for what they are — enduring works of art — but referred to in his business correspondence they appear almost as though they were mere everyday commodities — for which he required an appropriate remuneration. Beethoven resented the time he had to devote to the business-side of his affairs. He believed an agency should exist, for fellow artists such as himself, from which a reasonable sum could be paid for the work (composition) submitted, leaving more time for creative enterprises. In the event Beethoven, like Mozart before him, had to deal with publishers largely on his own. Beethoven, though, did benefit in his business dealings from the help he received from his younger brother Kasper Karl (Caspar Carl). From

1800, Carl worked as a clerk in Vienna's Department of Finance in which capacity he found time to correspond with publishers to offer his brother's works for sale and — importantly — to secure the best prices he could. In April 1802 Beethoven wrote to the Leipzig publishers Breitkopf & Härtel: '[You] can rely entirely on my brother who, in general, attends to my affairs.' Whilst Carl promoted Beethoven's interests with determination, he appears to have lacked tact and made enemies. For example, Beethoven's piano pupil Ferdinand Ries — who for a while also helped the composer with his business negotiations — is on record as describing Carl as being 'the biggest skinflint in the world'. The currencies most referred to in Beethoven's correspondence are as follows:

> silver gulden and florin: these were interchangeable and had a value of about two English/British shillings
> ducat: 4 1/2 gulden/florins: valued at about nine shillings
> louis d'or: This gold coin was adopted during the Napoleonic wars and the French occupation of Vienna and Austria more widely. It had a value of about two ducats or approximately twenty shillings or one-pound sterling.

Beethoven was never poor — in the romantic sense of 'an artist starving in a garret'. On arriving in Vienna in 1792, he was fortunate to receive financial support from his patron Prince Karl Lichnowsky who conferred on him an annuity of 600 florins that he maintained for several years. Between the months of February and July of 1796, Beethoven undertook a concert tour taking in Prague, Dresden, Leipzig and Berlin. He was well received and wrote to his other younger brother Nikolaus Johann: 'My art is winning me friends and what more do I want? ... I shall make a good deal of money.' Later on, in 1809, Napoleon Bonaparte's youngest brother Jérôme Bonaparte offered Beethoven an appointment at his Court with the promise of an income of 4,000 florins. Alarmed at the prospect of losing Beethoven — now the most celebrated composer in Europe — three of Vienna's most notable citizens, namely, the Archduke Rudolph (Beethoven's only composition pupil), Prince Kinsky and Prince Lobkowitz settled on the composer the same sum of 4,000 florins. Inflation, however, brought about by the Napoleonic wars, soon eroded its value; personal misfortune to Lobkowitz and Kinsky also took its toll.

Beethoven undoubtedly had to work hard to secure a reasonable standard of living. Notwithstanding, despite his occasional straitened circumstances, he contributed generously to the needs of others. For example, he allowed his works to be performed free of charge at charitable concerts; in 1815 his philanthropy earned for him the honour of Bürgerrecht — 'freedom of the City'.

Beethoven earned a great deal of money when his music was performed, to considerable acclaim, at several concerts held in association with the Congress of Vienna (1814-15). He did not though benefit from it personally; he invested it on behalf of his nephew Karl. It is one of the misfortunes of Beethoven's life that in money-matters he was culpably improvident. This is poignantly evident in a letter he wrote on 18 March 1827 to the Philharmonic Society of London just one week before his death; the Society had made him a gift of £100. He sent the Society 'his most heartfelt thanks for their particular sympathy and support'.

TMR

'In the entire Beethoven literature no other compositions have given rise to more argument or controversy, and we can hardly hope for agreement or a satisfactory explanation, at least not in the sense that other, earlier works have been explained. It is a fact that the contemporary critics, out of deference to the earlier works, were generally cautious and reserved in their evaluation of these quartets. But even then there were unbiased art connoisseurs who, after spending years studying this legacy, came to the conviction that in some parts (not all, as the attackers maintain) the combination of notes seemed to be carried to the furthest extreme of intellectual reflection, a circumstance that inevitably endangered the logic necessary to the relating of ideas. Everyone except the unconditional believer will have to concede that this situation will remain a permanent obstacle to a sure understanding of the music's poetic intentions, that all one can do is make random guesses and specious explanations.'

Anton Felix Schindler, *Beethoven as I knew him*, edited by Donald W. MacArdle and translated by Constance S. Jolly from the German edition of 1860, (reprint 1966), pp. 304–5.

> *'A fundamental difference of outlook separates the last quartets from those that preceded them, including the one in F minor, Op. 95, even though it approaches the spirit of the later works in a certain subjective intensity of emotion. Impassioned they may be, these earlier quartets, but they are primarily objective, and the later works are stamped with a profound and undeniable subjectivity; the mind that formed them is now wholly independent of external things for its inspiration, detached from the outside world, and careless of traditional form; the last quartets are essentially the direct expression of Beethoven's most intimate spirit, the channel of inspiration flowing from another sphere.'*

Joseph de Marliave, *Beethoven's quartets*, New York: Dover Publications 1925 (reprint 1961), p. 219.

> *'In coming to the late quartets we now pass over a period of fourteen years and reach the great last period of Beethoven's work. The deafness that threatened him about the time he began the composition of the first quartets has now become absolute, and his last quartets were never heard by his ears. Cut off as he was from the world of hearing, his thoughts necessarily turned inward and his music became more than ever a thing of the mind. During these last years he found the intimacy of the string quartet the medium in*

> *which he could best express himself, and his quartets more and more became to him refuge, consolation, one might almost say testament.'*

Rebecca Clarke — writing on the occasion of Beethoven's Death Centenary — The Beethoven quartets as a player sees them in: *Musical Times*, Special Issue, London: Vol. VIII, No. 2, 1927, pp. 184–90.

> *'With the passage of time, a consensus has emerged that sees Beethoven's later sonatas and quartets not as wayward productions of a deaf eccentric, as some early critics had seen them, but as some of the richest contributions ever made to musical art. The startling innovations of the last quartets may be said to centre on the musical symbolism in the A minor, paradoxical contrast in the B-flat major, and narrative design in the C-sharp minor ... The last quartets are bold, visionary works that seem to open a new creative period rather than close an old one.'*

William Kinderman, *Beethoven*, Oxford: Oxford University Press, 1997, pp. 323–4.

THE GALITZIN QUARTETS OP. 127, OP. 132 AND OP. 130

> 'I must admit that these eagerly-awaited Quartets were a source of deep disappointment in musical circles in St. Petersburg. They had been expecting music in the form and manner of Beethoven's first quartets; these were anything but that. Moreover, the demands upon technique were now further increased, so that perfect ensemble became a matter of long and hard study.'

Prince Nikolai Galitzin quoted in: Joseph de Marliave, *Beethoven's Quartets*, 1925 (1961 reprint), p. 225.

> 'I see heavenly forces intertwine with the world/See beautiful Eden of the first creation blossom/When like Apollo's magic harmonies/The wonderful

strings of the master of tones quiver.' Derived from a sonnet to Beethoven by Friederike Salzer, a contemporary prolific writer who published more than 600 poems and periodical articles. Originally published in the September 1817 issue of the *Allgemeine musikalische Zeitung.*

Quoted in: Wayne M. Senner, Robin Wallace and William Meredith, editors, *The Critical Reception of Beethoven's Compositions by his German Contemporaries,* 1999, Vol. 1, p. 45.

'He [Beethoven] can do everything, but we cannot yet understand all that he does ... No one understands Beethoven unless he has a high share of intelligence and even more of feeling and has been very unhappy in love or in some other way.' Attributed to Franz Schubert.

Otto E. Deutsche, *Schubert, Memoirs by his Friends,* 1958, pp. 249–50 and quoted by Martin Cooper in: *Beethoven: the last decade, 1817–1827,* 1970, p. 74.

'We have to thank Nikolai Borisovich, Prince Galitzin, for the late Quartets by Beethoven (Opp. 127, 132, and 130) which rank among the very greatest of their kind.' Sir John Russell writing in, *A tour in Germany and some of the southern provinces of the Austrian Empire, in the years 1820, 1821, 1822, 2 Vols. 3rd ed., Edinburgh, 1825, Vol. II,* p. 273.

Quoted in: H. C. Robbins Landon, *Beethoven: his life, work and world,* 1992, p. 208.

> 'One might say that your genius is centuries before its time and that there is no listener sufficiently enlightened to appreciate the full beauty of this music. But future generations will honour you and bless your memory more than your contemporaries are able.' Prince Nikolai Borisovich Galitzin writing to Beethoven from St. Petersburg on 8 April 1824 in connection with the String Quartets, Opp. 127, 132, and 130.

Quoted in: Anton Felix Schindler, *Beethoven as I knew him*, edited by Donald W. MacArdle and translated by Constance S. Jolly from the German edition of 1860, 1966 p. 302.

> 'You should know my dear Monnais, that Marseilles was the first town in France which understood the great works of Beethoven. It was five years ahead of Paris in this respect; Beethoven's late quartets were already being played and admired in Marseilles while we in Paris were still treating the sublime author of these extraordinary compositions as a madman.' Hector Berlioz writing in 1848 to his friend Édouard Monnais, Royal Superintendent at the Paris Opéra.

Quoted in: Hector Berlioz, *The Musical Madhouse* (*Les grotesques de la musique*), 2003, p. 159.

> 'Still today, among all the creations of Beethoven, [the late quartets] are the least understood and most in need of a psychological and musical commentary ... Unlike their predecessors, they were entirely individual, extremely personal,

subjective, and wholly divorced from the outside world.' As remarked by Theodore Helm, prominent Viennese music critic writing about Beethoven in a monograph of 1885.

Quoted in: in Leon Botstein, *The Patrons and Publics of the Quartets* in: Robert Winter and Robert Martin editors, *The Beethoven Quartet Companion*, 1994, p. 107.

'[The late quartets] grew to maturity in the midst of all the sufferings of mind and body that made these last three years [1824–27] one long agony ... He found in these intensely moving *Adagios* and pain-racked *Allegros* an outlet for his anguish ... The five works are intimately linked with the daily existence of one of the greatest and most desolate figures in history ... They are in every respect "the last revelations of his spirit", inspiring the listener to an admiration mingled with infinite pity and awe.'

Joseph de Marliave, *Beethoven's Quartets*, 1925 (1961 reprint), p. 197.

'Beethoven's last quartets are not the justification of modern music, but modern music has reached the point at which it justifies the quartets and proves Beethoven's genius to have been transcendental ... Their contents are so glorious, so interrelated and so metaphysical, that one might almost think Beethoven regarded them as an ABC [i.e., A minor (Op, 132), B-flat major (Op. 130), and C-sharp minor (Op. 131)] of the world to come.'

Marion M. Scott, *Beethoven: The Master Musicians*, 1940, p. 263 and p. 266.

> '[The] five quartets and the Great Fugue which occupied the end of Beethoven's composing life, after the Ninth Symphony, are drenched in evocations of the human voice. These evocations mean to sing or to speak instantly to the heart, like the songs imagined by Beethoven's poet at the climax of *An die ferne Geliebte*: "*Was mir aus der vollen Brust/ohne Kunstgepräng' erklungen/nur der Sehnsucht sich bewusst*".'

Joseph Kerman, *The Beethoven Quartets*, 1967, p. 195.

> 'For nearly all students of Beethoven [the late quartets] represent the final phase the ultimate in withdrawal from the world, a sort of communion between [Beethoven] and his Creator ... There is unfortunately a rather sentimental attraction for some people in this picture of a great man at the end of his life, writing his final message for the world at large, and no doubt it is helped by the dramatic nature of his own earlier career ... One nineteenth century conception — or misconception — resulted in isolating the late quartets: at first they were regarded reverently as a sort of last will and testament, separate from the rest of his work, regarded awesomely as utterances almost in an unknown tongue, scarcely meant for human ears.'

Harold Truscott, *Beethoven's Late String Quartets*, 1968, pp. 3–4.

> 'The last quartets are addressed to that inward ear which, like Wordsworth's inward eye [*viz.* 'I wandered lonely as a cloud'], may be called the "bliss of solitude".'

Martin Cooper, *Beethoven: the last decade, 1817–1827*, 1970, pp. 350–1.

> 'These three [quartets] are full of invention, personal in fact, where the late Beethoven seems to discover what already exists — a Newton organising the concepts that make the universe of music understandable.'

Basil Lam, *Beethoven string quartets*, 1975, p. 76.

> 'Perhaps a total acceptance of the late quartets would have required a rebelliousness of spirit, a refusal to accept the given conditions of life, which was beyond the reach of even the sensitive and the disaffected in Viennese society. They still preferred the Septet, with its harmless evocation of those better days before the [Napoleonic] war.'

Maynard Solomon, *Beethoven*, 1977, p, 320.

> 'In the last works [Beethoven's] imagination became increasingly subtle and far-reaching, as in the slow movement of Op. 132, wandering into mysterious and unfamiliar regions and sometimes, as in the *Grosse Fuge*, showing a structural power of unprecedented monumentality ... For very many years the posthumous quartets continued to be regarded with profound suspicion by a

large number of musicians. It is amusing to learn that Gounod, of all unlikely people, was accused in 1862 by the critic of the *Revue des Deux Mondes* of being a composer who "in company with all the bad musicians of modern Germany, be they Liszt, Wagner, Schumann, or even ... Mendelssohn, have drunk at the tainted spring of Beethoven's late quartets".'

Philip Radcliffe, *Beethoven's String Quartets*, 1978, pp. 177– and pp. 183–4.

'Apart from Shakespeare I can think of no other figure in Western culture who commands such supremacy and veneration in his own art yet is known to a universal public. What is it that still confers on Beethoven, more than 150 years after his death, the mantle of a prophet with a perennially vital message for each new generation? ... Why, when elevated by the Fifth Symphony's exaltation or absorbed in the questing mysteries of the late quartets or piano sonatas, do we feel the urge to wonder what Beethoven is saying or to ask what he means? ... If the Ninth Symphony addresses all mankind, the late sonatas and late quartets seem in places to represent a man talking to himself. We, his posthumous audience, are privileged to overhear a very lonely Beethoven communing with his inmost being — or with whatever external spiritual reality there may be.'

John Crabbe, *Beethoven's Empire of the Mind*, 1982, p. 9 and p. 121.

'As a series the late quartets were Beethoven's last testament and for many his greatest achievement, though for years they evoked bewilderment as well as admiration ... Time, however, has proved that Beethoven's late masterpieces are imbued with intellectual and spiritual qualities that invalidate any normal comparisons or assessments.'

Denis Matthews, *Beethoven, The Master Musicians*, 1985, p. 138.

'No final verdict was reached on Beethoven's late music during the years immediately following his death, either in the [contemporaneous] *Allgemeine musikalische Zeitung* or elsewhere.'

Robin Wallace, *Beethoven's Critics: aesthetic dilemmas and resolutions during the composer's lifetime*, 1986, p. 43.

'[Beethoven's last five quartets] carry not merely the string quartet but the art of music into new regions. Studies of them are innumerable. Like *Hamlet* they will never yield up their last secrets or admit of a "final" solution. They are inexhaustible.'

Gerald Abraham *Beethoven's Chamber Music* in: *The Age of Beethoven, The new Oxford history of music, Vol. VIII*, Gerald Abraham, editor, 1988, pp. 295–6.

'In his last works Beethoven has given up the struggle with the external world, so typical of the middle period symphonies, because he has

> fought and won a more important battle in his own spirit.'

Alec Harman with Anthony Milner and Wilfrid Mellers, *Man and his Music: the story of musical experience in the West*, 1988, p. 656.

> 'In part, Beethoven sought to be not only strikingly memorable on first hearing but sufficiently intriguing to ensure a magnetic residue that would stimulate a return to a work, thereby defying the inherently ephemeral aspect of musical communication.'

Leon Botstein, *The Patrons and Publics of the Quartets* in: Robert Winter and Robert Martin editors, *The Beethoven Quartet Companion*, 1994, p. 92.

> 'With Beethoven's last quartets ... the quartet assumed a new aesthetic stance. Though the late scores were played in public as soon as they were composed — indeed the composer took some trouble about this — directly afterwards they dropped ominously out of sight and sound. As Beethoven's musical imagination turned inward, the quartet turned away from its earlier audiences.'

Joseph Kerman, *Beethoven Quartet Audiences* in: Robert Winter and Robert Martin, editors, *The Beethoven Quartet Companion*, 1994, p. 21.

> 'The uniqueness of the last quartets is outwardly manifested in the growing number of movements, culminating in the seven-movement design of Op.

131. But no less striking is their expressive scope, which embraces moods ranging from whimsy and mocking humour to the sublime interiority of the slow movements – the *Adagio* of Op. 127, the *Cavatina* of Op. 130, and the *Heiliger Dankgesang*. The last quartets are bold, visionary works that seem to open a new creative period rather than an old one.'

William Kinderman, *Beethoven*, 1997, pp. 323–4.

'[In late Beethoven] harmony ... takes on something mask-like or husk-like. It becomes a convention keeping things upright, but largely drained of substance. In the last quartets, at least, one can hardly speak any longer of the construction of tonality ... It is no longer the autonomous law of motion, but remains behind a sound veil.'

Theodor W. Adorno, *Beethoven: the philosophy of music; fragments and texts*, 1998, pp. 138–9 and p. 156.

'Although [Beethoven's] late quartets were supposedly sparked off by a request from Galitzin and sustained by his own love of the genre, it was public demand, filtered through a number of publisher's, that fuelled this unprecedented burst of activity in a single genre.'

Barry Cooper, *Beethoven, The Master Musicians*, 2000, pp. 334–5.

'Beethoven set inhibitingly high standards in the string quartet, as in the symphony and also the piano sonata, the genres on which he had the most profound impact.'

Margaret Notely, *With Beethoven-like Sublimity* in: Glenn Stanley editor, *The Cambridge Companion to Beethoven*, 2000, p. 244.

'Beethoven's string quartets marked by opus numbers 127, 130, 131, 132, and 135 are usually bracketed under the group of "last" quartets. They belong to Beethoven's last three years, and in them greatness of inspiration is reflected in the greater length of the music itself, as though Beethoven needed a larger canvas and more manuscript paper to develop the dramatic expression of his last period ... Beethoven's sketchbooks show that he went from one quartet to another almost without an interval. It was a state of feverish activity; the extraordinary rhapsodic quality, the un-Classical fluidity of modulation, the innovating spirit of instrumental writing of the last quartets are explained by the fact that Beethoven ran a musical temperature when he was writing them.'

Electra Slonimsky Yourke editor: *Nicolas Slonimsky: Writings on Music*, 4 Vols., 2003–5, Vol. 1, pp. 163–4.

'Beethoven's series of late string quartets were his main creative preoccupation during the final three years of his life. To many listeners, these five works (six, if we count the original large-scale finale —the so-called *Grosse Fuge* — which Beethoven eventually removed from the Quartet

Op.130, and published as an independent piece) form the most profoundly personal and spiritual music he ever wrote.'

Misha Donat, *String Quartet in B-flat major, Op. 127: Notes to the BBC Radio Three Beethoven Experience*, Sunday 5 June 2005, www.bbc.co.uk/radio3/Beethoven

'Various authors, beginning with Paul Bekker [*Beethoven*, 1911], have described [The *Galitzin* Quartets] as a triptych, in view of their obvious thematic resemblances. These quartets represent Beethoven's boldest experiments with the formal design of a multi-movement composition going beyond the conventional framework of four movements ... [They] expand the cycle of movements beyond the conventional framework that had, with few exceptions, served Beethoven adequately throughout his career. Formal expansion beyond the four-movement framework is a remarkably consistent feature of this group of works ... The priority Beethoven granted to the imagination here comes to fulfilment in a manner that twists our expectations of the [quartet] genre even more than earlier works while advancing his art towards new creative perspectives.'

William Kinderman editor, *The String Quartets of Beethoven*, 2005, p. 279, p. 281, p. 301 and p. 317.

Before proceeding directly to our discussion of the Galitzin String Quartets, we open with a portrait of Beethoven at the period of their composition.

From the time of publication of the String Quartet, Op.

95 in 1816, a period of six years passed before Beethoven returned once more to the medium. During this interval the progressive deterioration in his hearing necessarily made him withdraw evermore from society. He last performed in public at the keyboard in the 1814 premier of the so-called *Archduke* Trio, Op. 97: this was to the mortification of his friends and admirers as he either jangled the strings excessively in the fortissimos or played inaudibly in the pianissimos. References to the effect the loss of hearing meant for Beethoven occur throughout his correspondence. For instance, in the summer of 1815 he wrote to Johann Xaver Brauchle, a minor composer who was then employed as the tutor to the children of the Countess Anna Maria Erdödy — an accomplished pianist and one of Beethoven's many aristocratic, women-friend admirers. He confides: 'I am not well ... Peevish about many things, more sensitive than all other mortals, and tormented by my poor hearing I often feel only *pain* in the society of others [Beethoven's italics].'[i]

The violist Rebecca Clarke, writing on the occasion of the composer's Death Centenary, felt disposed to remark: 'The deafness that threatened him about the time he began the composition of the first quartets [Op. 18] has now become absolute, and his last quartets were never heard by his ears. Cut off as he was from the world of hearing, his thoughts necessarily turned inward and his music became more than ever a thing of the mind.' Concerning his disposition to string quartet writing, she adds: 'During these last years he found the intimacy of the string quartet the medium in which he could best express himself, and his quartets more and more became to him refuge, consolation, one might almost say testament.'[ii] A few years later in her pioneering English-language study of the composer, Marion Scott expressed similar sentiments: '[The] string quartet was the medium towards which Beethoven's instinct was already drawing him, as the only one sufficiently pure and flexible for the expression of ideas now crowding upon him.'[iii]

At the close of 1817 Beethoven appears to have finally come to terms with his impaired hearing; he realized it would not improve. He became ever more reliant upon the ear trumpets devised for him by the pioneer of the metronome, Johann Mälzel (Maelzel) who had provided the composer with a variety of designs.[iv] With the passing of time, however, it seems Mälzel's ear trumpets proved to be of little practical benefit. By the following year Beethoven had to make recourse to notebooks — *conversation books* — so that instead of having to yell at him, friends and visitors could write down their thoughts. Perhaps it is not surprising that Beethoven would progressively turn away from composing piano sonatas such that the great trilogy Opp. 109, 110, and 111 would be his valedictory contribution to the genre — but not to the keyboard itself with such masterworks as the *Diabelli* Variations, Op. 120 and the Bagatelles, Op. 126 still to come.

It is generally considered that by Beethoven's standards the years 1815–18 were relatively unproductive and his detractors were murmuring 'Er hat sich ausgeschrieben, er vermag nichts mehr' — 'He can do nothing more'. Even the critic of the *Allgemeine musikalische Zeitung* felt disposed to remark: Beethoven seems now to be beyond writing great works'.[v] That said, these years witnessed the appearance of the pioneering song cycle *An die ferne Geliebte*, Op. 98, and the intellectually and technically challenging Piano Sonatas in A major, Op. 101 and B-flat major, Op. 106.[vi] Moreover, in 1817 and 1818 the Seventh and Eighth Symphonies respectively were published and Beethoven's celebrity was widely recognised — having already been elevated by the events of the Congress of Vienna some few years previously that also did much to promote the wider recognition of his work.[vii] As a consequence the composer's portrait was in demand. Sometime in 1818 the artist August von Kloeber made a crayon drawing of Beethoven that captures his intense gaze and resolute expression. Later that autumn the Austro-Hungarian artist Ferdinand Schimon painted a portrait of Beethoven. Anton Schindler, who was frequently in the composer's company at this time, considered it to be 'the most interesting' and 'full of characteristic truth'. In his typically fulsome manner he enthuses: 'In the rendering of that particular look, the majestic forehead, the dwelling-place of mighty, sublime ideas, of hues, in the drawing of the firmly shut mouth and the chin shaped like a shell, it is truer than any other picture.' This portrait is now in the possession of the Beethoven House in Bonn.[viii]

In March 1818, the English-born musician Cipriani Potter was on tour in Europe and when in Vienna he made a point of meeting the capitol's distinguished composer. Potter appears to have made a favourable impression on Beethoven: he was well qualified to do so being variously a composer, pianist, conductor, teacher and later Principal of the Royal Academy of Music, London. He wrote an account of his recollections of Beethoven that was subsequently published in *The Musical Times*, 1861. Potter recalled the composer's objection to unwelcome visitors, particularly those who were merely 'ambitious of contemplating the greatest genius in [Vienna] and of hearing him perform'. He regarded such visits as 'an intrusion and an impertinence' and exhibited his displeasure 'to those who were so unlucky as to expose themselves to rebuke'.[ix]

Recognition of Beethoven's celebrity came from other sources. On 15 March 1819 Beethoven was conferred Honorary Membership of the Philharmonic Society of Laibach, then in Hapsburg territory. Beethoven had been denied membership in 1808 on the grounds that a referee had complained: 'Beethoven is as full of moodiness as he is devoid of obligingness.' In 1819, however, the Laibach Society reconsidered Beethoven's name once more and on this occasion was disposed to remark: '[By] appointing you one of their Honorary Members, ask you, sir, to accept the strongest proof of their most profound admiration.'[x] Beethoven expressed his thanks in a letter of 4 May 1819, undertaking to send the Society an unpublished composition. There is no evidence though that he fulfilled this intention; instead he may have sent a copy of his *Pastoral Symphony*.[xi]

As Beethoven progressed towards his late string quartets, his musical language metamorphosed, becoming more psychologically complex and concerned with matters of 'theme, melody and texture'.[xii] As Maynard Solomon puts it: '[Struggle] is sublimated into ecstasy, as in the *Arietta* of the Sonata, Op. 111; chaos strives for lucid formation, as in the transition to the fugue of the *Hammerklavier* Sonata, Op. 106, and in the opening of the finale of the Ninth Symphony, Op. 126; victorious conclusions are incessantly sought after and discovered, as in the *Grosse Fuge* Op. 133, the Piano Sonata Op. 110, and the finale of the Quartet in C-sharp minor, Op. 131.' 'Beethoven', Solomon continues, 'could no longer confront such issues ... with his previous musical vocabulary or procedures.'[xiii] Charles Hubert Parry, in his capacity as musicologist, made similar observations: 'Beethoven [had by now found] the accepted scheme of organisation which he himself had brought to perfection, too constraining and restrictive to the impulse of his thought and therefore endeavoured to find new types of form to revive sundry earlier types of organisation and combine them in various ways which departed from the essential principles upon which composers had been working for generations.'[xiv]

In his discussion of Beethoven's evolving musical language, Joseph Kerman draws attention to what he refers to as the composer's 'wordless recitative' in his use of melody. He cites the celebrated passage that opens the finale of the Ninth Symphony 'where the cellos and bases reject a parade of themes [heard in the preceding movements] and then finally elects one, all in "wordless recitative".' Kerman contends the implied meaning of the cellos is then made evident when the baritone member of the vocal quartet proclaims: "O friends, not these sounds; let us rather strike up something more seemly, more joyful". Kerman argues this musical procedure infiltrates many passages of the late quartets and accompanying *Grosse Fuge*. In the first of the late quartets, Op. 127, he suggests an element of the wordless recitative may be heard in the work's third movement, 'the strange interruption that shakes up the *Scherzando vivace*'. In the Quartet in C-sharp minor, Op. 131, he cites 'the numerous touches of recitative – edging into rhapsodic or cadenza-like style – [that] help make wonderful transitions in and out of the A-major *Allegretto* Themes and Variations'. Of the finale to the Quartet in A major, Op. 132 he draws attention to the 'almost hysterical violin recitative, with tremolo and all the trimmings – the rawest that Beethoven ever conceived'. The original finale of the Quartet in B-flat major, Op. 130 – the Great Fugue, Op. 133 – Kerman describes as opening 'with an *Overtura* rattling through a parade of all the thematic shapes to be utilized in the piece'. And of the Quartet in F major, Op. 135, he characterises the slow introduction that precedes the finale, as adopting 'all the rhetorical tricks of a solemn *recitativo accompagnato*'.[xv]

In his wider reflections on Beethoven's late musical language, Kerman recalls examples from other of Beethoven's string quartets that he describes as *spiritualized dance parodies*: 'Already in Op. 18, a little *contredanse* parody scurries through the slow movement of the Quartet in G major [Op. 18, No. 2], and a *danza alla tedesca* alternates with *La Malinconia* in the oddly prophetic finale of the Quartet in B-flat major [Op. 18, No. 6].' He also cites the 'ethereal transformation' of the *Menuetto Grazioso* of the *Razumovsky* String Quartet, Op. 59, No. 3 – 'in mood, perhaps the clearest prophet of the late quartets'. In addition, Kerman makes reference to Beethoven's adoption of the variation form in the late quartets that he considers 'allowed Beethoven to work up to a luxuriance unparalleled in his earlier music ... [a] path for lyricism to travel ... the same technique [allowing] him unparalleled quietude, simplicity and ... sobriety'.[xvi]

Writing some forty years earlier, the French musicologist Joseph de Marliave expressed thoughts similar to the foregoing: 'As though unable to tear himself away from the task of interpreting his own inner consciousness, Beethoven extends it endlessly, delighting in his inexhaustible creative gift. For this reason he is especially drawn to the form known as the *Grand Variation*. From him it gains a new lyrical vitality and force, expressing all possible shades of emotional variety and contrast. He draws on the inmost subtleties of feeling from a theme already profoundly conceived and profoundly moving, and develops its expressive capacity with limitless musical resource.' He adds, in his typical fulsome style: 'The Master's genius seems to break its chains, and escaping from the restraint of the bar, it is even freed from the constraint of rhythm, for nothing now can confine nor set a limit to his powers ... In an ecstasy of freedom and creation he soars for a second into infinite time and space.'[xvii]

The variation form had been part of Beethoven's musical language throughout his career as a composer, and by about 1820 he had written some sixty sets of variations, either as separate works or as movements of larger cycles. In the context of the composer's evolving style and manner of expression, Solomon draws attention to the Piano Sonatas Op. 109 (1820) and Op. 111 (1822) in which he considers Beethoven 'imbued the form for the first time with a "transfigured" almost ecstatic content and a profundity of expression which indicated that he had found, in this basic musical form, a new vehicle for his imaginative thought'. Mindful of the composer's parallel interest in counterpoint and contrapuntal design, he adds: 'Thereby, variation form joins fugue as one of the leading characteristics of the late style, and variation movements appear in many of his last masterpieces, including the *Adagio* and finale of the Ninth symphony and crucial movements of the Quartets Opp. 127, 131, 132, and 135.' Of the Quartet Op. 127 he states: 'Beethoven adopted the melodic variation procedure and turned to it for the expression of his deepest meditations as in the [work's] *Adagio ma non troppo.* [xviii] Harold Truscott's summation is relevant here: 'Beethoven brought off a double achievement in the group of five string quartets which proved to be his last. He contrived to continue a line of thought coming directly from the works he had been occupied with immediately before writing them – the Mass in D, the Ninth Symphony and the last Piano Sonatas – while also continuing a totally different textural line coming directly from the earlier chamber music.'[xix]

Musicologists who have studied the sketches for the Galitzin string Quartets affirm the extent to which they reveal Beethoven's propensity not only for working on several compositions at the same time but also for exchanging, and inter-changing, ideas between them. One significant aspect of this was to find expression in the number of movements Beethoven assigned to each of the quartets – a process of extension that went beyond the confines of the conventional classical framework of four movements. In this context we draw on the observations of Beethoven authority William Kinderman. Beethoven's original intention conceived the formal design of Op. 127 to include perhaps as many as six movements, including 'a character piece in C major entitled *La gaité* that was planned at one point as a second movement, as well as a slow introduction, to the finale. In the end Beethoven retained the four-movement form in Op. 127, but, as Kinderman remarks 'his flirtation with such an expansion of the narrative chain of movements bore fruit in the following trilogy of quartets in A minor, Op. 132, B-flat major Op. 130, and C-sharp minor, Op. 131'.

The A minor Quartet, Op. 132, is performed today as a five-movement work but Beethoven himself initially regarded it as having six 'because he counted the recitative transition to the finale as a separate movement'. This is apparent from a letter he wrote to his nephew Karl on 11 August 1825 where he states: 'I am in mortal fright about the Quartet [Op. 132]. For Holz has taken away the third, fifth and sixth movements.' The violinist Karl Holz was then assisting Beethoven as his secretary-factotum (he had supplanted Anton Schindler in this capacity) and Beethoven had, uncharacteristically, allowed Holz to take away with him the original manuscript of the quartet in question.[ix]

The B-flat major Quartet, Op. 130, adopts a six-movement design which originally included the multi-sectional fugal finale — the *Grosse Fuge* ('Great Fugue') — that was subsequently removed in favour of a lighter-sounding substitute finale. Moreover, the B-flat major Quartet absorbed the *Alla danza tedesca* that was transposed for this purpose from A major to G major.

The C-sharp minor Quartet is unique in having seven movements. Kinderman summarizes Beethoven's creative process here in the following terms: 'Thus, in writing each of these works, Beethoven conceived material that spilled over beyond the composition immediately at hand. His fertility of invention refused to be contained within the boundaries of the singular work.'[xxi] Marion Scott writes in similar vein: 'Simultaneously with the A minor Quartet [Op. 132], Beethoven was evolving the great B-flat major Quartet [Op. 130]. It was finished about a month later. This relation went deeper than Beethoven's habit of working on several things at the same time; the two works are thematically joined, and so close is this connection that Beethoven was able to transfer a movement from one to the other — the *alla danza tedesca* — with perfect propriety. While still in the midst of the B-Flat major Quartet he began to work on the C-sharp minor [Op. 131], which occupied him till the summer of 1826.'[xxii]

The E-flat major Quartet, Op. 127 was completed in 1824 and was the only one of the 'late' quartets to be published in the composer's lifetime — hence the generic description of these compositions as the 'posthumous quartets'. The A minor Quartet, Op. 132, came next in order of composition with the B-flat major Quartet, Op. 130 following: this explains the sequence of the Galitzin string quartet opus numbers as Op. 127, Op. 132, and Op. 130. Later, but outside of our present discussion, came the C-sharp minor String Quartet, Op. 131 and the F major Quartet, Op. 135. The observations of Beethoven's biographer Anton Schindler are of relevance here when he writes: 'The opus numbers ought to conform to the sequence in which the quartets were composed. Once more we have an instance in which the three publishers [see later] who shared this work proceeded without consulting one another. The numbers should be as follows: Quartet in E-flat major, Op. 127; Quartet in A major (Op. 130 instead of Op. 132); Quartet in B-flat major (Op. 131 instead of Op. 130); Quartet in C-sharp minor (Op. 132 instead of Op. 131); and Quartet in F major (Op. 133 instead of Op. 135). The fugue in B-flat major, which the composer released as a separate work, should, in the proper order, have the number Op. 134.'[xxiii]

Karl Holz has left an impression of Beethoven from the period in question. He relates: 'When composing the three quartets requested by Prince Galitzin, such a wealth of ideas flowed from Beethoven's inexhaustible imagination that he virtually had to write the Quartets in C-sharp minor and F major involuntarily: "My dear fellow, I've just had another idea", he would say jocularly, and with glistening eyes, when we were out walking, would write down a few notes in his sketchbook.'[xxiv]

Gioacchino Rossini was in Vienna around April 1822 and has left a pen-portrait of Beethoven; he was then being lionised through the popularity of his *Il Barbiere di Seviglia*. He states he was familiar with some of the composer's string quartets, that he regarded 'with admiration', and, likewise, 'a number of his piano compositions'. Notwithstanding, he describes how he could barely master his emotions as he mounted the stairs to Beethoven's lodgings. He continues: 'When the door opened, I found myself in a sort of attic terribly disordered and dirty ... The portraits of Beethoven which we know, reproduce fairly well his physiognomy. But what no etcher's needle could not express was the indefinable sadness spread over his features — while from under heavy eyebrows his eyes shone as from out of caverns and, though small, seemed to pierce one.' When Rossini took leave of Beethoven, he encouraged his young contemporary 'to compose some more "barbers".'[xxv]

A description of Beethoven that accords with the popular image of him has been left by the English statesman Sir John Russell. In the years 1820–22, he travelled extensively in Europe and published an account of his journeys in *A Tour in Germany and Some of the Southern Provinces of the Austrian Empire*. In this he makes reference to Beethoven's appearance: 'The carelessness of his dress gives him a savage appearance; his features are marked and prominent; his eyes expressive; his hair, which looks as if it had not been touched by comb or scissors for some years, falls over his broad brow in a disorderly mass, being comparable only to the serpents on Medusa's head.' Also worthy of mention here is the likeness the artist Stephan Drecher took of Beethoven in 1824. This chalk and pencil study portrays the composer with a resolute expression and looking much older than his fifty-four years.

Russell heard the composer perform on the piano prompting him to comment: 'It required no little tact to induce him to play, so great is his dislike of anything like a pressing request.' When he was finally persuaded to perform Russell comments: 'Left to himself, Beethoven sat down at the piano. At first he struck a few short chords ... but soon he forgot his surroundings, and for about half an hour lost himself in an improvisation, the style of which was exceedingly varied, and especially distinguished by sudden transitions ... he revelled rather in bold stormy moods than in soft and gentle ones.'[xxvi]

Beethoven's improvisations at the keyboard were rare in his later years, as a consequence of his infirmity, and Russell was fortunate to hear the composer extemporize. News of this appears to have reached the correspondent of the *Allgemeine musikalische Zeitung* who enthused: 'Our Beethoven seems to be becoming more receptive to music again, which he has shunned almost like a misogynist since his worsening hearing ailment. He has already improvised masterfully a few times in a social gathering to everyone's delight and proved that he still knows how to handle his instrument with power, joy and love.'[xxvii]

Notwithstanding such occasional demonstrations of his prowess as a former keyboard executant, it was the medium of the string quartet that was now claiming Beethoven's attention. In this regard he was perhaps fortunate that he turned to this genre when he did — as a medium for his later style of musical expression. String quartet performance was becoming more popular with the musically-inclined public and less the preserve of wealthy aristocratic families who had previously enjoyed the exclusive privilege of hearing quartets performed in their grand salons, in some cases by liveried musicians in their employ. Within such an intimate environment, so enriched by the creations of Haydn and Mozart, the string quartet held sway where the interplay between the four instruments had the authority and interest of informed conversation.[xxviii] The contemporary mystical poet and musician Christian Schubart considered the string quartet expressed no less than 'the music-universe condensed into one work'.[xxix] Beethoven had first enriched this 'universe' with his own Op. 18 set of quartets. Now, with the experience of composing the quartets Opp. 59, 74, and 95, he was resolved to further stamp his authority on the medium by enhancing its stature and transforming it almost beyond recognition. In his pioneering study *Beethoven et ses trois styles* (1855), the German musicologist Wilhelm von Lenz described the five last quartets as being 'less quartets than discourses between four string instruments'. In these: 'Beethoven uses the instruments as four separate voices, each representing an idea with the utmost freedom and individuality, yet uniting in a perfect and significant whole.'[xxx]

The wider interest in the string quartet was given impetus by the emergence into the public domain of the professional string quartet. In this regard mention should be made of the pioneering influence of Ignaz Schuppanzigh and his fellow instrumentalists. Ignaz Schuppanzigh is a significant figure in the context of Beethoven's writing for the string quartet and also in connection with his role in the first performances of a number of his chamber and orchestral compositions. From 1794, when just eighteen years old, he led a quartet in the salon of Beethoven's patron Prince Lichnowsky. It was there, in April 1797, that he took part in a performance of the composer's Piano Quintet, Op. 16. At about this time he also gave Beethoven lessons in violin — an interesting experience for the composer given that Schuppanzigh was twenty-six years younger than himself. In 1804 he formed his own quartet that had the distinction of being the first to give subscription concerts to the wider public in Vienna. In 1805 he directed the first performance of Beethoven's Sextet, Op. 71 and in 1808 Count Razumovsky asked Schuppanzigh to assemble 'a fine string quartet' for him; this was at the prompting of Prince Lichnowsky who, through marriage, was Razumovsky's brother-in-law.

Schuppanzigh rendered service to Beethoven in the capacities of both orchestral leader and orchestral conductor. On 16 April 1812 he directed performances of the Overture *Egmont* and the Sixth Symphony and later in May the Overture *Coriolan*. The following year he similarly conducted performances of the Overture *Prometheus* and the Fifth Symphony (1 May). In May 1814 his Quartet gave the first performance of the String Quartet Op. 95 and later that year, on 8 December, he played first violin in a memorable performance of the Seventh Symphony that saw Beethoven enjoy his greatest public acclaim. Following a great fire at Razumovsky's palace, Schuppanzigh made plans to leave Vienna. On 11 February 1816 he gave a farewell concert at which the String Quartet Op. 59, No. 3 was performed. On his eventual return to Vienna, in 1823, Schuppanzigh became absorbed in the capital's musical life and, more significantly for our narrative, was soon reunited with Beethoven. He directed (as first violin) the first performances of the Ninth Symphony on 7 and 23 May 1824 and later gave the first renditions of the Quartets Op. 127 (6 March 1825); Op. 132 (6 November 1825); and Op. 130 (with fugue) on 21 March 1826. Beethoven did not have exclusive access to Schuppanzigh's Quartet though: it premiered the works of other composers including the youthful Franz Schubert's A minor, *Rosamunde* Quartet, D. 804 of 1824. Incidentally, it is known that Schubert, ever the admirer of Beethoven, attended all of Schuppanzigh's Beethoven-quartet premiers.[xxxi]

The composer and violinist Friedrich Reichardt has left an account of Schuppanzigh's style of playing. He writes: 'Herr Schuppanzigh himself has an original style most appropriate to the humorous quartets of Haydn, Mozart, and Beethoven — or, perhaps more accurately, a product of the capricious manner of performance suited to these masterpieces. He plays the most difficult passages clearly, although not always in tune ... He also accents very correctly and significantly, and his *cantabile*, too, is often quite singing. He is a good leader for his carefully chosen colleagues, who enter admirably into the spirit of the composer.'[xxxii] Schuppanzigh's occasionally playing out of tune may be explained by the fact that in later life he put on a great deal of weight — disposing Beethoven to confer on him the nickname *Falstaff*. This, combined with his very large hands, may have affected his intonation. Notwithstanding, as Robert Winter remarks: 'Whatever the virtues or defects of Schuppanzigh's playing, his two seminal contributions to the art of quartet playing — the pioneering of the permanent string quartet and the presentation of [a] regular series of chamber concerts — changed the landscape of quartet playing forever.'[xxxiii]

A further incentive to Beethoven to return to composing string quartets was the growing interest shown by publishers in commissioning such works and — in Beethoven's case — to be prepared to pay the high prices he demanded for them. Given Beethoven's standing as Vienna's, and Europe's, foremost composer, Beethoven could now request as much as 80 ducats (360 florins) for a string quartet 'not far short of the annual salary of such people as rank-and-file musicians at the Opera, school teachers, and junior lecturers at the University'.[xxiv] One publisher, eager to bring out Beethoven's works, was the Leipzig music publisher Carl Peters. In 1814 he became owner of the *Bureau de musique* and subsequently was keen to have the eminent composer on his books.[xxv] In a letter of 18 May, 1822 Peters introduced himself to Beethoven. He explained that since taking over his publishing business from the pervious owners, Hoffmeister and Kühnel, 'he had zealously endeavoured to issue excellent works in good printings and had long since wished to enter into an association with Beethoven'. Peters had refrained from approaching the composer sooner 'out of consideration for the Viennese publishers, so as not to make them angry' — an indication of the rivalry that was manifest amongst publishers eager to benefit from an association with Beethoven. Peters concludes that whatever the composer could send him would be welcome 'for I seek your association not from self interest, but rather from honour'.[xxxvi]

Beethoven replied to Peters on 5 June apologising for the delay in giving his reply on the grounds that he was occupied with the composition of his Mass (*Missa Solemnis*). Of significance in this letter is that Beethoven also makes reference to his preoccupation with his *Elegischer Gesang* ('Elegiac Song'), Op. 118, scored, significantly, for string quartet and four mixed voices — 'which may be taken as further evidence of the composer's putative orientation to the medium of the string quartet'. As for composing a string quartet for Peters — as requested by him — Beethoven responded: 'For a quartet for two violins, viola and violincello ... you could have one very soon [for] 50 ducats.'[xxxvii] Beethoven's words 'very soon' have been taken to infer that he already had such a composition in hand, although it is known he was disposed to offer publishers such reassurances even when the promised work existed only in sketch form. Ten days later Peters replied to Beethoven in a long letter in which he reaffirmed his awareness that such other publishers as Adolf Martin Schlesinger (in Berlin) and his son Moritz (in Paris), were also vying for Beethoven's attention. Nonetheless, he was still enthusiastic to bring out his editions of the composer's works. He cites his interest in trios, concert overtures, songs with piano accompaniment, and solo pieces for piano. Regarding string quartets, though, his response was more qualified: 'Finally, I would very much like to have your new quartet [the one Beethoven claimed to have in hand] ... but 50 ducats might exceed my capabilities.' He explained the highest he had ever paid for a quartet until then was 150 florins, and that he had to make that back before he could make any profit.[xxxviii]

On 3 July Peters once more wrote to Beethoven, this time to express his hope that through his publication of the composer's works he might thereby contribute to the improvement of his [Beethoven's] financial situation. He elaborates: '[It] is unjust that a man like you has to consider his economic circumstance; the great ones of the Earth should long ago have placed you in a completely worry-free position, so that you would no longer have to live *from* your Art, but only *for* Art.'[xxxix] In giving expression to such noble thoughts, Peters, living many miles distant from Vienna, was doubtless unaware that Beethoven was still receiving the Annuity conferred upon him in 1808 by his three benefactors, namely the Princes Kinsky and Lobkowitz and the Archduke Rudolph. Initially they had settled upon the composer the annual sum of 4,000 florins, although its purchasing power was diminished by inflation brought about as a consequence of the depredations of the Napoleonic conflicts. It is a measure of Peters' admiration of Beethoven, and the trust he placed in him, that he arranged for moneys to be deposited for the composer to meet the costs of such compositions as he hoped to receive.

On 6 July Beethoven replied to Peters' letter of 15 June in which he had expressed reservations about being able to meet his price of 50 ducats for a string quartet: 'As to the violin quartet, which is not quite finished [an understatement] ... it would be difficult for me to reduce the fee I am asking you for this work. For it is precisely for a composition of this kind that I am most highly paid.'[xl] Peters responded promptly on 12 July in a generous and enlightened manner. What he has to say sheds light on the challenges confronting such worthy publishers as himself and also the competition Beethoven faced from other composers — albeit of lesser creative standing but no less eager to get their works in print. Peters affirmed it was always his intention 'to pay the artist what I can' but how hard it was for him 'to procure the money that the many good works I print annually cost'. Anxious not to be misunderstood he continued: 'I am not taking into my head to bargain down [the price] that you demand [for a string quartet], for I certainly cannot equate an artistic product with a commodity.' Peters concluded: 'I do not blame you for setting your string quartet at a high price, but, as I just observed, I cannot bargain down, and since the fee asked for it is too high for my abilities to pay, I had better hold off.'[xli]

A further reason for Peters not entering into an agreement with Beethoven may have been the commitments he had entered into with other composers. For example, from this period Peters published a number of contemporary works that included: the String Quartets, Op. 58, Nos. 1–3 by Louis Spohr and his *Quatuor brillante*, Op. 61; Bernhard Romberg's Quartet No. 8, Op. 37 and Quartet No. 9, Op. 39; and Pierre Rode's four Quartets, Opp. 13–14.[xlii] Peters did eventually agree to accept other compositions by Beethoven, to be set against the money he had already deposited in the composer's account for this purpose. But the outcome was disappointing for both parties. The compositions Beethoven offered Peters included a set of piano pieces that he eventually declined to publish; he considered them to be too slight and unworthy of such a great composer. The works in question were eventually published by Schlesinger and later by Breitkopf & Härtel – the latter assigning to them the designation Bagatelles, Op. 119. Beethoven was duly obliged to return the payment he had received for the rejected compositions – but not until December 1825. With this, his dealings with Peters were terminated with no further undertaking to offer him the string quartet he had so desired.

Towards the end of 1822 Beethoven received a letter from the Italian-born Antonio Pacini. Its import provides further evidence of the eagerness on the part of publishers to secure Beethoven's favours and to coax chamber works from his pen. Pacini was variously a singer, manager and, more importantly for this part of our discussion, a Paris-based music publisher. Like Peters he was a Beethoven admirer and wanted to publish some of his compositions; he had already commissioned a string quintet adaptation of the First Symphony. In his letter he made particular mention of his enthusiasm to publish new string quartets 'by the Master'. Beethoven's younger brother Johann van Beethoven, then acting on the composer's behalf with regard to his business affairs, replied to Pacini on 27 December. He informed him his brother could not oblige since he was heavily occupied with work on the Ninth Symphony, the *Missa Solemnis* and the revision of his Opera *Fidelio*.[xliii]

With the breakdown in Beethoven's negotiations with Peters, and Pacini's approaches having to be declined, it is tempting to invoke the everyday expression, as one door closed (in effect two) another opened. A more fitting way of introducing the events that occurred is so say that Providence appeared before Beethoven in a new guise and whose timely intervention would indeed lead to the commission and composition of the three string quartets, Opp. 127, 132, and 130.

Nicholas (Nikolai) Galitzin(e) was a Russian nobleman — with the title of Count (later Prince) — and an accomplished amateur musician, his favoured instrument being the cello. He shared his love of music with his wife (Princess Helen Saltykow) who was his equal as a pianist — for example she secured and performed several of Beethoven's late piano sonatas. Thayer describes Helen as 'an admirable pianist' (p. 815). Galitzin's relative, Prince Dmitry, was the Russian ambassador in Vienna providing Nicholas with the incentive to visit the city where, doubtless, he became familiar with the music of Haydn, Mozart and Beethoven. Although outside the scope of the present discussion, worthy of remark is that Galitzin was one of the original subscribers, alongside the Czar of Russia, to Beethoven's *Missa Solemnis*. As further evidence of his disposition to things musical, it is known that when in Vienna, in 1822, Galitzin expressed an enthusiasm for Weber's opera *Der Freischütz* — then being performed — and made efforts to obtain a copy of the score to take back home with him to St. Petersburg. According to Joseph de Marliave, when Galitzin returned home from Vienna the violinist Zeuner — a member of the St. Petersburg Quartet — suggested to the Prince, somewhat contemptuously — but significantly, that the money spent on the score of *Der Freischütz* 'would be put to better use if Beethoven were commissioned to write three new quartets — by which the whole musical world would profit'.[xliv]

Whatever the precise origins that disposed Prince Galitzin to act as he did, on 9 November 1822 he wrote a fulsome letter to the composer in which he introduced himself in the French diplomatic language as 'passionné amateur de musique que grand admirateur de votre talent'. As a self-confessed admirer of Beethoven and his music, he asked if he would consent to compose 'one, two or three quartets' for which he states he would be glad to pay 'what you think proper'; the Prince clearly had greater wealth at his disposal that the publisher Peters who, as remarked, could not meet Beethoven's demands. As further indication of his enthusiasm and generosity, Galitzin undertook to have the agreed payment to be deposited at his bankers (Messrs. Stieglitz & Co.) upon which the composer was free to draw. To add emphasis to his request for string quartets, he revealed his personal enthusiasm for the cello — that might be taken as Galitzin inviting Beethoven to give a prominent part to this instrument in the works he was hoping to secure. In one other respect he was more direct: 'I will accept the dedication with gratitude'.[xlv]

Galitzin's correspondence with Beethoven disposed his amanuensis Anton Schindler to enthuse: 'These excerpts are enough to give us a picture of the Russian Prince as a noble-spirited patron of the arts, a character who could not fail to make a deep impression on our Master, for this Russian took the place among Germans and Poles we remember — Lichnowsky, Lobkowitz, Kinsky, Schwarzenberg — not to forget his compatriot Razumovsky, and others who in better days stood in the forefront of art patrons in the Austrian capital.'[xlvi]

As the wording in Galitzin's letter implies, regarding

'one, two or three quartets,' he was clearly commissioning three *individual* compositions and not a traditional *set* of three — as had been requested by Count Razumovsky. As we shall see, the differences between the three Galitzin Quartets was further emphasized by their being published by three different music publishers, namely Schott (Mainz), Artaria (Vienna) and Schlesinger (Paris/Berlin). In his commentary to the 'late quartets', taken to mean the three Galitzin Quartets together with Op. 131 and Op. 135, David Wyn Jones remarks: 'Their identity as five single works is a clear one, further borne out by the fact that each has a different overall movement pattern and, though extant sketches for the works reveal that certain characteristics ... were at one stage intended for a different quartet, nothing should ne allowed to detract from the formidable integrity of each of the five.'[xlvii]

It was not until 25 January 1823 that Beethoven responded to Galitzin, writing in French with the assistance of his nephew Karl. He expressed 'the great pleasure' he had derived from learning of the Prince's interest in his music and apologised for not having replied sooner due to 'pressure of work' — a reference to his preoccupation with the composition of the Ninth Symphony and the *Missa Solemnis*. He noted Galitzin's 'cultivation of the violincello' and, concerning the request for string quartets added, cryptically, 'I will take care to give you satisfaction in this regard'. He explained how as a composer he was obliged to live 'by the products of his mind' and therefore 'must take the liberty of setting the honorarium for one quartet at 50 ducats' that he trusted would be acceptable. Such, he anticipated, being the case he instructed payment should be made direct to his banker Hénikstein in Vienna. He concluded with a characteristically over-optimistic forecast: 'I bind myself to finish the first quartet by the end of the month of February or at the latest by the middle of March.'[xlviii]

In responding as Beethoven did to Nicolai Galitzin, we have an illustration of Louis Pasteur's proposition that 'Chance favours the prepared mind'. By this we mean it was fortunate indeed that the Russian music enthusiast should happen to request string quartets from Beethoven at the very moment when he was so disposed to work on such compositions, through a combination of his changing, inner musicological disposition and the external promptings of publishers — notably Carl Peters of Leipzig. Whilst, therefore, it is only fitting that the String Quartets Op. 127, 132, and 130 should be associated with the name of Prince Galitzin — and, for reasons of his nationality, should also be referred to as the 'Russian Quartets' — it is evident that Galitzin cannot lay claim to being the exclusive progenitor of these celebrated works. Kinderman makes the relevant observation: 'It is hardly credible that Beethoven's reawakened interest in quartet writing, after a lapse of fifteen years, is to be fully accounted for on the circumstances of Prince Galitzin's commission.' He posits: 'Is it not more plausible that the composer deliberately turned to the homogeneous timbre of the four stringed instruments as the medium best adapted to his mature thought?'[xlix]

Galitzin could hardly contain his delight when he received Beethoven's response to his proposals: 'Your letter of 25 January ... filled me with joy by making me hope I shall soon enjoy a new product of your sublime genius.' He arranged for the requested payment of 50 ducats to be made with the promise of a further 100 for the two others.[l] Over the next few months Galitzin appears to have established a bond of kinship with the composer — albeit it a rather (geographically) distant one — such that on 3 August he wrote to him remarking how his wife shared his love of music, 'is one of your great admirers', and how she looked forward to receiving and performing his latest piano sonatas.[li] Theodore Albrecht, whom we have just quoted, remarks: 'From Beethoven's putative exchanges with Peters, and his more conclusive negotiations with Galitzin, we can infer they must have encouraged the composer in his personal resolve to redirect his musical expression away from the medium of the piano sonata to that of the string quartet. Little wonder then, if such speculation has any foundation, that the C minor Piano Sonata, Op. 111 should be his last.'

Soon after, Beethoven learned from his former pupil Ferdinand Ries, then residing in London, that Charles Neate had expressed an interest in acquiring string quartets from him — yet further illustration of the extent to which his compositions were widely sought. Neate, pianist, cellist, composer and a founder member of the London (Royal) Philharmonic Society had made Beethoven's acquaintance on a visit to Vienna in 1815–16. On his return to England he had taken with him, on behalf of the Philharmonic Society, the three Concert Overtures *Die Ruinen von Athen*, *König Stephan* and *Zur Namensfier* for which the composer received the fee of 75 guineas. Beethoven got on well with Neate, described him to friends as 'an excellent musician and a charming man'.[lii] On 25 February Beethoven wrote to Neate informing him that he could have three string quartets and asked when would he like to receive them. A fee of 100 guineas was agreed. He concluded his letter with his often-expressed wish to visit England 'and meet all the splendid artists there'.[liii]

On 2 September, acting on his own behalf, Neate wrote to Beethoven: 'My intention was to ask some musical friends of mine to join with me in purchasing the manuscript of your three Quartets [Opp. 127, 132 and 130]; although I am not rich enough to undertake the venture alone, I am certainly ready to subscribe to my portion of the sum.'[liv] Neate explained he had raised £100 sterling on condition the money would be paid on receipt of the manuscripts. We discuss the English publication of the three Galitzin Quartets in our later remarks bearing on these works. Neate was only able to approach the composer in the way he did through Prince Galitzin's generosity. Although he had commissioned the String Quartets, Opp. 127, 132, and 130, he philanthropically allowed Beethoven to sell them as he wished; in so doing he was setting aside his privilege, under the copyright provisions of the period, to his exclusive use of them for a period of one year.

On 3 October Galitzin reaffirmed his intention to pay 50 ducats for the first of his commissioned quartets (Op. 127) and, further testimony to his good intentions, enquired of Beethoven what time-period would be acceptable for the payment of 150 ducats for all three Quartets.[iv] He then resolved to make the necessary financial arrangements. In the event, like so many good intentions, these financial undertakings would not be adequately fulfilled — at least not in the composer's lifetime. A combination of circumstances prevailed, outside the scope of our present discussion, which denied Beethoven the due reward for his labours. Suffice it to say: in the first instance Galitzin was distracted be being called away to attend a coronation ceremony; later he became embroiled in insurrections that broke out in Russia; and subsequently his personal fortune was much depleted. It was not until after Beethoven's death that Galitzin's heirs and legal representatives finally fulfilled the contract into which the two parties had originally entered. Reflecting on these circumstances, Schindler considered Beethoven may have been out of pocket by as much as 125 ducats — see later — but he acknowledged 'to say he was cheated is too strong an expression'.[vi]

Returning to the events of 1823, on 29 November

Galitzin wrote fulsomely to Beethoven: 'It was with inexpressible joy, dear sir, that I received the Mass [*Missa Solemnis*] that you recently composed, and though until now I have been able to judge it only from the score, I have found the same grandeur in it that distinguishes all your compositions and makes your works impossible of imitation. I am trying to get this work performed in a manner worthy of its creator.' In this instance he was as good as his word and the work received its world premier in St. Petersburg on 7 April, 1824. Revealing further evidence of his enthusiasm for the medium of the string quartet he adds: 'During my leisure moments, I even take pleasure in arranging some of your beautiful solo piano works as [string] quartets, and since I do not play this instrument, I take pleasure in performing them with the Quartet [a reference to his own group of instrumentalists].' Turning to the works he had commissioned, he continued: 'I am very impatient to possess a new quartet by you [Op. 127], but I beg you not to pay any attention to this, and to follow in that respect only your inspiration and the inclination of your mind, for no one knows better than I that one cannot command genius, rather must [one] leave it alone.'[lvii]

To 1823 belongs a portrait of Beethoven painted by the Austrian artist Georg Friedrich Waldmüller. It was commissioned by the music publisher Breitkopf & Härtel, further testimony to those in the music-publishing business eager to capitalise on the composer's celebrity; in engraved form, composers' portraits such as this were used to adorn sheet music. Waldmüller portrays Beethoven's countenance prematurely aged with no attempt having been made by him to idealize the composer as had other artists — albeit when he was much younger. According to Schindler, Beethoven was not in a good mood when the artist attempted to create the likeness; Beethoven resented being distracted from his work that may account for his sullen expression. Moreover, Waldmüller had to work quickly, being allowed only one sitting.[lviii] Also worthy of mention is the likeness the artist Stephan Drecher took of Beethoven in 1824. This chalk and pencil study portrays the composer with a resolute expression beneath the careworn countenance characteristic of his later years; it now belongs to the *Historisches Museum*, Vienna.[lix]

As 1824 approached Beethoven must have felt a twofold sense of relief; his creativity was once more rekindled and he was recovering from extended periods of illness. During the first months of 1821 he had been confined to bed with rheumatic fever and throughout July–August he suffered from jaundice. Similarly, during the first months of 1822, further bouts of Illness occurred undermining his capacity for creative work. The researches into Beethoven's many illnesses by the physician-musicologist Anton Neumayr, poignantly convey what Beethoven had to endure — despite the best efforts of his doctors to relieve his suffering.[lx]

1824 brought good news for Beethoven. On 24 February twenty-eight signatories sent the composer a fulsome letter expressing their esteem of him and his works. The signatories include several names that have appeared in our accompanying studies including: Artaria & Co., (one of the composer's first music publishers); Carl Czerny (Beethoven's former piano pupil and pianistic pedagogue); Anton Diabelli (composer and music publisher); Prince Eduard and Count Moritz Lichnowsky (respectively nephew and brother of Prince Carl Lichnowsky, Beethoven's friend and patron); and Andreas Streicher (piano manufacturer and long-time friend of Beethoven). We can only imagine how eagerly Beethoven's ardent admirer Franz Schubert would have added his name to this list had he been invited to do so. Collectively, Beethoven's devotees remark: 'Out of the wide circle of reverent admirers that surround your genius in your native city, a small number of disciples and lovers of art approach you today to express long-felt wishes.' They placed him on a level with Haydn and Mozart, regretted his enforced retirement from public life and looked forward to 'new blossoms' of his art and 'rejuvenated life'. In this context they reveal their awareness that 'a new flower grows in the garland of your glorious, still unequalled symphonies' [a reference to the Ninth Symphony, Op. 125] and of a 'grand sacred composition' [the *Missa Solemnis*, Op. 124]. Beethoven's admirers take leave of him by anticipating the spring in the hope that it will bring forth 'a twofold blossoming-time for us and the entire world of art'.[lxi]

The signatories to Beethoven's encomium make no mention of his preoccupation with Prince Galitzin's string quartets of which, doubtless, they would have been unaware. The Prince himself though still had them in mind since he wrote to Beethoven on 13 March: 'I pray you, let me know about when I may hope for the quartets I am awaiting so impatiently. If you want money, withdraw the amount from Messrs. Stieglitz & Co. in St. Petersburg; they will pay you any amount you wish.'[lxii] With the performance of the composer's *Missa Solemnis* on 7 April, Galitzin could not contain himself and, setting aside his concern regarding progress with the string quartets, he waxed eloquent: 'I haste, Monsieur, to give you news of the performance of your sublime masterpiece that we introduced to the public here ... The effect that this music made on the public is indescribable ... I never heard anything so sublime; I do not except even the masterpieces of Mozart.'[lxiii] He further enthused: 'One might say that your genius is centuries before its time and that there is no listener sufficiently enlightened to appreciate the full beauty of this music. But future generations will honour you and bless your memory more than your contemporaries are able.'[lxiv]

On 26 May Beethoven wrote once more to Galitzin. He thanked him for his 'many charming letters' and added 'You will soon receive your quartet [Op. 127], promised so long ago to you, perhaps also the others'. He offered to have the Ninth Symphony copied and sent to him. It was then Beethoven's turn to enthuse. He informed the Prince of a medal he had received from the French Emperor, Louis XVIII. Schindler writes: 'The first chancellor to the King, the Duc d'Achâts, announced in the most flattering terms that it had pleased his majesty to honour the artist with a gold medal showing the King's head.' This honorary gift had the weight of twenty-one louis d'or and inscribed on the reverse were the words: 'Donné par le Roi à Monsieur Beethoven.' Schindler considered this to be 'the greatest distinction conferred upon the master during his lifetime'. He conjectured: 'It could not fail to awaken in the artist a consciousness of his greatness and to raise his spirits to new heights.'[lxv]

In the summer of 1824, Beethoven commenced serious work on the first of Galitzin's quartets, the one in E-flat major, Op. 127. As was his habit he had taken residence in Baden to escape Vienna's oppressive heat, from whence he could enjoy the amenity of the countryside and benefit from the spa town's hydrotherapy facilities; illness was once more beginning to affect him to which Schindler attributed 'intestinal problems'. For several years Beethoven's physician had been Dr. Johann Malfatti; it was he who had recommended the curative powers of mineral springs. However, Beethoven subsequently fell out with him — an occupational hazard for anyone occupying such a position as Malfatti's — and the composer sought the advice of Dr. Jacob von Staudenheim. From what Schindler has to say, it appears that in collaborating with Staudenheim Beethoven met his match since 'this practitioner ... always insisted on the strictest observation of his prescriptions and would allow himself to speak sternly to his disobedient patient ... in fact, he brought to his task a degree of Viennese bluntness that impressed the patient and contributed to his recovery'.[lxvi] This was not, however, for several weeks and as a consequence work on Op. 127 was interrupted.

Amidst these circumstances, Beethoven received a letter on 16 August from the Leipzig music publisher Heinrich Probst. He was hoping to enter into a publishing agreement with the composer but felt obliged to approach him circumspectly since he was aware of Beethoven's earlier putative negotiations with Carl Peters, also of Leipzig — a reminder of the close world in which music publishers circulated and the competition that existed between them.[lxvii] In his reply of 28 August, Beethoven urged Probst not to pay too much attention 'to gossip' but intimated that his former negotiations with Peters were virtually at an end.[lxviii] As for Probst, Beethoven initially offered him the Bagatelles, Op. 126 but then, rather unprofessionally, changed his mind and sold them instead to the Mainz firm of Schotts. Perhaps, in order to keep good faith with Probst and to maintain his integrity, he later offered to sell him one or two of the quartets upon which he was working — the Galitzin Quartets — with the possibility also of the String Quartet, Op. 131. Probst, however, did not take up this proposal: his most significant gesture to Beethoven was his later publication of Carl Czerny's four-hand piano arrangements of the composer's nine symphonies.[lxix]

Beethoven returned from Baden in November but was still unwell. His doctor ordered him to stay indoors, however, typically strong willed, he ventured outside to take a walk in the fresh air and duly caught a chill. This made his condition all the worse, confining him to bed. His confinement at least absolved him from giving a prearranged composition lesion to his pupil the Archduke Rudolph that, notwithstanding the attention — and flattery — he bestowed upon him, was always a burdensome chore.[lxx]

Despite his many illnesses, Beethoven made progress with work on Galitzin's string quartets as his surviving sketchbooks reveal. It is estimated that perhaps as many as 8,000 pages of sketches are extant; many are from his later years with some relating to the late quartets.[lxxi] In Nicholas Cook's memorable summation: '[Beethoven] would write something [in sketch form] and then he would know [clarify] what he was trying to write. He used paper to improvise, to fight against — letting the paper speak back to him — whereas other composer's of the day would often work at the keyboard.'[lxxii] Those who have studied Beethoven's sketches have marvelled at the many-sided facets of the composer's genius they reveal. This was an aspect of his creativity considered by Roger Sessions in a lecture he gave in his capacity as Charles Eliot Norton Professor at the University of Harvard (1968–69). He remarked: 'Beethoven could have made a great deal out of any one of the earlier versions [of his sketches]. Obviously it would have been a different piece, and since that piece is not in existence we can never know what it would have been like.'[lxxiii] That said, musicologists such as Professor Giovanni Biamonti have reworked many of the composer's sketch-fragments to make greater musical sense of them and, operating on a larger scale, Professor Barrie Cooper may be cited in this context of his creation of a performing edition of the first movement of the Tenth Symphony extracted from the composer's many sketches.

Of his working method, Beethoven himself was disposed to say: 'I make many changes, and reject and try again until I am finished. Then the working-out in breadth, length, height and depth begins in my head and since I am conscious of what I want the underlying idea never deserts me.'[lxiv] Beethoven's contemporary Ignaz von Seyfried — a minor composer, cellist, pupil of Mozart and conductor at the *Theatre an der Wien* — is on record as saying: 'He was never seen out of doors without a little notebook, in which he jotted down his ideas. If anyone happened to remark upon it, he would parody Joan of Arc's words: "Nicht ohne meine Fahne darf ich kommen" — "I dare not come without my banner".' Von Seyfried concludes his recollections: 'He observed this rule with a firmness characteristic of great spirits.'[lxv]

From May 1823 to June 1824, Beethoven made use of a set of some forty sketch leaves now bound together and today known as Landsberg 11 after its one-time owner Ludwig Landsberg; it is now the property of the Berlin Deutsche Staatsbibliothek. From autumn 1824 to January 1825 he used a further thirty leaves that came into the possession of Anton Schindler who sold them in 1846 to the Berlin State Library. Today they exist as a sketchbook bound with a further sixteen leaves that date from around 1816; these now form part of the collection of the Berlin Staatsbibliothek Preussischer Kulturbesitz. Only a few sketches survive for the String Quartet in E-flat major, Op. 127, notably for the first movement, and belong to June 1824; these are shared with sketches for the six Bagatelles. Op. 126.

Further insights into the creation origins of the Galitzin Quartets are revealed in Beethoven's score sketches that also belong to his late period; prior to then he seldom worked in full score before proceeding to the final autograph. The sketches from the period 1824–26 reveal many such sketches and 'reflect an important development in Beethoven's compositional process'. To facilitate this, he made use of oblong-format leaves with typically 10, 12, 14, or 16 staves to a page. Unlike the pocket sketch leaves, Beethoven left the score sheets unbound. At the auction of the composer's effects in 1827, some 350 of these score sheets were purchased by the publisher Artaria & Co. and were acquired in 1901 by the Berlin State Library. Over another hundred such leaves were gifted over time by an unknown benefactor to the Gesellschaft der Musikfreunde. The score sketches for the late quartets, as listed in the original Artaria collection, is as follows: Op.127, 49 leaves; Op. 130, 24 leaves; Op. 131, 165 leaves; Op. 132, 22 leaves; Op. 133, 5 leaves; and Op. 135, 79 leaves.

From May to September 1825, Beethoven used a sketchbook originally consisting of 42 leaves (now reduced to 40) which today are known collectively as the De Roda Sketchbook that takes its name form its previous owner, the Spanish collector Cecilio de Roda. It was in the possession of his family until 1962 when it was acquired from his heirs by the Beethovenhaus. The cover is inscribed: 'Autograph e Louis van Beethoven. Livre d'esquisses des motifs du Quatour/en La Mineur et autre études/L'authenticié en est garantie par Artaria & Co. à Vienne/1847.' Its contents include sketches for the Quartets Opp. 130, 132, and 133.

From October to November 1825 belong some forty miscellaneous sheets known as the Kullak Sketchbook, this time deriving from the name of its former owner the collector Franz Kullak. It contains ideas for Opp. 130, 132 and 133. A further 62 leaves, Kullak SPK (Berlin Staatsbibliothek Preussischer Kulturbesitz) belong to 1825–26 and contain drafts for the following: Op. 130 (fifth, sixth and seventh movements); Op. 131 all movements: Op. 133 as the finale to Op. 130; and Op. 135 all movements.[lxxvi]

It will be recalled that in 1823 Charles Neate had approached Beethoven in the hope of securing from him some string quartets. Beethoven's correspondence with Neate provides insights into the progress he was making with what would eventually become the Galitzin Quartets.

On 20 December Neate wrote once more to Beethoven to reaffirm his interest in these compositions, moreover he hoped to revive Beethoven's aspirations to visit England. With this in mind he explained it was his pleasant duty to say: 'The Philharmonic Society is disposed to give you 300 guineas for your visit, and expects in return that you will take charge of the direction of your works, at least one of which will be performed at each [forthcoming] concert.' The Society also expressed the hope Beethoven would compose a symphony and a concerto, both of which would remain his property. Given the English public's growing awareness of Beethoven's celebrity — more correctly that of London concert-going audiences — the Society was convinced yet further opportunities existed 'to win honour and money from your great talent'. As for the string quartets, Neate added: 'If you bring along the Quartets of which I wrote to you, that is as good as £100 more.[lxxvii]

On 15 January 1825 Beethoven, who had only a modest command of English, replied to Neate in French, once again with the assistance of his nephew Karl who was then residing with his uncle. He opens: 'Ce fut avec le plus grand plaisir que je reçus votre letter ... par laquelle vous avez eu la bonté de m'avertir que la Société Philharmonique distinguée d'artistes m'invite à venir à Londres.' He expressed his satisfaction with the terms offered but requested additional funds to meet his travelling costs. He reassured Neate that the Ninth Symphony would not be published in Germany before the end of the year so as to ensure the Philharmonic Society would have performing-right priority. He stressed the composition should be rehearsed with care, preferably in small sections. He gave an undertaking to bring a new quartet with him but did not specify any details.[lxxviii]

On 1 February, Neate replied to Beethoven 'with great sorrow' that the Philharmonic Society could not meet his travelling expenses and that its offer of 300 guineas must stand. He explained the Society was not able to provide further payments on the grounds 'the directors must abide by the laws of the Society and were not masters of their conduct in all things'. He stated how willingly he would defray the costs himself if it were within his means. On a more positive note, he informed Beethoven the Ninth Symphony was soon to be rehearsed; it duly received its first English performance on 21 March. In this letter Neate made no reference though to string quartets.[lxxix] Thayer recounts that 'many prevailed upon Beethoven to make the trip to England' pointing out that Haydn had done so in the 1790s and when at a greater age than himself.[lxxx] Beethoven, however, had misgivings and on 19 March he informed Neate he would not be coming in the spring but 'peutêtre en automne'? He did, though, keep alive the prospect of publishing his new string quartets in England, provided he retained priority over them for a period of a year and-a-half or two years. As he explained it would be 'very advantageous to his finances'. Beethoven reassured Neate he had completed the first quartet, Op. 127 and that he was making progress with the other two, Op. 132 and Op. 130.[lxxxi]

On 25 May Beethoven wrote once more to Neate in London, reaffirming his satisfaction with the Philharmonic Society's offer of £100 pounds for the three quartets that he had in hand but warned that the first quartet, Op. 127, was much in demand ('est si cherché par les plus celebres artistes de Vienne') and had already been promised them for their benefit. He therefore urged Neate to let him know if he was satisfied with his conditions, so that he could send the first quartet right away; he stipulated the honorarium for this composition would not be due until he had reported the completion of the other two quartets.[lxxxii]

Evidence of Beethoven's progress with the composition of the Galitzin Quartets derives from other of the composer's correspondence. On 24 August he wrote to his then secretary-assistant Karl Holz: 'My dear fellow, the last Quartet too is to have six movements; and I hope to complete them [the set of three] by the end of the month.'[lxxxiii] He was referring to the B-flat major Quartet, Op. 130 that he had started to compose having finished the second one, Op. 132, in July. His anticipation to have the Op. 130 Quartet completed so soon proved to be wildly optimistic. He was still working on it as late as November. At this time he wrote in a conversation book: 'Title for the Quartet', and in another hand [probably to assist Beethoven with his French] is written '3 ième Quatuor, pour deux violins, viola et violincello composé aux désirs de S. A. Monseigneur le Prince Nicolas Galitzin et dédié au meme', to which Beethoven added: 'par L. v. B.'[lxxxiv]

Although Beethoven's relations with Carl Peters in Leipzig had by now become strained, he appears to have entertained the hope that his negotiations with him might still have a fruitful outcome. He wrote to him that he had a quartet 'lying ready ... and what is more a grand one'. This may be taken as a reference to the String Quartet, in A minor, Op. 132. He adds: 'Therefore, as soon as you let me know that you will take it for 360 gulden or 80 ducats, it will be sent to you at once.' He justified his price on the grounds: 'My compositions are now being paid for at higher rates than ever.' He urged Peters to make haste 'by the next post' for the reason 'someone else wants to have both this quartet and another one and also a new one I have just finished'.[lxxxv] Beethoven's references here are to Op. 132 and Op. 130, of the Galitzin set, and most likely Op. 131 on which he had just begun work.

The 'someone else' mentioned in Beethoven's letter was the publisher Schlesinger. Earlier in the year he had offered to publish all the composer's quartets 'and periodically to have from him each time a new one of these and to pay him what he wished'.[lxxxvi] Beethoven was reluctant to enter into such an agreement though since he believed it would harm his chances of having all his works published in a single collected edition — a thing he had long cherished. On 22 September Moritz (Maurice) Schlesinger, whose publishing house was based in Paris, did sign an agreement with Beethoven for the publication of the String Quartet, Op. 132 for which he paid 80 ducats in gold.[lxxxvii] At this time Beethoven may also have intended to let Schlesinger publish the Quartet, Op. 130 that was as yet unfinished; it was, however, subsequently brought out by Artaria & Co.

As for Peters, in the end nothing came of his protracted negotiations with Beethoven. Later in the year the composer returned the money he had previously received from the Leipzig publisher thereby putting an end to their relationship. Charles Neate's endeavours in connection with the publication of the Galitzin Quartets in England were no more successful. It was the Italian-born English composer, pianist, and pedagogue Muzio Clementi who eventually published the first of the Galitzin set, Op. 127. We consider the English publication of the other quartets in our later texts relating to the individual works concerned.

In a quite different context, 1825 ended memorably for Beethoven. On 29 November he was one of fifteen musicians that the Directors of the *Gesellschaft der Musikfreunde* elected to its Honorary Membership. Amongst the others, so honoured, was Luigi Cherubini whose music Beethoven then greatly admired. The election was confirmed by the Society on 26 January 1826, but the Diploma was not issued until 26 October and was not received by Beethoven until 7 March 1827, just a few weeks before his death.[lxxxviii][lxxxix]

1826 did not start well for Beethoven regarding his health; his abdominal pains returned and his work was hindered by a persistent eye infection. Circumstances were more auspicious though concerning the Galitzin Quartets. The A minor Quartet, Op. 132 had received its first public performance on 6 November 1825 in Vienna. News of this eventually reached St. Petersburg where the Prince himself read an account of its concert performance in the *Allgemeine musikalische Zeitung*. On 14 January he wrote enthusiastically: 'I am so impatient to become acquainted with this new masterpiece that I request you to send it to me without delay, by post, like the preceding one.'[xc] He arranged for payment of 75 ducats to be deposited with his banker Stieglitz; 50 ducats was for the Quartet and 25 ducats for the Overture, Op. 124 *Consecration of the House* that Beethoven had dedicated to Galitzin.

On 22 April Beethoven wrote to Moritz Schlesinger to clear up a misunderstanding. He explained he had allowed Mathias Artaria to publish the String Quartet, Op. 130 (see above) that Schlesinger thought was to be his. To exonerate himself, Beethoven told Schlesinger 'another quartet will be finished in two or three weeks' time' — a typical Beethovenian exaggeration.[xci] This is a reference to the String Quartet in F major, Op. 135 that was in fact not published until May 1827, after the composer's death, and did not receive its first public performance until March the following year.

It is from about this period that Beethoven's relations with Prince Galitzin became strained, due to a default in the promised payment for the string quartets that he had received in good faith. In response to Beethoven's request for the outstanding payment to be made, the Prince's Banker

Stieglitz & Co., in St. Petersburg, wrote to Beethoven on 13 August undertaking to remind their client of his obligations with the reassurance not to fail to inform Beethoven of the outcome.[xcii] Unknown to Beethoven, the Prince's fortunes had changed; he had been called away from St. Petersburg to Kozlov (Koslov), some 250 miles distant from Moscow, where he was embroiled in the conflict between Russia and Persia. Moreover he was involved in bankruptcy proceedings and his beloved wife was in her final illness.[xciii]

It was not until 22 November that Galitzin was in a position to write to Beethoven to apologize for his conduct. He touches upon 'the unfortunate circumstances' in which he found himself and cited 'some great losses' that had caused him 'several bankruptcies'. More positively, he acknowledged receipt of the composer's 'two new masterpieces' — the String Quartets, Opp. 132 and 130 — that he considered a product of Beethoven's 'immortal and inexhaustible genius'. Elsewhere, however, Galitzin expressed his recognition of the composer's achievements in more cautious terms. He found 'the poetic idea' was hidden beneath 'phrases of seeming angularity' and 'only revealed — even to the discerning — after long imaginative researches into the mind of the composer'. He recognised the need for 'perfect technical performance'. With this in view he held recitals in his own home at which nothing but Beethoven was played 'in all his various styles'. Such was Galitzin's enthusiasm he was reproached for 'this mania for Beethoven'. Notwithstanding, he writes: 'I was undeterred by disparaging criticism from my effort to make known among artists and amateurs the last works of a genius several decades ahead of his generation.' According to the Prince's testimony, his endeavours were successful: 'My perseverance was rewarded at last, because ten years later Beethoven's music, so far from being called extraordinary and harsh, was being played all over the capitol in drawing rooms and concert halls.'[xciv]

Concerning his financial obligations, Galitzin gave a further undertaking to have the outstanding 125 ducats (see previous) paid to Beethoven through Messrs Stieglitz.[xcv] Nothing came of this, however, and on 18 January 1827 the banking house was obliged to write to Beethoven once more: '[We] are notifying you that we have already written on your behalf to Prince Nicolas Galitzin in Koslov ... and reminded him of your demand for 125 ducats. We are still therefore awaiting his answer, of which we shall not fail to notify you after its receipt.'[xcvi] Beethoven persisted and on 21 March — on his deathbed and just five days before he passed away — he set forth in detail the circumstances of his financial dealings with Prince Galitzin and the latter's outstanding obligations to him. This was the last letter of any consequence written by Beethoven.[xcvii] As previously remarked, negotiations with Galitzin and his representatives dragged on for more than a quarter of a century before achieving resolution. This only came about after recriminatory letters appeared in the *Neue Zeitschrift für Musik* and the *Gazette musicale de Paris* together with the intervention of Count von Nesselrode, then Ambassador in Vienna. Prince Galitzin first paid fifty-five ducats, and later seventy-five more to Beethoven's nephew Karl — but too late to be of assistance to the composer.[xcviii]

In mid October 1826, Beethoven relocated from Baden to Vienna where he took up residence in the so-called *Schwarzspanierhaus* — usually translated as *The house of the black-robed Spaniard*. He occupied a spacious apartment on the second floor consisting of eight rooms. Although long demolished, some impression of the *Schwarzspanierhaus* is conveyed in Franz Xavier Stöber's lithograph showing the great crush of people who had assembled in front of it on the day of the composer's internment.[xcix] A fortuitous consequence of Beethoven's relocation to this property was that it reunited him with his old friend Stephan von Breuning who lived nearby. Beethoven developed a close friendship with Breuning's son Gerhard to whom he was wont to refer as his 'little trouser button' on account of the close attachment he had to him.

On 7 December, Beethoven wrote to his 'beloved old friend' to express his pleasure at being united with him once more. He regretted that illness had confined him to bed and was depriving him of the strength to write only a few lines. He told Stephan how, with the passing of the years, he had been elected both a member of the *Royal Society of Sweden* and the *Royal Institute of Science and Fine Arts* of Amsterdam, both in recognition of his international reputation, and also of being made an Honorary Citizen of Vienna for his contributions to various charitable causes.[c]

A great comfort to Beethoven in his last weeks came via Johann Andreas Stumpff. Although of German descent, he lived and worked in London where he acquired a considerable fortune as a harp maker — although by inclination he was a poet — being on friendly terms with none other that Goethe.[ci] Stumpff first made Beethoven's acquaintance in 1824 during his travels on the continent, having secured the necessary letter of introduction to the aloof composer from the piano maker Andreas Streicher. It was at this time that Stumpff learned of Beethoven's great admiration for Handel and his music. According to the composer-pianist Cipriani Potter, like Stumpff based in London, it was from about 1817 that Beethoven became absorbed in Handel's music — to the extent he once confessed that Handel had now supplanted Mozart in his estimation as 'the greatest composer that ever lived'. Stumpff, learning of Beethoven's condition, purchased Samuel Arnold's forty-volume set of Handel's works and arranged for them to be sent to the ailing composer. This was undertaken, free of charge, by the Viennese piano maker Johann Streicher who informed Stumpff 'you will be greatly pleased to learn your gift gave the greatest joy to our poor Beethoven, who is confined in such misery to his sickbed, and made him forget his woeful condition'.[cii] Such indeed was Beethoven's 'great joy' that he resolved to dedicate a composition to Stumpff but which regrettably he was not able to fulfil.[ciii]

Dr. Andreas Wawruch, formerly a professor and surgeon at the University of Prague, attempted to alleviate Beethoven's symptom's through a combination of the administration of frozen punch (fruit juice with alcohol) and massaging the abdomen with ice-cold water; Beethoven's stomach was so swollen by dropsy that it required periodic drainage — a painful procedure that Beethoven is said to have endured with his characteristic fortitude.[civ]

Beethoven wrote to Johann Stumpff on 8 February to express his pleasure and gratitude at receiving Handel's works, to which he referred as his 'royal gift'. More importantly, for this part of our narrative, he drew attention to his worsening financial circumstances. He intimated how beneficial it would be to him if Sir George Smart could arrange for the Philharmonic Society of London to hold a concert for his benefit — Smart being a founder member of the Society.[cv] On 22 February he wrote in a similar manner to Ignaz Moscheles enclosing a further letter intended for Sir George. In this he supplicates: 'I live on what I can earn by my intellectual works; and at the moment I just cannot think of composing.'[cvi] Such was Beethoven's concern that on 6 March he wrote once more to Smart to encourage him to exert his influence with the Philharmonic Society 'to carry out their former decision to give a concert for my benefit'.[cvii]

In the closing months of Beethoven's life, Anton Schindler was restored to favour as the composer's unpaid secretary-assistant — having been temporarily supplanted in this role by Karl Holz. He relates how Beethoven had consulted with both himself and his friend Stephan von Breuning as to the prudence of seeking financial assistance from abroad. Schindler writes: 'We did not conceal our fears that such a step was bound to become public knowledge sooner or later and would create a bad impression. We made so bold as to remind our sick friend of the government bonds he still had in his possession, and recommended he postpone for some time asking aid from a foreign quarter.'[cviii] Schindler is referring here to the investments Beethoven had made following the highly successful series of concerts he had given at the period of the Congress of Vienna. However, he no longer regarded these as being his own property, having set them aside as an inheritance for his Nephew.

On learning of Beethoven's parlous state, Stumpff wrote to Beethoven on 1 March informing him he had consulted with Smart and Moscheles who had told him that a benefit concert of the kind the composer so desired 'could not be accomplished at a moment's notice'. However, Stumpff bore the good news that the Directors of the Philharmonic Society had authorised £100 to be paid to the Rothschild Banking House in Vienna upon which Beethoven could draw as he needed. The Directors ardently wished Beethoven a good recovery and trusted 'the hearts of [his] admirers would soon be uplifted on the waves of a *Symphony of Thanks* [italics added] streaming from [his] breast'.[cix] This gesture of the Philharmonic Society is recognised for being one of music's most praiseworthy charitable acts; the sum made available to Beethoven would be the equivalent today of about £8,000.[cx]

Beethoven was of course in no position to even contemplate the composition of a 'Symphony of Thanks' — had he lived we can assume he would almost certainly have done so. He did, however, find the strength on 18 March to dictate a letter to Ignaz Moscheles with the assistance of Anton Schindler. He told the Directors he was profoundly moved by the Philharmonic Society's generosity to his 'innermost soul'. Such was his need he drew on the £100 at once: it was the equivalent of 1,000 florins in the Viennese currency of the period. It also amounted to the same sum he had requested of various publishers for his *Missa Solemnis* — on which he had worked over a number of years. Still musically alert, in his letter to Moscheles he included a set of metronome markings for the Ninth Symphony, Op. 125 that he still hoped would be performed at a future London benefit concert.[cxi]

We take leave now of Beethoven and his personal circumstances and recount some of the responses his new and daring string-quartet writing provoked.

In 1812, Louis Spohr was in Vienna where he was scheduled to conduct some of his oratorios. In his *Autobiography* he writes how he wished to meet the composer at one of Vienna's many musical parties but learned Beethoven had withdrawn from such reunions 'for his deafness had so much increased that he could not hear music readily or clearly, and he had become exceedingly shy of society'. Spohr eventually encountered Beethoven by chance in a restaurant, recalling: 'One had to shout loud enough to be heard three rooms off.' He describes the composer as being a little abrupt 'but a pair of sparkling eyes gleamed under his shaggy eyebrows'. Spohr then expresses his opinion of Beethoven's music that he states was current at the time, and with which he concurred for many years afterwards: 'His ear could no longer guide him in his constant strivings after originality and new forms. Was it, then, wonderful [not surprising] that his works should become more and more strange, incoherent and incomprehensible? ... I ... freely confess that I have never been able to acquire a taste for Beethoven's later works.'[cxii]

An entry from the diary of the nineteen-year old Franz Schubert, from 16 June 1816, records his impressions of contemporary music. He cites the 'bizzarrerie' of current musical trends and attributes these to the influence of 'one of our greatest living artists'. This is certainly a reference to Beethoven who he considered — notwithstanding his profound admiration of him — 'unites and confuses the tragic and the comic, the pleasant and the repulsive without compunction'.[cxiii]

Beethoven's conceptions were clearly too modern for Carl Maria von Weber as he appears to suggest, albeit somewhat indirectly, in an appreciation he wrote on 23 July 1818, in support of the music of Friedrich Fesca, a contemporary violinist and composer. Weber makes the following indirect reference to Beethoven: 'Herr Fesca can be gay, even witty ... He is scrupulous in detail and his music recalls Spohr ... but he is by nature too gentle to seize the listener unexpectedly, as Beethoven does, and suddenly hold him in his giant fist over the edge of a precipice'.[cxiv]

In 1827 the correspondent of the *Berliner Allgemeine musikalische Zeitung* reviewed the String Quartet, Op. 127. He advised his readers the work required 'repeated hearings in order to be understood' and only after such careful study would 'the unfamiliar harmonies seem like the streaks of the Milky Way'.[cxv]

In the winter of 1829, Anton Schindler — a competent violinist — studied the Galitzin Quartets with Count Franz von Brunsvik with whom Beethoven had enjoyed a particularly warm friendship; it was to the Count that he had dedicated the *Appassionata* Piano Sonata. Schindler describes Brunsvik as being 'one of the most perceptive connoisseur's of Beethoven's compositions'. The reading through of the Quartets, however, proved a challenge as Schindler admitted: 'Our study revealed the harmonic and technical beauties of the music, but, as for recognizing a logical sequence of ideas, our efforts here and elsewhere remained fruitless.'[cxvi]

In later years when at work on his study of the composer, Schindler reflected more generally on the Galitzin String Quartets: 'In the entire Beethoven literature no other compositions have given rise to more argument or controversy, and we can hardly hope for agreement or a satisfactory explanation, at least not in the sense that other, earlier works, have been explained.' He considered contemporary critics 'were generally cautious and reserved in their evaluation of these quartets'. He also acknowledged though there were 'unbiased art connoisseurs' who, 'after spending years studying this legacy, came to the conviction that in some parts (not all, as the attackers maintain) the combination of notes seemed to be carried to the furthest extreme of intellectual reflection'. Perhaps with a mind to future performers and hearers, Schindler concluded: 'Everyone, except the unconditional believer, will have to concede that this situation will remain a permanent obstacle to a sure understanding of the music's poetic intentions, that all one can do is make random guesses and specious explanations.'[cxvii]

Karl Holz once remarked to Beethoven that of the three Galitzin Quartets he most preferred the String Quartet in B-flat major, Op. 130. When he ventured to ask Beethoven himself which he most favoured, he replied laconically: 'Each in its own way. Art demands of us that we shall not stand still.' Later, after further reflection, Holz states 'he declared the C-sharp minor to be his greatest'.[cxviii]

In his study of the patrons and publics of Beethoven's late quartets, Leon Botstein remarks that these new and innovative compositions could not be readily mastered by performers or easily assimilated by audiences without diligent rehearsal by the former and frequent hearings by the latter: "The quartets demanded repeated playings and rehearsings and study to permit a deeper appreciation of their coherence and shape.'[cxix] Tchaikovsky, whose idol was Mozart, found in these last works of Beethoven 'glimmers and nothing more', dismissing the rest as 'chaos'.[cxx]

We have seen that Ignaz Schuppanzigh and his fellow instrumentalists were pioneers in bringing these works into the public domain. Other string-quartet performers of the early nineteenth century also took up the challenge. In 1819 the Hungarian violinist Joseph Böhm assembled a quartet consisting of three of the previous members of Schuppanzigh's group, namely Holz, Weiss, and Linke. In 1834, following the death of Ignaz Schuppanzigh, Holz and Linke formed a new quartet under the direction of the violinist Leopold Jansa. These players had the honour of giving the first performance, in Vienna, of the String Quartet in C-sharp minor, Op. 131. The Müller Quartet consisted of four brothers who initially performed for the Duke of Brunswick. Later, as a quartet playing under their own name, they are credited with 'bringing the art of string-quartet playing to a degree of perfection previously unknown'. They had such works as the *Razumovsky* String Quartets in their repertoire and gave one of the early pubic renderings of the String Quartet Op. 131. In England *The Beethoven Quartet Society* was established in 1845 by Thomas Alsager, a pioneering music critic of *The Times*. The Society was based in the *Beethoven Rooms* in London's Harley Street where it held recitals 'to honour Beethoven'. One of its stated aims was to encourage the study of the composer's quartets 'from score'. In its first season, the society gave the first performance of the complete cycle of Beethoven string quartets in a series of concerts that ran from April–June.[cxxi]

Of the initial reception of the Galitzin Quartets in France, Joseph de Marliave writes that most critics emphasized 'the curious blending of genius and extravagance' they seemed to present. The compositions were recognized for their 'extraordinary beauty' but were held to be 'marred by blemishes and by passages of inexplicable obscurity'. De Marliave concludes: 'One gains the impression of admiration mixed with an uneasy, even awestruck, astonishment ... contemporary opinion was entirely bewildered by these works, which are still fascinating mysteries to us after a century of advance in musical thought.'[cxxii]

We consider the fortunes of the three individual Galitzin String Quartets, and the related *Grosse Fuge*, in our following texts. Although we have previously cited Sir Charles Hubert Parry's summation of Beethoven's later compositional style, given its appositeness it makes a fitting conclusion to our present study. It will be recalled he stated: 'Beethoven had by now found the accepted scheme of organisation which he himself had brought to perfection too constraining and restrictive to the impulse of his thought, and therefore endeavoured to find new types of form to revive sundry earlier types of organisation and combine them in various ways which departed from the essential principles upon which composers had been working for generations.'[cxxiii]

---

[i] Emily Anderson, 1961, Vol. 2, Letter No. 550, pp. 519–20.
[ii] Rebecca Clarke *The Beethoven quartets as a player sees them* in: *Musical Times*, Special Issue, London: Vol. VIII, No. 2, 1927, pp. 184–90.
[iii] Marion M. Scott, 1940, p. 263.
[iv] Mälzel evolved a number of designs. The first was a conical-shaped device made from copper; another was a piped-shaped trumpet with a perforated

cover — to keep insects out; and two others were of similar design but supplied with a headpiece to help bear their weight. They are thought to have been of little use but Beethoven continued to place his trust in future innovations from which he did not, alas, live to benefit. Beethoven's hearing aids are illustrated on the Beethoven House, Digital Archives, Library Document, R 2. See also: Derek Melville in: Denis Arnold and Nigel Fortune, editors, 1973, plate 8.

[v] Quoted by Joseph de Marliave, 1925, (1961 reprint), p. 199.

[vi] See, for example: Anton Felix Schindler, edited by Donald W. MacArdle and translated by Constance S. Jolly from the German edition of 1860, 1966, 341 and endnote 149.

[vii] For the opening of the Congress of Vienna in 1814, Beethoven either conducted or took part in the performance of several of his compositions. The series had commenced on 8 December 1813 and before the Congress on 27 February, he gave — to great acclaim — the final of four *Akademie* (benefit) Concerts at Vienna's Grosser Redoutensaal.

[viii] Both images are illustrated in: Oscar George Theodore Sonneck, 1927. For discussion of these see: Thayer-Forbes, p. 742 and H. C. Robbins Landon, 1970, p. 16 and plate 11.

[ix] As recalled in: Oscar George Theodore Sonneck, 1927, p. 109.

[x] As recalled in: Ludwig Nohl, 1880, pp. 174– 9. The Styrian Musical Society was founded in 1815 and in 1820 its list of members included Beethoven, alongside such other composers as Diabelli, Moscheles and Salieri. In 1823 it elected Franz Schubert to its membership, one of the few honours conferred on Beethoven's gifted young contemporary in his lifetime.

[xi] Emily Anderson, 1961, Vol. 2, Letter No. 943, p. 808, note 2.

[xii] Harold Truscott, 1968, p. 22.

[xiii] Maynard Solomon, 1977, pp. 294.

[xiv] C. H. H Parry, *Style in Musical Art*, 1911, p. 95; quoted by Maynard Solomon — see preceding.

[xv] Joseph Kerman, 1967, p. 200.

[xvi] *Ibid*, p. 131 and pp. 218–22.

[xvii] Joseph de Marliave, 1925, (1961 reprint), p. 219 and footnote 1.

[xviii] Maynard Solomon, 1977, p. 302.

[xix] Harold Truscott, 1968, pp. 38–9.

[xx] Emily Anderson, 1961, Vol. 3, Letter No. 1410, pp. 1231–2.

[xxi] William Kinderman, 1997, pp. 282–3.

[xxii] Marion M. Scott, 1940, p. 266.

[xxiii] Anton Schindler, 1860, English edition: Donald MacArdle, 1966, p. 309.

[xxiv] Quoted in: H. C. Robbins Landon, 1970, p. 180.

[xxv] Quoted in: Oscar George Theodore Sonneck, 1927, pp. 116–20.

[xxvi] Derived from Ludwig Nohl, 1880, pp. 200–1. See also: Oscar George Theodore Sonneck, 1927, pp. 114–16 and Peter Clive, 2001, pp. 298–99.

[xxvii] Wayne M. Senner, Robin Wallace and William Meredith editors, 1999, Vol. 1, p. 65.

[xxviii] See, for example: Leon Botstein, *Music, culture and society in Beethoven's Vienna*, in: Robert Winter and Robert Martin, editors, 1994, pp. 91–2.

[xxix] Christian Schubart outlined his views in: *Ideen zu einer Aesthetik der Tonkunst* (1806). Beethoven was interested in Schubart's writings, particularly his theory in which he characterised the musical keys with feelings and ascribed to them a certain 'psyche'. For example, he considered A-flat minor implied 'difficult struggle' and 'wailing lament' and B minor suggested 'patience' and 'calm awaiting one's fate'. In comparison, C major was the key with the connotation 'completely pure'. For an account of Schubart's theories and Beethoven's attachment to them, see: Anton Schindler, 1860,

English edition: Donald MacArdle, 1966, pp. 366-7. As expressed by Leon Botstein, *Music, culture and society in Beethoven's Vienna*, in: Robert Winter and Robert Martin, editors, 1994, pp. 91–2.

xxx Quoted in: Joseph de Marliave, *Beethoven's quartets*, 1925 (reprint 1961), p. 221.

xxxi See Martin Cooper, 1970, p. 74.

xxxii Robert Winter, *Performing the Beethoven quartets in their first century* in: Robert Winter and Robert Martin editors, 1994, pp. 37–41.

xxxiii *Ibid*.

xxxiv Barry Cooper, 1990, p. 35.

xxxv For an account of Carl Peters and his negotiations with Beethoven see: Peter Clive, 2001, p. 260.

xxxvi Theodore Albrecht, translator and editor, 1996, Vol. 2, Letter No. 286, pp. 204–6.

xxxvii Emily Anderson, editor and translator, Vol. 2, Letter No. 1079, pp. 947–50, 1961.

xxxviii Theodore Albrecht, translator and editor, 1996, Vol. 2 Letter No. 290, pp. 211–14.

xxxix *Ibid*, 1996, Vol. 2 Letter No. 294, pp. 220–22.

xl Emily Anderson, editor and translator, 1961, Vol. 3, Letter No.1085, pp. 955–6.

xli Theodore Albrecht, translator and editor, 1996, Vol. 2 Letter No. 295 pp. 222–5.

xlii See Theodore Albrecht's commentary to Letter No. 295, pp. 222–5.

xliii *Ibid*, 1996, Vol. 2 Letter No. 300, pp. 230–2.

xliv Joseph de Marliave, 1925, (reprint 1961), p. 207. See also: Marion M. Scott, 1940, p. 264.

xlv Theodore Albrecht, translator and editor, 1996, Vol. 2 Letter No. 299, pp. 228–9. See also: Thayer-Forbes, 1967, p. 815 and Anton Schindler, 1860 (1966), p. 251. For a lithographic representation of Prince Nicholas Galitzin, see: Beethoven House, Digital Archives, Library Document, B. 1560. Galitzin looks rather portly as he stands wielding a short baton as though conducting an orchestra.

xlvi Anton Felix Schindler edited by Donald W. MacArdle and translated by Constance S. Jolly from the German edition of 1860, 1966, p. 302.

xlvii David Wyn Jones, *Beethoven and the Viennese legacy* in: Robin Stowell editor, *The Cambridge companion to the string quartet*, 2003, pp. 221–2.

xlviii Emily Anderson, editor and translator, 1961, Vol. 3, Letter No. 1123, pp. 988–9. See also: Thayer-Forbes, 1967, pp. 815–16.

xlix William Kinderman, editor, 2005, p. 50.

l Theodore Albrecht, translator and editor, 1996, Vol. 2, Letter No. 310, pp. 244–5.

li *Ibid*, Letter No. 333, pp. 277–8.

lii Peter Clive, 2001, pp. 245–6.

liii Emily Anderson, editor and translator, 1961, Vol. 3, Letter No. 1144, pp. 1007–8.

liv Theodore Albrecht, translator and editor, 1996, Vol. 2 Letter No. 334, pp. 279–80.

lv *Ibid*, Vol. 2 Letter No. 336, pp. 281–2.

lvi Anton Felix Schindler edited by Donald W. MacArdle and translated by Constance S. Jolly from the German edition of 1860, 1966, p. 309 and pp. 459–64. See also: Thayer-Forbes, 1967, p. 978.

lvii Theodore Albrecht, translator and editor, 1996, Vol. 2 Letter No. 338, pp.283–5. For a facsimile reproduction of this letter together with the original German text, see: Beethoven House, Digital Archives, Library

Document, NE 54.
[lviii] For a commentary to the circumstances surrounding the Waldmüller portrait and contemporary opinions of it, see: Peter Clive, 2001, pp. 283–5.
[lix] This is a frequently reproduced study of the composer. See, for example: Frontispiece to Theodore Albrecht, translator and editor, 1996, Vol. 3.
[lx] Anton Neumayr, *Music and medicine*, 1994–1997. In addition to his study of Beethoven's illnesses, Neumayr also includes those endured by Haydn, Mozart and Schubert.
[lxi] Quoted in: Theodore Albrecht, translator and editor, 1996, Vol. 3, Document No. 344, pp. 4–11.
[lxii] Anton Schindler, from whom the quoted words derive, remarks: 'This note bears the unmistakable mark of a princely character, not to mention the *pseudo brother*, to have such a generous music-lover as a patron.' Anton Felix Schindler edited by Donald W. MacArdle and translated by Constance S. Jolly from the German edition of 1860, 1966 p. 302. Galitzin's letter is reproduced in full in: Theodore Albrecht, translator and editor, 1996, Vol. 3 Letter No. 379, pp. 52–4.
[lxiii] Theodore Albrecht, translator and editor, 1996, Vol. 3 Letter No. 355, pp. 23–4.
[lxiv] Cited by Anton Felix Schindler edited by Donald W. MacArdle and translated by Constance S. Jolly from the German edition of 1860, 1966 p. 302. See also: Marion M. Scott, 1940, p. 263 who includes a commentary relating to the late quartets. Galitzin's letter, combined with a scholarly commentary, is included in Theodore Albrecht, translator and editor, 1996, Vol. 3, Letter No. 355, pp. 23–4.
[lxv] Anton Felix Schindler edited by Donald W. MacArdle and translated by Constance S. Jolly from the German edition of 1860, 1966, p. 242. See also: Thayer-Forbes, 1967, pp. 923–6 and Emily Anderson, editor and translator, 1961, Vol. 3, Letter No. 1292, pp. 1127–29. The medal is now a prized possession of the Gesellschaft der Musikfreunde.
[lxvi] *Ibid*, p. 305.
[lxvii] Theodore Albrecht, translator and editor, 1996, Vol. 3 Letter No. 379, pp. 52–4.
[lxviii] Emily Anderson, editor and translator, 1961, Vol. 3, Letter No. 1305, pp. 1137–8.
[lxix] Peter Clive, 2001, pp. 271–2.
[lxx] See: Emily Anderson, editor and translator, 1961, Vol. 3, Letter No. 1300, p. 1150. The wider context of Beethoven's circumstances at this period are discussed in: Thayer-Forbes, 1967, p. 923.
[lxxi] Barry Cooper, *The compositional act: sketches and autographs*, in: Glenn Stanley, editor, *The Cambridge companion to Beethoven*, 2000, pp. 32–42.
[lxxii] Quoted in: Michael Oliver editor, *Settling the score: a journey through the music of the twentieth century*, 1999, p. 224.
[lxxiii] Roger Sessions, *Questions about music*, 1970, p. 85.
[lxxiv] Beethoven in conversation in 1823 with Louis Schlösser, quoted by Alan Tyson *Sketches and autographs* in: Denis Arnold and Nigel Fortune, editors, *The Beethoven companion*, 1973, pp. 443–5.
[lxxv] Quoted in: Ludwig Nohl, *Beethoven depicted by his contemporaries*, 1880, p. 55.
[lxxvi] Douglas Porter Johnson, editor, 1985, p. 73, p. 292, pp. 294–5, pp. 299–304, pp. 306–7, pp. 309–10, p. 313, p. 317, and pp. 463–8.
[lxxvii] Theodore Albrecht, translator and editor, 1996, Vol. 3 Letter No. 388, pp. 67–8.
[lxxviii] Emily Anderson, editor and translator, 1961, Vol. 3, Letter No. 1344, pp. 1166–7.

[lxix] Theodore Albrecht, translator and editor, 1996, Vol. 3 Letter No. 393, pp. 75–6.
[lxx] Thayer-Forbes, 1967, p. 929–37.
[lxxi] Emily Anderson, editor and translator, 1961, Vol. 3, Letter No. 1352, p. 1179.
[lxxii] *Ibid*, Letter No. 1378, p. 1201.
[lxxiii] *Ibid*, Letter No. 1415, pp. 1236–7.
[lxxiv] Thayer Forbes, 1967, p. 970.
[lxxv] Emily Anderson, editor and translator, 1961, Vol. 3, Letter No. 1420, pp. 1240–1. This letter is undated but is considered to belong to August 1825.
[lxxvi] Thayer-Forbes, 1967, p. 929–37.
[lxxvii] Theodore Albrecht, translator and editor, 1996, Vol. 3 Letter No. 417, pp. 114–5.
[lxxviii] Thayer-Forbes, pp. 968–9.
[lxxix] For a copy of the letter of 7 March 1827 sent to Beethoven by the *Gesellschaft der Musikfreunde* see: Theodore Albrecht, translator and editor, 1996, Vol. 3 Letter No.465, pp. 190–1.
[xc] *Ibid*, 1996, Vol. 3 Letter No. 425, pp. 129–30. See also: Thayer-Forbes, 1967, p. 978.
[xci] Emily Anderson, editor and translator, 1961, Vol. 3, Letter No. 1481, pp. 1283–2. See also: Thayer-Forbes, 1967, p. 1009.
[xcii] Theodore Albrecht, translator and editor, 1996, Vol. 3 Letter No. 434, p. 140.
[xciii] Anton Felix Schindler edited by Donald W. MacArdle and translated by Constance S. Jolly from the German edition of 1860, 1966, pp. 321–2.
[xciv] Quoted in: Joseph de Marliave, *Beethoven's quartets*, 1925 (1961 reprint), p. 225.
[xcv] Theodore Albrecht, translator and editor, 1996, Vol. 3 Letter No. 444, pp. 152–3.
[xcvi] *Ibid*, Letter No. 456, p. 174
[xcvii] Emily Anderson, editor and translator, 1961, Vol. 3, Letter No. 1567, p. 1345.
[xcviii] See: Thayer-Forbes, Appendix H: 'The later history of Prince Galitzin's payments', pp. 1100–02.
[xcix] For a virtual reality creation of the *Schwarzspanierhaus* see: Website *Beethoven a small museum*.
[c] Emily Anderson, editor and translator, 1961, Vol. 3, Letter No. 1542, pp. 1321–3.
[ci] Anton Felix Schindler edited by Donald W. MacArdle and translated by Constance S. Jolly from the German edition of 1860, 1966, p. 323.
[cii] Theodore Albrecht, translator and editor, 1996, Vol. 3 Letter No. 453, pp. 169–70.
[ciii] Peter Clive, 2001, pp. 148–9, p. 260, and pp. 359–60.
[civ] For a brief account of Beethoven's treatment at this time, see the correspondence relating to the composer dated 12 January 1827 in: Theodore Albrecht, translator and editor, 1996, Vol. 3 Letter No. 454, pp. 170–1.
[cv] Emily Anderson, editor and translator, 1961, Vol. 3, Letter No. 1550, pp. 1332–3.
[cvi] *Ibid*, Letter No. 1544, pp. 1335 and Letter No. 1555, pp. 1336–7. See also: Theodore Albrecht, translator and editor, 1996, Vol. 3 Letter No. 460, pp. 179–83.
[cvii] *Ibid*, Letter No. 1559, p. 1355. Beethoven being too week, this letter was written by his amanuensis Anton Schindler.
[cviii] Anton Felix Schindler, *Beethoven as I knew him*, edited by Donald W. MacArdle and translated by Constance S. Jolly from the German edition of 1860, 1966 pp. 322–3.
[cix] Theodore Albrecht, translator and editor, 1996, Vol. 3 Letter No. 462, pp. 185–8.

cx Website: *CPI Inflation Calculator*.
cxi Emily Anderson, editor and translator, 1961, Vol. 3, Letter No. 1566, pp. 1343–5.
cxii Louis Spohr quoted in: Ludwig Nohl, *Beethoven depicted by his contemporaries*, 1880, p. 121.
cxiii Adapted from John Daverio, *Manner, tone, and tendency in Beethoven's chamber music for strings* in: Glenn Stanley editor, *The Cambridge companion to Beethoven*, 2000, pp. 147–64.
cxiv Quoted in: John Hamilton Warrack, 1981, p. 270.
cxv Adapted from John Daverio, *Manner, tone, and tendency in Beethoven's chamber music for strings* in: Glenn Stanley editor, *The Cambridge companion to Beethoven*, 2000, pp. 147–64.
cxvi Anton Felix Schindler, *Beethoven as I knew him*, edited by Donald W. MacArdle and translated by Constance S. Jolly from the German edition of 1860, 1966, p. 305.
cxvii *Ibid*, pp. 302–5.
cxviii Quoted in: Thayer-Forbes, 1967, p. 982.
cxix Leon Botstein *The patrons and publics of the quartets* in: Robert Winter and Robert Martin editors *The Beethoven quartet companion*, 1994, 92.
cxx Quoted in: Denis Matthews, 1985, p. 138.
cxxi With acknowledgment to Website: *The Beethoven project* and James Keller, *A listener's guide*, Oxford, 2011.
cxxii Joseph de Marliave, 1925 (1961 reprint), p. 228.
cxxiii C. H. H Parry, *Style in Musical Art*, 1911, p. 95.

STRING QUARTET IN E–FLAT MAJOR, OP. 127

'Beethoven's brother Johann put it like this when he first heard the E-flat major Quartet: "In everything, there was a mood that exists in no other quartet. The interweaving [of voices] is so rich that one is fully occupied just observing a single voice: therefore one wishes that he could hear the Quartet four times".' Quoted in:

Daniel K. L. Chua, *The "Galitzin" Quartets of Beethoven: Opp.127, 132, 130,* 1995, p. 13.

'Beethoven has spoken to us in a way that is awe-inspiring and moves us to the depths. It is a sombre message ... the calm expression of suffering by a soul that is deeply wounded but equally inspired by hope.' Ludwig Rellstab, on hearing a performance of the E-flat major String Quartet in 1825.

Cited by: Leon Botstein, *The Patrons and Publics of the Quartets* in: Robert Winter and Martin Robert editors, *The Beethoven Quartet Companion*, 1994, p. 106.

'Judgments about the last works of this master are very divergent, indeed not seldom completely contradictory. One person says that one can find nothing more beautiful and marvellous than this very Quartet, which represents the highest that music can offer. Another person says on the other hand: "No, everything is unclear here, all is confused; there is no clear idea that is developed since in every measure there are sins against accepted rules, the already deaf composer must indeed have been unbalanced to bring this piece into being".' Anonymous review published in Issue 28 of the *Allgemeine musikalische Zeitung*, 1827 cited in:

William Kinderman, *Beethoven*, 1997, p. 7.

'A feeling of reverence for its creator took possession of every heart; perhaps no one understood the work (this is a task for all time), or found the same thing in it; it is characteristic of the sublime that we do not comprehend it — that like a mysterious superior power, it exalts and impels us forward.' Ludwig Rellstab on hearing the E-flat major String Quartet played at its first performance. Originally published, with various other writings, in *Aus Meinem Leben*, 1861, and reproduced, in part, in:

Ludwig Nohl, *Beethoven depicted by his Contemporaries*, 1880, pp. 260–91.

'[The] E-flat major Quartet, Op. 127 ... represents a summoning up of the forces of personality, a statement of a new attitude towards life and its problems.'

Paul Bekker, *Beethoven*, 1925, p. 326.

'In this work, the first in the manner of his later quartets, Beethoven revels himself — not only his power of psychological expression, but his genius — as a creator of musical form ... The apparently complex construction of the work, in which every note is of vital importance, is never merely the result of technical art, but springs from the artist's brain as a normal flowering of his complex emotions and aspirations.'

Joseph de Marliave, *Beethoven's Quartets*, 1925, (reprint 1961), p. 236.

'[The late quartets] are so great that one hesitates to write about them; for the beauty of music lies in the very fact that it postulates itself only and cannot be expressed in any other way. What can one say about the force and tenderness in the very first movement of the Quartet in E-flat major, Op. 127, the elevation of the *Adagio*, with its wonderful variations, or the elemental freakishness of the

Scherzo, that is not far better conveyed by studying the work itself?'

Rebecca Clarke *The Beethoven quartets as a player sees them* in: *Musical Times*, Special Issue (Beethoven's Death Centenary), Vol. VIII, No. 2, 1927, pp. 184—90.

> 'With this mighty work [Op. 127] we enter a realm, the like of which is not to be found in the whole range of the tone-art. The last five quartets of Beethoven ... constitute a mystical testament of that spark that lighted the composer through darkness to the flame of immortality — *per aspera ad astra.*'

Arthur Shepherd, *The String Quartets of Ludwig van Beethoven*, 1935, p. 44.

> 'By the time Beethoven composed his next Quartet, No. 12 in E-flat major, Op. 127 (1824), he had travelled far from the world to which *The Harp* Quartet belonged ... While at work on his *Missa Solemnis* he had been studying the music of Palestrina and pure modal counterpoint ... The beauty of modal harmonies and the marvellous effects obtainable from the juxtaposition of common chords were revealed to him.'

Marion M. Scott, *Beethoven: (The Master Musicians)*, 1940, p. 262.

> 'The first of the series of late quartets, the Quartet in E-flat major, Op. 127, is of all works his crowning monument to lyricism ... Lyricism — it

has been said many times – is at the heart of this Quartet, inspiring the intimate *aveu* [confession/declaration] of the opening movement, the popular swing of the Finale, and the stream of melody in the *Adagio* variations.'

Joseph Kerman, *The Beethoven Quartets*, 1967, pp. 195–6 and p. 239.

'[When] Beethoven began Op. 127 in 1824 he picked up a thread of continuity so firm that he might have completed Op. 95 only the day before.'

Harold Truscott, *Beethoven's Late String Quartets*, 1968, p. 38.

'The E flat and the larger and more innovatory C-sharp minor, are the most unified, consistent, satisfying of the late quartets ... What the quartets ... share, incontrovertibly, is an influence on Wagner. "Who comes after him will not continue him but must begin anew, for he who went before left off only where art leaves off." Thus Grillparzer, orating at Beethoven's funeral, and if the poet seems to have been writing with Wagner in mind, so does Beethoven himself in the *Adagio molto espressivo variation* in this Quartet in E flat.'

Igor Stravinsky, *Themes and Conclusions*, 1972, p. 257.

'The late E-flat major Quartet ... is even greater in scale than that eminently exploratory work, the first

> *Razumovsky*, yet the work is self-contained, compact, economical — in a word "classical" — while at the same time the sound world is utterly new.'

Robert Simpson, *The Chamber Music for Strings* in: Denis Arnold and Nigel Fortune editors, *The Beethoven Companion*, 1973, p. 265.

> 'Op. 127 has always been considered the most "normal" of the five [last] quartets and has therefore escaped the attentions of those musical philosophers who have soared into the "intense inane" in their attempts to elucidate the meaning of the middle three of the five. Its greatness is beyond question, but the simplification of the idea apparent in the last three Piano Sonatas [Opp. 109, 110 and 111] is continued to such a degree that the difficulty of comprehension is to come to terms not so much with extreme complexity as with a blinding simplicity.'

Basil Lam, *Beethoven String Quartets*, 1975, p. 76.

> 'Despite its unenigmatic approachability and lyricism, the Quartet [Op. 127] is not without its "late style" characteristics — the driving dotted rhythms of the *Scherzo*; the contrapuntal textures; the fantastic, idealized, occasionally violent dance rhythms of the pastoral finale; and, especially, the luxuriously ornamental variations of the *Adagio*, in the course of which the theme itself is transformed into a new entity.'

Maynard Solomon, *Beethoven*, 1977, pp. 321–2.

> 'It is the combination of lyrical beauty with harmonic and rhythmic subtlety of Beethoven's latest style that gives this Quartet [Op. 127] its peculiar individuality. It contains much, especially in the first and last movements, that makes a ready appeal even at a first hearing, and the meditations of the slow movement and the capricious high spirits of the *Scherzo* are more accessible to the listener than similar things in some of the later quartets.'

Philip Radcliffe, *Beethoven's String Quartets*, 1978, p. 108.

> 'Op. 127 is the most traditional and, for that reason, approachable of the late quartets. It has the conventional four movements, a sonata-form allegro, a slow movement cast as a set of variations, a scherzo and trio, and a finale in sonata form.'

David Wyn Jones, *Beethoven and the Viennese Legacy* in: Robin Stowell editor, *The Cambridge Companion to the String Quartet*, 2003, p. 222.

By the time Beethoven commenced work on the String Quartet in E-flat major, Op. 127 he had, in the words of Robert Simpson, 'entered another phase of prodigious creative energy'. Manifestations of this had already appeared in such works as the intensely concentrated String Quartet, Op. 95 – *Quartetto Serioso*, and the technically challenging Piano Sonata, Op, 106 – the *Hammerklavier*. Moreover, at the period in question, Beethoven was turning his mind to the Ninth Symphony, Op. 125 – the *Choral*, and, what he considered to be his greatest work, his Mass in D minor,

Op. 123 — the *Missa Solemnis*. Additionally, and not too distant in the future, were the *Diabelli* Variations Op. 120 that the ardent Beethovenian Donald Tovey considered to be 'the greatest set of piano variations ever written'. To quote Simpson once more: 'When one considers the magnitude and the exploratory nature of most of these works, this period, though longer, becomes comparable with the burst of [creative energy] of 1803—6.'[i]

In his preparation for work on the *Missa Solemnis*, Beethoven spent hours of study in the Library of his composition pupil the Archduke Rudolph. Here, he became acquainted with the music of Palestrina and enlarged his understanding of modal counterpoint and model harmonies that would, in due course, infiltrate his writing for the string quartet. On a deeper level: 'Years of pondering and experience ... had brought him to a position in which he had something of the vision and knowledge of Truth ... Life in its metaphysical reality had become clear to him.'[ii]

Beethoven's tendency to expand his musical style is evident in the E-flat major Quartet, notwithstanding that its format is confined to the traditional four movements; in a spacious interpretation it has a playing time approaching forty minutes. Expansion is even more evident in the three following quartets: the A minor Quartet, Op. 132 has five movements; the B-flat major Quartet. Op. 130 has six movements; and the C-sharp minor Quartet, Op. 131 has seven movements — all with corresponding extended performing times. It must be conceded that in the very last of this set of late quartets, namely the String Quartet in F major, Op. 135, Beethoven was content to adopt a four-movement structure in which each of the movements is shorter and less discursive than in those just mentioned.

With the composition of the three great Piano Sonatas

Opp. 109, 110 and 111 (1820—22), Beethoven turned to the genre of the string quartet as his most personal medium of musical expression. In this regard he was perhaps fortunate. String quartet performance was becoming more popular with the musically inclined public and less the preserve of wealthy aristocratic families who had previously enjoyed the exclusive privilege of hearing quartets performed in their grand salons. Within such an intimate environment, so enriched by the creations of Haydn and Mozart, the string quartet held sway where the interplay between the four instruments had the authority and interest of informed conversation.[iii] Beethoven's late string quartets would change all that. In his pioneering study *Beethoven et ses trois styles* (1855), the German musicologist Wilhelm von Lenz described the five last quartets as being 'less quartets than discourses between four string instruments'. In these: 'Beethoven uses the instruments as four separate voices, each representing an idea with the utmost freedom and individuality, yet uniting in a perfect and significant whole.'[iv]

The wider interest in the string quartet in the second decade of the nineteenth century was given impetus by the emergence into the public domain of the professional string quartet. In this regard mention should be made of the pioneering influence of Ignaz Schuppanzigh and his fellow instrumentalists. Schuppanzigh is a significant figure in the context of Beethoven's writing for the string quartet and also in connection with his role in the first performances of a number of his chamber and orchestral compositions.[v] On his return to Vienna in 1823, following a period of time in Germany, Poland and Russia — where he did much to promote Beethoven's chamber music — he soon became absorbed in the capital's musical life. For example, he was *Konzertmeister* (first violin) of the first performances of the

Ninth Symphony on 7 and 23 May 1824 and, more significant to our narrative, he gave the first rendition of the String Quartet Op. 127 (see later).

As we shall in due course see, a further stimulus to Beethoven's composing string quartets was the desire on the part of music publishers to commission such works from him — and be willing to pay the high prices he demanded for them.[vi]

Beethoven's previous exploration of the key of E-flat major, in the medium of the string quartet, was in 1809 when he had composed the so-called *Harp* String Quartet. This has been variously described as being: 'a lyrical contemplative, and expressive work' (Maynard Solomon); 'genial and inviting' (Michael Steinberg); a work of 'sheer delight' (Paul Bekker); and 'full and mellow in sound, but for the most part more intimate and thoughtful than any of the *Razumovsky* Quartets (Philip Radcliffe). How far Beethoven had journeyed since then in his tonal kingdom is captured in Paul Bekker's observation: '[There] is a wide difference between the Beethoven of 1809 and the Beethoven of 1824. In the earlier work he had been content with clever playful variations, a simple witty song theme. Here [in Op. 127] it is the mystery of artistic conception which concentrates him and we are reminded of the *Benedictus* of the *Mass*.'[vii]

Music critics and Beethoven admirers alike were quick to seize upon and acknowledge the innovations to be found in the composer's late music. The German poet and music critic Ludwig Rellstab, writing in 1825 in Adolf Schlesinger's romantic journal, the *Berliner Allgemeine musikalische Zeitung*, praised the 'exaltation and fervour of the String Quartet, Op. 127, and saw in it the soul of 'the genius who desires only self-realization' and whose struggle to express his sufferings evoked 'the manly anguish of a Laocoon'. [A reference to the Trojan priest who, racked with agony, sought to defend himself and his sons from the grip of giant serpents] Some years later the Belgian musicologist-composer François-Joseph Fétis — founder of the influential *Revue musicale* — wrote in his monumental *Biographie universelle des musiciens et bibliographie générale de la musique* (Brussels, 1833-1844, 8 vols.) how Beethoven's late music represented a definitive break with that of his predecessors: 'He had a different object than to charm the ear by the successive development of some principal phrase, by happy melodies or by beautiful harmonic combinations.' Rellstab contended that Beethoven 'found the ordinary forms of music too symmetrical, too conventional, and too proper to adequately encompass his thought'. Reflecting on the views expressed by Beethoven's contemporary critic-admirers, Maynard Solomon remarks: '[The] later Beethoven ... had his romantic defenders who freely acknowledged and rejoiced in his subjectivity, in the free play of his imagination, and in his new organizing conception of musical form.'[viii]

In his admiration of Beethoven's craftsmanship, as evident in the E-flat major Quartet, the French musicologist Joseph de Marliave enthused: 'The apparently complex construction of the work, in which every note is of vital importance, is never merely the result of technical art, but springs from the artist's brain as a normal flowering of his complex emotions and aspirations.'[ix] Here, however, we have an instance of art concealing art. The complex construction, as in so much of Beethoven, came about only after much study and reflection. At first he was uncertain as to how many movements the Op. 127 should contain; he initially planned two additional movements, one between the first and second, and another between the third and fourth. As we have seen, he reserved such an expanded format for the companion Quartets Opp. 130, 131 and 132.

In the case of the Op. 127 the *extra* movements would have been a character piece entitled *La gaieté* and a brief *Adagio* before the finale. To quote the American Beethoven authority William Kinderman: 'In the end, Beethoven retained the four movement form in Op. 127, but his flirtation with such an expansion of the narrative chain of movements bore fruit in the following trilogy of quartets in A minor, Op. 132, B-flat major Op. 130 and C-sharp minor, Op. 131.' His, and others', study of the composer's sketches (see later) reveal the gestation of much of the music for the late quartets was conceived within the same sketchbooks, and ideas for different compositions are to be found on the same page. To quote Kinderman once more: 'Thus in writing each of these works, Beethoven conceived material that spilled over beyond the composition immediately at hand. His fertility of invention refused to be contained within the boundaries of the singular work.'[x] An illustration of this is that the spirit of the putative movement that Beethoven designated *La gaieté*, ultimately found expression in the variation theme he used as a basis for the slow movement of Op. 127. Initially possessing a light hearted theme (hence the expression *La gaieté*), it appears to have been conceived with a prominent part for the cello; could Beethoven, perhaps, have had in mind that the work's dedicatee was an accomplished cellist? Be this as it may, Beethoven eventually transformed the melody into 'the sublime variation theme of the work's slow movement'.[xi xii]

The English writer on music Paul Griffiths describes the 'newness' in Op. 127 is an indicator of what is to follow in other of the late quartets, in particular the 'song-like nature' of so much of the music that is found in the work's outer movements. He elaborates: 'The tradition of the "singing allegro" belonged very much to Italian composers of quartets and symphonies, and to Mozart, but decidedly not to

Haydn, whose expressiveness comes wherever possible from musical action, not evocation.' He concludes: 'Beethoven, the inheritor of both, had been more like Haydn in his quartets, but now, in Op. 127 and its successors, the pressure to make the quartet sing becomes irresistible. Haydn, the typical classist, expressed himself through what his music *is*; Beethoven, now beyond question a Romantic, expresses himself through what music *says*.' [italics added][xiii]

Before proceeding to a discussion of the creation-origins of the E-flat major String Quartet, we present a selection of views (estimations) of the work, as expressed from the time of its first appearance, through the nineteenth century, and from thereon to our own times.

The German-born composer and conductor (Sir) Julius Benedict was introduced to Beethoven by Carl Maria von Weber in the autumn of 1823. It so chanced that he (Benedict) was present at the first performance of the E-flat Quartet of which he later wrote: 'I heard the first performance of one of the so-called "posthumous" quartets ... Schuppanzigh and his companions, who had been his interpreters before, were scarcely equal to this occasion: as they did not seem to understand the music themselves, they failed to entirely impart its meaning to the audience.' Benedict closed his recollections: 'The general impression was most unsatisfactory.'[xiv] The music correspondent to the Leipzig *Allgemeine musikalische Zeitung* (issue XXVII) expressed similar thoughts, implying that on the whole the audience 'was baffled by the work'. The reviewer in the sister journal the *Berliner Allgemeine musikalische Zeitung* similarly described the great difficulty experienced by both the performers and audience in understanding the Quartet which he considered could become familiar only through repeated hearings. He did though acknowledge 'one must always give Beethoven credit for artistic integrity'.[xv]

Amongst the early interpreters of Beethoven's chamber music can be listed the Bohrer String Quartet, consisting of the brothers Anton, Max, Tilmont and Urhan. Hector Berlioz heard them in a rehearsal of the Op. 127 when the Bohrer Quartet was in Paris preparing to give concerts in February-March 1830. According to Berlioz, Anton (first violin) 'became so possessed with the divine fire of [the *Adagio*]' that he 'suddenly took on a new force and eloquence of expression' such that he had to leave off from playing for a while so as to retain his composure. Notwithstanding the Bohrer brothers' personal enthusiasm for the quartets of Beethoven and their attempts to promote his chamber works in France met with little success. In the following 1831 Paris music season they performed the Op. 59 *Razumovsky* Quartets but aroused little public interest.[xvi] In the same year, Giacomo Meyerbeer chanced to hear the Bohrer String Quartet in a recital devoted to a selection of Beethoven's chamber music. A diary entry of his from 3 April 1831 reads: 'Attended a performance of the Anton Bohrer Quartet Concert [that] included the wonderful Violincello Sonata by Beethoven in A major, Op. 69; the *scherzo* is elfin and ghostly.' Turning to the main work of the evening he relates: 'Finally they played Beethoven's Quartet in E-flat major, Op. 127 ... the first movement is difficult to grasp, perhaps even incomprehensible. The *Scherzo* that is part of the *Andante* is, however, splendid.'[xvii]

The Joseph Hellmesberger String Quartet played an important role in Vienna's musical life. Established in the 1840s it did much to promote an awareness and appreciation of Beethoven's works alongside those of Schubert and Brahms. The Quartet earned a reputation for playing in 'an unabashedly subjective and emotional manner', especially well suited to the late quartets of Beethoven. After hearing a performance of the Hellmesberger Quartet in 1859, the music critic of the *Neue Zeitschrift für Musik* (issue 26) wrote: 'The masterworks of [Beethoven's] last period, the C-sharp minor, Op. 131 and E-flat major, Op. 127 Quartets, as well as the first performance here of the *Grosse Fuge*, Op. 133 [were featured]. It is Hellmesberger's great service to have made this prophetic and progressive artist so popular among us.' Concerning Op. 133, the critic in question considered Hellmesberger's Quartet could hold the attention of an audience even when playing the 'many-faceted structure [of] Beethoven's Quartet Fuge' and, moreover, 'after its completion [to be] greeted so warmly and with so much applause'.[xviii]

Following a performance of the E-flat major Quartet sometime in Vienna in 1881, Hugo Wolf, in his role as music critic, remarked how the music 'spoke to the assemblage and shared with them the wonders of [Beethoven's] dreamworld'.[xix]

Turning to the estimation of Beethoven's string quartet music, as expressed in the early part of the twentieth century, we find Romain Rolland coming to the composer's defence: 'To say that string-quartet writing is only an imperfectly filled-in sketch of orchestral idiom is not correct; otherwise, when Beethoven had four instruments at his disposal, would he have written some of those spacious passages for three, or even two instruments only?'[xx]

In 1902, Donald Tovey heard a performance of the E-flat major String Quartet played by the Joachim String Quartet at James's Hall, London. Their recital was part of a festival of chamber music that included several Beethoven quartets. Joseph Joachim founded the Quartet in 1869 with the intention of providing opportunities for his music students at the Königliche Hochschule für Musik, Berlin to hear professional performances of the classical quartet repertoire; Beethoven and Schubert featured prominently.

Tovey, in his capacity as music correspondent to the *Times Literary Supplement*, reserved particular praise for the Joachim Quartet's interpretation of the closing passages of the final movement of Op. 127: 'The performance ... of the *Allegro commodo* at the end of Beethoven's Quartet in E-flat major, Op. 127, was a stupendous feat of technique.' Tovey acknowledged that any four young players 'with musical ears might with patience – *and much practice* [our italics] – acquire the skill to play the passage in question at the required speed and uniform degree of loudness and softness'. However, with regard to the musical prowess of the Joachim String Quartet, he concluded: 'But it would be many years before they might play it steadily ... before their technique would help them to put anything like the variety of light and shade that Dr. Joachim and his colleagues seem as a matter of course to put into three pages of a most intense pianissimo.'[xxi]

On 21 March 1918, the expatriate poet and sometime music-critic Ezra Pound heard a rendering of the E-flat major Quartet in the Wigmore Hall; the work had been performed by the Catterall String Quartet. Founded in 1910 by Arthur Catterall, the Quartet made pioneering recordings in the 1920s of Beethoven's string quartets for *His Master's Voice* using the so-called 'acoustic process'. This required the players to gather round a large exponential horn as a means of capturing the sound of the instruments. Pound could do no more than describe the Catterall Quartet's performance of the Op. 127 Quartet as 'solid' and 'business-like' – notwithstanding that their leader, Arthur Catterall, was acknowledged for being one of the best-known English classical violinists of the first half of the twentieth century. Worse was to follow in Pound's review – he was clearly no ardent Beethovenian. He railed: 'Beethoven was, doubtless in his day, a relief from too many trills: he towered as a colossus over the delicate derivativeness of Steibelt [one of Beethoven's pianistic rivals]; he was a Titan, but he is now rather too much the daily ... roast beef of music. The effect of deliverance that he may have given to his contemporaries is no more to be had from him. He seems verbose, not nonsensical but verbose.'[xxii]

Beethoven found an ally when the English violinist and musicologist Marion Scott published her pioneering study *Beethoven* in 1934 as part of the *Music Masters Series* of J. M. Dent & Sons, Ltd. Received to much acclaim, although now superseded and reworked by Denis Matthews (1985) and Barry Cooper (2000), Scott's study of the composer is still highly regarded today. We give testimony to this by citing her cryptic but fulsome remarks concerning Op. 127: 'It is a glorious work, in which the gallantly ringing heroism of Beethoven's E-flat mood is suffused by an indescribable happiness.'[xxiii]

In the late 1950s the American conductor and writer Robert Craft invited Igor Stravinsky to express his views on aspects of Beethoven's chamber music. Of the E-flat major Quartet he declared: 'My particular pleasures in Op. 127 are the modulation in the second movement, measures 75–8; measure 91, measures 97–101; and the whole *presto* of the *Scherzando*, but above all measures 244–70.' Like Ezra Pound, though, Stravinsky was not in awe of Beethoven and his comments are occasionally spiced with acerbic put-downs. It is no surprise, therefore, he added to the foregoing remarks: 'Like the greatest beauties, they [the late quartets] are a little flawed except for Op. 127 and the *Great Fugue*, each has its *ennuis*.'[xxiv]

The English music scholar Basil Lam placed his estimation of Beethoven's late quartets, considered as a group, within the wider context of other of the composer's contemporaneous works: 'The Mass [*Missa Solemnis*] and the

Symphony [the *Choral*] are the utterances of a man speaking to men, but in the last quartets Beethoven is as indifferent to communication as to self-expression.'[xxv] Alongside Lam, the English composer-musicologist Philip Radcliffe found Op. 127 to be 'full of lyrical beauty of the gentlest and most approachable kind'. Like Lam, he compared Op. 127 with other of the composer's works: 'Its nearest equivalent among the last five piano sonatas is Op. 110, but there the moods are more varied and probably more direct in expression. But both works are among the most genial and approachable of Beethoven's third period, with only occasional glimpses of its more enigmatic and elusive features.'[xxvi]

Dennis Matthews, setting aside his prowess as a concert pianist and adopting the mantle of musicologist, expressed his enthusiasm for the E-flat major Quartet. He first endorses Joseph Kerman's description of the composition as 'Beethoven's crowning monument to lyricism'. Then he adds: 'This could certainly apply to the first two movements and perhaps the finale too, where the animated main theme is stretched out ... in an unconventional coda that reveals its lyrical potential against a murmuring background of triplet semiquavers.'[xxvii]

It is perhaps fitting we should conclude our brief survey of responses to Beethoven's String Quartet in E-flat major — albeit a recollection of a light-hearted nature — by making reference to one of the twentieth century's most respected group of instrumentalists. The *Amadeus Quartet* gave a performance of Op. 127 in Staines Town Hall, Middlesex during which the stage lighting failed. Not wishing to disrupt the flow of the music, and therefore spoil the audience's enjoyment, they heroically continued to play. At the conclusion of the recital the stage manger apologised and asked how they had managed to continue. First violin Norbert Brainin responded saying they so had the music within themselves: 'We could have played it in complete darkness.'[xxviii]

We direct our attention now to the creation origins of the E-flat major String Quartet as revealed in the composer's surviving sketchbooks and autographs.

Beethoven composed the Quartet between the summer of 1824 and the spring of 1825. Consistent with his well-established working method, he preserved his thoughts in sketch form. Those that are extant survive in various forms and are today preserved in several archives. Significant amongst these are the so-called pocket sketchbooks that consist of random sheets of music paper stitched together by the composer. These enabled him to jot down his ideas in pencil when out and about in the summer on his strolls in the countryside; the fugitive nature of the pencil medium now poses challenges to scholar-musicologists attempting to decipher his intentions. When indoors Beethoven could work in ink at his writing desk in pre-formed 'desk-sketchbooks' that have, for the most part, retained their legibility. Sketchbooks also survive in bound format. These typically consist of miscellaneous gatherings of music sheets compiled by music dealers and collectors after the sale of Beethoven's possessions in the auction that took place in November 1827 following his death earlier in the year.

In his work on the Quartets Opp. 127, 132, 130, 131 and 135, Beethoven introduced an innovation into his sketching procedures. He made use of manuscript paper that was ruled in the form of quartet-score sheets. These enabled him to set down more extended compositional drafts encompassing all four instruments – doubtless prompted, in part, by the challenges posed by the growing contrapuntal complexity of the music evolving in his mind.[xxix] As Cooper remarks, the composer's 'limitless aspirations' required a new method of composing: '[He] began making frequent use of sketching in open score on four staves, instead of merely on one or two as before.' This was to assist with what Beethoven himself described as 'a new kind of part writing'. Cooper adds: 'The score sketches did not supplant other types of sketching, but ran in parallel with them.'[xxx]

Beethoven authority Douglas Porter Johnson remarks that Beethoven rarely worked in full score prior to working on the autograph of the work under consideration. Consistent with what we have just said he states: 'The enormous body of such [full score] sketches from the years 1824–26, when he was occupied almost exclusively with the late quartets, must therefore reflect an important development in Beethoven's compositional process.' His researches, and those of others, reveal the paper Beethoven used for these late score sketches is similar to that found in the sketchbooks and autographs. These take the form of oblong-format leaves with 10, 12, 14, or 16 staves to a page, usually pre-ruled but sometimes lined by Beethoven himself. Unlike the sketchbooks, Beethoven left the score sketches loose. At his death about 350 of these leaves were purchased by the music publisher Domenico Artaria. These were acquired by the Berlin State Library in 1901 (catalogued as Artaria 206 MS). Another hundred or so such leaves were gifted over time by an unknown benefactor to the Gesellschaft der Musikfreunde (catalogued as MSS A51 and A55). Their sheer number is testimony to the great effort Beethoven expended in the creation of the late quartets.[xxxi]

As the creative process neared completion, Beethoven worked in autograph-score format. Of the last five quartets and the Great Fugue, only the autograph of the String Quartet in A minor, Op. 132 has survived intact. 'The autographs of Opp. 127, 130, 131 and 135 were, early in their history, dismembered and sold off, movement by movement, in some cases to different buyers.'[xxxii] The Autograph Score of the last movement of Op. 127 survives today in the archive of the Beethoven House in Bonn. It is bound in a handsome cover probably supplied by a collector after Domenico Artaria had dismembered the manuscript when it was in his possession complete with all four movements. The text consists of 27 pages that are purposefully clear and legible to assist the copyist to make his copperplate engraving.[xxxiii] The first and second movements form part of the collection of the Biblioteka Jagiellońska, Kraków. The third movement was owned by the Stiftelsen Musikkulturens Främjande, Stockholm until it was acquired by a private collector in a Sotheby's sale in December 2003 (see later).[xxxiv]

From May 1823 until June 1824 Beethoven used a sketchbook now designated Landsberg 8 Bundle 2 (8/2). Its name derives from its one-time owner the avid collector of Beethoven manuscripts Ludwig Landsberg. This is a compilation collated into fifteen 'gatherings', of some forty leaves, bearing the Roman numerals I–XV. The closing pages contain ideas for the first movement of Op. 127 and belong to early June 1824. Typical of the composer, sketches are also found for Op. 125 (Ninth Symphony) and Op. 126 (Six Bagatelles). Landsberg 8/2 is today housed in the archive of the Deutsche Staatsbibliothek, Berlin.[xxxv]

From February to September 1824 Beethoven used a pocket sketchbook designated Artaria 205 Bundle 4 (205/4) that once formed part of the collection of Domenico Artaria; it was acquired by the Berlin State Library in 1879. Its principal contents are sketches for the Ninth Symphony but ideas for Op. 127 are also included: first movement, pp. 2–11, pp. 14–16 and pp. 19–22; second movement, pp. 14–16 and pp. 17–36; fourth movement pp. 34–35. It is believed Beethoven worked on the first movement in this pocket sketchbook during the early summer months when he was in Baden; later on he expanded his thoughts using the separate score leaves to which we have made reference.[xxxvi]

From about October to December 1824 Beethoven used the so-called Grasnick 4 Sketchbook, formerly in the collection of F. A. Grasnick and acquired by the Berlin State Library in 1879. It is now preserved in the special collections archive of the Biblioteka Jagiellońska, Kraków. Sketches for Op. 127 are well represented: second movement, folios 1r, 4v–6r, 23r–24v; third movement, folios, 1r–4r, 6r–19v, 25v; and fourth movement, folios 2v–3r, 13r–14r, 15r–16r.[xxxvii]

From the autumn of 1824 until January 1825 Beethoven used a sketchbook styled as Autograph 11/2 (q.v. Autograph 11, Bundle 2). This consists of two sketchbooks that Anton Schindler had bound together to form a single sketchbook of thirty leaves. He acquired them from Beethoven's effects following his death and in 1846 sold them to the Berlin State Library (in Schindler's time the Königliche Bibliothek). The thirty surviving leaves are held today in the Staatsbibliothek zu Preussischer Kulturbesitz. The sketchbook is typical insofar as Beethoven assembled it from leftover leaves of manuscript paper. With regard to the E-flat major Quartet, sketches are included for the last three movements: second movement folios 2r–17v passim; third movement folios 1r–v, 16r–17v and 21 r–v; third movement folios 21v–22v and 27r–28r. Of interest is that Beethoven appears to have set aside work on the final movement of Op. 127 in favour of turning his attention to ideas for the first movement of the String Quartet in A minor, Op. 132. In addition, the theme for the *Grosse Fuge*, Op. 133 appears amongst the sketches for Op. 127 as do sketches for the Bagatelles, Op. 126 – bearing testimony to Kinderman's assertion that Beethoven's fertility of invention 'refused to be contained within the boundaries of the singular work'.[xxxviii]

From May to September of 1825 Beethoven confided his musical thoughts to the De Roda Sketchbook that derives it name from the Spanish collector Cecilio de Roda. He owned it until early in the twentieth century from whose heirs the Beethovenhaus acquired it in 1962. During Beethoven's lifetime it contained 42 leaves of which 40 have survived – only the outer cover is presumed missing. Domenico Artaria acquired the book at the auction of Beethoven's effects in November 1827. The present-day cover bears the inscription: 'Autograph e Louis van Beethoven/Livre d'esquisses des motifs du Quatour/en La Mineur et autre études/L'authenticié en est garantie par Artaria & Co. à Vienne/1847.' Once more Beethoven assembled the sketchbook from remnants of blank pages of music paper removed from other manuscripts. No fewer than thirteen different types of paper have been identified from various periods, some dating as far back as 1808 – testimony to the care Beethoven exercised in preserving his sketch-manuscripts. The De Roda Sketchbook contains ideas for the String Quartets Opp. 127, 132, 130 and the *Grosse Fuge* Op. 133: fourth movement, Op. 127; second, third, fourth and fifth movements, Op. 132; and first, second and third movements, Op. 130. This sketchbook also contains the draft of a letter Beethoven later sent to Prince Galitzin concerning the String Quartet, Op. 127 – characteristic of the manner in which the composer made occasional use of his sketch books for purposes other than setting down his musical thoughts.[xxix]

A number of single sketch leaves survive that may or may not once have belonged to sketchbooks; in the case of the former it is known that Anton Schindler gave away single sketch leaves to friends as souvenirs. One such leaf shows the last movement of the String Quartet, Op. 127 at an early stage in its composition.[xl] By way of contrast another leaf contains sketches mainly for the second movement of the String Quartet, Op. 127 but which reveal the composition at an advanced stage. To quote from the Beethoven's House text that accompanies this sketch: 'Unlike sketches made at the beginning of a project, which are mainly very short and generally do not yet hang together, in this case, Beethoven has written down extensive passages. He has also noted down the four instruments of the Quartet in the score [with the remark] a "new" method when making sketches, which he only began to use systematically in the year before his death beginning with this String Quartet, Op. 127.'[xli]

We pause here in our discussion of the creation origins of the String Quartet in E-flat major, Op. 127 and consider how his contemporaries viewed its creator.

The Stuttgart *Morgenblatt für gebildete Stände* was a pioneering journal of the day and enjoyed a wide circulation. In October 1819 it published an article about the composer that gives a flavour of how he was perceived at this time: 'Our Beethoven is, we may say, among musicians what Goethe is among poets ... It is impossible to give an adequate description of Beethoven's free, simple, and hermit-like life, and his only tribute to society is the fruit of his genius.'[xlii] Implicit in these words is the realisation of the composer's enforced isolation as a consequence of his, by now, profound deafness.

One who succeeded in encroaching upon Beethoven's reclusiveness was Dr. Wilhelm Christian Müller of Bremen. A theologian by training he earned his living by teaching and writing about music. Whilst travelling to Italy he and his daughter Elise — an accomplished pianist — were favoured with a meeting with Beethoven sometime in October 1820. Recalling this experience in later years, Müller wrote: 'Beethoven is perhaps the greatest aesthetic artist. His profound works are far in advance of their time, and just as

Sebastian Bach's compositions have been revived a hundred years after they were written, so will Beethoven's be. Many of his earlier works are much appreciated by the fashionable world ... He seems less understood in Vienna ... They do certainly express unfavourable opinions about his peculiarities and strange manners, but they all agree that he is a genius, although few are acquainted with him. Those who know the soundness of his understanding and the purity of his heart, entertain the sincerest friendship for him. This much is certain: he is a stranger to the world, the court, politics, and the art of dissimulation. He lives in his own art-world like a monarch in the kingdom of music.'[xliii]

In the years 1820–22, the English statesman Sir John Russell travelled extensively in Europe and published an account of his journeys in *A Tour in Germany and Some of the Southern Provinces of the Austrian Empire.* In this he makes reference to Beethoven's appearance: 'The carelessness of his dress gives him a savage appearance; his features are marked and prominent; his eyes expressive; his hair, which looks as if it had not been touched by comb or scissors for some years, falls over his broad brow in a disorderly mass, being comparable only to the serpents on Medusa's head.'[xliv]

The artist Joseph Carl Stieler took a likeness of Beethoven in the spring of 1820 that enables us to place Russell's remarks into their rightful context. Contemporaries, including Anton Schindler, thought Stieler had made a good likeness. Stieler requested the composer to 'sit as if you were writing' and to add authenticity to his creation he introduced manuscript pages of the *Missa Solemnis* on which Beethoven was then at work. Commentators value Stieler's portrait for its thoughtful expression, others though regard it as being somewhat idealized. The music publisher Mathias Artaria later published a lithograph of the portrait that promoted its popularity.[xlv] In his recollections of Beethoven, Gerhard von Breuning, the son Stephan von Breuning — one of the composer's closest friends — records his father remarking that 'although none of Beethoven's portraits was a perfect likeness, this one resembled him more than any other of recent times'.[xlvi]

On the occasion of his meeting with Beethoven, Sir John Russell heard him perform on the piano commenting: 'It required no little tact to induce him to play, so great is his dislike of anything like a pressing request.' When he was finally induced to perform, Russell comments: 'Left to himself, Beethoven sat down at the piano. At first he struck a few short chords ... but soon he forgot his surroundings, and for about half an hour lost himself in an improvisation, the style of which was exceedingly varied, and especially distinguished by sudden transitions ... he revelled rather in bold stormy moods than in soft and gentle ones.' Of the composer's working methods, Russell remarks: 'He has always a small paper book with him, and what conversation takes place is carried on in writing. In this, too, although it is not lined, he instantly jots down any musical idea which strikes him. These notes would be utterly unintelligible even to another musician, for they have thus no comparative value; he alone has in his own mind the thread by which he brings out of this labyrinth of dots and circles the richest and most astounding harmonies.'[xlvii]

Our final pen-portrait of Beethoven, at the period when he was contemplating turning to the medium of writing for the string quartet, is derived from the meeting Gioacchino Rossini had with the composer in 1822. Rossini was then being lionised in Vienna through the popularity of his *Il Barbiere di Seviglia*. He states he was familiar with some the composer's string quartets, that he regarded 'with admiration', and, likewise, 'a number of his piano compositions'.

Notwithstanding, he describes how he could barely master his emotions as he mounted the stairs to Beethoven's lodgings. He continues: 'When the door opened, I found myself in a sort of attic, terribly disordered and dirty ... The portraits of Beethoven which we know, reproduce fairly well his physiognomy. But what no etcher's needle could not express was the indefinable sadness spread over his features – while from under heavy eyebrows his eyes shone as from out of caverns and, though small, seemed to pierce one.' When Rossini took leave of Beethoven, he encouraged his young contemporary to compose 'some more barbers'.[xlviii]

With these images of the composer in our mind, we continue our discussion of the emergence of the Op. 127 String Quartet.

In 1814 Carl F. Peters had purchased the *Bureau de Musique* that had been founded in 1798 by Hoffmeister and Kühnel; this publishing house had the distinction of publishing a number of Beethoven's early compositions including the First Symphony. For some years Peters cherished the idea of publishing other works of the composer but initially hesitated. Being based in Leipzig, Peters was outside of the somewhat closed circle of Viennese music publishers and did not want to be seen as 'attempting to rival them in having the first claim on the composer's latest creations'.[xlix] After seeking the advice of his friend the instrument maker Johann Andreas Streicher, advantageously based in Vienna and being an acquaintance of Beethoven, he pursued his objective by writing to the composer on 18 May 1822. He expressed his interest in the composer's works and included a list of the particular compositions he wished to have. He rather grandly states: 'I seek your association not from self-interest but from honour.' Among Peters' wish-list he cites string quartets.[l] It is tempting to infer this request provided a stimulus to Beethoven's imagination and disposed him to think seriously about writing for the medium of the string quartet. Be this as it may, Beethoven replied to Peters on 5 July listing several types of composition he could offer him and the prices he wanted. In particular he stated he could have a string quartet 'very soon' for 50 ducats.[li] The words 'very soon' may be interpreted two ways; were they a typical Beethoven-style promise or was he in fact turning his mind already to writing for the string quartet? Ten days after receiving Beethoven's offer, Peters responded. Although he would like to have a quartet from Beethoven 'very much' he considered the asking price to be too high since the most he had ever paid for such a composition was 150 florins (roughly 40 ducats) — a reminder Beethoven had a reputation for demanding top prices for his works.[lii]

On 6 July Beethoven wrote once more to Peters: 'As to the violin quartet, which is not quite finished [an exaggeration], because something else intervened [a reference to work on the Ninth Symphony and *Missa Solemnis*], it would be difficult for me to reduce the fee I am asking you for this work. For it is precisely for a composition of this kind that I am most highly paid.' He expressed regret that compositions such as this are not justly regarded by the public at large.[liii] The following month (12 July) Peters felt obliged to apologise to the composer for declining to publish his quartet. He did not blame him for asking a high price and, in any event, he explained he was already fully committed in publishing four new string quartets by Louis Spohr. He concluded 'I had better hold off' and consequently nothing more came of the venture.[liv]

A few months later Providence beckoned from another quarter that would indeed precipitate Beethoven into writing for the medium of the string quartet and, moreover, would elevate the genre to unprecedented heights that many would say have seldom been equalled and never surpassed.

Prince Nikolay Galitzin was a Russian nobleman domiciled in St. Petersburg who had family connections in Vienna with the Russian ambassador to the Austrian Court. Galitzin was an accomplished cellist and on 9 November 1822 he wrote to Beethoven introducing himself as 'a great admirer' of the composer. More significantly, he requested 'two or three' new quartets for which he would be 'honoured to receive the dedication'.[lv]

In the New Year, on 25 January 1823, Beethoven responded to Galitzin's letter writing in French with the help of his nephew Karl: 'Etant contraint de vivre des produits de mon esprit, il faut que je prenne la liberté de fixer l'honoraire de 50 ducats pour un quatuor.' Beethoven's French-language letters were often written by a third party and only signed by the composer himself. From the foregoing it can be seen he was still seeking 50 ducats for a string quartet.[lvi] Galitzin could hardly contain his delight. He replied on 23 February: 'Your letter of 25 January ... filled me with joy by making me hope I shall soon enjoy a new product of your sublime genius.' He arranged for the payment of 50 ducats to be made with the promise of a further 100 for the two others.[lvii]

On 5 May Galitzin informed Beethoven he had arranged for the payment of 50 ducats for the String Quartet Op. 127 through his agent Henikstein. He intimated how anxious he was to receive the composition so that he could 'enjoy a sublime product of [the composer's] spirit' and reaffirmed his wish to receive the dedication to the work. In his enthusiasm, he continued: 'Please begin the second Quartet and notify me of it; them I shall send you 50 more ducats at once.' The work in question was the String Quartet, Op. 132.[lviii]

We next learn of the E-flat major Quartet in a letter Beethoven wrote on 16 July to his former piano pupil

Ferdinand Ries. Ries was then living in London and making his own way in the world as a composer; his considerable output included symphonies, concertos, string quartets and numerous works for solo piano; being blind in one eye did not prevent him from achieving quasi virtuoso standing as a concert pianist. In his letter, Beethoven reveals he had in mind dedicating his newly composed *Diabelli* Variations, Op. 120 to Ries's wife; in the event Antonia Brentano received the dedication. During his studies with Beethoven in Vienna, Ries had rendered many practical services to Beethoven, acting as his secretary and assisting him with negotiations with publishers. With this in mind, Beethoven expressed the hope that Ries might be able to sell the Variations to an English publisher 'for a good price'. He closes 'I am also composing a new string quartet [Op. 127]' and asks if it would be possible to offer it for sale in London.[lix] Ries appears to have had some initial success in this regard through the offices of fellow pianist and composer Charles Neate. Like Ries, he had a close association with the (Royal) Philharmonic Society, London. In the event, however, despite Neate's efforts to have the Op. 127 Quartet published – together with Opp. 132 and 130 – he could not find sufficient support amongst the London publishers.[lx]

As for Galitzin, over the next few months, he appears to have established a bond of friendship with Beethoven, albeit of a rather tenuous kind – the two never met. (Perhaps there is a parallel to be found here between Beethoven and Prince Galitzin and Tchaikovsky and his patroness Countess Nadezhda von Meck?) In a letter of 3 August, Galitzin revealed to Beethoven how his wife Elena, a talented pianist, shared his love of music, 'is one of your great admirers' and how she looked forward to receiving and performing his latest piano sonatas.[lxi] On 3 October he reaffirmed his intention to pay 50 ducats for the String Quartet Op. 127, confirming (see above) that he would be prepared to pay 150 ducats for this and two additional quartets, namely Op. 132 in A minor and Op. 130 in B-flat major.[lxii]

The following month it was Beethoven's *Missa Solemnis* that seized Galitzin's attention. On 29 November he wrote enthusiastically: 'It was with inexpressible joy, dear sir, that I received the Mass that you recently composed, and though until now I have been able to judge it only from the score, I have found the same grandeur in it that distinguishes all your compositions and makes your works impossible of imitation. I am trying to get this work performed in a manner worthy of its creator.' He still hoped to receive Beethoven's recently composed Piano Sonatas, Opp. 109, 110 and 111. As further evidence of his enthusiasm for the medium of the string quartet he adds: 'During my leisure moments, I even take pleasure in arranging some of your beautiful solo piano works as [string] quartets, and since I do not play this instrument, I take pleasure in performing them with the quartet.' Trying to contain his enthusiasm he concludes: 'I am very impatient to possess [my] new quartet by you [Op. 127], but I beg you not to pay any attention to this, and to follow in that respect only your inspiration and the inclination of your mind, for no one knows better than I that one cannot command genius, rather must [one] leave it alone.'[lxiii]

We turn now to 1824 to trace the composer's progress with the E-flat major String Quartet. As we do, we make passing reference to related events and circumstances bearing on his life and work.

The year opened auspiciously for Beethoven in the form of the recognition of his achievements from the musically inclined both at home and abroad. On 20 February he received a letter from the Duc d'Achâts, the first chancellor to the French Emperor Louis XVIII, announcing 'it had pleased his majesty to honour the artist with a gold medal showing the King's head'. This honorary gift had the weight of twenty-one louis d'or and inscribed on the reverse were the words: 'Donné par le Roi à Monsieur Beethoven.'[lxiv] Beethoven was clearly touched by this as is evident from a letter he wrote some time later (early March) to the journalist and editor Joseph Karl Bernard. He requested news of his honour should be made more widely known by being announced in the *Wiener Zeitung*, of which Bernard was then editor. Beethoven refers to Louis XVIII as being 'a generous King and a man of refined feeling'.[lxv]

Just four days after receiving his gold medal, on 24 February Beethoven was honoured once more in the form of a fulsome letter signed by twenty-four admirers of his art expressing their esteem of him and his works. The signatories included: Artaria & Co., (one of the composer's first music publishers); Carl Czerny (Beethoven's former piano pupil and pianistic pedagogue); Anton Diabelli (composer and music publisher); and Prince Eduard and Count Moritz Lichnowsky (respectively nephew and brother of Prince Carl Lichnowsky). Beethoven's devotees remark: 'Out of the wide circle of reverent admirers that surround your genius in your native city, a small number of disciples and lovers of art approach you today to express long-felt wishes.' They placed him on a level with Haydn and Mozart, regretted his enforced retirement from public life and looked forward to 'new blossoms' of his art and 'rejuvenated life'.[lxvi]

Of greater significance to the progress of our narrative is that around this time the Mainz publisher Schott (Schott's and Sons) approached Beethoven with the prospect that he might be prepared to contribute to their journal *Cäcilia* (*Cecilia*, patroness of musicians).[lxvii] The Mainz firm of music publishers was founded by Bernhard Schott in the days of Mozart; following Bernhard's death the business was carried on by his sons Johann Andreas and Johann Joseph under the title B. Schott's Söhne. In their letter to the composer (now thought to be lost)[lxviii] Schotts (as we shall refer to the publisher) also expressed their wish to bring out some of his more recent compositions.

Beethoven responded on 10 March. He first declined the invitation to contribute to *Cäcilia* on the grounds that he preferred to reveal himself to the world by means of his compositions. He did, though, give an undertaking to find a Viennese music correspondent to fill this role. More significantly for our narrative, he offered Schotts a number of works: 'I could offer you the following: a grand new solemn Mass with solo voices, chorus and full orchestra ... I must say that I consider this to be my greatest work.' Beethoven also offered 'a new grand symphony', the *Choral*, which he explained concludes with a finale 'in the style of my *Fantasia* for piano and orchestra [Op. 80] but on a far grander scale'. He closed his letter offering: 'A new quartet for two violins, viola and cello' — the String Quartet, Op. 127 for which Beethoven requested the fee of 50 gold ducats.[lxix] The composer's association with Schotts would eventually prove fruitful to both parties. Between 1825 and 1827, Schotts published first editions of the String Quartets Op. 127 and Op. 131 together with the *Missa Solemnis*, the Ninth Symphony, the Six Bagatelles, Op. 126 and the Overture *The Consecration of the House*. Initially, however, the Schotts brothers were rather cautious. On 24 March, Johann Joseph Schott responded to Beethoven's letter. He expressed regret that his firm could not undertake such a large scale undertaking all at once, given the great financial outlay involved; Johann Joseph was referring to the Mass, Choral Symphony and the String Quartet, Op. 127. Concerning the latter, though, his publishing house was prepared to accept the E-flat major Quartet as their exclusive property, for the requested fee of 50 ducats in gold, upon receipt of the manuscript. In business-like manner Johann Joseph concluded: 'If you want to withdraw the amount through a business house [in Vienna] immediately upon dispatch of the manuscript to us, then we shall render *prompt* payment. We wish, however, to come into possession of the manuscript very soon.'[lxx]

On 20 May Beethoven wrote to Schotts primarily to confirm the prices he wanted for his *Missa Solemnis* (1000 gulden) and the Ninth Symphony (600 gulden) but he also makes reference to his writing for the string quartet. He regretted he could not give a definite promise for the delivery of his new quartet (Op. 127); he excused himself for reasons that 'this correspondence with publishers at home and abroad has become very heavy'. Of passing interest in this letter is that Beethoven undertook to assist the pianist-violinist Christian Rummel — as Schotts had requested sometime in April. The interest here is that later on Rummel made piano-duet arrangements of both the composer's Ninth Symphony and the String Quartet, Op. 127.[lxxi]

By way of confirmation of the demanding business-side of the composer's life, Beethoven felt obliged just six days later to write to Prince Galitzin. He excused his failure to respond to a number of the Prince's 'amiable communications' for reason of being heavily committed to two concerts. In a letter of 26 May he promised Galitzin: 'You will soon receive the quartet [Op. 127] I promised to you so long ago, and perhaps the others as well [Opp. 132 and 130].' This reassurance prompted Galitzin on 16 June to convey his 'inexpressible pleasure' at receiving the composer's letter: 'It is with very real impatience that I await the shipment of the Quartet that you promised me ...'.[lxxii] On 28 June the Prince wrote once more, this time expressing the wish that he could be in Vienna so as to be in closer reach of the composer's 'sublime masterworks'. He added: 'As for my Quartets, my impatience requests them out of your friendship for me.'[lxxiii] One wonders if Galitzin's repeated expressions of enthusiasm may have tested Beethoven's own patience?

On 3 July, Beethoven renewed his connection with Schotts stating: 'I am willing to send you the Quartet [Op. 127] ... for a fee of 50 ducats. You will certainly receive the quartet within six weeks.'[lxxiv] 'Despite this promise of an early delivery, the first quartet did not reach Galitzin until April 1825. The other two quartets commissioned by him and dedicated to him, Op. 132 and Op. 130, were not completed until the summer and autumn of that year.'[lxxv]

Schotts responded to Beethoven's proposal on 19 July. It is a measure of their esteem of him that they greeted him with the salutation 'Herr Kapellmeister!' — a title, incidentally, that Beethoven never possessed but did covertly desire. Schotts first gave an undertaking to proofread the manuscripts of the *Missa Solemnis* and Ninth Symphony 'with the utmost care' so as to have them ready for publication. Regarding the Op. 127 they add: '[We] can surely count on the String Quartet as our property, it gladdens us all the more that we shall receive it in six weeks' time, and you may rest assured that, according to the time schedule of payments that you designated, this shall be accomplished through Herr Fries & Co. just as punctually.'[lxxvi]

Beethoven's progress was seriously impeded by illness as Schindler relates: 'Beethoven began the planning of the first of [the Galitzin] Quartets in the summer of 1824 in Baden, and upon his return in October he set himself to writing it down. For the first time in many years he took an apartment in the city.' The reason for this was to enable him to be close to the University where his nephew Karl was then studying. Schindler continues: 'The revision of the score had not been completed when the master fell ill of a sickness that lasted for several weeks. The cause of his illness was the trouble with his intestines that had bothered him almost constantly.' Since Beethoven's falling out with Dr. Malfatti in 1815, his physician had been the highly respected Dr. Jacob von Staudenheim. As a practitioner, he insisted on the strictest observation of his prescriptions 'and would allow himself to speak sternly to his disobedient patient'. It so chanced that such was the severity of the composer's stomach pains that Beethoven, unable to consult with Staudenheim, called upon the services of Professor Anton Braunhofer. It would seem that once more, in personality terms, Beethoven met his match as Schindler infers: '[Braunhofer] was no more lenient than his predecessor in handling his stubborn patient; in fact, he brought to his task a degree of Viennese bluntness that impressed the patient and contributed to his recovery. Still, it was not until his next summer's vacation in Baden that Beethoven's illness disappeared entirely.'[lxxvii]

Meanwhile, on 17 September, Beethoven felt obliged to write to Schotts to explain his circumstances. He informed the publisher he was staying in Baden on account of his health, or, as put it, 'on account of his poor health'. This time he promised the Quartet would be ready 'by October'. He asked Schotts to be 'just a little bit patient'. He ended his letter with a typical Beethovenian flourish: 'Apollo and the Muses are not yet going to let me be handed over to Death, for I still owe them so much ...'.[lxxviii] Beethoven's October deadline passed and the contrite composer wrote to Schotts once again on 16 November to further explain that his lack of progress was due to illness. He promised: 'By the end of the month, the Quartet will follow.' His (largely self-imposed)[lxxix] straightened circumstances prompted him to add: 'I would be pleased if, by then, I could receive the fee designated for it directly upon delivery of the Quartet.'[lxxx]

Carl Peters we recall had approached Beethoven in 1822 with the hope of securing a string quartet from the composer but had declined because he deemed the price requested was beyond his means. On 12 December Beethoven resumed his correspondence once more with the Leipzig publisher. He expressed regret he had now passed the E-flat major Quartet to another publisher (Schotts) 'since he particularly asked for it'. He sought to placate Peters, saying: 'But you will certainly get another one soon or I shall make a proposal to you about a greater work.' He closes: 'Please be patient ... for I will certainly satisfy you.'[lxxxi] Nothing, however, came of this proposal. A year later Beethoven repaid money he owed Peters, thereby terminating what had started out as a potentially fruitful working relationship.

As 1824 drew to a close Beethoven was obliged to write to Schotts once more. On 17 December he reassured his publisher that progress was well in hand with the Op. 127 Quartet but explained 'there is only a slight addition to be made to the last movement'. He took leave of Schotts 'otherwise [the Quartet] is finished and can be dispatched as soon as I have made the additions'.[lxxxii]

Early in 1825, Schuppanzigh was eager to promote his subscription series of quartet concerts and was anxious to have his Quartet (Karl Holz, second violin, Franz Weiss, viola and Joseph Linke cello) give the first performance of the E-flat major String Quartet. An entry in Beethoven's Conversation Book for the period reveals he consented to Schuppanzigh's request; the two were on good terms for reasons already outlined. For some reason, however, Beethoven's brother Johann and his nephew Karl urged

Beethoven to let Linke have the honour of the first performance and to allow Schuppanzigh to perform the Quartet later on as frequently as he wished. Schuppanzigh eventually prevailed to secure the first performance of the Op. 127 with an undertaking that Linke could perform the A minor Quartet, Op. 132 later in the autumn. The way ahead thus being clear, Schuppanzigh wasted no time and promptly made an announcement of his forthcoming concert that was scheduled to be held on 20 January in Vienna's *Vereinssaal* – a small concert hall. By mid January, however, Beethoven still had more work to do and Schuppanzigh had to substitute the Quartet in F minor, Op. 95 in place of the intended Op. 127.[lxxxiii]

It is apparent from a letter Beethoven sent to Schuppanzigh (undated but thought to be between 21–26 February) that the E-flat major Quartet was still not ready for performance. Beethoven explained he could not let Schuppanzigh have the work since he now had access to only one copyist. He reassured him though that the Quartet would not be published 'for a long time' and would therefore be available to him for his exclusive performance. In this letter Beethoven seized the opportunity to poke fun at his friend. Schuppanzigh had put on considerable weight and in view of his corpulence Beethoven wrote: 'As soon as my machine is finished, which will be able to transport you quite leisurely up to me on the fourth floor, I will let you know.'[lxxxiv] More seriously, as we shall see, the delay in letting Schuppanzigh and his fellow instrumentalists have sight of the Quartet reduced the time available to them for the proper rehearsal of this difficult work; this had consequences for the quality of the eventual first performance. Concerning the delay in releasing the work to Schuppanzigh, Barry Cooper makes the observation: 'It seems that Beethoven was becoming increasingly self-critical, and reluctant to release a work until he was fully satisfied (which of course he never was, as he aimed for that unattainable goal of absolute perfection).'[lxxxv]

Beethoven was clearly aware of the technical challenges to performers posed by his latest string quartet. With work on the composition complete, in March he wrote to Schuppanzigh, Weiss, Linke and Holz in quasi-humorous terms urging them to do their best in performing the work: 'Excellent Fellows! Each of you is receiving his part. And each of you undertakes to do his duty and, what is more, pledges himself on his word of honour to acquit himself as well as possible ...'.[lxxxvi] Writing of the 'newness' that Beethoven anticipated the performers would encounter, Griffiths remarks: 'A greater independence of the four parts is one of the striking new features brought into the string quartet by Op. 127.' He adds: 'And though even Beethoven's style of the 1820s could not allow the four members of a quartet to speak wholly different languages ... they are much less ready to concur in his late quartets than ever before, much more prone to stake and maintain individual positions.'[lxxxvii]

The first performance of the E-flat major String Quartet eventually initiated Schuppanzigh's subscription concerts. This was advertised in the *Bäuerles Theaterzeitung* on 3 March 1825: 'The first of these concerts is to be held on 6 March and will be honoured by an entirely new and masterly quartet of Beethoven's composition. This work (still in manuscript) should afford all the more pleasure to all lovers of fine music, as it is the only quartet which the celebrated composer has written for fifteen years.'[lxxxviii]

Of the event itself, Anton Schindler writes: 'The first performance of the first of these quartets [the Galitzin Quartets], in E-flat major, by Schuppanzigh and his companions took place ... in March 1825. It was an almost total failure, and the audience that had come with high expectations left the concert hall in a state of bewilderment. People asked one another what it was they had just heard.'[lxxxix] Beethoven was not present at the concert and news of its failure reached him via a somewhat jaundiced account by his brother Johann. Beethoven's biographer Alexander Wheelock Thayer reflects: 'Schuppanzigh was held responsible and his patience must have been severely tested by Beethoven's upbraidings and his determination to have an immediate repetition by other players. Schuppanzigh defended himself as vigorously as possible and was particularly vexed because Beethoven cited his brother's opinion of the performance — that of a musical ignoramus.' Schuppanzigh protested that the fault of the fiasco was not his individually, as Beethoven had been told. He assured Beethoven 'he could easily master the technical difficulties, but it was hard to arrive at the spirit of the work'. He acknowledged the ensemble was faulty 'because of this fact and too few rehearsals'.[xc]

Joseph Böhm, who had been leader of the quartet concerts in Vienna during Schuppanzigh's absence in St. Petersburg, was at the first performance and relates: 'The affair did not come off well. Schuppanzigh, who played first violin, was weary from much rehearsing, there was no finish in the performance and the Quartet did not appeal to him, he was not well disposed towards the performance and the Quartet did not please. Few were moved, it was a weak *succès d'estime.*' When Beethoven heard of this — for he was not present at the performance — he became furious and let both performers and the public in for some harsh words.'[xci]

Cooper cites some of the particular circumstances that probably contributed to the poor performance: 'There were inevitably some copying errors that only gradually came to light, for Beethoven had been unable to find an adequate replacement for Schlemmer [Beethoven's most reliable copyist who had recently died].' He also singles out 'the irregular figurations and numerous ledger lines for the first violin' that made reading of the music more difficult. Of the poor ensemble he remarks: 'The metrically disruptive opening, followed by numerous changes of metre during the work, needed much more rehearsal time than normal, and the performance was inevitably ragged in places.'[xcii]

The correspondent writing in issue XXVII, 1825 of the *Allgemeine musikalische Zeitung* acknowledged that the Quartet was 'symphonically conceived' but required 'study by the performers down to the smallest detail'. He reported the work had been understood and completely comprehended by only a very few, and confessed: 'We were not one of them.' Schuppanzigh was blamed (somewhat unfairly) for the failure, for he was 'no longer considered capable of playing correctly or understanding fully the difficult task he had undertaken'.[xciii]

Schindler relates how Beethoven remonstrated with Schuppanzigh on hearing of the failure of his new quartet to make a favourable impression and that he was unwilling to let matters rest 'and sought an honourable vindication of his work'.[xciv] Accordingly, he approached Joseph Böhm to whom we have made brief reference. He requires further introduction. He was the first professor of violin to be appointed at the Vienna Conservatoire and was active in the musical scene at the *Gesellschaft der Musikfreunde*. Moreover, he shared Beethoven's enthusiasm for the works of Goethe, Schiller and Shakespeare and rendered assistance to the composer in copying out the parts of Op. 127.[xcv] It is a measure of the regard in which Böhm held Beethoven that he was a torchbearer at his funeral and, on the occasion of the memorial concert held in his honour on May 1827, he performed the composer's Violin Concerto.[xcvi] Beethoven asked Böhm to direct further performances of the work that subsequently took place on 18 and 23 March — but only after intensive rehearsal under Beethoven's personal supervision; Beethoven could not hear the music but judged the interpretation by keenly observing the bowing action of the players. The 23 March concert was particularly significant insofar as the Quartet was performed twice — probably at the suggestion of Karl Holz.

Various accounts have been left of these early performances of the E-flat major Quartet. The musical correspondent Alfred Ebert was disposed to enthuse: 'This professor [Joseph Böhm] now performed the marvellous quartet twice on the same evening, before the same very numerous assembly of artists and critics to the entire satisfaction of all ... and the magnificent work of art shone forth in all its blinding glory.'[xcvii] Thayer, although not a witness himself, based his account of the events in question on the (reliable) recollections of those who were present. He comments: 'The Quartet was performed finally and received with a real storm of applause. Now Beethoven was satisfied. Steiner [publisher], who had attended one or more of the rehearsals, was particularly enraptured by it and at once offered to buy it for publication for 60 ducats — a fact that Beethoven did not fail to report to Schott and Sons when he sent the manuscript to them.'[xcviii]

We have already cited the impressions the Op. 127 String Quartet made upon Ludwig Rellstab (see above) but his views regarding the composition, and of his meeting with the composer, are worthy of further comment. Rellstab's recollections derive from his *Aus meinem Leben* that were published a year after his death in 1861. He writes: 'There was not space enough to sit ... The four players had barely enough room for their stands ... [These] were some of the most admirable younger Vienna virtuosos, who had dedicated themselves to their important task with all the enthusiasm of youth, and had held seventeen (or even more) rehearsals before daring to give the enigmatic new composition even a semi-public performance before a number of connoisseurs.' Rellstab describes the atmosphere and sense of eager expectation: 'The performance began amid the most intense silence and rapt attention ... Everyone in this select assembly understood what he heard, which produced a most significant community of sentiment; and there was present the thought ... that the creator of the profound work was still living near to us ...'. Of the challenges posed by the composition — to both performers and audience — he comments: 'And just as the players had been obliged to study, moil and toil until they had clambered up its precipitous heights, so did the listeners find it was not to be taken too lightly — and with this presumption in mind, it had at once been settled in advance that the work should be played twice in succession.'

Rellstab's subsequently made a visit to see Beethoven and disclosed he had heard the Op. 127 performed to such effect. At this he relates 'a happy smile vivified [the composer's] languid glance' and he spoke as though in self-reproof: "It is so difficult that they probably played it badly?" He enquired: "Did it go at all?" In response Rellstab had to weigh his words with care since the work had challenged his expectations. He confessed: '[In] this work are to be found only the ruins of the erstwhile youthful and virile exaltation of his genius; that it is often buried beneath the most disordered rubble and wreckage.' Notwithstanding, regarding the effect the performance had made upon him, and many others in the audience, he wrote in the composer's Conversation Book: 'I was devoutly and profoundly moved to the depth of my soul!' At this, Rellstab narrates how Beethoven went to the window where he gazed for a long time in silent contemplation.[xcix]

Throughout these events Schuppanzigh had to bear the misfortune of having been displaced by Böhm — but his downfall was temporary. Such was Beethoven's estimation of him and his musicianship that he took part in the premiers of both the String Quartet in A minor, Op. 132 and the String Quartet in B-flat major, Op. 130 both with the fugue, Op. 133 and with the new finale. We provide details of these in our later accounts.

With the E-flat major Quartet now performed and shaped to the composer's satisfaction, his thoughts and energy turned to having the work published. Accordingly, he resumed his correspondence with Schotts; it will be recalled on 10 March the previous year he had promised the Mainz publisher 'A new quartet for two violins, viola and cello.' On 19 March 1825 Beethoven wrote to Schotts: 'The violin Quartet [Op. 127] will be delivered 'during the next few days.' He drew attention to the 'favourable offers' he had received from rival publishers in Vienna but gave an undertaking to let Schotts have priority as he had promised. Of related interest is that Beethoven revealed to Schotts that he was working on the other two remaining Galitzin Quartets, namely, Op. 132 and Op. 130. He made the exaggerated claim that 'the second one' [Op. 132] was 'almost finished'; in fact this composition was not completed until the end of July.[c] Towards the end of the month he provided Schotts with a list of the opus numbers for his most recent compositions including that for the E-flat major String Quartet, Op. 127.[ci] In late March, Beethoven was obliged to write once more to Schotts with the reassurance he would 'certainly receive the works [including Op. 127] next week'. He excused his delay for reasons once more of not having access to a reliable copyist. He urged Schotts to send him the fee for the Quartet as soon as possible since he was 'in need of a good deal of money'.^{cii} It was not until 7 May that Beethoven was satisfied that Schotts had received the manuscript copy of the E-flat major Quartet. In this letter he once more mentioned the interest shown by other publishers in the composition and of their willingness to pay 60 ducats for it. Notwithstanding, he held firm to his undertaking with Schotts to allow his firm to bring out the work for the agreed sum of 50 ducats.^{ciii}

Beethoven fell ill again at this time and his condition threatened to undermine work of any kind. Such was his concern that he wrote to his then physician Dr. Anton Braunhofer requesting stronger medicine to help with his catarrhal condition. He also complained of spitting up blood, nose bleeds and of a 'dreadfully weak stomach'. He was concerned that without Braunhofer's assistance his strength would not be restored. He informed Braunhofer that he wanted one thing only which was 'to being able to sit soon at his writing table'.^{civ} Despite the seriousness of his condition, Braunhofer's medication appears to have restored Beethoven's health since he wrote to him in late May: 'We thank you for the advice *which was well given and well followed'.* [Beethoven's italics]^{cv}

Meanwhile, as Beethoven's negotiations with Schotts were taking place, Prince Galitzin gently urged the composer to make progress in sending him the first of his commissions: 'I cannot express with what impatience I await the first of the Quartets.' He also requested a copy of the Ninth Symphony, the expense of which he undertook to reimburse the composer.^{cvi} In the New Year 1825, Galitzin duly received his copy of the Op. 127 Quartet. This prompted him to write to the composer on 29 April in characteristically fulsome terms: 'I have many thanks to give you, worthy Monsieur de Beethoven, for the precious parcel with the sublime Quartet that I have just received. I have already had it played several times, and I find in it all the genius of the master, and when the playing of it becomes more perfect, the pleasure will be all the greater.' He added: 'For a few days we shall play your new Quartet with Bernhard Romberg, who has been here a month.' Romberg was a violoncellist, composer, conductor and a friend of Beethoven since their youth together in Bonn. Galitzin concluded his letter: 'Do not delay, I ask you, in having it printed; such a beautiful masterpiece ought not to remain hidden for a single moment.'[cvii] It would not, however, be until 1826 that Schotts published the Op. 127 Quartet, first in parts (March) and then in score (June). It was the only one of the Galitzin Quartets to be published in the composer's lifetime – hence their sometimes-applied sobriquet 'posthumous quartets'.

When he had assimilated the E-flat major Quartet, Galitzin, in his enthusiasm, sent the original manuscript of the composition to Pierre Marie de Baillot – then newly established as professor of violin at the Conservatoire de Paris. He had established a reputation for the quartet concerts he had initiated there in the concert season 1821–22, news of which had clearly reached the musically minded Prince. He writes: 'I believed this famous artist would prove one of the first to appreciate this new work of the celebrated composer.' When de Baillot sent back the manuscript he expressed the following opinion: 'Beethoven translates one to a new world, where one wanders in wild desolation, on the edge of chasms, in the darkness of night. One awakes in an early paradise of ravishing beauty, and all the splendour of life shines in the sunlight.' Galitzin responded: 'No metaphor could better describe the last works of Beethoven; the arid stretches of dimly understood obscurity only throw into greater relief the sunlit passages, where divine harmonies seem to break out of chaos, reflecting the soul of the artist in all its variety of emotion.'[cviii]

It was at the time of Beethoven's illness that Ludwig Rellstab made several visits to see the composer. On one of these he told him how deeply moved he had been on hearing a performance of the E-flat major Quartet that he had heard played twice in succession – a reference to the performance under Böhm's direction to which we have made reference. The encounter with Beethoven had a poignant moment. Rellstab recounts how Beethoven noticed him gazing at the piano that he had received as a gift from the English maker John Broadwood. He proudly pointed to the crossbeam on which were inscribed the names Moscheles, Kalkbrenner, Cramer, Clementi and Broadwood himself. Beethoven struck a chord, hoping thereby to reveal the instrument's fine tone. Instead, he created a dissonance compounding his error by striking the false chord several times. Rellstab movingly observed: 'The greatest musician on earth did not hear the dissonance.'[cix]

In St. Petersburg at this time was the violin virtuoso Karol Lipiski; he was then making a tour of Poland, Russia and Germany. Prince Galitzin seized the opportunity to perform the Op. 127 Quartet with Lipiski and could not restrain himself from sharing this experience in a letter to Beethoven on 21 June.

On 10 July Beethoven found time to write a long letter to his Nephew Karl; by then Beethoven had in effect adopted the young man and consequently he addressed him as 'Dear Son'. He reflected on the poor performance and consequent indifferent reception of his Op. 127 Quartet on 6 March. He recognised the work had been inadequately rehearsed but he also considered Schuppanzigh's Quartet was not as versatile as in earlier days when it was known as the 'Razumovsky Quartet'. In happier mood he says: 'On the other hand the Quartet has been splendidly performed six times by other artists and received with great applause.'

He informed Karl: 'On one evening it was played twice in succession.' He also refers to a performance by Böhm at his benefit concert and enthused that other musicians wanted the composition.[cx]

On 2 August, Beethoven informed Schotts that the String Quartet Op. 127 was to be dedicated to Prince Galitzin.[cxi] The following month he sent Galitzin the instrumentalists' parts for the companion String Quartet Op. 132 and politely asked for the required payment to be sent to him via his banker Henikstein — adding that at present his expenses were high. He informed Galitzin the third Quartet (Op. 130) 'will soon be finished' — it was completed in December. Beethoven expressed his delight with the Prince's praise for the first Quartet (Op. 127) and now hoped he would find equal pleasure with the second one that he had just sent.[cxii]

On 25 November Beethoven, in his business-affairs capacity, wrote to Schotts: 'I herewith confirm by my signature that Herren Bernhard Schotts Söhne have received from me a quartet in E flat for two violins, viola and violincello and that this quartet is *entirely their property.*' [Beethoven's italics][cxiii]

In 1826 Beethoven was in a position to complete the arrangements necessary for Schotts to proceed with publication of the E-flat major Quartet. On 28 January he wrote to the publisher: 'Please do not forget the first quartet [Op. 127] is dedicated to Prince Galitzin.' He also requested several copies of the work for him to give — as was his custom — to impecunious artists he held 'in high regard'.[cxiv]

The Op. 127 String Quartet was among the compositions to benefit from Beethoven's interest in the recently invented metronome. On 28 March he promised to send Schotts the required metronome designations together with those for the *Missa Solemnis* and the Ninth Symphony. He tempted Schotts with the possibility of him writing a further quartet, asserting he would require '*at least 80 gold ducats*' [Beethoven's italics] in view of the 'very great competition' for a composition of this kind.[cv] Schotts duly published the instrumental parts for the E-flat major Quartet in March 1825 and the score in the following June. The Title page for the latter reads: 'GRAND QUATOR/pour deux Violins, Alto et Violincelle/composé et dédié/á Son Altesse Monseigneur le Prince/Nicolas de Galitzin/Lieutenant-Colonel de la Garde de S.A.Mgr. de toutes les Russien/PAR/LOUIS V. BEETHOVEN/Oeuvre 127/À PARIS/chez les Fils de B. SCHOTT, Editeurs et Marchands de Musique.'[cxvi]

In 1827, Clementi & Co. published the parts of the Op. 127 String Quartet in England.

Errors inevitably appeared in the first edition for which Beethoven chastised Schotts. He supplied a list of the required corrections that he demanded should be made public in the publisher's journal *Caecilia*.[cxvii] After these had been made good Schotts wrote to the composer on 28 November with the welcome news: 'We have now received the Paris *Journal général d'annonces*, No. 94 of 25 November. An article says: "Vienna. There has appeared here a new Quartet by Beethoven, entitled *Grand quatuor pour deux Violons, alto et Violoncello*, composé et dédié a S. A. Mgr. le Prince de Galitzin par Beethoven, *Oeuvre* 127".'[cxviii]

Writing in 1827, and echoing the outlook of many nineteenth-century critics that the late quartets did not divulge their secrets easily, the reviewer of the Op. 127 String Quartet for the *Berliner Allgemeine musikalische Zeitung* maintained that the work required repeated hearings in order to be understood: 'Only after careful study of the score will the unfamiliar harmonies [of the Quartet] seem like the streaks of the Milky Way.'[cxix] The spirit of this contention prevailed well into the nineteenth century. In 1861 the music correspondent of the *Revue et Gazette musicales de Paris* reported on a performance of the E-flat major Quartet performed under the direction of Jean-Pierre Maurin

The music could not have been in more reliable hands. Maurin was professor of violin at the Conservatoire de Paris and founder of the *Society for the last Quartets of Beethoven*. Maurin's musicianship earned the admiration of none other than Richard Wagner. Notwithstanding possessing these credentials, the music critic of the *Revue* opined: 'M. Maurin presented his audience with a performance of [Beethoven's] twelfth Quartet ... the work belongs to [the composer's] last period, when deafness had overtaken him, and his broken faith in humanity had driven him to take refuge in a half-defined religious mysticism ... his last works have a sort of analogy with the *Rêveries* of J.-J. Rousseau. The grammatical and musical forms are respectively observed, but the inspiration flickers.' The critic acknowledged that Beethoven's late works had merit but qualified his praise: 'It cannot, however, be denied that there are still, in these last compositions, qualities which have always marked his quartet writing – splendour of inspiration, broad curves of melody, and daring harmonies; but he seems no longer careful of the formal excellence to be found in his earlier work; his idea wanders in a waste of formless development.' The reviewer closed his piece with words of caution: 'Those who worship [Beethoven] blindly see in this the ecstasy of a misunderstood genius; his true admirers pity him, and realize that it is now the dying fire of genius still bursting fitfully into flames.'[cx]

We set aside these bleak estimations of the composer's achievement with the observation that with the Galitzin String Quartets – alongside the C-sharp minor Quartet and the F major Quartet – Beethoven bequeathed a legacy to the string-quartet medium that would remain without equal until Bella Bartók contributed his own set of six masterpieces to the genre in the twentieth century.

The fist movement of Op. 127 is designated *Maestoso* – 'stately, dignified and in majestic fashion' and to be played 'quickly'. Beethoven also marked the score here *teneramente* – 'tenderly'. *Maestoso* refers particularly to the sonorous chords that open the piece and which several times serve to halt, or temporarily interrupt, the progress of the music. More generally the movement has 'a tender, lyrical quality' perhaps with evocations of the mood prevailing in the Piano Sonata in A flat, Op. 110.[cxxi] Michael Steinberg suggests 'the wistful mood of this music' and the first violin's melody 'of touching sweetness', are 'perhaps illuminated by the knowledge that some of the early sketches were headed *La gaieté*.[cxxii] The 'sonorous chords' take the form of a six-bar introduction, 'a wonderful idea ... a touchstone of sheer beauty and depth in Beethoven's music'.[cxxiii] Paul Bekker likened the opening to a 'stately prelude ... a proclamation of indomitable willpower, triumphant after many past conflicts'. In his view the opening chords do more than usher in a new quartet, they are no less than 'the portal to the whole artistic kingdom of Beethoven's last years'.[cxxiv]

David Wyn Jones finds a parallel with Beethoven's six-bar introduction and the manner in which Haydn opens his String quartets Op. 71 and Op. 74. Here, in the E-flat major Quartet, he maintains they serve 'to launch the movement rather than to provide a formally complete section'. Furthermore, in his view the later appearance of the chords acts as 'a clear aural landmark before the development section'.[cxxv] Arthur Shepherd suggests the *maestoso* introductory phrase serves to provide not only 'a striking contrast to the persistently regular flow of the ensuing three-four rhythm' but also functions to determine 'the tonal architecture of the whole movement'.[cxxvi] De

Marliave describes the *maestoso* chords, when vigorously struck, as being possessed of 'throbbing energy' that emanates from 'the sinewy *sforzandi* of the bass' and whose intermittent repetitions give the movement 'an air characteristic of Beethoven'.[xxvii] For Simpson, the opening 'is a new blend of formality and rhythmic ambiguity'.[xxviii]

Many commenters have remarked that for Beethoven the key of E-flat major is often a key of 'grand rhetoric' and 'emphatic gestures', such as may be found in the opening of the *Eroica* Symphony and the *Emperor* Piano Concerto. Michael Steinberg is one who finds the declamatory first measures of the Op. 127 Quartet to be fashioned in a similar manner. He states: 'Few composers, told to write alternating tonic and dominant chords ... would come up with something so arresting, yet so unfussy, as what Beethoven gives us here.' He invites us to regard the opening to the first movement as being something akin to 'an illuminated initial at the head of a chapter'. The six measures he believes are in essence a form of 'pseudo-introduction' that nonetheless 'convey a powerful sense of direction and intention'.[xxix] In similar manner, Harold Truscott asserts that whilst the opening sounds like an introduction, not least by reason of its 'slow, majestic pace', it is not really an introduction at all; 'It is part of a larger idea which is completed with the beginning of the *Allegro.*'[xxx]

Terse as the opening introduction may be, it is anything but perfunctory. Martin Cooper suggests Beethoven's manner here looks back to the slow introductions of Haydn's symphonies — rather than forward 'to the atmospheric, improvisatory introductions of Liszt and the later Romantics'. He also believes there is a parallel to be found between the opening of the E-flat major Quartet and that of the Piano Sonata, Op. 81a, 'in which a slow introduction in E flat leads to a statement of the main theme'. In Cooper's estimation, however, a close comparison between the two passages reveals the composer's 'change in concentration' and, as it were, 'the tempo of Beethoven's thought-process in these last years'. He elaborates: 'Whereas in the Sonata there is still a large degree of symmetry, repetition and extended, song-like melody, all the rhetorical element has entirely disappeared.' He concludes: 'If such a pruned, chastened style is characteristic of advancing age, it does not denote a falling-off so much as a redirection of creative energy, an interiorization and concentration of the powers that were previously directed outwards to charm, persuade, or convince a hypothetical listener.'[cxxxi]

In the programme notes Donald Tovey wrote to accompany a performance of the Op. 127 String Quartet on 17 February 1915, he states: 'The first movement, after an unfinished phrase of *Maestoso* introduction, starts its opening so quietly and in a rhythm so different from that of the introduction that we soon feel the special beauty of the steady maintenance of this rhythm.'[cxxxii] The American composer and writer on music Arthur Shepherd declared the principal theme to be 'genial and ingratiating', serving to establish a mood of 'pastoral serenity' that he believed to be 'testimony of the composer's gospel of Tonality'.[cxxxiii] Alongside him de Marliave perceived the predominant effect of the first movement to be one of 'mystical contemplation'.[cxxxiv] Could the atmosphere that prevails here perhaps have affinities with the *Arietta* of the Piano Sonata in C minor, Op. 111? — as suggested by Phillip Radcliffe.[cxxxv] In Joseph Kerman's opinion song, not drama, grounds the tender movement of this Quartet, song that is 'superbly and strongly moulded' such as to inspire the theme and variations of the following *Adagio*. He elaborates: 'By chamber standards the first movement is delicate and retiring and by any standards at all, for sonata form, it minimizes dramatic contrast to a remarkable extent.'[cxxxvi]

The opening theme of the first movement, a broad melody, is announced by the first violin and is then repeated, with greater emphasis, by the cello. Truscott regards the theme to be more of 'a tuneful fragment' as typical of Beethoven's later style and one that Robert Schumann would make personal to his own later musical idiom. He defends his proposition saying: 'These fragments are melodic, but not complete; they have this quality of a theme, that they can rise to growth beyond themselves. They are the result of Beethoven's preoccupation with counterpoint.'[cxxxvii] De Marliave considered the composer's style here to be 'new' and 'far from true sonata form' and yet showing itself 'to be as coherent and unified as the old'. Regarding the form of the composition he considered it to be 'more condensed' and, from a psychological aspect, he perceived the work as broadening and progressing as though to a goal 'that constantly recedes as it is approached'.[cxxxviii] Simpson is more direct: '[The] ensuing *Allegro* is thematically one of the most close-fisted [Beethoven] ever wrote, yet still giving a sense of superb ease and expansiveness out of all proportion to its length.'[cxxxix] To cite Truscott once more: 'In spite of the reputed complexity of these [late] works the truth is that Beethoven's harmonies here are just as simple as in his earliest works; at times even simpler.' With regard to the working out in Op. 127 he states: 'So far the music has revolved around tonic, dominant and subdominant, but this is obscured to a great extent by the freedom of the melodic lines, the tendency to counterpoint.' Truscott considered no other composer, with the exception of Franz Schubert, had the ability 'to make such homely harmonies sound so much as though they had dropped from another planet'.[cxl]

For the origins of the composer's inspiration, Stephen

Rumph looks back to earlier Beethoven string-quartet creations: 'The first movement of Op. 127 harvests oats sown long before in *The Harp* Quartet.' But, he maintains: 'The contrasts are sharper, the counterpoint more rigorous, and the form more paradoxical than ever.' Then, looking forward to later creations, he proposes this movement and its contrapuntal treatment 'looks ahead to the *Grosse Fuge*'.[cxli] Steinberg is similarly inclined to recall earlier of Beethoven's works and finds parallels between them: 'Now the music moves forward with captivating verve, resembling in spirit the first movement of the great Piano Trio in the same key, Op. 70, No. 2.'[cxlii] Kerman cites similarities between the first movements of the String Quartet, Op. 74 (*The Harp*) and that of the Op. 127 String Quartet, both of which, as remarked, share the same key of E-flat major. He observes: 'The composite theme of Op. 127 can be thought of as a more "extreme" version of the theme-type employed in Op. 74, namely, an antecedent-consequent idea passing from force to goodness.'[cxliii] As the first movement continues in its 'lilting three-four time ... harmonised with the subtlest fluidity'[cxliv], we give the last words here to Truscott: 'Nothing is permanent; all is directed to one end, conveyed through some of the most beautiful counterpoint in all classical music.'[cxlv]

Tovey, in his programme notes to which we have made reference, perceived the tranquillity that permeates the fist movement having to brace itself, as it were, 'so as to withstand the rhythmic shock of the twofold reappearance of the opening chords'.[cxlvi] Marion Scott also alludes to the these chords and to their musical significance: '[An] *allegro* with singularly gracious, lovely subjects, is ushered in by a short prelude in E flat — *maestoso* — used twice again in G and C during the course of the movement, and always with an effect like the immense weight-bearing strength of

Norman pillars and arches — one of its purposes being to dominate the "tonal structure" of the movement.'[cxlvii] Of Beethoven's craftsmanship Truscott remarks: 'Part of the successful alternation of chordal and contrapuntal treatment is achieved by subtle phrasing, managed so skilfully that it conveys its effects to us without drawing attention to itself.'[cxlviii]

'A simple and touching epilogue closes the movement.'[cxlix] In de Marliave's estimation: 'This entire first movement of the Quartet is a delicate ad subtle portrayal of the artist's soul.'[cl]

The second movement of the E-flat major String Quartet is designated *Adagio, ma non troppo e molto cantabile* — 'slowly, but not too much so and very songlike'. Romain Rolland described the *Adagio* as 'dreamy'[cli] but it was clearly too much so for a fellow countryman of his writing of the music in 1844 in the 18 February issue of the *Revue et Gazette musicales de Paris*. He protested: 'Frankly, we can declare that the *Adagio* of the twelfth Beethoven Quartet, except for the opening passage of grave religious fervour, is intolerably long without sequence of ideas, in spite of the long inscription which explains the emotions of the writer, and might well be considered the forerunner of the "Programmes" of the great Romantic composers.'[clii] With the benefit of deeper insight and understanding, the A flat *Adagio* disposed the Jewish-Austrian musicologist Viktor Zuckerkandl to the view that the functioning of a musical composition has a close analogy with the functioning of life itself: 'We act as we do because we are what we are; we become what we are because we act as we do. The process is a gradual one of progression from amorphous beginnings towards ever more sharply defined forms and is complete only when the last step has been taken.'[cliii] Joseph Kerman praises Beethoven's musical construction: 'Speaking purely of architectural eloquence ... this movement goes deeper and further than any other slow movement of the last period. In terms of structure, the Ninth Symphony seems bulging by comparison, Op, 130 merely happy and correct, Op. 131 permissive. Only the *Lento assai* of the last quartet, the Quartet in F, Op. 135, inscrutably the simplest of all, is built so perfectly and so eloquently.'[cliv]

The second movement is the variations movement of the Quartet, although not so described by the composer. Beethoven was attracted to the variation form throughout his life; it has been estimated he composed some sixty sets of variations of one kind or another. Early in his career, as a piano virtuoso, he composed what may be described as 'occasional pieces' and others styled in the prevailing fashion of the day — but bearing the distinctive hallmark of his (unrivalled) improvisatory manner. His later variations, of the kind with which we are here concerned, have been described as 'the vehicles of his most intimate emotion'.[clv] Evidence of the latter may be found in the Piano Sonata in E major, Op. 109, its companion the Piano Sonata in C minor, Op. 111, and, more significantly, in the *33 Variations on a waltz by Anton Diabelli*, Op. 120. Commonly known as the *Diabelli Variations*; these were composed between 1819 and 1823, making them a close neighbour — both in terms of chronology and kinship of spirit — of the E-flat major String Quartet.

Beethoven had made sparing use of the variation form in his String Quartet in A, Op. 18 (1799—1800) and in the allegretto *variation* in the finale of the Quartet in E-flat major, Op. 74 (1809). Writing of the composer's subsequent preoccupation with the variation form, Steinberg comments: 'Late in life, Beethoven turned to variation form more and more, often using it as he does here [in the Quartet Op. 127], in contemplative breadth as a contrast to the terseness and drive of his sonata forms.'[clvi] Cooper observes: 'Variation form, used in the second movement, is also prominent in his late style, but is treated with great diversity [see later].'[clvii] Basil Lam argues: 'The suggestion that Beethoven's latest style evolved through simplification might seem to be invalidated by the growing prominence of variations in the music of his last years, but the themes out of which these variations grow [here in the Op. 127 Quartet] are themselves precisely those final simplicities, purified of all expressive alloy.'[clviii]

Steinberg describes the opening of the movement as 'an act of preparation'. It commences with the cello that sounds its lowest E flat, following which the other instruments are heard in turn; viola, second violin and first violin make their entries in their respective low registers. As Steinberg comments: 'Beethoven would again use the same device of building up a first chord note by note at the beginning of the variations movement of the last quartet, Op. 135.' Here, as he further comments, the theme is 'a rapt and expansive melody', reminding us of the composer's directions to the performer 'to play slowly and songlike'. Eventually the second violin 'sings a duet with the cello'.[clix] Regarding the second movement as a whole, Truscott regards the *Adagio* to be both 'the most intricate movement' in the Quartet and yet 'the simplest as well'. He justifies this for the reason: 'It is easy to be misled by the long-drawn nature of the beautiful complex tune which is part basis of [the following] set of variation[s]; complex as it is, it is simple fundamentally as everything else in the work.' With an intellectual twist in the tail he adds: 'But one thing needs to be stressed: simplicity makes complexity.'[clx] Setting aside musicological technicalities and other such considerations, Lam is content to remark: '[The] theme in its unworldly calm is as nearly timeless as music can be.'[clxi]

The E-flat major Quartet exemplifies Beethoven's

expansion of musical form that is found in his later compositions. Writing of this, de Marliave makes the generalisation: 'It is not only that each movement of these [late] quartets assumes gigantic proportions, by reason of [Beethoven's] uninterrupted flood of musical ideas, but each main theme is itself on a larger scale, occupying a greater number of bars than before.' The theme of the *Adagio* of the Op. 127 Quartet extends over eighteen bars. For de Marliave these eighteen bars 'rise out of a depth of concentrated feeling' and enclose 'one of those indescribable passages only Beethoven could write'. In support of this contention he cites the *Adagio* of the Ninth Symphony, the *Benedictus* of the Mass in D and the *Adagio* of the monumental Piano Sonata in B flat major, Op. 106.[clxii] Scott finds evidence, in the opening of the second movement, of the studies Beethoven made of Palestrina when he was at work on the *Missa Solemnis*. In particular she draws attention to the manner in which the individual voices of the four instruments enter, as mentioned, in turn; this she considers 'fitted perfectly with Beethoven's predilections'.[clxiii] The philosopher-musicologist Theodore Adorno also makes reference here to Beethoven's D minor Mass and finds a connection with it and the slow movement of the Op. 127 String Quartet: '[The] *Missa* holds a place entirely apart from the rest of Beethoven's *oeuvre*, even the late ones ... there are *hardly* any connections to his other works, even the late ones — neither formally, nor thematically, nor in the characters ... The sole exception, perhaps, is the variations movement from Op. 127 — itself extremely obscure — which is reminiscent of the *Benedictus*.'[clxiv] Kerman describes the movement not so much as obscure but 'organic in conception' from which, as we later remark, a set of variations develop.[clxv]

When the composer's second-movement tempo

marking *molto cantabile is* respected, an expansive performance extends to fifteen or more minutes — the equivalent of that of an entire string quartet of the classical era. The sense of expansiveness is progressively conveyed through the medium of the opening theme and the following set of variations. As Wyn Jones comments, 'Beethoven does not label the constituent sections of the movement ... but the sentence structure is clearly articulated and each variation has a highly distinctive rhythmic configuration'.[clxvi]

Establishing the final form of the theme for the slow movement posed a challenge to Beethoven. Lam comments: 'In Op. 127, the numerous sketches for the slow movement theme make a strange sequence quite unlike the continuous process, generally attributed to Beethoven, of perfecting a rough outline.' After establishing the opening bar of the melody, in his first sketch, what Lam describes as 'pages of useless variants' follow until the required phrase was completed. He concludes: 'All this is not so much invention as the clarifying of vision, so that something already known can be realised.'[clxvii] Cooper makes similar observations: 'The theme cost Beethoven endless trouble, as the sketchbooks show. Only the opening seems to have been an initial "inspiration" or *Einfall* — what Paul Valéry called a "vers donné".' The composer's tribulations were not, however, in vain since, as Cooper further remarks: 'Beethoven tried, as usual, a number of different keys and rhythms; and a phrase from an idea eventually rejected in one place often occurs somewhere else later in the theme.' He additionally reflects: 'The situation seems to have been complicated by the fact that two different works seem to have been maturing together in Beethoven's mind at this time — this slow movement in A-flat major and an entirely different movement, which was never completed, in C major and bearing the title *La gaieté.*'[clxviii] Radcliffe also comments on this aspect of the composer's creative process: 'The theme appears to have given Beethoven endless trouble; there are innumerable sketches, including a number that are in a different key and tempo.' The endeavour though he also believed to be worthy of the effort: 'The theme in its final form has extraordinary beauty and subtlety.'clxix

Kerman describes the melody that generates the second movement of the Quartet in E-flat major — *Adagio, ma non troppo e molto cantabile* — as 'a famous miracle of beauty'. He quotes the American composer and music critic Daniel Gregory Mason: 'Were some malignant power to permit us to retain but a single page of Beethoven this page, which gave him such endless trouble in the writing, might well be the one we should cherish for our solace and delight.' Mason is referring to the extensive sketches for the melody that prompt Kerman to remark: '[Beethoven's] best music was the most laboriously sketched, and the most laboriously sketched the most spontaneously sounding.' He adds: 'The melody has a natural vocal quality that bears a resemblance to an early draft for Leonore's aria *Komm, Hoffnung* in *Fidelio*.'clxx

Kerman is fulsome in his praise for 'the consummate lyric art' of this *Adagio* and its 'quite extreme luxuriance of texture'. At the same time he argues the strength of the movement's structure should not be overlooked: 'No other Beethoven slow movement, I would judge, quite matches it in this respect. It is a structure based less on contrast than on similarity, emanating from variations on a single theme.' For Kerman, however, lyric art is given the last word: 'In the middle, serenity deepens to prayer, and luxuriance deepens to intensity.'clxxi Arthur Shepherd was no less fulsome in his praise for what Beethoven had achieved, albeit at the same time recognising that it posed the listener with a challenge that had so bewildered the first audience: 'So far removed is the exalted music of this second movement, from the ordinary or normal variation form (the external decorative treatment of a theme), that it becomes difficult for the casual hearer to apprehend the composer's structural and expressive purposes.' He further comments: 'Decoration and manipulation have given way entirely to the most subtle *idealization*. The wealth of detail, exuberant and ethereal by turns, that it is only through feeling rather than through intellectual perception that one remains aware of the basic relationship of the theme and arabesque.'[clxxii] Recalling Beethoven's preoccupation with writing liturgical music, at the period when he was composing the E-flat major Quartet, Radcliffe maintains: 'The flowing 12/8 time inevitably suggests the *Benedictus* of the Mass in D major.'[clxxiii]

In his discussion of Beethoven's constructional procedures, Griffiths draws attention to precedents that he finds in the earlier E flat String Quartet: 'The opening *Allegro* [of the first movement] is followed by an *Adagio* in A flat, exactly as in Beethoven's previous E flat Quartet, Op. 74, only the expressive richness is greatly increased, and music is set on a road towards the *Heiliger Dankgesang* of Op. 132 and the *Cavatina* of Op. 130.'[clxxiv] Although Beethoven was not a proficient string player — unlike Haydn and Mozart — Radcliffe pays tribute to the sympathetic manner in which the music is laid out: 'The slow movements of the Ninth Symphony and the Quartet, Op. 127, contain passages of a similarly ornate character which are equally suited to the violin in their widely sweeping melodic curves.'[clxxv] Beethoven took particular care to ensure his intentions to the performer were clear by writing out repeats in full.[clxxvi] Rumph finds much of the slow movement to be a 'sustained exercise in double counterpoint'.[clxxvii] Not surprisingly, former concert pianist turned musicologist, Denis Matthews found parallels between Beethoven's writing for the medium of the string quartet and that seen in the late piano sonatas; in particular he draws attention to Beethoven's 'absorption in trills'.[clxxviii]

We direct our attention now to the set of variations that are at the heart of the second movement.

We have remarked that in his late period Beethoven became drawn ever closer to the variation form as a medium for his more contemplative style of musical expression. The American musicologist Daniel Chua discusses Beethoven's disposition to transform and decorate counterpoint in the context of the adoption of variation form. He reminds us that the idea of adopting such a procedure was already germinating in the comoser's mind as early as 1802 and found expression in the so-called *Eroica Variations*, Op. 35; Beethoven himself considered these to be 'distinctly different' from his earlier ones. Chua reasons: 'In Op. 35 he was groping towards a concept of contrapuntal variation by introducing the bare bones of the bass first and only later adding the tune.' Technically, Chua maintains, the Op. 35 Variations represented a new departure for the variation form insofar as 'the bass is not so much the *theme* as a *bass* for the theme'. In his opinion this idea of 1802 'reaches its fruition in this movement in 1824'.[clxxix] Simpson recalls the expansive nature of the opening theme of the slow movement and describes Beethoven's reworking of it in variation form as 'the utmost subtle elaboration, contrasted in character with surprising sharpness, every note inspired'.[clxxx] Describing the manner in which the opening theme leads to the variations, de Marliave enthuses 'the original theme shines through a brightness of rarefied purity'. He likens Beethoven's transformation of the theme to a form of musical *melopoeia* – the process whereby, in language, words are charged beyond their normal meaning with some musical property that further directs their meaning, inducing emotional correlations by sound and rhythm of speech. He maintains this melopoeia is to be the theme of the variations. Invoking the views of the pioneering Beethoven authority Adolf Bernhard Marx, he likens the transformation as 'an increasingly sublime transfiguration of the melody'. From the point of view of musical style, de Marliave compares the Op. 127 Quartet variations with those found in the Ninth Symphony and the Piano Sonatas Opp. 109 and 111. He adds the caveat: 'But in detail of formal construction they are quite different; the variations here are purely contrapuntal, and wholly in the genre of the quartet.'[clxxxi]

Kerman likens the variations to 'an iridescent chain' in which each one seems to cleave a little to its predecessors. He is one of a number of authorities who consider Beethoven's musical structure can be considered as having six variations – depending upon how one dissects Beethoven's somewhat homogenous musical fabric. He states: '[In] Op. 127 the six variations and coda are formed, not like a chain with seven links and a plummet, but like a symmetrical *A B A* design with a very significant gap in the coda.' The opening theme and Variations 1 and 2 he considers constitute the first element in the chain; Variation 3 constitutes the second; and Variations 4, 5, and 6 serve 'as a unit' to complete the design. Setting aside such analytical technicalities, he concludes: 'What one cherishes is [the movement's] calm directness, its sense of freedom, its simplicity and its economy. The form is spare, the harmony plain.'[clxxxii] Matthews enters into this same spirit of warm endorsement: 'The slow movement was to explore the richness of variations in a continuum unimaginable in the neatly articulated set in Op. 18, No. 5 or *The Harp.*' He makes reference to Beethoven's painstaking working out: '[The Quartet's] *Adagio* theme, the result of many reworkings and character changes in the sketches, is warmly lyrical on the broadest scale'. He suggests 'the rapt manner' of the introduction must have appealed to many Romantics 'who were otherwise unable to enter into Beethoven's spiritual world'.[clxxxiii] Bekker considered the series of variations to be nothing less than 'marvellous' in which Beethoven 'attempts to embody and set forth the revelation which has been granted to his seeking soul'.[clxxxiv]

Truscott maintains Variation three is at 'the real heart of the movement' but acknowledges the others for the manner in which they, in their different ways, 'draw out the tune [opening melody] into rich and varied decoration, with beautiful counterpoint'.[clxxxv] In her summative assessment Scott avers the variations 'contain a wealth of inspiration expressed with consummate mastery'. She invites the student of Beethoven to view these in relation to the *Agnus Dei* and *Dona nobis* of the *Missa Solemnis*.[clxxxvi]

Barry Cooper describes the first and second variations as being of the decorative variety but which are enriched 'with a profusion of ornamental figures and motivic fragments' that generate what he regards as 'some of the most elaborate and intricate textures that had ever been seen in quartet writing'.[clxxxvii] Martin Cooper expresses similar thoughts: 'The contrapuntal texture is unusually close-knit; there is not an otiose, unaccounted note anywhere and the cadence of one phrase is inextricably tied to the opening of the next, as so often in Beethoven's works.'[clxxxviii] Kerman considers the first variation to be one of the most complex that Beethoven ever wrote with its 'tiny moments of intensity' and 'spontaneous invention', everything 'burgeoning freely' and whose 'lush vibrant texture' is sustained to the very last bar.[clxxxix] Some find the treatment of Variation 1 reminiscent of the first variation of the *Arietta* of the Piano Sonata Op. 111.[cxc] The youthful Felix Mendelssohn is known to have had a particular fondness for this music and, more generally, was one of the first to absorb the spirit of Beethoven's late string-quartet music into his own chamber compositions. The first variation gives the opening melody 'a new rhythmic shape'[cxci] together with an effect of 'added animation' and 'a restless intensity of thought' by the substitution of semiquavers for quavers.[cxcii] Of the mood prevailing in the new music, Lam comments: 'The first variation, while faithful to the structure of the theme, dwells joyfully on some of its melodic phrases, infused with chromatic inflections so harmonised as to exclude pathos.'[cxciii]

Beethoven heads Variation 2 with the performer's direction to play *Andante con moto* – 'moderately slow with movement'. Tovey, writing for an audience in 1915, described the character prevailing as having 'a mysterious marching rhythm' that he describes as pervading the music with its 'glitter of delicate ornamentation' and 'rich repeats'.[cxciv] The two violins commence a 'playful dialogue'.[cxcv] Beethoven allows these two instruments to have prominence for eighteen of the twenty-three bars of the variation. In Cooper's words: '[The] first and second violins execute an elaborate duo, either answering each other antiphonally, imitating each other's figuration, or providing a countersubject to each other's melody ... trills, suspensions, syncopations ... mercurial in character.' Meanwhile, the two lower instruments provide 'simple harmonic and rhythmic support'.[cxcvi] Radcliffe suggests the general mood that prevails anticipates that of the *Andante con motto* of the String Quartet Op. 130.[cxcvii] Kerman is in agreement and also finds 'the light *obbligato* style' to be typical of that of the *Heiliger Dankgesang* passage in the String Quartet Op. 132. He also makes reference to the composer's use of syncopations, trills and, for the technically minded, how the 'fast-dancing dialogue' requires recourse to sixteenth, thirty-second and sixty-fourth notes.[cxcviii]

In Lam's estimation: 'A heavenly levity pervades the

Andante con moto with its naïve serenade-like accompaniment to the fantastically elaborate duet of the two violins.' With regard to Beethoven's level of invention he asserts: '[Nothing] like this had been heard since the *Dominie Deus* of the B minor Mass.'[ccix] In his description of the music, de Marliave indulges in some nineteenth-century musicological imagery: 'The inspiration becomes almost martial and heroic, but still as though enshrouded in a half-light. Shades of heroes seem to cross the path of the imagination, ethereal and shadowy. As the development extends, this impression deepens ... the half-light persists, with barely perceptible changing nuance.' Of the music's construction, he states: 'The modulation to the minor ... casts a passing shadow of melancholy over the theme, now adorned with imitations, trills and turns, on the two violins alternately, against the monotonous beating of the base.' And of the transition to the next transformation of the theme, he writes: 'This restless variation, a dream-like fantasy of the imagination is linked to the next by a modulation in a unison of the four instruments.'[cc]

At the period when Beethoven was turning his attention to string-quartet writing, Rossini was enjoying considerable public success in Vienna with his stage works. Fellow composers were somewhat less enamoured of the Italian's success, regarding him as being something of an interloper. Schubert, for one, responded to the Rossinian challenge with his *Overture in the Italian Style*. As for Beethoven, Truscott finds him also responding to Rossini in this variation. He observes: 'Beethoven does much more than just imitate – he creates and carries the Rossinian mood much further than Rossini ever thought of doing ... [Beethoven] simply appropriated for his own purposes and in his own way.' By way of illustration, he cites 'the steady but jerky dance rhythms' and 'the most remarkable interlacing counterpoint' shared between the two violins.[cci]

The hymn-like character of Variation 3 makes for many 'a spiritual crown for the movement' if not, for that matter, for the whole quartet. Kerman, whose words we have just quoted, also detects in the music recollections of the 'mystical E-major hymn' in the second *Razumovsky* Quartet and the slow variation finale of the Piano Sonata in E, Op. 109.[ccii] Radcliffe also finds a parallel between the 'serene tenderness of mood' in the Quartet and the character of the theme in the Op. 109 Piano Sonata.[cciii] For de Marliave, eighteen entire bars of this variation 'breathe a deep religious feeling'. He contends the notes of the sustained melody on the first violin 'fall slowly upon the ear ... like a prayer'. In his estimation: 'This section combines the fullness of inspiration of the first variation with the subdued melancholy of the second.'[cciv] Vincent d'Indy, writing of Beethoven's compositional procedures in his biography of the composer (1913), remarks: 'In order the better to mark the change of state, Beethoven places his character theme in the key of E major, giving by this means the effect of a mysterious, almost celestial radiance.'[ccv] With the change of key (F flat written as E) 'we are brought back to the human world of aspiration and prayer'. Lam whose words we have cited here adds: 'Significantly, Beethoven's *cantabile*, always reserved for the inexpressive sublime, is now replaced by *molto espressivo*, with wide melodic intervals and highly charged harmony.' It is known that Anton Bruckner was a great admirer of Beethoven and, with this in mind, Lam reflects: 'Bruckner was surely inspired by this variation in the profound *Adagio* of his Sixth Symphony, and the possibility of such an association is indicative of its remoteness from the rest of the Quartet.'[ccvi]

De Marliave described the third variation as 'a sort of progressive movement' that is urged on by the use of short trills that, as we have noted, Beethoven so often adopts in his later works.[ccvii] Whilst all the instruments democratically share the main theme and the accompaniment, Beethoven allows the first violin and cello to share, in alternation, what Steinberg describes as 'an ecstatic, high-flying song'.[ccviii] Placing the third variation in its wider context, with regard to Beethoven's compositional procedures, Truscott contends: 'Where the other variations move in wonderful decorating counterpoint, and so increase the melodic depth of the whole, the third variation is harmonic rather than melodic and, instead of decorating, reduces the theme to its harmonic skeleton.'[ccix]

The thirteen measures that follow have been described as more of an 'episode' than a full variation.[ccx] In Cooper's estimation, their 'solemn recollected quality' anticipates episodes to be found in Chopin's *Barcarolle* and the late *Barcarolles* of Fauré'.[ccxi] Kerman is amongst those who also describe 'this wonderful passage' as not so much a variation 'as an episode' of just thirteen bars that are characterised by 'the rich use of trills ... a Beethoven hallmark at this period'.[ccxii] These trills, against a background of chords, although 'very simple' make for an episode that is 'curiously exciting after the stillness of the preceding variation'.[ccxiii] As mentioned, the melody forms the basis of a duet between the cello and first violin[ccxiv] while the second violin and viola 'support the harmony and maintain a steady rhythmic flow of even quavers'.[ccxv] As this variation draws to a close Beethoven develops chordal passages that serve as a link to the fifth and final variation. Discussing this link, Truscott considers it contains 'one of the profoundest passages in the whole work, not least for its very bare writing in the midst of harmonic richness ... with the tune varied in a continuous stream of semiquavers for first violin, and an accompaniment divided between the other three instruments to give suggestion of counterpoint'.[ccxvi]

Beethoven writes *sotto voce* at the beginning of variation five — the final full variation — and, in Steinberg's words, 'this sets the tone for the whole of this mysterious episode. It is unpredictable — tentative, almost'.[ccxvii] In Simpson's estimation: 'Its great striding arpeggios [march] skywards past the slow soaring of the theme, the air alive with the singing of birds.' He considers the mood prevailing surpasses even 'the scene by the brook in the *Pastoral* Symphony 'as a response to nature'.[ccxviii] Several authorities compare Beethoven's treatment of the closing variation with similar procedures he adopts in the *Choral* Symphony. De Marliave describes the first violin as giving 'a metamorphosed statement of the principal theme' which, as he considers, is typical of the *Adagio* in the Ninth Symphony. This is then taken-up by the other three instruments 'above a wave of melody'.[ccxix] Kerman concurs: 'The last, simplest and shortest variation glides over the melody in continuous flowing sixteenth notes [having] affinities with the second variation in the *Adagio* of the Ninth Symphony and just as serene.' He further avows if we were able to retain but a single bar of Beethoven 'we might take this last variation of the chromatic close'.[ccx] The semi-quaver ornamentation of the theme and the manner in which it is 'passed from instrument to instrument' against 'a syncopated accompaniment', is suggestive to Cooper of the third variation in the slow movement to the Ninth Symphony.[ccxxi] Radcliffe describes the closing variation as being 'luxuriously ornate' and whose 'flowing semi-quavers [are] similar to the those in the *Adagio* of the Ninth Symphony'.[ccxxii]

We take leave of the variations and the movement in the words of de Marliave: '[A] last figure on the first violin, joined by the cello, murmurs a farewell as the dream slips away ... So fades from view this vision of a supernatural existence, where [quoting Robert Schumann] "one seems to have lingered, not fifteen short minutes, but an eternity".'ccxxiii

The third movement is a Beethoven *scherzo* that he heads *Scherzando vivace – Presto*. De Marliave was unequivocal in his praise for the composer's achievement here: 'With those of the Ninth Symphony and the Quartet Op. 59, No. 1, this *Scherzo* is the most advanced work Beethoven ever wrote.' He qualifies his observation: 'But while the *Allegretto Scherzando* of the Op. 59 derives its highly developed construction from variety and musical treatment of *motifs*, the *Scherzo* of the Quartet in E flat is evolved from the germ of an idea gradually developed to complex maturity.'ccxxiv De Marliave's 'germ of an idea' is a reference to the four-note motivic configuration with which the movement opens and which, to some, connects all of the composer's late string quartets. Kinderman is one such authority. He cites additional evidence of the extent to which the motif in question seized the composer's imagination; a version of it is found in sketches for the slow introduction of a projected piano sonata for four hands that Beethoven, regrettably, never completed. Kerman adds: '[The] motivic material and sequential [note] pattern transposed from C minor [in the sketches] to E-flat major [in the Quartet], found its way into the *Scherzo* of the Quartet in E-flat major, Op. 127.'ccxxv

The sketches for this movement date from around August 1824 and both their extent and complexity suggest they once again gave Beethoven considerable difficulty in resolving them into their final version. Writing of this, and of the composer's wish to make his intentions to performers clear, Cooper notes: 'Beethoven emphasizes the rhythmic peculiarity by marking it *ritmo di tre battute* ['rhythm of three bars'] to signify that the rhythm goes in groups of three bars or four bars respectively (as in the *Scherzo* of the Ninth Symphony).'[ccxxvi]

Beethoven's opens the Op. 127 *Scherzo* with the sound of plucked strings, the four chords of which 'in the neatest possible way define rhythm, key, character, and speed'.[ccxxvii] They are little more than tonic, dominant, tonic, dominant[ccxxviii] prompting Lam to observe. 'The most commonplace formula of tonic and dominant chords having been glorified in the slow movement, a second such makes an enchantingly witty introduction to the *Scherzo*, but it looks back, not forward.'[ccxxix] Jones agrees: '[The] four pizzicato chords set up one of those gently jesting movements by Beethoven that consist of short phrases that move in one direction followed by similar phrases in the opposite direction.'[ccxxx] Misha Donat describes the start as 'a flourish tapped out by the pizzicato strings' but with scoring 'as rich as that of the opening movement's initial chords' – a 'toy fanfare' but which 'could hardly be more different'.[ccxxxi] For Arthur Shepherd the transition from the slow movement to the *scherzando vivace* reveals a trait 'that is at once enigmatic and fascinating'. He remarks: 'The composer almost catapults one from the heights to the hard material surface of the earth.' He quotes the nineteenth-century musicologist Julius Spitta: 'It would seem impossible that any sound from earth could penetrate this calm and serene air. But we find that Beethoven, after he has worked on the *Adagio* for a time, is suddenly possessed by his demon. He changes the key and the tempo, and the theme becomes a gay *allegro* movement through which his humour goes leaping merrily.'[ccxxxii]

The *Scherzando* is an extended movement that has the second longest performing time of the Quartet. Simpson describes it as 'one of the largest and strangest of Beethoven's scherzos, contrasting fragmentary counterpoint with vivid jagged unisons – the supressed disturbances of the first movement rising to the surface'.[cxxxiii] Notwithstanding, commentators observe how in its construction Beethoven adheres closely to 'near normal procedure'[cxxxiv] and even to 'the old classical form'.[cxxxv] Despite the movement 'being large in scale and possessed of elaborate detail'[cxxxvi], some detractors have dismissed these virtues as 'dry, academic' and even 'full of calculated tricks that merely trivialise the Quartet'.[cxxxvii]

Beethoven's would-be detractors are silenced by the many who admire his *Scherzando* humour. As early as 1825, the music critic Ludwig Rellstab remarked 'even in the profound *Scherzo* where it seems to make fun of itself ... in so doing [it] only moves us to a deeper and more stirring response'.[cxxxviii] 'The persistent dotted-note rhythm of its main section recalls the third movement of Op. 95, but its drily humorous, conversational mood is much more akin to that of the second movement of Op. 59, No. 1, though there is more counterpoint and less lyrical relief.'[cxxxix] Radcliffe, whose words we have quoted further elaborates: 'The movement as a whole is the only part of Op. 127 that gives full expression to the abrupt and capricious side of Beethoven's latest style and it stands out with remarkable effect against the lyrical beauty of its neighbours.'

With Beethoven's changing (darkening) mood that is characteristic of his final period, Griffiths states 'like all those of Beethoven's late quartets, [the humour] is not so much jokey as possessed — and the gesture with which it starts, four pizzicato chords, reaches far beyond joking to mock the very opening of the work'. More generally he comments: 'The central movements thus range across the whole spectrum of musical seriousness, from the profound subjectivity of the slow movement to, immediately following, the brisk deflation at the start of the *Scherzo.*'[ccxl] Bekker's analysis leaves no doubt as to the many layered complexity of the music: 'The subsequent *Scherzo*, with its alternations of wild, almost rough humour and eeriness, is something of a riddle. It is the richest in content and the most prolix of Beethoven's *scherzi*, and may represent a last uprush of the powers of darkness before they succumb finally to the spirit of joy.'[ccxli] Kerman comments in the same manner: '[The] *Scherzando vivace* is one of Beethoven's most explosive pieces, bursting with energy and malice, crackling with dry intelligence ... It is the *Scherzando vivace* that supplies the intellectual, mordant note ... Even a note of parody: the cryptic introductory *pizzicato* fanfare seems to make light of the *pizzicatos* introduced at the very end of the *Adagio* variations.'[ccxlii] Tovey was in no doubt of the earnestness of Beethoven's intentions here, describing the *Scherzo* as 'one of Beethoven's most humorous examples of its kind' but adding 'the humour is specially profound and abstruse'.[ccxliii] Lam makes a similarly inclined commentary. He acknowledges that the *Scherzando vivace* has been likened to the *Allegretto vivace e sempre scherzando* of Op. 59, No. 1, but consider the resemblance to be superficial. He reasons: 'The earlier piece, splendidly wilful in the extremity of its contrasts, convinces by expressing the personality of its composer, but the Beethoven of 1825 is no more concerned with self-expression than was Bach of the Goldberg Variations, where the same sense of intellectual joy comes from the awareness of a freedom so absolute that it can create its own limitations for the pure pleasure of transcending them.'[ccxliv]

The 'absorbingly capricious' *Scherzo* gives way, 'to a wild Trio in the minor that disappears as suddenly as it came'.[ccxlv] It is in the form of a *presto*, rather rare in Beethoven, but having similarities 'in sound and phrasing' to some of the composer's Bagatelles from his contemporary Op. 126.[ccxlvi] Tovey described the Trio as 'a round-dance', having typical Beethovenian characteristics.[ccxlvii] To de Marliave's ears 'the Trio ripples on in a stream of sound essentially melodic in type, in turn ethereal and misty, decisive and heroic'.[ccxlviii] It is quite some 'ripple' extending, with repeats, for approaching 150 bars. Donat describes the character of the Trio as being 'an agitated *minore' of a kind used elsewhere by the composer. He explains:* 'The scheme is similar to the one Beethoven had used in the *Scherzo* of his Ninth Symphony, and both pieces play on the listener's expectations of encountering the expanded scherzo form he had used so often during the preceding decade, in which the trio was played twice in full, between three statements of the scherzo.[ccxlix]

Radcliffe believes Beethoven wanted to have the last laugh on the first performers, playing, it will be recalled, under the direction of the overweight Ignaz Schuppanzigh. He comments: 'The final notes of the *Scherzo* of Op. 127 are reminiscent of the vivid imitation of a donkey's bray — *hihiya* — that occurs at the end of a comic part-song written by Beethoven many years previously for the corpulent violinist Schuppanzigh.'[ccl]

We take leave of the *Scherzo* to the String Quartet in E-flat major, Op. 127 with an observation of the extent to which Beethoven's original manuscripts are now valued as cultural artefacts. The thirty-one page manuscript scherzo-section of the Quartet, including alterations and additions by the composer, sold at auction on 6 December 2003 for £1,181,600. A few months previously, Beethoven's working manuscript of his Ninth symphony, for which he earned a mere £100, fetched £2.1m at Sotheby's.

The finale movement opens with four bars of unison introduction that Cooper likens to a 'curtain raiser in the good-humoured style of Haydn; his studies of the sketches do indeed suggest Beethoven initially had in mind 'an unmistakably rustic idea' for this movement. On reflection though, he feels: 'If this can be called rustic, it is nearer to Bartók's stylized realism than to the idealized village scenes of Beethoven's own Sixth Symphony' [viz. 'Merry gathering of country folk].[ccli] De Marliave found the spirit of Haydn hovering unequivocally about the closing movement: 'In this finale the passionate and bitter emotions of the first movement, the unearthly twilights of the *Adagio*, and the fantastic movement of the *Scherzo* are set aside; here all is gaiety and charm recalling the genial wit of Haydn, in which the imaginative intensity of the preceding movements is relaxed.'[cclii] However, the spirit of Haydn does not so much hover as march: 'The whole movement has the character of a march. A spirit of indomitable happiness dominates it. Some adventurer from the heavens seems to visit the earth he has left, with tidings of gladness to return to his home in the heavens once more.'[ccliii] Also with Haydn in mind — consider for example his Piano Trio No. 39 — Steinberg draws attention to the music's 'robust rhythms' that he considers are 'almost gypsy-like' and the atmosphere 'decidedly more rustic'. He regards the movement, initially at least, suggestive of a reversion 'to an older, lighter type of finale'.[ccliv]

It is alleged one of the composer's friends, on hearing the closing pages of the E-flat major Quartet, remarked: 'Beethoven is inspired by the ecstasy of his joy, and the joy of his ecstasy.' Commenting on this, Shepherd proposes: 'The joy of the finale is not the cosmic, world-embracing rapture of the Ninth Symphony, but, rather, a simple rustic vigour that was just as surely part and parcel of Beethoven's healthy nature as those transcendent impulses that sent him soaring with the poet Schiller and his "Tochter aus Elysium".' He makes the further assertion: 'But the joy of the Quartet finale is not earth-bound, for at the very end it is transformed into one of the master's many most ecstatic pages. Through the subtle alchemy of genius, the rollicking figure of the opening theme now becomes a celestial call that once more echoes among the heights.'[cclv]

Haydn has been mentioned as a source of possible influence on Beethoven, but perhaps the spirit of Mozart also exerted its sway: 'In the first twelve bars the whole content of the movement is revealed. The first four bars of unison (presenting something of a resemblance ... of Mozart's Quartet in E flat) appear at first as a simple introduction, but later it is seen that they contain germs of thematic material.'[cclvi] Perhaps, as Tovey once suggested, Beethoven was drawing inspiration from compositions of his own creation. He found affinities with the movement in question and the finale of the Trio in B flat, Op. 97. He cites the 'narrow circle of keys', the movement's 'rhythmic subtlety', and 'the gorgeous modulations'.[cclvii]

In his estimation of the character of the music, Truscott sets aside musicological refinement seeing the music for what it is: 'So far from being recondite or incomprehensible the harmony has been an almost unbroken alternation of tonic and dominant, and the themes themselves are of an utter simplicity ... the whole thing *sounds* simpler because it is not concerned with elaborate counterpoint, as the first movement.' He refers to the procedure as: 'The old classical habit ... of making the finale echo the first movement in a simpler way.'[cclviii] Alluding once more to vernacular musical idiom, Simpson singles out for mention Beethoven's predilection for the use of 'simple folk-like couplets' and the application of 'weaving tonal ambiguity.' Together, he maintains, these add 'a dimension to what would otherwise be a charming but plain-sailing finale'.[cclix] Whilst Beethoven's motifs may be 'simple and almost popular in form' his development of them has 'a unique originality'. De Marliave invites the student to study the score at the fifty-fifth bar where, he asserts, there occurs 'a passage rippling with gaiety, after Haydn's manner, but revealing Beethoven's own essential humour in the vigorous rhythmic descent of the bass from E flat to F'.[cclx]

The final movement, rich in 'subtle and unexpected features', is more approachable than the extended slow movement. Radcliffe remarks that the character of the music has sometimes been described as Haydnesque that he himself considered appropriate to its 'good humour'. He also makes mention of the 'lilting and leisurely tune' of the kind generally associated with Haydn rondos — that Beethoven develops in sonata form.'[cclxi] Lam describes the finale as having something of the composer's 'second-period harmonic breadth'. Of Beethoven's workmanship he adds: 'The deaf master's imagination invents a quartet-texture quite unlike anything he or anyone else had ever heard ... contrasts [that] alternate between *Eroica* Symphony grandeur and quite lyricism.'[cclxii] Kerman is fulsome in his praise for this movement, considering it to be 'one of Beethoven's sweetest and simplest-sounding, as well as one of the most perfectly conceived and executed'. He likens the main theme to a folk tune 'so magical and true, so lively and calm' but what he finds most striking is 'the combination of an evocation of childishness, on the one hand, and almost utterly refined treatment of melodic and harmonic detail, on the other'. With Beethoven's legacy of Haydn's string-quartet writing once more in mind, Kerman evokes a sustained metaphor by way of characterising the movement: 'The folk dances suddenly become dreamed or disembodied, the clay on the dancers' shoes whitened into some kind of glittering dust. The exquisitely calculated journey leads to a castle in the clouds, a fantasy world; but by many magic casements open from it into the real world. The main theme, of course, remains in a spiritual transformation.'[cclxiii]

We pause for a moment in our discussion of the final movement to recall an incident bearing on the Quartet's gestation. We have remarked that the first performance, under the direction of Ignaz Schuppanzigh, was unsatisfactory and that Beethoven subsequently called upon the services of Joseph Böhm to have the work repeated. At one of the rehearsals an interesting moment occurred, the outcome of which suggests Beethoven was, on occasions, amenable to making changes to his compositions. Böhm recalls how Beethoven sent for him in his usual curt way and said: 'You must play my Quartet'. Thereafter, Böhm relates how the Quartet 'was studied industriously and rehearsed frequently under Beethoven's own eyes'. He adds: 'I said *eyes* intentionally, for the unhappy man was so deaf that he could not hear the heavenly sound of his compositions.' Notwithstanding, Böhm tells how rehearsing in the composer's presence was not easy: 'With close attention, his eyes followed the bows and therefore he was able to judge the smallest fluctuations in tempo or rhythm and correct them immediately.' At the close of the last movement, a passage occurs which Beethoven had directed should be played *meno vivace* — 'less lively'. Böhm considered this weakened the effect and, summoning up his courage, he advised his fellow instrumentalists to maintain the original tempo. This was brought about and, to Böhm's ears, 'to the betterment of the effect'. He relates: 'Beethoven, crouched in a corner, heard nothing, but watched with strained attention.' After the last stroke of the bows Beethoven, having become aware of Böhm's change of tempo, strode over to the players' desks, crossed out the *meno vivace* in the four parts and said laconically 'Let it remain so'.[cclxiv]

From a purely psychological point of view, the Coda to the final movement 'epitomizes the emotional content of the entire work'.[cclxv] Beethoven expands his thoughts at length in a manner 'strange and most original'. 'The modulation to the remote key of C major brought about by raising the higher note of a trill, is magical; and the change of key brings with it a new and mysterious atmosphere.' Radcliffe, whom we are quoting, sees Beethoven luxuriating 'to an unusual degree in delicately sensuous colour ... wandering through a typically Romantic succession of keys'.[cclxvi] Although Beethoven adopts a slower tempo than in the rest of the movement, Tovey was in no doubt that the 'outward slackening of speed' imparts to the music 'an immense accession of energy in movement, and an enormous breadth of effect'.[cclxvii]

Truscott writes of the work moving 'gradually but inevitably to its crowning glory, the coda of this finale'.[cclxviii] By way of interest this was Igor Stravinsky's favourite movement in all of Beethoven's quartets.[cclxix] Tovey was similarly generously disposed: 'The last pages of this Quartet are the most ethereal tone painting in all quartet literature; technically of alarming difficulty, they amply justify their risks, and represent the most brilliant as well as the most profound art in instrumental music.'[cclxx] '[The] music dissolves into a long trill, there is a new sense of motion ... Garlands of scales move mysteriously about an altogether unearthly transformation of the main theme ... With an easy and assured breadth, wholly purified of rhetorical gestures, the Quartet moves to its conclusion, a miracle to the last of rhythmic and harmonic delicacy.'[cclxxi] '[Two] vigorous chords of the tonic ... conclude the movement, and with which [they] bring the Quartet to an end, with its wealth of inspiration and spiritual power, its overflowing vitality and brilliance of technique.'[cclxxii]

---

[i] Robert Simpson, 1973, p. 265.

[ii] Marion M. Scott, 1940, pp. 262–3. In her discussion of Beethoven's interest in the ecclesiastical music of the past, Scott remarks: 'The texture of

sixteenth-century polyphony (with those melodies which are so much shorter than the "subjects" of Viennese symphonic music and which yet are endless) modified his style perceptibly.'

[iii] See, for example, Leon Botstein, *Music, culture and society in Beethoven's Vienna*, in: Robert Winter and Robert Martin, editors, 1994, pp. 91–2.

[iv] Quoted in: Joseph de Marliave, *Beethoven's quartets*, 1925 (reprint 1961), p. 221.

[v] For a fuller account of Schuppanzigh's contribution to the musical life of Vienna, and in particular his association with Beethoven, see the accompanying text *The Galitzin Quartets*.

[vi] In his discussion of this aspect of Beethoven's pre-occupation with writing for the string quartet, Barry Cooper describes music publishers as yielding to their 'marketing instincts' as stirred by both amateur and professional players. Barry Cooper, 2000, p. 341.

[vii] Paul Bekker, 1925, pp. 326–7.

[viii] Maynard Solomon, *Beethoven: Beyond Classicism* in: Robert Winter and Robert Martin editors, *The Beethoven quartet companion*, 1994, p. 70. The references to Rellstab and Fétis are derived from this source.

[ix] Joseph de Marliave, 1925 (reprint 1961), p. 236.

[x] William Kinderman, 1997, pp. 282–3.

[xi] Misha Donat, *String Quartet in B-flat major, Op. 127: Notes to the BBC Radio Three Beethoven Experience*, Sunday 5 June 2005, www.bbc.co.uk/radio3/Beethoven

[xii] For a discussion of Beethoven's constructional procedures as employed in the late quartets, see, for example: Paul Griffiths, 1983, pp. 103–5; Barry Cooper, 1991, p. 236 and 2000, p. 323; and John Daverio, *Manner, tone, and tendency in Beethoven's chamber music for strings* in: Glenn Stanley editor, *The Cambridge companion to Beethoven*, 2000, pp. 147–64.

[xiii] Paul Griffiths, 1983, p. 104.

[xiv] As recorded in: Arthur Shepherd, 1935, p. 45.

[xv] Robin Wallace, 1986, p. 42 and p. 61.

[xvi] *The Cambridge companion to Berlioz*, 2000.

[xvii] As quoted in Robert Ignatius Letellier editor and translator, *The diaries of Giacomo Meyerbeer*, 4 Vols., 1999–2004, derived from Vol. 1, pp. 414–5.

[xviii] Robert Winter and Robert Martin editors, *The Beethoven quartet companion*, 1994, pp. 41–3 and p. 52. See also: *Elias String Quartet, The Beethoven project: The early performers of the Quartets of Beethoven*, website text.

[xix] *Ibid*, (Winter and Martin) p. 93.

[xx] Romain Rolland, 1917, p. 187.

[xxi] As quoted in: Michael Tilmouth editor, *Donald Francis Tovey: The classics of music: talks, essays, and other writings previously uncollected*, 2001, p. 257. The words quoted have been slightly adapted.

[xxii] Originally published on 21 March 1918 in *Music in the New Age* and reproduced in: R. Murray Schafer editor, *Ezra Pound and music: the complete criticism*, 1978, pp. 88–9.

[xxiii] Marion M. Scott, 1940, p. 264.

[xxiv] Igor Stravinsky and Robert Craft, *Conversations with Igor Stravinsky*, 1959, pp. 114–5.

[xxv] Basil Lam, 1975, pp. 75–6.

[xxvi] Philip Radcliffe, 1978, p. 99 and p. 108.

[xxvii] Denis Matthews, 1985, p. 139.

[xxviii] Daniel Snowman, *The Amadeus Quartet: the men and the music*, 1981, p. 110.

[xxix] Richard Kramer in: Christoph Wolff and Robert Riggs, *The string quartets of Haydn, Mozart and Beethoven: studies of the autograph manuscripts: a*

xxx Barry Cooper, 2000, pp. 322—3.
xxxi Douglas Porter Johnson, editor, 1985, pp. 471—4 and William Kinderman editor, 2005, p. 327.
xxxii Richard Kramer in: Christoph Wolff and Robert Riggs, *The string quartets of Haydn, Mozart and Beethoven: studies of the autograph manuscripts: a conference at Isham Memorial Library*, March 15—17, 1979, pp. 234—5.
xxxiii For a facsimile representation of the Autograph Score in question see: Beethoven House, Digital Archives Library Document, BH 72.
xxxiv William Kinderman, editor 2005, p. 327
xxxv Douglas Porter Johnson, editor, 1985, pp. 294—6.
xxxvi *Ibid*, pp. 411—18. See also: William Kinderman, editor 2005, p. 327.
xxxvii *Ibid*, Johnson, pp. 415—18 and Kinderman, p. 327.
xxxviii Douglas Porter Johnson, editor, 1985, pp. 299—305; William Kinderman editor, 2005, p. 327; and Barry Cooper, 1990, p. 124. For a facsimile reproduction of a sketch leaf from Autograph 11/2, see: Beethoven House, Digital Archives Library Document, NE 98. A facsimile reproduction of a sketch leaf intended for one of the Bagatelles from the Op. 126 set is also illustrated on the Beethoven House, Digital Archives Library Document, NE 98.
xxxix Douglas Porter Johnson, editor, 1985, pp. 309—10 and William Kinderman editor, 2005, p. 327.
xl For a facsimile reproduction of the sketch leaf in question, see: Beethoven House, Digital Archives Library Document, NE 98.
xli For a facsimile representation of the sketch leaf in question see: Beethoven House, Digital Archives Library Document, HCB Mh 97.
xlii Derived from Ludwig Nohl, *Beethoven depicted by his contemporaries*, 1880, p. 180.
xliii *Ibid*, p. 183 and Peter Clive, 2001, pp. 242—3.
xliv Ludwig Nohl, 1880, pp. 200—1. See also: Oscar George Theodore Sonneck, 1927, pp. 114—16 and Peter Clive, 2001, pp. 298—99.
xlv H. C. Robbins Landon, 1970, pp. 16—17 and plate 12. See also: Beethoven House, Digital Archives, Library Documents, B 1083/c.
xlvi Gerhard von Breuning, *Memories of Beethoven: from the house of the black-robed Spaniards*, 1874, reprinted and edited by Maynard Solomon, 1992, p. 78.
xlvii Oscar George Theodore Sonneck, *Beethoven: impressions of contemporaries*, 1927, pp. 114—5.
xlviii *Ibid*, pp. 116—20. Rossini's visit to see Beethoven so seized the mind of Richard Wagner as to dispose him to meet the Italian composer in Paris in 1860. The meeting subsequently took place in the presence of a number of others including the wealthy amateur pianist-composer Edmond Michotte. He took notes of the ensuing conversation that he subsequently published in 1906 as *La visite de Wagner à Rossini*. This is available today as *Richard Wagner's visit to Rossini* (Paris 1860) and *An evening at Rossini's in Beau-Séjour (Passy)* (1858), translated by Herbert Weinstock (1968.) In this work, Michotte's text is of interest in providing an insight into Wagner's theories about music drama and, relevant to the present study, Rossini's impressions of Beethoven.
xlix For an account of Peters' negotiations with Beethoven, see: Thayer-Forbes, pp. 787—91.
l Theodore Albrecht, translator and editor, 1996, Vol. 2, Letter No. 286, pp. 204—6.
li Emily Anderson, 1961, Vol. 2, Letter No. 1079, pp. 947—50.
lii Theodore Albrecht, translator and editor, 1996, Vol. 2, Letter No. 290, pp.

211–14.
[liii] Emily Anderson, editor and translator, 1961, Vol. 3, Letter No.1085, pp. 955–6.
[liv] Theodore Albrecht, translator and editor, 1996, Vol. 2, Letter No. 295, pp. 222–5.
[lv] *Ibid*, Letter No. 299, pp. 288–9. For a facsimile representation of Prince Galitzin's letter to Beethoven, together with a translation of the original text, see: Beethoven House, Digital Archives Document H. C. Bodmer, HCB Br 286.
[lvi] Emily Anderson, 1961, Vol. 3, Letter No. 1123, pp. 988–9.
[lvii] Theodore Albrecht, translator and editor, 1996, Vol. 2, Letter No. 310, pp. 244–5.
[lviii] *Ibid*, Vol. 2, Letter No. 319, pp. 259–60.
[lix] Emily Anderson, editor and translator, 1961, Vol. 3, Letter No. 1209, pp. 11064–5.
[lx] Anton Schindler, 1860, English edition: Donald MacArdle, 1966, p. 300, p. 354 and endnote 230. See also our accompanying text *The Galitzin Quartets*. Neate made Beethoven's acquaintance on a visit to Vienna in 1815–16. On his return to England he took with him, on behalf of the (Royal) Philharmonic Society, the three Concert Overtures *Die Ruinen von Athen*, *König Stephan* and *Zur Namensfier* for which the composer received the fee of 75 guineas. Beethoven got on well with Neate and described him to friends as 'an excellent musician and a charming man'.
[lxi] Theodore Albrecht, translator and editor, 1996, Vol. 2, Letter No. 333, pp. 277–8.
[lxii] *Ibid*, Vol. 2, Letter No. 336, pp. 281–2.
[lxiii] *Ibid*, Vol. 2, Letter No. 338, pp. 283–5. See also: Anton Schindler, 1860, English edition: Donald MacArdle, 1966, pp. 300–1.
[lxiv] Anton Felix Schindler edited by Donald W. MacArdle and translated by Constance S. Jolly from the German edition of 1860, 1966, p. 242. See also Thayer-Forbes, 1967, pp. 923–6 and Emily Anderson, editor and translator, 1961, Vol. 3, Letter No. 1292, pp. 1127–29. The medal is now a prized possession of the Gesellschaft der Musikfreunde.
[lxv] Emily Anderson, editor and translator, 1961, Vol. 3, Letter No. 1271, p. 1115.
[lxvi] Quoted in: Theodore Albrecht, translator and editor, 1996, Vol. 3, Document No. 344, pp. 4–11.
[lxvii] Thayer-Forbes, 1967, pp. 915–6.
[lxviii] It is thought Schotts wrote to Beethoven early in 1824.
[lxix] Emily Anderson, editor and translator, 1961, Vol. 3, Letter No.1270, pp. 114–5.
[lxx] Theodore Albrecht, translator and editor, 1996, Vol. 3, Letter No.350, pp. 18–19.
[lxxi] Emily Anderson, editor and translator, 1961, Vol. 3, Letter No. 1290, p. 1126, footnote 3.
[lxxii] Theodore Albrecht, translator and editor, 1996, Vol. 3, Letter No. 370, pp. 40–3.
[lxxiii] *Ibid*, Vol. 3, Letter No. 374, pp. 47–8.
[lxxiv] Emily Anderson, editor and translator, 1961, Vol. 3, Letter No. 1132, pp. 1132–3.
[lxxv] *Ibid*, Letter No. 1292, pp. 1127–9.
[lxxvi] Theodore Albrecht, translator and editor, 1996, Vol. 3, Letter No. 372, pp. 44–5.
[lxxvii] Anton Felix Schindler, *Beethoven as I knew him*, edited by Donald W. MacArdle and translated by Constance S. Jolly from the German edition of 1860, 1966, p. 305.

lxxviii Emily Anderson, editor and translator, 1961, Vol. 3, Letter No. 1308, p. 1141. See also: Joseph de Marliave, 1925 (reprint 1961), p. 210.

lxxix Beethoven had a number of bank shares that derived from the considerable money he earned from the various concerts he gave at the period of the Congress of Vienna of 1815. He resisted benefitting from these, however, since he considered them to be his nephew Karl's inheritance.

lxxx Theodore Albrecht, translator and editor, 1996, Vol. 3, Letter No. 384, pp. 61–2.

lxxxi Emily Anderson, editor and translator, 1961, Vol. 3, Letter No. 1324, p. 1154.

lxxxii *Ibid*. Letter No. 1325, pp. 1155–6.

lxxxiii Thayer-Forbes, 1967, pp. 937–39.

lxxxiv Emily Anderson, editor and translator, 1961, Vol. 3, Letter No.1350, p. 1177. For a facsimile representation of Beethoven's letter to Schuppanzigh, see: Beethoven House, Digital Archives Document HCB Br 217

lxxxv Barry Cooper, 2000, p. 324.

lxxxvi Emily Anderson, Vol. 3, Letter No. 1356, pp. 1182–3. See also: Thayer-Forbes, 1967, p. 940.

lxxxvii Paul Griffiths, 1983, pp. 101–2.

lxxxviii Paul Bekker, 1925, p. 325.

lxxxix Anton Felix Schindler, *Beethoven as I knew him*, edited by Donald W. MacArdle and translated by Constance S. Jolly from the German edition of 1860, 1966, pp. 305–6.

xc Thayer-Forbes, 1967, pp. 940–41.

xci *Ibid*.

xcii Barry Cooper, 2000, p. 325.

xciii Robert Winter, *Performing the Beethoven quartets in their first century* in: Robert Winter and Robert Martin editors, *The Beethoven quartet companion*, 1994, p. 40 and Anton Felix Schindler, *Beethoven as I knew him*, edited by Donald W. MacArdle and translated by Constance S. Jolly from the German edition of 1860, 1966, p. 306.

xciv Anton Felix Schindler, *Beethoven as I knew him*, edited by Donald W. MacArdle and translated by Constance S. Jolly from the German edition of 1860, 1966, pp. 305–6.

xcv Barry Cooper, 2000, p. 330.

xcvi For a facsimile representation of Böhm, see: Beethoven House, Digital Archives Document B 2250. For an account of Böhm and his principal achievements, see: Peter Clive, 2001, p. 38.

xcvii As quoted in: Paul Bekker, 1925, p. 326. For a comprehensive account of the early reception of the Op. 127, see: Robert Adelson, *Beethoven's string quartet in E flat, Op. 127: A study of the first performances, Music and letters*, Vol. 79, No. 2, May 1998, pp. 218–24.

xcviii Thayer-Forbes, 1967, p. 941.

xcix Derived from, Oscar George Theodore Sonneck, *Beethoven: impressions of contemporaries*, 1927, pp. 176–91. Originally published in: Ludwig Nohl *Beethoven depicted by his contemporaries*, 1880, pp. 260–91.

c Emily Anderson, editor and translator, 1961, Vol. 3, Letter No. 1354, pp. 1180–1.

ci *Ibid*, Letter No. 1355, pp. 1181–2. Also included were opus numbers for the *Missa Solemnis* (Op. 123), the *Choral* Symphony (Op. 125) and the Bagatelles (Op. 126).

cii *Ibid*, Letter No. 1357, pp. 1183–4.

ciii *Ibid*, Letter No. 1368, pp. 1192–3.

civ *Ibid*, Letter No. 1371, pp. 1195–6.

cv *Ibid*, Letter No. 1383, p. 1204.

[cvi] Theodore Albrecht, translator and editor, 1996, Vol. 3, Letter No. 385, pp. 62–4.
[cvii] *Ibid*, Letter No. 405, pp. 95–6.
[cviii] Quoted in: Joseph de Marliave, 1925 (reprint1961), p. 226.
[cix] Thayer-Forbes, 1967, pp. 947–8.
[cx] Emily Anderson, editor and translator, 1961, Vol. 3, Letter No. 1394, pp. 1213–5.
[cxi] *Ibid*, Letter No. 1407, pp. 1227–9.
[cxii] For a facsimile representation of Beethoven's letter to Galitzin see: Beethoven House, Digital Archives Library Document NE 163.
[cxiii] Emily Anderson, editor and translator, 1961, Vol. 3, Letter No.1452, pp. 1263–4.
[cxiv] *Ibid*, Letter No. 1466, pp. 1273–4.
[cxv] *Ibid*, Letter No. 1472, pp. 1278–9.
[cxvi] For a facsimile representation of the Title Page of String Quartet, Op. 127 in the first edition by Schott, see: Beethoven House, Digital Archives Documents C 127/9 and HCB C Md 79/8. The related pages (pp. 1–51) reproduce the quartet as styled in its original musical orthography.
[cxvii] Emily Anderson, editor and translator, 1961, Vol. 3, Letter No. 1548, pp. 1329–31.
[cxviii] Theodore Albrecht, translator and editor, 1996, Vol. 3, Letter No. 447, pp.156–9.
[cxix] Quoted in John Daverio, *Manner, tone, and tendency in Beethoven's chamber music for strings* in: Glenn Stanley editor, *The Cambridge companion to Beethoven*, 2000, pp. 147–64. Daverio adds: 'An organization such as the *Beethoven Quartet Society*, founded in London during the 1840s, even took as one of its express aims the study of the late quartets *from score.*' [italics added]
[cxx] Quoted in: Joseph de Marliave, 1925 (reprint1961), pp. 229–30.
[cxxi] As suggested by Barry Cooper, 2000, p. 323.
[cxxii] Michael Steinberg, *The late quartets* in: Robert Winter and Robert Martin, editors, *The Beethoven quartet companion*, 1994, pp. 218–9.
[cxxiii] Harold Truscott, 1968, p. 43.
[cxxiv] Paul Bekker, 1925, p. 326.
[cxxv] David Wyn Jones, *Beethoven and the Viennese legacy* in: Robin Stowell editor, *The Cambridge companion to the string quartet*, 2003, p. 222.
[cxxvi] Arthur Shepherd, 1935, p, 46.
[cxxvii] Joseph de Marliave, 1925 (reprint 1961), pp. 231–2.
[cxxviii] Robert Simpson, *The chamber music for strings* in: Denis Arnold and Nigel Fortune editors, *The Beethoven companion*, 1973, p. 265.
[cxxix] Michael Steinberg, *The late quartets* in: Robert Winter and Robert Martin editor, *The Beethoven quartet companion*, 1994, pp. 218–9.
[cxxx] Harold Truscott, 1968, p. 43.
[cxxxi] Martin Cooper, 1970, p. 350.
[cxxxii] Quoted in: Michael Tilmouth editor, *Donald Francis Tovey: The classics of music: talks, essays, and other writings previously uncollected*, 2001, p. 76.
[cxxxiii] Arthur Shepherd, 1935, p. 47.
[cxxxiv] Joseph de Marliave, 1925 (reprint 1961), p. 236.
[cxxxv] Philip Radcliffe, 1978, p. 102.
[cxxxvi] Joseph Kerman, 1967, p. 230 and p. 239.
[cxxxvii] Harold Truscott, 1968, p. 44.
[cxxxviii] Joseph de Marliave, 1925 (reprint 1961), p. 236.
[cxxxix] Robert Simpson, *The chamber music for strings* in: Denis Arnold and Nigel Fortune editors, *The Beethoven companion*, 1973, p. 265.

[cxl] Harold Truscott, 1968, p. 46.
[cxli] Stephen C. Rumph, 2004, p. 123 and p. 150.
[cxlii] Michael Steinberg, *The late quartets* in: Robert Winter and Robert Martin editor, *The Beethoven quartet companion*, 1994, pp. 218–9.
[cxliii] Joseph Kerman, 1967, p. 204.
[cxliv] Denis Matthews, 1985, p. 139.
[cxlv] Harold Truscott, 1968, pp. 48–9.
[cxlvi] Quoted in: Michael Tilmouth editor, *Donald Francis Tovey: The classics of music: talks, essays, and other writings previously uncollected*, 2001, p. 76.
[cxlvii] Marion M. Scott, 1940, p. 264.
[cxlviii] Harold Truscott, 1968, p. 45.
[cxlix] Paul Bekker, 1925, p. 327.
[cl] Joseph de Marliave, 1925 (reprint 1961), p. 236.
[cli] Romain Rolland, 1917, p. 187.
[clii] Quoted in: Joseph de Marliave, 1925 (reprint 1961), pp. 229–30.
[cliii] Originally published in Viktor Zuckerkandl, *Man the musician* (1973) and quoted in: John Paynter, editor, *Between old worlds and new: occasional writings on music by Wilfrid Mellers,* 1997, p. 43.
[cliv] Joseph Kerman, 1967, p. 218.
[clv] For an overview of Beethoven's contribution to the genre of the variation form, see: William Henry Hadow's pioneering centenary article, *Beethoven, Music and Letters*, Vol. 8, No. 2, April, 1927, pp. 213-26.
[clvi] Michael Steinberg, *The late quartets* in: Robert Winter and Robert Martin editor, *The Beethoven quartet companion*, 1994, p. 223.
[clvii] Barry Cooper, 2000, p. 324.
[clviii] Basil Lam, 1975, p. 78.
[clix] Michael Steinberg, *The late quartets* in: Robert Winter and Robert Martin editor, *The Beethoven quartet companion*, 1994, p. 223.
[clx] Harold Truscott, 1968, pp. 51–2.
[clxi] Basil Lam, 1975, p. 79.
[clxii] Joseph de Marliave, 1925 (reprint 1961), p. 220 and p. 226.
[clxiii] Marion M. Scott, 1940, pp. 264–5.
[clxiv] Theodor W. Adorno, 1998, pp. 138–9 and p. 140.
[clxv] Joseph Kerman, 1967, p. 212.
[clxvi] David Wyn Jones, *Beethoven and the Viennese legacy* in: Robin Stowell editor, *The Cambridge companion to the string quartet*, 2003, p. 223.
[clxvii] Basil Lam, 1975, pp. 78–9.
[clxviii] Martin Cooper, 1970, p. 351.
[clxix] Philip Radcliffe, 1978, p. 103.
[clxx] Joseph Kerman, 1967, 210. Beethoven's use of instrumental melody that he adopted in the late string quartets, disposed Kerman to reflect on the concept of what he describes as 'wordless recitative'. He first cites the celebrated passage beginning the Finale of the Ninth Symphony 'where the cellos and bases reject a parade of themes [previously heard form the preceding movements] and then finally elects one, all in *wordless recitative'*. [italics added] The implied meaning of the cellos is then made evident when the baritone member of the vocal quartet proclaims: 'O friends, not these sounds; let us rather strike up something more seemly, more joyful.' Kerman argues this musical procedure infiltrates many passages of the late quartets and accompanying *Grosse Fuge*. Of the Op. 127 – third movement, the *Scherzando vivace* – Kerman remarks: 'The first of the late quartets, the highly lyrical Quartet in E-flat major, does not contain any wordless recitative, unless one counts the strange interruption that shakes up the third movement, the *Scherzando vivace*.' Of Op. 131 – *Allegretto Themes and Variations* – *G-sharp minor Adagio* Kerman states: 'In the Quartet in

C-sharp minor, Op. 131, numerous touches of recitative — edging into rhapsodic or cadenza-like style — help make wonderful transitions in and out of the A-major *Allegretto* Themes and Variations, and also in and out of the G-sharp minor *Adagio* (which sounds, by the way, as though in another context it might have grown into another *Cavatina*).' Kerman remarks that each of the three other quartets shows the influence of the Ninth Symphony at the beginning of the Finale:Op. 133 — original finale to Op. 130; 'The original finale of the Quartet in B-flat major, the Great Fugue, opens with an *Overtura* rattling through a parade of all the thematic shapes to be utilized in the piece.'Op. 132 — 'The Finale of the Quartet in A minor, Op. 132, is led by an almost hysterical violin recitative, with tremolo and all the trimmings — the rawest that Beethoven ever conceived.'Op. 135 — 'The Quartet in F, Op. 135, precedes its Finale with a regular slow introduction adopting all the rhetorical tricks of a solemn *recitativo accompagnato*.'

[clxxi] *Ibid*, 1967, pp. 241–2.
[clxxii] Arthur Shepherd, 1935, p. 47.
[clxxiii] Philip Radcliffe, 1978, p. 103.
[clxxiv] Paul Griffiths, 1983, p. 104.
[clxxv] Philip Radcliffe, 1978, p. 19.
[clxxvi] As Donald Tovey observes in his study of the E-flat major Quartet, see: Donald Francis Tovey, 1944, p. 134.
[clxxvii] Stephen C. Rumph, 2004, p. 123 and p. 150.
[clxxviii] Denis Matthews, 1985, p. 140.
[clxxix] Daniel K. L. Chua, 1995, pp. 24–5.
[clxxx] Robert Simpson, *The chamber music for strings* in: Denis Arnold and Nigel Fortune editors, *The Beethoven companion*, 1973, p. 266.
[clxxxi] Joseph de Marliave, 1925 (reprint 1961), p. 220 and p. 237.
[clxxxii] Joseph Kerman, 1967, p. 210 and pp. 214–5.
[clxxxiii] Denis Matthews, 1985, p. 140.
[clxxxiv] Paul Bekker, 1925, p. 327.
[clxxxv] Harold Truscott, 1968, p. 52.
[clxxxvi] Marion M. Scott, 1940, p. 265.
[clxxxvii] Barry Cooper, 2000, p. 234.
[clxxxviii] Martin Cooper, 1970, p. 352.
[clxxxix] Joseph Kerman, 1967, p. 215.
[cxc] See, for example, Philip Radcliffe 1978, p. 103.
[cxci] Harold Truscott, 1968, pp. 52–3.
[cxcii] Joseph de Marliave, 1925 (reprint 1961), pp. 238–9.
[cxciii] Basil Lam, 1975, p. 79.
[cxciv] Donald Francis Tovey, Programme notes for a recital held on 17 February 1915, in: Michael Tilmouth editor, *Donald Francis Tovey: The classics of music: talks, essays, and other writings previously uncollected*, 2001, p. 76.
[cxcv] Michael Steinberg, *The late quartets* in: Robert Winter and Robert Martin editor, *The Beethoven quartet companion*, 1994, p. 223.
[cxcvi] Martin Cooper, 1970, p. 353.
[cxcvii] Phillip Radcliffe, 1978, pp. 103–4.
[cxcviii] Joseph Kerman, 1967, p. 215.
[cxcix] Basil Lam, 1975, p. 79.
[cc] Joseph de Marliave, 1925 (reprint 1961), p. 238.
[cci] Harold Truscott, 1968, pp. 52–3.
[ccii] Joseph Kerman, 1967, p. 215.
[cciii] Phillip Radcliffe, 1978, p. 104. Martin Cooper likewise remarks: '[Throughout] the harmony of these seventeen bars is a very striking parallel in the theme of the finale in Op. 109, another E major movement.' See: Martin Cooper,

ᶜᶦᵛ 1970, p. 354.
ᶜᶦᵛ Joseph de Marliave, 1925 (reprint 1961), pp. 238–9.
ᶜᵛ Quoted in Arthur Shepherd, 1935, p. 47.
ᶜᵛᶦ Basil Lam, 1975, pp. 79–80.
ᶜᵛᶦᶦ Joseph de Marliave, 1925 (reprint 1961), p. 239.
ᶜᵛᶦᶦᶦ Michael Steinberg, *The late quartets* in: Robert Winter and Robert Martin editor, *The Beethoven quartet companion*, 1994, p. 224.
ᶜᶦˣ Harold Truscott, 1968, pp. 53–4.
ᶜˣ See, for example, Joseph de Marliave, 1925 (reprint 1961), p. 240.
ᶜˣᶦ Martin Cooper, 1970, p. 355.
ᶜˣᶦᶦ Joseph Kerman, 1967, p. 217.
ᶜˣᶦᶦᶦ Phillip Radcliffe, 1978, pp. 104–5.
ᶜˣᶦᵛ Harold Truscott, 1968, pp. 54–5.
ᶜˣᵛ Martin Cooper, 1970, p. 354.
ᶜˣᵛᶦ Harold Truscott, 1968, pp. 54–5.
ᶜˣᵛᶦᶦ Michael Steinberg, *The late quartets* in: Robert Winter and Robert Martin editor, *The Beethoven quartet companion*, 1994, p. 224.
ᶜˣᵛᶦᶦᶦ Robert Simpson, *The chamber music for strings* in: Denis Arnold and Nigel Fortune editors, *The Beethoven companion*, 1973, p. 266.
ᶜˣᶦˣ Joseph de Marliave, 1925 (reprint 1961), p. 240.
ᶜˣˣ Joseph Kerman, 1967, p. 218.
ᶜˣˣᶦ Martin Cooper, 1970, p. 355.
ᶜˣˣᶦᶦ Phillip Radcliffe, 1978, p. 105.
ᶜˣˣᶦᶦᶦ Joseph de Marliave, 1925 (reprint 1961), p. 241.
ᶜˣˣᶦᵛ *Ibid*, pp. 141–3.
ᶜˣˣᵛ William Kinderman, editor, 2005, p. 282.
ᶜˣˣᵛᶦ Martin Cooper, 1970, p. 355. See also: Romain Rolland, 1917, p. 187.
ᶜˣˣᵛᶦᶦ Michael Steinberg, *The late quartets* in: Robert Winter and Robert Martin editor, *The Beethoven quartet companion*, 1994, p. 224.
ᶜˣˣᵛᶦᶦᶦ As described by Harold Truscott, 1968, p. 51.
ᶜˣˣᶦˣ Basil Lam, 1975, p. 81.
ᶜˣˣˣ David Wyn Jones, *Beethoven and the Viennese legacy* in: Robin Stowell editor, *The Cambridge companion to the string quartet*, 2003, p. 223.
ᶜˣˣˣᶦ *Misha Donat, String Quartet in B-flat major, Op. 127:Notes to the BBC Radio Three Beethoven Experience*, Sunday 5 June 2005, www.bbc.co.uk/radio3/Beethoven
ᶜˣˣˣᶦᶦ Arthur Shepherd, 1935, pp. 47–8.
ᶜˣˣˣᶦᶦᶦ Robert Simpson, *The chamber music for strings* in: Denis Arnold and Nigel Fortune editors, *The Beethoven companion*, 1973, p. 266–7.
ᶜˣˣˣᶦᵛ Marion M. Scott, 1940, p. 265.
ᶜˣˣˣᵛ Joseph de Marliave, 1925 (reprint 1961), pp. 141–3.
ᶜˣˣˣᵛᶦ Philip Radcliffe, 1978, p. 105 – with some adaptation of wording.
ᶜˣˣˣᵛᶦᶦ One such critic is Daniel Gregory Mason, as cited by Daniel K. L. Chua, 1995, p. 13.
ᶜˣˣˣᵛᶦᶦᶦ Quoted by Leon Botstein, *The patrons and publics of the quartets* in: Robert Winter and Robert Martin editors, *The Beethoven quartet companion. Berkeley*, 1994, pp. 92–3.
ᶜˣˣˣᶦˣ Philip Radcliffe, 1978, pp. 105–6.
ᶜˣˡ Paul Griffiths, 1983, p. 104.
ᶜˣˡᶦ Paul Bekker, 1925, p. 327.
ᶜˣˡᶦᶦ Joseph Kerman, 1967, p. 230 and p. 241.
ᶜˣˡᶦᶦᶦ Quoted in: Michael Tilmouth editor, *Donald Francis Tovey: The classics of music: talks, essays, and other writings previously uncollected*, 2001, p. 76–7.
ᶜˣˡᶦᵛ Basil Lam, 1975, pp. 81–2.

ccxlv Robert Simpson, *The chamber music for strings* in: Denis Arnold and Nigel Fortune editors, *The Beethoven companion*, 1973, p. 267.
ccxlvi *Beethoven*, String Quartet Op. 127, website text.
ccxlvii Quoted in: Michael Tilmouth editor, *Donald Francis Tovey: The classics of music: talks, essays, and other writings previously uncollected*, 2001, p. 77.
ccxlviii Joseph de Marliave, 1925 (reprint 1961), p. 248.
ccxlix *Misha Donat, String Quartet in B-flat major, Op. 127:Notes to the BBC Radio Three Beethoven Experience*, Sunday 5 June 2005, www.bbc.co.uk/radio3/Beethoven
ccl Philip Radcliffe, 1978, pp. 106.
ccli Martin Cooper, 1970, p. 356.
cclii Joseph de Marliave, 1925 (reprint 1961), p. 248.
ccliii Paul Bekker, 1925, p. 327.
ccliv Michael Steinberg, *The late quartets* in: Robert Winter and Robert Martin editor, *The Beethoven quartet companion*, 1994, p. 226.
cclv Arthur Shepherd, 1935, p. 48.
cclvi Joseph de Marliave, 1925 (reprint 1961), p. 248.
cclvii Quoted in: Michael Tilmouth editor, *Donald Francis Tovey: The classics of music: talks, essays, and other writings previously uncollected*, 2001, p. 77. Joseph de Marliave, 1925 (reprint 1961), p. 77.
cclviii Harold Truscott 1968, pp. 57–8.
cclix Robert Simpson, 1973, p. 267.
cclx Joseph de Marliave, 1925 (reprint 1961), p. 250.
cclxi Philip Radcliffe, 1978, p. 107.
cclxii Basil Lam, 1975, pp. 82–3.
cclxiii Joseph Kerman, 1967, p. 234, p. 236 and 242.
cclxiv See: Thayer-Forbes, 1967, pp. 940–41 and Robert Winter and Robert Martin editors, 1994, p. 40.
cclxv Joseph de Marliave, 1925 (reprint 1961), p. 255.
cclxvi Philip Radcliffe, 1978, p. 108.
cclxvii Quoted in: Michael Tilmouth editor, *Donald Francis Tovey: The classics of music: talks, essays, and other writings previously uncollected*, 2001, p. 77.
cclxviii Harold Truscott 1968, p. 63.
cclxix Igor Stravinsky, 1972, p. 257.
cclxx Quoted in: Michael Tilmouth editor, *Donald Francis Tovey: The classics of music: talks, essays, and other writings previously uncollected*, 2001, p. 77.
cclxxi Michael Steinberg, *The late quartets* in: Robert Winter and Robert Martin editor, *The Beethoven quartet companion*, 1994, p. 226.
cclxxii Joseph de Marliave, 1925 (reprint 1961), pp. 255–6.

STRING QUARTET IN A MINOR, OP. 132

> 'There was a numerous assembly of professors to hear Beethoven's second new manuscript quartet, bought by Mr. Schlesinger. This quartet is three-quarters of an hour long. They played it twice ... It is most chromatic and there is a slow movement entitled "Praise for the recovery of an invalid". Beethoven intended to allude to himself ... for he was very ill during the early part of this year.'

As recalled by the English musician Sir George Smart on hearing an early performance of the A minor Quartet; first recounted in *Leaves from the Journal of Sir George Smart*, Longmans, 1907 and recollected in:
 Oscar George Theodore Sonneck, *Beethoven: Impres-*

sions of Contemporaries, 1927, pp.191–6.

Writing of the Greek modes as a potential source of richness of invention for his fellow countrymen to explore, the Russian writer on music César Cui remarked:

> 'Couldn't the composer in quest for new effects, tired of the uniformity of our harmonic and melodic constructions, exploit this fertile mine? Must not the new, in certain measure, come out of the old, isn't the germ of flourishing youth in what we call decay? More than once have the potent masters had recourse to the old modes; let us cite only Beethoven, who, in his Quartet Op. 132, wrote an *Adagio* in the Lydian mode; it is one of the most admirable productions in musical art.'

Original source derived from an article in the *Revue et gazette musicale*, Paris, 1878–79. Quoted in:
  Sam Morgenstern editor, *Composers on Music: An anthology of composers' writings*, 1956, p. 222.

> 'The scene of the entire work is laid in an atmosphere of suffering; the music restless, morbid, and nervous: creating effects that the sinewy wailing tone of the stringed instruments is peculiarly fitted to express.'

Derived from the writings of Adolph Bernhard Marx and quoted in:
  Joseph de Marliave, *Beethoven's Quartets*, 1925, (reprint 1961), p. 328.

De Marliave himself states:

> '[The Quartet] contains passages of wonderful loveliness, and the *Adagio* especially is one of the summits of achievement in quartet writing and indeed in all music: *Ibid*,' (p. 329).

> 'Concert at R.C.M. at 8.15 pm. Beethoven A minor (Op. 132) Quartet. Divine Work!' From the diary entry of Benjamin Britten (age 18) 26 February 1931 in:

Donald Mitchell editor, *Letters from a Life: The selected letters and diaries of Benjamin Britten 1913–1976*, Vol. 1, 1991, p. 163.

> 'The programmatic attributes discernible in Beethoven's last works are nowhere more clearly focused than in the A minor Quartet. No aesthetic speculation can reasonably disregard the deepened personal accent and the autobiographical emphasis that underlines these exalted pages. If the composer's increasing usage of superscriptions be taken as the hallmarks of typical nineteenth-century romanticism, one may come to a clearer understanding of the sympathy and enthusiasm for these works on the part of such arch-romanticists as Berlioz, Liszt and Wagner.'

Arthur Shepherd, *The String Quartets of Ludwig van Beethoven*, 1935, p. 62.

> 'With the works immediately following Op. 127, Beethoven passed beyond any semblance of

quartet form as it was then understood. For over a century his three greatest quartets, in A minor, Op. 132, B-flat major, Op. 130, and C-sharp minor, Op. 131, remained more or less unsolved enigmas.'

Marion M. Scott, *Beethoven: (The Master Musicians)*, 1940, p. 265.

'The world of play and the world of song are not lost to Beethoven's later compositions; nothing is ever lost. But in turning from the Quartet in E-flat major to the Quartet in A minor, Op. 132, the listener could hardly be blamed if he imagined himself witness to some great reaction, some act of revulsion against the very sources of the lyric vision. In sentiment these two adjacent quartets differ as categorically as other well-known twins: the Fifth and Sixth Symphonies, or the earlier Quartet in E flat, Op. 74 and the *Quartetto serioso* in F minor.'

Joseph Kerman, *The Beethoven Quartets*, 1967, p. 242.

'Beethoven describes himself in the epigraph to the third movement as "One recovered" (*eines Genesenden*), but the continuing trauma of the illness is more apparent in the music. "Hysterical", Mr. Kerman's word for the violin outburst with which the *Adagio* begins, applies as well, I think, to the oscillations of mood throughout the Quartet.' Igor Stravinsky quoting Joseph Kerman, *The Beethoven quartets*, 1967, p. 200.

Igor Stravinsky, *Themes and Conclusions*, 1972, pp. 257–8.

> 'No greater contrast could be imagined than between the E-flat major Quartet, Op. 127 and the one Beethoven composed next, the A minor, Op. 132. Even the keys are poles apart; the A minor is predominantly dark, though it rises in the *Adagio* to a luminosity that makes the E-flat major seem like a coal fire compared with the sun.'

Robert Simpson, *The Chamber Music for Strings* in: Denis Arnold and Nigel Fortune editors, *The Beethoven Companion*, 1973, p. 267.

> 'The greatest Western music — Bach's great organ chorales, Beethoven's Fifteenth Quartet — has taught us that the highest forms of musical expression stem from that miraculous phenomenon, "evolutive contemplation".

André Hodeir, *Since Debussy: a view of contemporary music*, 1975, p. 114.

> 'No other composition in all of Beethoven's works shows the unintegrated contrasts of this Quartet, but once he had become possessed by this unique vision of the *Heiliger Dankgesang*, no solution of the formal problem was available other than to surround it with sound-images united only by their tonal diversity.'

Basil Lam, *Beethoven String Quartets*, 1975, p. 98.

> '[The] subject matter of this quartet is pain and its

transcendence ... Perhaps Beethoven considered this Quartet a summary work, ending the exploration of the set of musical problems to which the late quartets (and perhaps all late works) were devoted; and this may explain what appear to be numerous references to other works — from the ... similarity of the opening fugue to themes from Op. 132 and the Fugue of Op. 130, to what I hear as conscious recollections of the *Heiliger Dankgesang* in the fourth variation of the *Andante* (bars 1–4), and of the main theme of the opening *Allegro* of Op. 132 in the third variation (bars 1–2, 9–10). The raging, victorious finale is surely the *Grosse Fuge* revisited — and conquered.'

Maynard Solomon, *Beethoven*, 1977, p. 322 and p. 325.

'The unusual proportions of the first movement and the almost hypnotically persistent treatment of the main theme of the second movement show Beethoven in a wayward mood in which he is less than ever inclined to come to meet his audience, and in the *Heiliger Dankgesang* he soars still further away into his own imagination, exploring a strange and solemn region of his own discovering; coming after it the little march, for all its brisk and cheerful manner, sounds half ironical. But it is in the finale, with its sweeping melody, that the music comes out finally into the open without in any way lowering the standard of inspiration.'

Philip Radcliffe, *Beethoven's String Quartets*, 1978, p. 121.

'[The] elements adopted from church music [in

> the String Quartet Op. 132] are integrated into the language of Classical form ... From this point of view one can agree wholeheartedly with Adolph Bernhard Marx [*Ludwig van Beethoven*, Berlin 1859]: according to him, in the *Dankgesang* Beethoven "had not been aiming at antiquarianism or bookish learning, but had been led merely by the intuition of the artist".'

Sieghard Brandenburg, *Historical background to the Heiliger Dankgesang*, in:
Alan Tyson editor, *Beethoven Studies 3*, 1982, p. 191.

> 'From my place [in St. James Hall, London] I used to watch George Eliot and her husband sitting together in the stalls like two elderly love-birds, and was irritated by Lewis's habit of beating time on her arm with his pince-nez. There is a well-known syncopated passage in Beethoven's Quartet Op. 132, and I noted with scornful amusement how the eyeglass, after a moment of hesitation, would begin marking the wrong beat, again hover uncertainly, and presently resume the right one with triumphant emphasis as if nothing had happened.'

Ronald Crichton editor, *The Memoirs of Ethel Smyth*, 1987, p. 57.

> 'Beethoven's imagination for sonority and texture — the imagination, one is once again startled to remember, of a deaf man — is unsurpassed in freedom and freshness.'

Michael Steinberg, *String Quartet, Op. 132*, in: Robert Winter and Robert Martin editors, *The Beethoven Quartet Companion*, 1994, p. 265.

> 'Obviously, something new was happening in Beethoven's technique. It was not that Beethoven abandoned the logic of motivic development; rather ... he complicated it by a process of variation and counterpoint, so that the logic did not quite connect, allowing chaos to break through the cracks in the structure. With these techniques of thematic penetration, he seriously questioned the validity of his own style and all that he had inherited ... The music turned in on itself and against its own public ... This was difficult music, and the accusations of madness by his critics were a defence against this musical attack.'

Daniel K. L. Chua, *The "Galitzin" Quartets of Beethoven: Opp.127, 132, 130*, 1995, pp. 54–5.

> '[The] very first postmodernist was Beethoven himself, in a work like the A minor Quartet Op. 132. In this extraordinary piece things not only happen that did not have to happen, but which are indeed opposite of what might have been predicted. No wonder Beethoven's late quartets puzzled his contemporaries, potently animated by aspirations and resolutions.'

John Paynter editor, *Between old Worlds and New: occasional writings on music by Wilfrid Mellers*, 1997, p. 221.

> 'Even today Beethoven's late quartets are a challenge for the listener to whom they disclose themselves in their full fascination only after the said listener has dedicated himself with some intensity to their study.'

Daniel Brandenburg, *Liner notes to Ludwig van Beethoven, String Quartets*, Vol. 9, Arte Nova (undated).

> 'This music soars high above all material things — the purest expression of a lofty spirit which dwells serenely beyond all earthly things, indeed beyond the limits of music itself. It is music such as probably could be written only by one who, like Beethoven of that period [1825–26] was no longer of this world: one who had for years been barred from perceiving the voices of the surrounding world, who listened only to his own inner voice — one who was alone with himself and with his Creator.'

'H.G.', *Ludwig van Beethoven, String Quartet in A minor, Op. 132*, Preface to: Philharmonia Score, No. 324 (undated).

In fulfilment of Prince Borissowitsch Galitzin's request for three quartets from Beethoven, on completion of the E-flat major Quartet, Op. 127, he commenced work on the String Quartet in A minor, Op. 132. As a consequence of its opus number it is sometimes referred to as the 'fifteenth' quartet but this does not correspond to the order of its composition; it was completed before the String Quartet in B-flat major, Op. 130 and the String Quartet in C-sharp minor, Op. 131.

The key of A minor is found in only a few of

Beethoven's major compositions. Two worthy examples are the slow movement of the third *Rasumovsky* String Quartet and that of the Seventh Symphony, both of which, in common with passages of the A minor String Quartet, 'express a kind of subdued and restrained melancholy, elegiac rather than passionate in character'.[i] Sketches for the A minor Quartet date from 1824 with much of the composition being undertaken between the spring and early summer of 1825. Beethoven's severe illness at this time both delayed progress with its creation and left a profound influence on the character of the music.

The music theorist and writer on music Adolf Bernhard Marx was one of Beethoven's most ardent admirers. When Adolph Martin Schlesinger — whom we will encounter later — founded his weekly journal the *Berliner Allgemeine musikalische Zeitung* (1824) he appointed Marx as its editor. He soon became known for his informed reviews of Beethoven's compositions even earning the composer's respect as 'the clever Herr Marx'.[ii] In the fifth volume of the *Zeitung*, Marx reviewed both the A minor and B-flat major Quartets. He opened his account by recognising Beethoven's latest quartets went 'far beyond' other compositions in the quartet repertoire and how they represented 'a significant step in the progress of musical art'. He predicted in the future their difficulties and challenges (to both performer and listener) would be assimilated just as the quartets of Haydn had been. Interestingly, he compared Beethoven's latest creations to a painting by Rubens 'in which one must first become acquainted with a mass of detail before proceeding to understand the sense of the whole'. He concluded by urging patience on his readers.[iii]

In the manner characteristic of much early nineteenth-century music criticism, Marx characterised the A minor Quartet as being set 'in an atmosphere of suffering ... the music restless, morbid, and nervous creating effects that the sinewy wailing tone of the stringed instruments is peculiarly fitted to express'. Joseph de Marliave, from whom we have just quoted, accepted Beethoven was a precursor of Romantic music, but chastised Marx for 'finding in every musical work an appropriate *programme*' [de Marliave's italics]. Of the A minor Quartet he writes: 'Here it is not the case.' He defends his assertion: 'Admittedly, Beethoven was a composer of *programme* music, but always in the highest and psychological sense. In this respect the XVth Quartet only translates through the medium of sound the artist's permanent habit of spiritual thought, like all the last works: the struggle against destiny, and the triumph of happiness over sorrow ... It is only a coincidence that the composition of the Op. 132 stretched over a period in which health for a time overcame disease.'[iv]

The youthful Felix Mendelsohn was influenced by Beethoven's late style: his engagement with the composer's music is particularly evident in his own A minor String Quartet, Op. 13. Mendelssohn worked on the A minor Quartet around the time of Beethoven's death (26 March 1827) and indicated in the score that he had completed the first movement on 28 July 1827 and the finale on 26 October of the same year. These circumstances have inclined some musicologists to the view: 'Certain passages in the Quartet so clearly echo string quartets by Beethoven that they must be understood as homage.'[v]

For Joseph Kerman: 'Beethoven's unique achievement here was the creation of a psychological progress perhaps more arresting than in any other work.' In support of his contention he quotes Romain Rolland for whom the A minor Quartet was 'l'oeuvre la plus ardue peut-être et la plus profonde de Beethoven'.[vi] Writing shortly after the French man-of-letters, the American composer and writer on music

Arthur Shepherd similarly enthused: 'This Quartet is a matchless fusion of life and art which was pre-eminently the province of this master.'[vii] Nearer our own time, musicologist Daniel Chua has written: 'There is something not only surprising but dangerously experimental about the contrast in the work [Op. 132], as Beethoven plays with the positioning and numbering of movements, breaking out of the four-movement scheme for the first time in his quartets. Never before had the composer provoked such a sense of heterogeneity, in which the parts do not correspond to the whole but coalesce into autonomous objects, juxtaposed to stress the lacunae between them.'[viii]

By way of illustration of the far-reaching influence of Beethoven's music in popular culture, we may cite the work the film composer Alex North — celebrated (Academy Award) for such scores as *2001 A Space Odyssey*. When invited to provide a musical score to the film adaptation of Edward Albee's *Who's Afraid of Virginia Woolf?*, he originally conceived the notion of adapting themes from Beethoven's String Quartet Op. 132. This idea was eventually abandoned in favour of North composing his own score.[ix]

We direct our attention now to the creation origins of the A minor String Quartet as revealed in the composer's surviving sketchbooks, score sketches and autographs.

Beethoven worked intensively on the second of the Galitzin Quartets through May and June of 1825 during his customary sojourn at Baden. The artist Theodor Weiser made a watercolour study of the small house where the composer did much of his deskwork after returning from his walks in the neighbouring countryside, armed with his pocket sketchbooks. To add authenticity to his image, Weiser included the opening bars to the theme of the *Heiliger Dankgesang*.[x]

Consistent with his well-established working method,

Beethoven preserved his thoughts in sketch form. Those that are extant survive in various forms and are today preserved in several archives. Most commonly are the so-called pocket sketchbooks that consist of random sheets of music paper stitched together by the composer. These enabled him to jot down his ideas in pencil when out and about in the summer on his strolls in the countryside; the fugitive nature of the pencil medium now poses challenges to scholar-musicologists attempting to decipher his intentions. When indoors Beethoven could work in ink at his writing desk in pre-formed 'desk-sketchbooks' that have, for the most part, retained their legibility. Sketchbooks also survive in bound format. These typically consist of miscellaneous gatherings of music sheets compiled by music dealers and collectors after the sale of Beethoven's possessions in the auction that took place in November 1827 following his death earlier in the year.

In his work on the Quartets Opp. 127, 132, 130, 131 and 135, Beethoven introduced an innovation into his sketching procedures. He made use of manuscript paper that was ruled in the form of quartet-score sheets. These enabled him to set down more extended compositional drafts encompassing all four instruments — doubtless prompted, in part, by the challenges posed by the growing contrapuntal complexity of the music evolving in his mind.[xi] As Barry Cooper remarks, the composer's 'limitless aspirations' required a new method of composing'. He elaborates: '[Beethoven] began making frequent use of sketching in open score on four staves, instead of merely on one or two as before.' This was to assist with what Beethoven himself described as 'a new kind of part writing'. Cooper adds: 'The score sketches did not supplant other types of sketching, but ran in parallel with them.'[xii]

Throughout May-September 1825, Beethoven made

use of a miscellaneous gathering of sketch leaves (forty in number) that are preserved today in the Beethoven Archive, Bonn as the De Roda sketchbook. It takes its name from the Spanish collector Cecilio de Roda who owned it in the twentieth century and from whose descendants it was acquired by the Beethovenhaus in 1962. The cover bears the inscription – testimony to its previous owner Artaria – 'Autograph e Louis van Beethoven. Livre d'esquisses des motifs du Quatour/en La Mineur et autre études/L'authenticié en est garantie par Artaria & Co. à Vienne/1847.'[xiii] Beethoven compiled the De Roda sketchbook from thirteen different paper types, some partially used and others dating back to 1808, testimony to the care he took in the preservation of his sketch materials – despite his numerous changes of address.[xiv] Sketches for Op. 132 in the De Roda sketchbook are: second movement, folio 5v; third movement, folios 5v–11v passim; fourth movement, folios 9v–14v passim; and fifth movement, folios 3v–18v passim. The 'autre études' referred to on the cover include Op. 130 – first, second, third and fourth movements, and ideas for the *Grosse Fuge*, Op. 133.[xv]

The so-called 'Autograph 11, Bundle 2' sketchbook is devoted largely to the last three movements of the Quartet in E-flat major, Op. 127, but it also includes several pages of sketches for the first movement of the Quartet in A minor: first movement folios 23r–25r, 26v, 28v–30r and plans for other movements at folios 25v–26r. Beethoven also carried forward his ideas for the *Grosse Fuge* at folios 26v and 27r.[xvi] In 1895 the British Museum acquired a collection of sixteen pocket sketch leaves now catalogued (British Library) as 'Egerton 2795'. This improvised sketchbook is devoted primarily to movements I–III and V of the third Galitzin String Quartet in B-flat major, Op. 130, but it also includes brief notations for the first and last movements of the A-minor Quartet, Op. 132 (folios 13v—16v).[xvii] The Central Glinka Museum for Music culture, Moscow possesses a pocket sketchbook of 25 leaves that is believed to have once been owned by Felix Mendelssohn; Beethoven made use of these leaves between May and July 1825. Op. 132 is represented as follows: third movement, pp. 1—3; fourth movement, pp. 3—13 passim, 18; fifth movement, pp. 6—28 passim. Amongst the sketches are also ideas for the first movement of Op. 130 and sketches for the *Credo* of the *Missa Solemnis*.[xviii] A bifolium, considered to have once formed part of the Moscow collection, is now preserved in the Beethoven Archive, Bonn.[xix] Other sketch sources in the Beethoven archive include the following: A single leaf, not thought to have belonged originally to a miscellany, was inscribed by Beethoven in the top right-hand corner 'Quartet 2' — possibly jotted down on the spur of the moment when he was out strolling in the countryside.[xx] A single sketch leaf from 1824—25 contains sketches for the first and second movements of Op. 132.[xxi] The first page of a bifolium, once owned by Beethoven's amanuensis Anton Schindler, contains score sketches for the third movement — *Heiliger Dankgesang* — from Op. 132. The remaining three pages contain drafts for a movement in A major which was actually intended as the final movement for Op 132 but which is known today, in the key of G major, as the fourth movement *Alla danza tedesca* of the String Quartet Op. 130. These bifolium sketches bear testimony to how closely connected are the creation origins of the Quartets Opp. 132 and 130.[xxii]

Score sketches are an additional source of information to the pocket sketchbooks and desk sketchbooks. Beethoven only rarely worked in full score prior to his first attempt at the Autograph itself. The considerable number of such sketches from the years 1824—26, when he was occupied almost exclusively with the late quartets, reflects — as we have just noted when quoting Cooper — an important development in Beethoven's compositional process. The paper Beethoven used for his late score sketches is similar to that found in the sketchbooks and autographs: oblong-format leaves with 10, 12, 14, or 16 staves to a page are typical. Beethoven did not stich them together, as he did his improvised sketchbooks, but left them loose. This is as they were found and sold at the auction following his death. Many were purchased by the publisher Artaria — almost 350 leaves — that were later acquired by the Berlin State Library in 1901. Over another hundred such leaves were later gifted to the Gesellschaft der Musikfreunde. Op. 132 is represented in the score sketches.[xxiii]

Contemporary studies have established that of the last five quartets and the Great Fugue, only the Autograph of the Quartet in A minor Op. 132 has survived intact. 'The autographs of Opus 127, Op. 130, Op. 131 and Op. 135 were, early in their history, dismembered and sold off, movement by movement in some cases, to different buyers.'[xxiv] Beethoven completed work on the Autograph Score (Staatsbibliothek Preussischer Kulturbesitz, Berlin) in July 1825 and continued to make revisions (Beethoven House, Bonn, Document SBH 741) with copies that date from July to October.[xxv] William Kinderman remarks: 'The incorporation of the *Alla danza tedesca* as the fourth of the sixth movements of Op. 130 marked a decisive development in the genesis of the A minor and B-flat major quartets.' Beethoven appears to have been undecided as to what kind of movement should follow the celebrated *Heiliger Dankgesang* — the celebrated slow movement of the A minor Quartet — that he composed in his summer lodgings in May of 1825, following recovery from serious illness earlier in April (see later). A version of the Autograph with the *Alla danza tedesca* as fourth movement was considered for Op. 132 but by August Beethoven had resolved on a six-movement format for the following Quartet in B-flat major, Op. 130 – 'in which the *Alla danza tedesca* found its new home'.[xxvi]

From the foregoing it can be seen that the three Galitzin string quartets share closely related creation origins. Following completion of the E-flat major Quartet, Op. 127 Beethoven commenced work on the A minor Quartet, Op. 132 with studies for the B-flat major Quartet, Op. 130 finding expression at almost the same time. Writing of this connection Marion Scott remarks: 'This relation went deeper than Beethoven's habit of working on several things at the same time; the two works are thematically joined, and so close is this connection that Beethoven was able to transfer a movement from one to the other – the *alla danza tedesca* – with perfect propriety.'[xxvii] While still in the midst of the B-flat major Quartet he began to work on the C-sharp minor, which occupied him until the summer of 1826. The remaining two 'late' quartets followed soon after: while working on the B-flat major Quartet, Beethoven commenced studies for the C-sharp minor Quartet. Paul Bekker offers the following summation: 'The five quartets thus fall into three groups, the introductory Op. 127, the closely associated Op. 132, Op. 130, Op. 131 and the final Op. 135.'[xxviii]

From his study of Beethoven's sketches for the late quartets, William Kinderman suggests they reveal 'particular affinities connected to their extension beyond the conventional classical framework of four movements'. Beethoven's original intention was to conceive the formal design of the Quartet Op. 127 in perhaps as many as six movements, including 'a character piece' in C major entitled *La gaité*, planned at one point as a second movement, as well as a slow introduction to the finale. In the end, as we have seen in our discussion of this work, he returned to the traditional four-movement structure. However, as Kinderman further observes, 'his flirtation with such an expansion of the narrative chain of movements bore fruit in the following trilogy of quartets in A minor, Op. 132, B-flat major Op. 130 and C-sharp minor, Op. 131'.[xxix]

The A minor Quartet is today performed as a five-movement work but Beethoven himself perceived it as having six movements; he regarded the recitative transition to the finale as a separate movement. This may be inferred from a letter he wrote to his Nephew Karl on 11 August 1825 when he was anxious about the possible loss of the 'third to sixth' movements in the Autograph Score (see later). Op. 132 as we know it today might have been on an even more expansive scale. To quote Kinderman once more: 'The A Minor Quartet, Op. 132, was initially larger because of its inclusion of the *Alla danza tedesca* movement in penultimate position, which he replaced only at the autograph stage by the concise march-like intermezzo, the *Alla Marcia, assai vivace*.' In the B-flat major Quartet, Beethoven employs a six-movement design. The C-sharp minor Quartet uniquely expands to seven movements. Thus, in writing each of these works, 'Beethoven conceived material that spilled over beyond the composition immediately at hand. His fertility of invention refused to be contained within the boundaries of the singular work'.[xxx]

Commenting on the structure of Op. 132, Maynard Solomon invokes architectural imagery: 'The A-minor Quartet, Op. 132, expands the framework to five movements, with a *scherzo* and a brief march-like movement filling both of the usual alternative positions for the dance movement and serving as necessary and "normal" transitions into and out of the unearthly *Molto Adagio* in the archaic Lydian mode ... They serve also to help form what appears to be a consciously wrought arch structure, which is in turn mirrored and capped by the five-sectioned arch construction of the *Heiliger Dankgesang*.'[xxxi] Beethoven authority David Wyn Jones expresses similar thoughts: 'The arch structure of the slow movement is placed within an overall five-movement structure that reveals a strong sense of symmetry; one layer out are two dance movements in A major, a *scherzo* and trio (movement 2) and a march (movement 4); the outer layers consist of allegro movements in a sonata-form first movement and a sonata-rondo finale.'[xxxii]

In his description of the A Minor Quartet's sequence of movements, American musicologist Daniel Chua contends: 'The emotional intensity of the opening is shrugged off by the niceties of the minuet and the naivety of the musette; the supplication to the Godhead in the *Heiliger Dankgesang* is ridiculed by the banality of a miniature march, which in turn breaks down into an impassioned recitative.' He follows this with a characteristic example of his musicological psychoanalysis: 'There is a peculiar narrative pattern of social estrangement. The individual and the institutional are alienated in this impasse of emotions, as prayer and passion are mixed with the aristocratic, the bucolic, and the military ... Beethoven snatches indifferent objects from the real world to invade the privacy of the quartet; the minuet, musette, and march deliberately mimic the social formalities of an ideal world, and perhaps the way they are used would have signified radical changes in society at the time.'[xxxiii]

The pioneering Beethoven musicologist Gustav Nottebohm is acknowledged for being the first to suggest that a thematic-organic connection links the A minor Quartet, Op. 132 to its companions Op. 130, Op. 131 and Op. 133. Bekker was also convinced of this proposition. Citing his forebear he remarks: 'Nottebohm has shown that the fugue theme of Op. 130 and the opening of the A minor are contemporaneous and closely associated.' He expands: 'Nottebohm believed there can scarcely be a doubt that Beethoven drew from the studies for the fugue theme the motive of four long notes with which he opens the first movement of the A minor Quartet and which he uses again later in that work. The fugue studies thus served a double purpose.' (Becker is quoting from: Nottebohm, *Beethoveniana*, Leipzig, 1872, 1887 and 1925.) Bekker himself maintains the purpose was in fact threefold: 'This theme formed not only the main subject of the first movement of Op. 132 and the fugue subject of Op. 130 (now Op. 133), but by a change from ascending sixths to descending thirds it became the principal theme of the first, and, reversed, of the last movement of Op. 131.' He summarizes: 'It is the leading idea of the whole group of Beethoven's three greatest quartets ... and throws light on the composer's train of thought.'[xxxiv]

Scott enters into the spirit of Bekker's analysis and argues that Opp. 132, 130 and 131 should be regarded as a *triptych* (our italics). Firstly, she remarks: 'Their contents are so glorious, so inter-related and metaphysical, that one might almost think Beethoven regarded them as an ABC of the world to come.' She draws a parallel with the manner in which Russian melodies unify the *Razumovsky* Quartets and how a fugal subject (fugal device) here joins the Opp. 132, 130 and 131 triad. She illustrates her assertion: 'It forms the starting-point at the beginning of the A minor Quartet ... It recurs in many guises and adumbrations throughout the work ... its rising sixth haunts the subject matter of the B-flat major Quartet ... and the theme, expanded, appears as one of the two subjects in the double fugue which originally formed the finale of the B-flat major ... Finally, the theme, now changed from an ascending sixth to a descending third, forms the fugue subject of the first movement and (reversed) the principal subject of the last movement of the C-sharp minor.'[xxxv]

Harold Truscott though urges caution in perceiving too much into the nature of the inter-relatedness between the Opp. 132, 130 and 131 Quartets. He makes the generalization: 'No composition on any sizeable scale is founded on one or even many themes only ... Even within a work or even a movement, two things which have a common origin may well not show that origin — in sound. So much of this sort of connection can only be seen, not heard ... Music is for hearing: nothing else, musically, matters a jot. The finest performer in the world is there merely as a means to be heard.'[xxxvi] Basil Lam expresses similar views: 'These facts [the perceived quartet connections] though interesting as evidence of Beethoven's working methods, do little more than exemplify the scarcely surprising truth that a composer who, as he said on various occasions, liked to occupy himself with several compositions at the same time, exploited divers aspects of a basic note-set that happened to interest him during these last few years of his life.' He concludes: 'There is no evidence of any kind to suggest that these quartets were considered by Beethoven to be connected or related, and the listener's awareness of the integrity of any one of them can only be confused by the suggestion that thematic coincidences of identity imply relatedness of the works themselves.'[xxxvii]

The violinist Ignaz Schuppanzigh will feature shortly in our narrative and therefore requires a few words of introduction. Since we have already encountered him in our preceding discussions of the Galitzin Quartets and the text to the String Quartet, Op. 127, we confine the following remarks to a brief outline of some of the circumstances that make him such an important figure in Beethoven's development of the string-quartet ensemble. He was violinist to

Beethoven's benefactor Prince Karl Lichnowsky from 1794 to 1799 when he regularly led quartet sessions. In the winter of 1804–5 he pioneered the concept of subscription concerts. In 1808 Beethoven's patron Count Razumovsky invited Schuppanzigh to assemble a quartet for him that subsequently premiered the *Razumovsky* Quartets, Op. 59. It was Schuppanzigh's Quartet that also gave the first performance in May 1814 of the composer's String Quartet, Op. 95. With the calamitous loss of Razumovsky's palace in a great fire – that deprived the Count of much of his fortune – Schuppanzigh was obliged to disbanded his Quartet and leave Vienna. After a period of concert touring he returned to Vienna in 1823 and was soon once more absorbed in the city's musical life. As Tully Potter states 'the knowledge that this faithful servant was once again available was undoubtedly a stimulus to Beethoven, who always had performance in mind for even his most advanced music'.[xxxviii] Moreover, Schuppanzigh's second violinist was Karl Holz; a close friend of Beethoven at this time, he had temporarily supplanted Anton Schindler as his amanuensis and secretary-assistant. Both Schuppanzigh and Holtz will assume a sharper focus as our narrative proceeds.

We recall on 27 May 1824 that Beethoven had written to Prince Galitzin in order to reassure him: 'You will soon receive the quartet I promised you [Op. 127] and perhaps the others as well' [Op. 132 and Op. 130].[xxix] Reference is next made to the A minor Quartet in Beethoven's affairs the following year. In January 1825 Schuppanzigh was commencing another of his subscription concerts with his newly formed Quartet: Karl Holz, second violin; Franz Weiss, viola; and Joseph Linke cello. Beethoven's Conversation Book for the period reveals the composer consented to Schuppanzigh's request to premier the E-flat major Quartet on 20 January in Vienna's *Vereinssaal* – a small concert hall. He gave the further undertaking that Linke would have the privilege of performing the A minor Quartet later in the autumn.[xl]

On 29 April Galitzin wrote to Beethoven enthusing over 'the sublime Quartet [Op. 127]' that he had just received and which he had 'played several times'. Optimistically he added he was 'delighted to hear that the other quartets [Op. 132 and Op. 130] will soon be finished'. It appears Beethoven had given Galitzin this reassurance in a letter that is now considered lost.[xli] April 1825 was not, however, a good month for Beethoven as a consequence of debilitating illness. He was diagnosed with serious intestinal inflammation for which, on 18 April, he consulted his physician Dr. Anton Braunhofer: 'I am not feeling well ... for I am in great pain ... I do most earnestly beg you to come.'[xlii] Braunhofer prescribed a strict diet that precluded wine, coffee and spiced food. Beethoven, for once, did as he was told and held to this strict regimen. In the event Braunhofer's prescription did much to alleviate the condition such that on 7 May Beethoven was able to relocate to Baden to recuperate. We recall the house where he spent the summer months was later depicted in a watercolour study by the artist Theodor Weiser.[xliii]

Beethoven's relief appears to have been temporary since, despite relocating to Baden, illness continued to afflict him such that on 13 May he was obliged to write to Braunhofer once more. He complained of a catarrhal condition, heavy nose bleeds and a weakened stomach. He was concerned that without assistance his constitution and strength would not be restored. In his letter he expressed the hope that with Braunhofer's guidance he could forward 'to being able soon to sit at his writing table'.[xliv] His condition does appear to have eased somewhat since a few days later (17 May) he wrote to his adopted nephew – addressing him

'Dear Son' — that he was now 'beginning to compose a fair amount again' although the weather was so cold he complained 'I can scarcely move my fingers to write'.[xlv] The work on which Beethoven was making progress was the A minor Quartet. In a Conversation Book he used at this time he wrote: Dankhimne eines Kranken an *Gott bei seiner Genesung Gefühl neurer Kraft und wiederwachtes Gefühl* — 'Hymn of Thanksgiving to God of an Invalid on his Convalescence. Feeling of new strength and reawakened feeling.' As will be discussed in due course, these words, in modified form, were subsequently inscribed at the head of the third movement of the A minor Quartet by way of conveying, to performers and listeners, the depth of its profound feeling.[xlvi]

As Beethoven's health improved so were his entrepreneurial instincts roused — doubtless impelled, as ever, by the need to increase his income. On 16 July the previous year, with the completion of the first Galitzin Quartet Op. 127, he had written to his former piano pupil Ferdinand Ries in the hope that his new quartets would be of interest to a London publisher.[xlvii] Ries appears to have had some initial success in this regard through the offices of fellow pianist and composer Charles Neate. Like Ries, he had a close association with the (Royal) Philharmonic Society, London. In the event, however, despite Neate's efforts to have the Op. 127 Quartet published — together with Opp. 132 and 130 — he could not find sufficient support amongst the London publishers.[xlviii]

Undeterred, Beethoven wrote to Neate again on 25 May 1825 in the hope that once more he could offer the three Galitzin Quartets for sale in London for the price of £100 sterling. In this letter — written in French by another hand — he drew attention to the fact that he had already handed over exclusive rights for the first Quartet (Op. 127) that, he proudly asserted, 'is cherished by the most celebrated artists in Vienna'. He asked Neate to inform him as soon as possible whether he wanted to accept his offer 'as other publishers were also interested in the quartets'. At this time Op. 127 had already been sold to Schotts although the engraver's model had not yet been delivered. Beethoven assured Neate he would ask for payment 'only when the other two Quartets, Op. 132 and Op. 130, were completed'.[xlix]

In a further attempt to find an outlet for his quartets, Beethoven wrote, sometime between 15–19 July, to the Berlin publisher Adolf Martin Schlesinger. He first expressed his pleasure in reading favourable reviews in the *Berliner Allgemeine musikalische Zeitung* of his Piano Sonatas Op. 110 and Op. 111. The music critic in question was Adolph Bernhard Marx who, we recall, was also editor of the influential *Berliner AmZ* that Schlesinger had founded the previous year. Beethoven thought highly of Marx, describing him as 'gifted', and enthused: 'I hope that he will continue to reveal more and more of what is noble and true in the sphere of art'. In response to Schlesinger's requests for compositions, Beethoven informed him of the progress he was making with 'two grand violin quartets' for which the fee would be '80 ducats *for each work*' (Beethoven's emphasis) – the works in question being Op. 132 and Op. 130. He emphasised – in the manner of Beethoven the business-man: 'I must add that for some time now people everywhere have been clamouring for my works. Thus for each of these quartets I have already been offered the sum of 80 ducats. So if you would like to have them at this price, I will gladly give you preference.' Beethoven enticed Schlesinger with the prospect of being able to sell the quartets in Paris and London.[l]

We learn of the progress Beethoven made with the composition of the A minor Quartet from a letter he wrote to his nephew Karl on 19 July. Karl was to receive a visit in Vienna from a Herr Thal, the son of a prominent businessman in St. Petersburg, who was acting on behalf of Prince Galitzin. Beethoven informed Karl: 'In regard to the copying of the Quartet [Op. 132] you may tell [Thal] that I write quite differently now, much more legibly than during my illness and that the Quartet would have to be copied twice.' Mindful of the importance of this for his business negotiations with Galitzin, he urged Karl to be on his 'most mannerly behaviour in the company of this man'. He could not resist exhorting his nephew with a typical Beethovenian aphorism: '[The] best and noblest people are united through art and science.'[li]

On the same day that Karl was being asked to receive Thal in Vienna, he wrote to the Leipzig publisher Carl Peters, at Beethoven's request, to see if he was interested in publishing the A minor Quartet; an illustration of Beethoven's preparedness to open business negotiations with several publishers at once. Karl informed Peters that he was taking the liberty of informing him, according to written instructions from Beethoven, that he had recently finished a new *Grand String Quartet* (Beethoven's own description and italics) and wished to offer it to him. Concerning payment, Karl explained that Beethoven would draw on the 360 gulden that Peters had deposited with Beethoven some years before. Beethoven instructed Karl to inform Peters he was offering him '*the best that I have at present*' (Beethoven's emphasis). Notwithstanding, Karl added a little Beethovenian arm-twisting: 'Should you not be inclined to do this [publish the Quartet], my uncle must therefore turn it over to another publisher who has offered him the same amount for it.' As we have just seen, Beethoven was in fact negotiating at this time with Adolf Martin Schlesinger in Berlin and, shortly thereafter, with

Schlesinger's son Maurice (Moritz) Schlesinger, in Paris.[lii]

The following August saw Beethoven making progress with the correction and copying of the manuscript for the A minor Quartet. On the second of the month he exhorted Karl: 'On account of proof-reading *it is still extremely necessary to hurry as much as possible*' [Beethoven's emphasis].[liii] To assist with the copying Beethoven enlisted the services of the violinist Karl Holtz. Holz took possession of the original score of the third, fourth, fifth and sixth movements of the music since the composer's copyist, Wenzel Rampl, required it to copy out the four instrumental parts.[liv] The realization he had allowed the original score out of his possession caused Beethoven considerable anxiety. On 11 August he wrote once more to his nephew: 'I am in mortal fright about the Quartet ... What a terrible misfortune if [Holz] has lost the manuscript.' What Beethoven said next to Karl sheds light on his working method and the importance to him of his sketches. He states: 'The ideas for [the Quartet] are only jotted down on small scraps of paper; and I shall never be able to compose the whole Quartet again in the same way.'[lv] Reflecting on Beethoven's concern, Cooper suggests the composer's sketches – what he describes as 'das Concept' – on this occasion were more fragmentary than those typical for other of his compositions.[lvi] Beethoven's fears proved to be groundless. Holtz did in fact take care of the score and undertook the proofreading – though not to the composer's satisfaction. On 15 August Beethoven had to send Holz a detailed set of corrections. Writing these out vexed him: 'I have spent no less than the whole of this morning and the whole afternoon of the day before yesterday correcting these two movements [first *Allegro* and *Adagio*] and I am quite hoarse from cursing and stamping my feet.'[lvii] Despite his cursing and stamping, Beethoven kept his peace with Holz and later in the month invited him to dinner — despite believing 'his cook should be burnt to death'! More seriously, mindful of the interest being expressed in his work by various music publishers, Beethoven cautioned Holz 'not to let anyone see or hear the Quartet'.[lviii]

A letter to Karl Holz dated 24 August provides evidence Beethoven was trying to make up his mind as to which publisher should bring out his new quartets. He addressed Holz 'Most excellent piece of mahogany' — a typical Beethoven pun; holz in German meaning 'wood'. Beethoven intimated he was telling his nephew to cease corresponding for the time being with Peters and Schlesinger since he was now waiting for a reply from the music dealer Artaria. From this letter it is also evident Beethoven was working on the third of the Galitzin Quartets, Op. 130 in B-flat major, since he remarks 'the last Quartet is to have six movements' that he hoped to complete by the end of the month. Disabling illness was once more a problem though since he complained of a sick stomach and the wish that someone could give him something for it.[lix]

Beethoven seems to have quickly reached a decision regarding the nomination of a publisher. On the same day that he wrote to Holz he wrote to his nephew: 'I have already made up my mind. We will give this Quartet [Op. 132] to Artaria and the last one [Op. 130] to Peters'.[lx] (In the end Op. 132 was published by Moritz Schlesinger in Paris and Op. 130 by Artaria — both after Beethoven's death.) He affirmed the belief that the third Quartet would be finished in 'ten, or at most, twelve days'; work on it, however, extended well into the autumn. Poor health once more played its part since Beethoven complained to Karl of the little he had had to eat, of drinking only water, of a yellow tongue and of poor bowel movements.

In his negotiations with Beethoven, Adolf Schlesinger

made it known he was eager to become familiar with the composer's latest quartet compositions. In particular he wanted to attend a rehearsal of the A minor Quartet. It is to these events therefore that we now direct our attention.

Schuppanzigh's Quartet had the privilege of rehearsing and giving the first performance of Op. 132. Beethoven originally wanted the players to travel from Vienna to be with him at his lodgings in Baden. However, he soon realised this was impractical as he explained to his nephew on 6 September: 'I quite see how inconvenient it is for everyone to come out here.' He therefore asked Karl to make arrangements for the Quartet to be rehearsed in Vienna adding: 'I really ought to be present in case something goes wrong.'[lxi] In anticipation of these forthcoming events, several worthy individuals assembled to hear the composer's latest creation. These included: the violinist Karl Holz; the music dealer and composer Tobias Haslinger; and the music lover Johann Wolfmayer — one of Beethoven's staunchest admirers — to whom the composer originally intended the dedication of the String Quartet in C-sharp minor.[lxii]

Rehearsals duly took place on 9 and 11 September in Vienna at the *Gasthaus Zum wilden Mann* in the Prater. Beethoven's biographer Alexander Thayer derived an account of the rehearsals from the eminent English conductor Sir George Smart. In the summer of 1825 Smart was on a tour of Germany and wished to meet Beethoven, primarily to verify with him the exact times (metronome indications) he desired for his symphonies — notably the Ninth that he had directed at its first London performance on 2 March 1825. (Smart's recollections were later edited by H. Bertram Cox and C. Cox that were published as *Leaves from the Journal of Sir George Smart*, 1907.)

Of the 9 September performance Smart relates: 'There

was a numerous assembly of professors to hear Beethoven's second new manuscript quartet, bought by Mr. Schlesinger.' The instrumentalists were those previously mentioned, namely Schuppanzigh, Holz, Weiss, and Linke. Smart identified Beethoven's piano pupil Karl Czerny in the audience. Of the music itself Smart recalled: 'It is most chromatic and there is a slow movement entitled "Praise for the recovery of an invalid" ... All paid [Beethoven] the greatest attention.' It is reported that on hearing the music, Haslinger 'scratched his head [in perplexity]' but at the *Adagio* 'Wolfmayer wept like a child'. The audience for the 11 September rehearsal was larger. At this, Beethoven's Trios Op. 70 and Op. 97 were performed together with the Quartet Op. 132 — played by the same performers and given two renderings for its better assimilation by the audience. Smart recalls: 'Beethoven was seated near the pianoforte beating time during the performance of these pieces.' Later he was coaxed to extemporize: '[He] played for about twenty minutes in a most extraordinary manner, sometimes very fortissimo, but full of genius.' The audience was fortunate to be so favoured since this must have been one of the composer's very last public demonstrations of his powers of keyboard improvisation.[lxiii]

To establish his right to publish the A minor Quartet, Maurice Schlesinger wrote to Beethoven on 22 September in the following formal terms: 'I the undersigned attest that I have acquired two Quartets as my property for one of which [Op. 132] I will immediately pay 80 ducats in gold here and now, and the other Herr Biedermann here in Vienna will take over on my behalf, and likewise will pay the fee of 80 ducats in gold upon delivery.' The inference here is that Beethoven may have intended to sell Schlesinger the Quartet Op. 130, which was still unfinished. As remarked, Op. 130 went to Artaria and Schlesinger received

Op. 135 as his second quartet.[lxiv] At the same time that he was negotiating with Schlesinger, Beethoven sent copies of the parts for Op. 132 to Prince Galitzin. He politely asked his majesty to pay the money he owed him via the company Henikstein, stating 'at present his expenses were high'. He reassured the Prince the third Quartet would soon be finished — in fact Op. 130 was not completed until December. Beethoven once more expressed delight with the Prince's praise for the first Quartet, Op. 127, and now hoped the second one he had just sent would give equal pleasure.[lxv]

After the private rehearsals of the Op.132 Quartet, its first public performance was duly advertised: 'L. van Beethoven's newest A minor Quartet will be performed on Sunday 6 November 1825 in the *Gesellschaft der Musikfreunde's* hall in the Rother Igel, in a benefit concert for Herr Joseph Linke. Also Beethoven's great Trio in B-flat major for pianoforte, violin and cello.'[lxvi] On 10 November Tobias Haslinger wrote to Nepomuk Hummel in Weimar about Vienna's musical life. He made particular reference to the events of 6 November: 'Last Sunday, in his own benefit concert, Linke performed [took part in] Beethoven's recently completed thirteenth Quartet in A minor to great applause.'[lxvii] Anton Schindler was present at the first performance and recalls: 'The second Quartet in A minor was first performed in November 1825. The reception was far more favourable than in the case of the first [Op. 127], since Schuppanzigh and his group practised it with great care.'[lxviii] Karl Holtz and Karl van Beethoven conveyed news of the work's favourable reception to the composer who sanctioned a further performance on 20 November.[lxix]

A review of the 6 November premier of the A minor Quartet duly appeared in the December 1825 issue of the *Allgemeine musikalische Zeitung*. On reading this, when it eventually reached St. Petersburg, it prompted Prince Galitzin to write to Beethoven on 14 January 1826 in his characteristically fulsome manner: 'I have just read in the *musical Gazette* [*AmZ*] of Leipzig that the new Quartet in A minor was performed in Vienna, and I am so impatient to get acquainted with this new masterpiece that I beg you to send it to me by post, like the preceding one [Op. 127], without delay.' He further enthused: 'The Leipzig journal referred to your new quartet in such flattering terms that I could not be more impatient to get acquainted with it.' He concludes his letter by confirming his intention to arrange for payment of the Quartet to be made through his banker M. Stieglitz.[lxx]

Beethoven sent the A minor Quartet to Galitzin the following February but waited in vain for his payment. The protracted and acrimonious events that eventually played out disposed Anton Schindler to write: 'If only the Russian nobleman had remained constant in the role he had begun so promisingly, it would have behoved the biographer to write nothing but praise of the encouragement that he afforded our master and his behavior towards the composer in the matter of works he had commissioned. Alas, it was not so!'[lxxi] As late as 21 March 1827, just five days before his death, Beethoven was still in communication with Stieglitz and Co. endeavouring to secure his payment. The matter was not settled until the autumn of 1858 when Galitzin's son made a final payment of 125 ducats into Beethoven's estate. However, given Prince Borissowitsch Galitzin's role in bringing into being the three quartets with which his name is so closely associated, it is perhaps only fitting to take leave of him with Peter Clive's words of endorsement: 'In one way or another, Galitzin made a significant contribution to the growth of Beethoven's reputation in Russia' – despite, we may add, the fact that Galitzin and Beethoven never met.[lxxii]

The Title Page to the first edition of the A minor String Quartet, Op. 132 proclaimed: 'Douzième / QUATOUR / pour deux Violons, Alto & Violoncelle, / COMPOSÉ / et Dédié à Monseigneur le Prince / Nicolas de Galitzin / Lieutenant-Colonel de la Garde de S. m. Impériale de toutes les Russies, / PAR / L. VAN BEETHOVEN. / ŒUV. 132. PRIX: 12f. / Œuvre Posthume. / À PARIS, chez Maurice SCHLESINGER, Md. De Musique du ROI, Éditeur des Œuv. De Mozart, Hummel, Rossini, etc. /Rue de Richelieu, No. 97 / BERLIN, chez A. M. SCHLESINGER — LONDRES, chez CLEMENTI, COLLARD et COLLARD. / Propriété des Éditeurs.'[lxxiii]

The Schlesinger's, Adolf and Maurice, brought out the score and parts in Berlin and Paris respectively. The French edition appears to have been based on a copyist's set of parts corrected by Beethoven that Maurice Schlesinger acquired from the composer in 1825.[lxxiv] Beethoven authority Alan Tyson comments: 'The editions of the Berlin Schlesinger, which was published by September 1827, have always been considered to be the first editions of these two quartets [Op. 132 and 135]. In fact, however, the Paris and Berlin editions are both authentic [contemporaneous], and both appeared at about the same time — if anything, the Paris was a little earlier.'[lxxv]

An English edition was entered at Stationers Hall on 11 October 1827 by Clementi and his Partners as their property. In England at this time the Law of Copyright required eleven copies of newly printed works to be deposited at Stationers Hall, the London home of the Worshipful Company of Stationers and Newspaper Makers, a Livery Company that regulated the affairs of the printing and publishing industry. On receipt of new works, the Company then passed these to the eleven libraries that were privileged to exercise their right of demand to receive new works — the equivalent of today's system of Legal Deposit. As Pamela Willets explains in her study *Beethoven and England*: 'This is the principal source of the collections of the English Beethoven [first] editions preserved in the British Museum, the Bodleian Library at Oxford, [and] the University Library at Cambridge.[lxxvi] For the English edition, the French-wording (see above) was adapted to include that of Clementi, Collard & Collard in London.[lxxvii]

The American musicologist Robert Winter has made a study of the early reception of Beethoven's string quartets. In this context he cites the pioneering role of the Berlin composer and violinist Karl Möser. By 1812 he had been appointed Konzertmeister of the Berlin Hofkapelle from which time he offered regular quartet evenings — much as Ignaz Schuppanzigh was doing in Vienna. In 1825 he was elected as Director of the Hofkapelle from which time his chamber and orchestral series 'became the hub of Berlin musical life'. Winter remarks that Möser 'was not afraid of audacious programing'. He cites a review from issue 30 of the *Allgemeine musikalische Zeitung* for 1828. Works by Haydn and Spohr were performed and were well received. The reviewer then remarks: '[A] very difficult and new quartet of Beethoven in A minor, Op. 132 [followed], which, in spite of individual beautiful thoughts, did not please in its total effect owing principally to the exhausting length of the movements and the overly rhapsodic development.'[lxxviii] Beethoven's latest quartet creations were clearly being perceived as a challenge even to an informed musical audience.

We have remarked that the youthful Felix Mendelssohn was not intimidated by the difficulties posed by Beethoven's string-quartet writing. On the contrary, he confronted their challenges and assimilated them into his own chamber music style. Although clearly steeped in the influence of the late composer, Mendelssohn revealed 'he could write music of considerable power and individuality'.[lxxix]

We close these prefatory remarks bearing on the creation origins of the String Quartet in A minor, Op. 132, with the prophetic words of Adolf Bernhard Marx from 1824: 'In the future their difficulties and challenges (to both performer and listener) will be assimilated just as the quartets of Haydn had been.'[lxxx]

Beethoven designates the first movement *Assai sostenuto — Allegro*, 'very sustained' progressing to 'fast'. It is in A minor set in common time. 'An *allegro* of extraordinary, passionate regretful beauty, cast in the very remarkable form of three expositions interrupted by developments of the introductory theme.'[lxxxi] '[It] is the voice of an oracle speaking of things beyond reach of thought ... a splendid imaginative hymn to *Fate*, conceived not as a destructive but a constructive character-moulding force, the whole expressed in a remarkable, perfect close-knit form.'[lxxxii] 'No other piece by Beethoven carries a sense of suffering so close to the skin and treats the experience so deeply and so objectively, at least to my apprehension ... [For] once Beethoven seems to be dealing with pain itself, rather than with attitudes or responses to pain. The first movement is concerned not with action but with passion.'[lxxxiii] 'The first movement of Op. 132 — is a work of extremes — is full of unresolved tensions; unlike any other of Beethoven's tragedies it brings a sense of oppressiveness, being as sombre as the beginning of Op. 95, with neither grand rage nor lyrical ardour of that splendid outburst.'[lxxxiv]

In common with the preceding String Quartet Op. 127, the A minor Quartet opens with a slow introduction and shares its 'changing moods'.[lxxxv] Marx likened its opening eight bars to a 'mysterious procession of minims' in which he discerned 'long drawn agony' rising from the lowest register 'like creeping mists from a river' that in his estimation convey 'a sense of uneasiness' and which are 'poignant with meaning'.[lxxxvi] The opening bars are germane to the music and take on the role of a motif or motto theme that recurs throughout the movement. Beethoven exploits this theme variously as 'a contemplative curb on his main action' or 'to impart impetus to the music'.[lxxxvii] The viola is given the notes A, G sharp, C and B which, it has been observed, have a direct bearing on the name *BACH* (B flat, A, C, B or, transposed, A, G sharp, B and A sharp).[lxxxviii] As the introduction is announced *Assai sostenuto*, the different instruments announce their putative fugal entries in ascending order reminiscent of Bach's musical symbolism. This calls to mind that at this time Beethoven was planning an overture in homage to the older composer to whose fugal and contrapuntal studies he had devoted so much time and effort in his apprentice years with Albrechtsberger and Haydn.

Some consider the elements of the texture of the later *Grosse Fuge* are to be found in the A minor Quartet's opening notes.[lxxxix] Be this as it may, they underpin the psychology of the entire movement 'casting a shadow' over it and conferring 'the motivic texture' and 'the white-note notation' that provide an anticipation of the *Heiliger Dankgesang*.[xc] Beethoven's sketches reveal he worked on the slow introduction to the A minor Quartet at about the same time that he was conceiving the opening subject of the *Grosse Fuge* — originally intended for the finale of Op. 130. When working on the Op. 127 Quartet Beethoven had noted down a four-note motif in the form of various canons and inversions that would appear, in different guises — what John Daverio describes as a 'four-note cell'[xci] — throughout the next three quartets and most notably as the subject of the *Grosse Fuge*.[xcii]

We recall from our opening remarks that Paul Bekker, following the pioneering researches of Gustav Nottebohm, believed the first four notes of the opening to the A minor Quartet can be considered as being related to the *Grosse Fugue* and, in modified form, to the fugue theme with which Op. 131 opens. Vincent d'Indy was convinced of such unifying musical connections and described the opening motif to Op. 132 as 'the master-key without which none can enter the superb edifice which forms the first movement'.[xciii] Philip Radcliffe offers words of caution, arguing since Beethoven was working on these works more-or-less at the same time, 'thematic resemblances are not surprising'. He cites how some twenty years previously Beethoven had been seized by the possibilities inherent within an 'insistent rhythm' that had ultimately found expression in the Fifth Symphony, the *Appassionata* Sonata and the Fourth Piano Concerto. He concludes, in the case of the late quartets, 'there is a possibility that the thematic connections might have been contrived deliberately, but it is far more likely that they came about subconsciously'.[xciv] Robert Simpson expresses similar views: 'A great deal has been written about the ramifications of the phrase with which the A minor begins, not only in that work itself but in the two following quartets, the B-flat major and the C-sharp minor.' He maintains: 'It is not unnatural that Beethoven should have found various meanings and possibilities in this series of notes, both melodically and harmonically, and even tonally.' He reasons: 'I do not see, however, that our understanding of any one of these masterpieces as a work of art is substantially increased by an awareness of any elements it may have in common with the others.' He concludes: 'Each is self-contained, an organism; we must grasp each individually as such before generalising further.[xcv]

When the *Allegro* makes its appearance it 'bursts in as though propelled by the similar tension of its opening bars, whose four-note motif is threaded into the *Allegro's* main theme'.[xcvi] As the *Allegro* progresses the opening motif is taken up first by the cello, in its high register, and then by the first violin. They form a dialogue with the other instruments reminding us, thereby, of the eighteenth-century string-quartet concept of musicians engaged in conversation: 'The instruments convey the impression almost of the speaking voice.' The first violin 'darts away with a rapid phrase, halts for a second, assumes a plaintive air, then reasserts itself with renewed vigour, before fading away into space.'[xcvii]

The first movement has three successive expositions that are, in a manner of speaking, interrupted by developments of the introductory motif. Arthur Shepherd likens Beethoven's procedures here to a key being used to open a sequence of chambers: 'It is the motif which throws open each chamber of the palace and gives rise to the appearance of the two constituent ideas, the first of which reflects the hours of suffering, while the second, in F major, bearing the impress of hopeful charm, combines, in its third phase, the rhythm of the initial idea with the rather peculiar harmony of the key-phrase of the introduction.'[xcviii] De Marliave praises Beethoven's workmanship here and cites it for being one of the many instances in the late quartets where 'the fusion of the laws of logical formal construction [are unified] with an unimpeded imaginative force.'[xcix] Kerman concurs describing the A minor recapitulation as 'the most brilliant thing in the whole movement' that betrays no suggestion of relaxation 'but rather of obsession, increased intensity, and pathos'.[c] Basil Lam considers the motif that appears in canon at bar 92 is nothing less than 'a quasi-vocal reminiscence' from the 1805 *Leonora* text that was subsequently deleted in the

Fidelio revision.[ci]

In Bekker's imagery: 'The close of the movement suggests to the hearer Dürer's Knight, *Death and the Devil*; it is an apotheosis of ethical heroism, a restrained, unpretentious heroism, without so much as a pathetic gesture.'[cii] To quote Kerman once more: 'The movement leaves an unforgettable aftertaste. Principally it is the bittersweet flavour of the main theme, the omnipresent march-like counterpoint etched against its grave invariable *cantus firmus*. The inherent conflict has been seized, but it has not been settled; its world of frustration is left for the later movements of the Quartet to cope with.'[ciii] With passion finally spent, the movement ends with a single abrupt chord — testimony to Beethoven's willingness to be succinct when he chose.

During the years 1830 and 1831, the Anton Bohrer Quartet pioneered Beethoven's late string quartets in France. A popular venue for their concerts was the salon of the piano manufacturer A. Pope. The *Revue musicale* published an account of the concert given on 6 March 1831 when the Op. 132 Quartet was played. The music critic found the work a challenge: 'Here, I must confess, it seemed to me that genius was overwhelmed by fantastic extravagance. Without doubt the work could only have been written by Beethoven, and one recognizes his style from time to time, but these moments are few and far between.' He found the first movement to be 'the least involved of them all' but which he nevertheless considered to be 'full of harmonic vagueness which offends a sensitive ear'.[civ] The Russian composer Alexander Glazunov was not intimidated though by the 'harmonic vagueness' of Beethoven's Op. 132. In 1894 he composed his own A minor Quartet that authorities consider show the influence of Beethoven's pioneering work.[cv]

Comparing the difference of character between the composer's Op. 127 and Op. 132, Radcliffe considers 'it is as marked as that between the first and second *Rasumovsky* Quartets and can be felt vividly in the slow introductions of the first movements'. In the Op. 127 he remarks how the tonic 'is asserted boldly at the outset' whereas in the Op. 132 it is carefully avoided in the mysterious passage of eight bars to which we have made reference. Commenting further on the Op. 132 he suggests the 'restless energy' of the music recalls the *Allegro con brio* of Op. 95, but in the Op. 132 'everything is laid out on a more spacious scale and the themes are for the most part developed at greater length'. In his final summation he asserts: 'But, even in a movement of this size, Beethoven does not allow the lyrical mood to luxuriate as a later composer would have done; it soon is made to give way to music of a more energetic character ... there is a decided foretaste of Schumann in the cadence with which the exposition ends.'[cvi]

Igor Stravinsky had reservations about the first movement of the Op. 132 String Quartet characterising it as 'slow in starting, and patchy and spasmodic much of the way'.[cvii] For him the delights of Op. 132 were what he describes as 'the Schubertian *Allegro appassionato* and the quarter-note canon' that he further believed influenced Schoenberg when he was composing his String Trio Op. 45.[cviii]

We close this part of our account with de Marliave's summation of the character of the music that opens the A minor String Quartet: '[The] first movement ... conveys the effect of darkness lit by fitful gleams, and crossed by shifting moods of passion. But in all this there is an etherealised spiritual restlessness, by no means an expression of pathological disorder.'[cix]

The second movement is headed *Allegro ma non tanto* – 'fast but not swift/rapid'. It has been likened variously to an *intermezzo* (de Marliave), in parts to a scherzo (Bekker), elsewhere (the trio) to being 'folk-like and a minuet' (Lam). '[After] the oppressed first movement of Op. 132, ruled as sternly as any fugue by its grim four-note motif, the contrast had to be an evocation of rural peace and simplicity.'[cx] 'Of the five movements of the Quartet in A minor, the second and fourth are experienced in a curious and unique way as subsidiary. They are way-stations on the total journey, *intermezzi* in the total action, point of stasis in the total experience.'[cxi] Some authorities consider the second movement fulfils the role of a *scherzo*. Romain Rolland, for example, states: 'The *Allegro* in A major is in ternary form and takes the place of the *scherzo*.'[cxii] Likewise Truscott: 'The second movement is an easy-going *scherzo*, almost a German *Ländler* in style.'[cxiii] Misha Donat though offers words of caution: 'The second movement is not a *scherzo*, as it was to be in the Quartet Op. 130, but to all intents and purposes an old-fashioned minuet.'[cxiv] Scott mediates, describing the second movement as a substitute for a *scherzo* being 'graceful and not very quick'.[cxv]

'The mood is serene, almost playful, as relaxed as that of the first movement was tense and often distraught.'[cxvi] Both in 'metrics' and in 'tonality' the 'ghost of the Mozartian *menuetto*' is discernable but 'subdued, without contrasts, without climax'.[cxvii] Philip Radcliffe draws attention to Roger Fiske's writing in the *Pelican Chamber Music*. Fiske finds a parallel between Beethoven's second movement and the Minuet from Mozart's Quartet in A major, K. 464, which, he suggests, 'has something of the same air of elegant, perhaps slightly aloof concentration'.[cxviii] Kerman elucidates: 'A model for the *Allegro ma non tanto* can be found in Mozart's Quartet in A major, K. 464.' He recalls: 'This was the piece that Beethoven studied twenty-five years earlier in connection with his other Quartet in A, the Quartet in A major, Op. 18, No.5.' One specific similarity between the two lies in the way their openings share a 'slow unison motif'. But is Beethoven's manner quite that of Mozart, aske Kerman? 'No' is his response: 'Beethoven's composition is not quite that; but one cannot help feeling that if Mozart had still been living (aged 69), he would have found it to his taste, more than most of Beethoven's other music.'[cix]

Beethoven's sketches indicate he explored and rejected various ideas when composing the second movement *Allegro*. They included the theme he used later for the *Danza alla tedesca* of Op. 130 and a much-modified theme that found expression in the slow movement of Op. 135. The opening theme of the *Allegro* has been likened to a reminiscence of the first movement, adopting the same notes but in different guise and contributing to establishing its eventual character.[cx] A leisurely march-like tune is heard, shared at first between the cello and first violin and then by the three upper voices. The main section of the movement has been described as 'an exhaustive and highly refined contrapuntal study' though not, perhaps, sounding as such at first hearing. Writing of this, Kerman remarks: 'Beethoven achieved a range of variety ... only minute scrutiny will reveal all the facets of this superbly polished piece of musical jewellery.'[cxi] Chua is equally effusive: 'The psychological implications of this little *tonbild* are very moving to whomsoever is capable of seeing beneath the surface of the simply ordered dance rhythms.'[cxii] The dance-like episodes recall passages from the German dances (*Deutschen*) that Beethoven composed between 1795 and 1800 for the annual ball held in Vienna's Assembly Rooms. These have been identified as: *Deutscher Tanz* WoO 8, No, 8; *Ländler* WoO 13, No. 11; and *Allemande* for keyboard WoO 81.[cxiii] Beethoven adopted a similar compositional procedure when writing his String Quartet Op. 131.

In his negotiations with his publisher Schott, he initially caused him considerable anxiety by implying the work was not an original piece but had been 'patched together from stolen bits of this and that'. Reflecting on Beethoven's later compositional working methods, Radcliffe remarks: 'It is significant that, even at this late stage in his career, Beethoven was able to use material from a much earlier work without any feeling of incongruity.'[cxxiv]

Michael Steinberg praises Beethoven in the second movement for his ability 'to turn the most ordinary things into miracles'. Nowhere, he asserts, does he do it more touchingly than in the Trio, 'where a country dance tune, with bagpipe drone and all, becomes transfigured as at great height into something distant, mysterious, free of the pull of gravity'. He elaborates: 'Here, too, is one of the moments at which Beethoven's imagination for sonority and texture – the imagination, one is once again startled to remember, of a deaf man – is unsurpassed in freedom and freshness.'[cxxv] Adolf Bernhard Marx described this movement as an *intermezzo* and, mindful of the circumstances under which it was composed, regarded it as an illustration of 'feeling born of approaching convalescence'. Inspired by the breath of 'renewed vitality' he perceived the composer once more 'taking courage'. De Marliave cautioned against such a subjective interpretation: 'Without giving this statement more credence than it deserves, it cannot be gainsaid that from the very first bars of this movement, with its simple four-voice unison, its vivid dance rhythm, and its clear tone, an impression is created of health regained, and of untroubled well-being following the feverish restlessness of the first movement.' Less dispassionately he viewed the movement as 'an entirely characteristic work, in which Beethoven extracts the last ounce of development from each *motif,* sometimes in whimsical fashion with a transformation ...

sometimes with added animation within the structure of the theme'. He invited the listener to compare the movement 'from an imaginative point of view' with the *scherzo* of the String Quartet, Op. 127.[cxxvi] The *Allegro ma non tanto* did not appeal to Stravinsky who considered it did not stop in time, or seem to, on the grounds 'the subject matter is not grippingly interesting in the first place, and for a moment (m. 63—68) is actually dull'.[cxxvii]

Mention has been made of the putative influence on Beethoven of passages from Mozart's much admired A major String Quartet, K. 464. In his discussion of the second movement of Op. 132, Denis Matthews remarks it retains the outward form of a minuet and trio, momentarily recalling Mozart, but on a much expanded time scale derived from the two opening figures.[cxxviii] At the period of composition of Beethoven's A minor Quartet, the courtly minuet of Haydn and Mozart was becoming something of an anachronism. In his discussion of the social change in Vienna following the period of the Napoleonic Wars, Chua observes: '[With] the toppling of the aristocrats, their favourite dance music, the minuet, was also overthrown.' He asserts: 'For Beethoven to revive such an overtly eighteenth-century minuet in 1825 was to force pre-revolutionary music upon post-revolutionary ears ... Indeed, the social distinctiveness in the second movement of the A minor Quartet glances back at the eighteenth-century French court.'[cxxix] 'A mood of dreamy reminiscence is [thereby] suggested.'[cxxx]

Beethoven's economy of workmanship in the second movement has been much admired: 'It is based entirely on two tiny melodic fragments which are presented over and over again, in every conceivable combination.'[cxxxi] 'Another example of remarkable thematic economy.'[cxxxii] 'The *scherzo* itself is a triumph in the art of extracting much from practically nothing.'[cxxxiii] These observations call to mind the humorous remark of the musicologist Claude Egerton Lowe. Commenting on Beethoven's capacity to develop ideas from simple material, he likened his ability to that of a French chef 'who can make an excellent soup from a couple of old bones'![cxxxiv] The parallel is not flattering but it would have appealed to Beethoven's sense of humour. We recall how, when invited to elaborate a waltz theme of Anton Diabelli – contemporaneous with the Galitzin Quartets, he initially dismissed Diabelli's subject matter as 'a cobbler's patch' before eventually creating from it arguably the greatest ever set of piano variations.

The central section of the movement finds Beethoven in a relaxed mood 'luxuriating in the delights of colour'. Could Borodin perhaps have been influenced by this when composing an equivalent passage in the *scherzo* of his String Quartet in A major?[cxxxv] And does the music here have associations personal to the composer? Lam believed so commenting: 'For once Beethoven allows an extra-musical, even autobiographical, motive to determine a musical scheme.' He invites the listener to bear in mind on hearing the long viola solo (bars 149–73), that Beethoven himself played the viola in the Bonn Court orchestra during the years 1788–92.'[cxxxvi]

In the trio section the first violin suggest a popular song in the manner in with which its open A string produces the effect of a bagpipe-like rustic drone. Martin Cooper likens this to a street *savoyardlied* of the kind Beethoven would have heard wafting into the courtyard of the house where he lived in his younger days.[cxxxvii] Be this as it may, the *ländler* that is heard has been traced to an unpublished piano *Allemande* that Beethoven had composed in the early 1790s.[cxxxviii] The theme, shared between the viola and violin, commencing at bar 141 has also been identified with the *Largo* of the Piano Trio Op. 1, No. 2. Writing of the overall effect of the trio, Lam movingly observes: '[The] rustic trio brings a deeply moving sense of renewed awareness and acceptance of the ordinary human world. Evocations of the musette or of the *zampogna* (bagpipe) that were fashionable in the Baroque era.' In this context he recalls that Beethoven knew — and greatly admired — Handel's *Messiah*. Lam refers to the *Pastoral Symphony* from this work and cites it as 'a pure example of the most poetic use of this convention' — that is of infiltrating a folk idiom into a great piece of music. Turning to the A minor Quartet he remarks 'the ethereal melody over the trio section in drone bass in Op. 132 is no less wonderful.'[cxxxix]

Kerman remarks how: 'The trio works with off-beat accents ... with the effect of spiritualising tawdry *allemande* clichés into a strangely insubstantial distillate of popular lyricism.'[cxl] Beethoven designates the trio *Alternativo*. De Marliave characterises it as 'an elaborately worked-out *musette* of an unexpected and wholly alien character that breaks the logical sequence of the work'. He draws attention to Beethoven's 'gay and lively dance tune' in which he gives 'brilliant arabesques' for the four instruments. In more down to earth fashion de Marliave considers the music calls to mind the 'rather clumsy rhythms' found in Haydn's symphonies and the *Zusammensein der Landleute* in the composer's own *Pastoral* Symphony. De Marliave invites the listener to embrace the style of Marx: 'If for once we were to follow Marx's *programme*, let us suppose this passage to express the realistic description of the invalid's fist convalescence in the country, as he takes the fresh air while watching the country-folk making holiday.'[cxli]

The American musicologist and musician David Blum discussed the interpretation of the A minor String Quartet with members of the Guarneri String Quartet. Michael Tree (viola) remarked on the Quartet's attitude to tempo and how it had changed over the years with growing familiarity and insight: 'The second movement of Op. 132 is ... a case in point. We now convey more of its restless, agitated feeling. We used to play it in three beats per bar, but now we feel it in one.' Blum interjected: 'A slower tempo might sound expressive at the beginning, but given the constant repetition of motifs, the movement retains more interest throughout if played in a more rapid tempo.' Arnold Steinhardt (first violin) responded: 'It takes a great deal of courage for a man to write a whole movement with so little variety of material.' To which John Dalley (second violin) quipped: 'It takes more courage to play it!'[cxlii]

Beethoven headed the third movement with words of personal significance: *Heiliger Dankgesang eines Genesenden an die Gottheit, in der lydischen Tonart. Molto adagio* – 'Hymn of thanks in the Lydian mode offered to the Deity by a convalescent' or 'Sacred song of thanksgiving to the Deity from a convalescent, in the Lydian mode.' The tempo indications are: *Andante – Molto adagio – Andante – Molto adagio* Then follow the additional superscriptions: *Mit innigster Empfindung* and *Neue Kraft fühlend* – 'Renewed strength'. Beethoven's adoption of the German language here is significant. This was the period when he was endeavouring to give fuller expression to his native language in the terminology of his compositions; the most enduring example of this is the designation to the Piano Sonata Op. 106 as being for the *Hammerclavier*. Philosopher John Crabbe elucidates: 'Although the literary and emotional influences which helped to mould his instrumental art always found expression in purely musical terms, it is clear from the many elaborations of traditional instructions and titles in his scores that Beethoven wished to convey degrees of meaning which transcend the mechanics of performance ... [When] he could no longer trust his Italian he broke with tradition and employed German.' In the context of Beethoven's late quartets he adds: 'Notes such as "Hymn of thanksgiving to the Divinity from a convalescent" or "Resolution in face of difficulty" (appended to Op. 132 and Op. 135) suggest a need to acquaint performers with particular emotional frameworks before the music can find full expression.'[cxliii] Of related interest is that the original Autograph bears, in another hand than the composer's, the added Italian superscription: '*Canzona di ringraziamento offerta alla divinità da un guarito, in modo lidico.*'[cxliv]

Beethoven makes apparent the movement was inspired — perhaps one should say prompted — by the relief of recovery from illness. Much has been written about this movement. Kerman contends: '[There] are certain superlatives that Beethoven invites or rather demands. Like the *Great Fugue* this movement is utterly radical in conception, a fantastic vision — a devastating, *unerhört.*'[cxlv] The mood prevailing disposed Bekker to be allegorical: 'The movement opens with a prayer to which the answer comes in a fresh up-springing of the joy of life. The sick man, restored in body and soul, returns to face the world again with renewed courage, with zest and confidence.'[cxlvi] Cooper is more orthodox: 'Serenity in ... an august sense is the hallmark of the *Molto adagio* ...'.[cxlvii]

Significantly no sketches for the *Adagio* are known before the onset of Beethoven's illness, the implication being that the wellspring source for the music was indeed recovery from illness. Preliminary studies for the A minor Quartet and the and B-flat major Quartet were commenced immediately after the conclusion of the E-flat major Quartet. As we have seen, serious illness interrupted work on the Op. 132 that was not resumed until Beethoven's sojourn in Baden at the beginning of May 1825. Bekker remarks: 'The content of the A minor Quartet shows that the work was not merely interrupted but considerably altered as a direct result of Beethoven's illness.'[cxlviii] At the end of May, Beethoven made some sketches in a conversation book headed 'Hymn of thanksgiving from a sick man to God on his recovery — leading to new strength and reawakened feeling', subsequently reworked as 'Sacred song of thanks from a convalescent to the Godhead in the Lydian mode.'[cxlix]

Also of significance — for the eventual musical expression found in the great third movement — is Beethoven's preoccupation with matters of a spiritual kind. For example, he wanted to be better acquainted with ancient Hebrew texts and wished to own Luther's translation of the Bible.[cl] In his discussion of the melodic and harmonic influences on Beethoven's style, Barry Cooper draws attention to Beethoven's interest in the treatises of various musicological theorists. He cites Georg Joseph Vogler's *Chorale-System* and Daniel Gottlob Türk's *Von dem wichtigsten Pflichten eines Organisten* and to his early compositional exercises under the direction Johann Georg Albrechtsberger. Jones considers Beethoven's outlook was further shaped by his reading of Gioseffo Zarlino's *Le Istitutioni Harmoniche* in which the mode is described as 'a remedy for fatigue of the mind and likewise for that of the body'.[cli] We have referred to Beethoven's work on the great *Missa Solemnis* (1819–23). In preparation for this it is believed he resorted to the work of the *Dodecachordo* of the Swiss music theorist Heinrich Glarean. In this he expounded on the system of church modes then prevailing; copy of this rare work was shelved in the Library of Beethoven's former patron the Prince Lobkowitz to which the composer had access.[clii]

Beethoven's absorption in church music found further expression in the *Lydian* sections of the *Heiliger Dankgesang*, yielding 'a choral in slow minims, interwoven with imitative figures and elaborated in two variations'. Two interludes on and the *Lydian* F major transforms to D major expressed in an animated three-eight tempo over which Beethoven wrote 'neue Kraft fühlend' — 'feeling new strength'. Matthews asks: 'Is it coincidental that this sudden joyfulness of spirit should turn the key of the *Joy* theme in the finale of the Ninth Symphony?'[cliii] Furthermore, at the period under consideration, Beethoven was formulating tentative plans for the composition of an oratorio (never fulfilled). In addition the idea of Beethoven giving expression to a song of praise, expressed in the musical language of the ancient modes, may have its origins as early as 1818 in sketches for a symphony. Gustav Nottebohm is credited with being the first to draw attention to a sketch leaf from this time in which Beethoven declared his intention of introducing 'an *Adagio Cantique* or *Cantique Eclesiastique*' into a symphony 'in the old modes'.[cliv] Additional evidence of Beethoven's receptivity to antiquarian influences is evident in an exchange of letters between himself and Carl Gottlieb von Tucher, the son of the mayor of Nuremberg who had a fondness for Renascence and Baroque music. In 1824 Tucher travelled through Italy collecting early church music. On his return to Nuremberg in 1825, he sent a two-volume collection of music by Palestrina and his school to Beethoven's publisher Artaria in Vienna. In a letter of 28 February 1827, among the last he wrote, Beethoven accepted Tucher's request to have the volumes dedicated to him — further testimony to his identification with the ecclesiastical music of the past.[clv]

Chua contends: 'The composer's experience of 1825, bringing him to grips with the adversary [of illness], recalled the earlier ideas which now seemed applicable.'[clvi] In his summation of Beethoven's musicological inclination, as found in his later compositions, Martin Cooper reasons: 'The first hymn-like theme [in Op. 132] is the clearest reflection that we posses of Beethoven's interest in the modes, which prompted a number of passages in both the *Missa Solemnis* and the Ninth Symphony. Here, however, he does not use modal harmony as a spice, to give a few bars a specifically different colouring. He contrasts a complete archaic, ecclesiastical-sounding hymn – in fact a chorale in five strains, separated by short contrapuntal *ritornellos* – with a completely modern, secular dance-like movement.' He concludes: 'It is as though Beethoven were aware of two aspects of his recovery; the feeling of objective gratitude, which he found it natural to express in a hymn to the God whom he always instinctively envisaged as a father, and the subjective physical and emotional sensations of a *retour à la vie*.'[clvii] Basil Lam, an authority on early church music writes: 'The polyphony here [in Op. 132] has been called medieval but the description is neither accurate nor adequate to the remoteness of this music from all historical styles. Beethoven intuitively rediscovers the severe diatonic dissonances of thirteenth-century *Ars Antiqua*, combined with a non-harmonic counterpoint in which parts cross like tenor and contra-tenor in the early fifteenth century.'[clviii]

The third movement alternates slow sections in modal F with faster passages, the essential features being a great chorale elaboration and grand variation. Shepherd likened the movement to 'a grand *lied*' in five sections: '(1) Chorale in five phrases; (2) Episode in D; (3) Chorale with variations; (4) Episode in D; (5) Chorale.'[clix] Beethoven headed the *Credo* in the *Missa Solemnis* 'God above all – God has never deserted me' and the *Kyrie* 'From the heart, may it go to the heart'. Remarking on these deeply personal expressions of feeling, Crabbe suggests: 'One could well imagine Beethoven applying this second dictum to parts of the late quartets, and indeed both mottos would be appropriate for the deeply felt *Adagio* of Op. 132, the movement called "Hymn of thanksgiving to the Divinity from a convalescent".'[clx] Also in the *Missa Solemnis*, as Cooper reminds us, Beethoven had adopted a form of 'quasi-modal harmony' at the *Et incarnates*. He describes the third movement as a 'double variation form' whose main theme is cast in the form of a chorale in the Lydian mode — 'F major [F G A B flat C D E] but with B naturals — creating an antique, religious flavour'. Cooper likens the prevailing atmosphere as being 'of timeless piety', perhaps owing something to contemporary organ improvisation; we recall as a boy Beethoven had played the organ in his Bonn days and by the age of twelve could play many of Bach's *forty-eight* from memory.[clxi]

As befitting the serene nature of the music, Beethoven lays out the melody in spacious minims with interludes in crotchets with the main section of the *Adagio* extending for some thirty bars. Reflecting on Beethoven's workmanship, Truscott contends: 'Although the *Molto Adagio* ... is emotionally the most complex in the work, structurally it is extremely simple. We need not be concerned as to whether or not it is a good piece of writing in the Lydian mode. What maters is that the main parts of the piece are pitched on a scale of F with a B natural (the normal Lydian mode), and that the music in its own natural movement gravitates to an emphasis on C — so that the tonal effect of the whole is a somewhat distorted C major.'[clxii] Marion Scott praises Beethoven for his enterprise: 'Beethoven's thank-offering to God and the use of the Lydian mode is memorable at a period when to [other] musicians the modes were a book closed and obsolete. In re-opening it Beethoven showed a prophetic spirit.' Of his musicianship she enthuses: 'Beethoven alternates the Lydian sections with more human, personal sections in D major, and the movement is developed with a power and wealth of meaning that fills with awe.'[clxiii]

With the transition to *Neue Kraft fühlend* — 'renewed strength' — Beethoven symbolizes his newly recovered vitality by requiring the instruments to play in a higher pitch. As though to embolden himself he noted in his manuscript workings: 'Doch du gabst mir wieder Kräftemich des Abends zu finden' — 'You returned to my strength to find me again in the evening' — a derivative from the classical Sibylline oracles with which he was acquainted.[clxiv] 'The change of rhythm and pace, the animation of the theme, the technical character of accent, bowing, and trills, all give a very real sense of the joy of the convalescent on indeed "regaining vitality".' De Marliave, whom we have just quoted, cites Marx in support of his contention: 'Intellectual power is wonderfully revealed in this *Andante*. This is no expression of physical energy, but of a nervous force, a subtle sensibility. The first violin, mingling with the melody of the second, takes the theme and brings it to a conclusion that ravishes the ear; throbbing with a youthful vitality and vigour that makes the pulse beat quicker as one listens.' De Marliave concludes: 'The passage is rather an echo of the Mass in D; it is a fifteen-bar melody growing in fervour that expresses the very spirit of the words of thanksgiving.'[clxv] The *Adagio* returns for the last time: 'Here again a new modification of the twofold theme is involved by the redoubled imaginative force of the artist in whose hand is written in the manuscript: *Mit innigster Empfindung* (*Con intimissimo sentimento*) ... It is a passage of unspeakable beauty ... a new religious fervour ... *sforzato* accentuations of each note seem to proclaim an unshakable conviction of belief.'[clxvi]

We have said that much has been written about Beethoven's A minor String Quartet, Op. 132. With this in mind we draw our remarks here concerning the third movement to a close with a section of aphoristic endorsements drawn from this great body of writings.

> '*Recovery* is not to be understood merely in the narrower sense of physical convalescence, but as victory by the grace of God over the assault of fate.' Paul Bekker, 1925, p. 330.
>
> 'This famous movement is the climax of the Quartet and, in a way, the pivot upon which its spiritual inspiration turns. It is an "act of grace" of matchless fervour, perhaps more deeply expressive of Beethoven's spirit of devotion than the Mass in D itself.'
>
> 'The impression is heightened by the fact that the artist has chosen to express his sense of gladness to the Almighty in the musical form of one of the ecclesiastical modes.'
>
> 'The musician reaches so sublime a level of creative imagination that he is indifferent to passing harmonic harshness that Fuchs or an Albrechtsberger would undoubtedly have condemned. These angularities only serve to stress the character of [the composer's] rugged faith.

Joseph de Marliave, 1925 (reprint 1961), pp. 343–4.

> 'Beethoven obviously meant to give the impression of a "programme". The hymn-like opening leads to an andante marked *Neue Kraft fühlend* which with its rustling, whispering and twittering, gives a wonderful picture of re-awakening life.' Rebecca Clarke, *The Beethoven quartets as a*

player sees them in: *Musical Times*, Special Issue, London: Vol. VIII, No. 2, 1927, pp. 184—90.

'The piece is neither operatic nor churchy, nor excessively humble either; it may look plain, but sonority is so calculated that the term *sobriety* hardly seems to do justice to the fullness of the effect.'

'[The movement is] *contemporary* in that the piece makes up its own new language — in spite of the fact that the Lydian mode was an archaism, and a sufficiently remarkable one ... No one had ever used the Lydian mode in this way. To accommodate it, Beethoven imagined a unique harmonic, rhythmic dynamic and textual order.'

'The Lydian hymn summons up some infinitely remote liturgy, a ritual music of romance that tenuously looks ahead to *Parsifal* and the Fauré Requiem.'

'The Lydian mode gave him a rarefied atmosphere for his hymn of thanks, whispered by a convalescent who has just and barely, passed a supreme crisis ... The hymn is twice interrupted by a thrilling vision of new strength (*Neue Kraft fühlend*), strength which has been attained, and which perhaps never will be attained.' Joseph Kerman, 1967, p. 221 and p.254.

In the interests of objectivity, a dissentient voice must be allowed its place:

> 'Two slices of "minuet" and three of hymn of praise pile up like a five-decker Dagwood sandwich, except that the hymn decks and minuet decks fail to integrate, even to react on each other. In consequence, the listener forgets the minuet and therefore that Beethoven ever did feel any "new strength".' Igor Stravinsky, 1972, p. 258.

(A Dagwood sandwich is a tall, multilayered sandwich made with a variety of meats, cheeses, and condiments. It was named after Dagwood Bumstead.)

'I cannot attempt to describe the wonderful static power of this slow movement; too many have tried already.' Robert Simpson, *The Chamber Music for Strings* in: Denis Arnold and Nigel Fortune editors, *The Beethoven Companion*, 1973, p. 270.

'Music here appears to become an implicit agency of healing, a talisman against death.' Maynard Solomon, 1977, p. 322.

> 'In his last works [Beethoven's] imagination became increasingly subtle and far-reaching, sometimes as in the slow movement of Op. 132, wandering into mysterious and unfamiliar regions and sometimes, as in the *Grosse Fuge*, showing a structural power of unprecedented monumentality.'

> 'The *Heiliger Dankgesang* ... is the strangest piece of music that Beethoven ever wrote, and this strangeness is emphasised by the fact that it comes between the quietly precise end of the previous

movement and a prosaically vigorous march.'

Philip Radcliffe, 1978, p. 115 and p. 177.

'The heart of Op. 132 ... lies in its extraordinary slow movement, explicitly entitled "Hymn of Thanks-giving from a Convalescent to the Deity, in the Lydian Mode". Knowing of Beethoven's own sufferings, it is impossible not to respond to the music's subjective overtones, though the expression, more than in the *Arioso dolente* of the Op. 110 Piano Sonata and the *Cavatina* of the Op. 130 Quartet, seems sublimated into the universal.'

Denis Matthews, 1985, p. 141.

' ... one of Beethoven's great humane categories ...'.

Theodor W. Adorno, 1998, p. 175.

'Slowly, slowly, the melody unfolded itself. The archaic Lydian harmonies hung on the air. It was an unimpassioned music, transparent, pure and crystalline, like a tropical sea, an Alpine lake. Water on water, calm sliding over calm; the according of level horizons and waveless expanses, a counterpoint of serenities. And everything clear and bright; no mists, no vague twilights. It was the calm of still and rapturous contemplation, not of drowsiness or sleep. It was the serenity of a convalescent who wakes from fever and finds himself born again into a realm of beauty. But the fever was "the fever called living" and the rebirth was not into

> this world; the beauty was unearthly, convalescent serenity was the peace of God. The interweaving of Lydian melodies was heaven.'

Aldous Huxley, *Point Counterpoint*, 1928, quoted in: Martin Geck, 2003, p. 121.

The conclusion of the deeply personal third movement posed Beethoven a problem — how to follow such an expressive piece of music? He originally considered an *Alla danza tedesca* but finally settled on a march — *Alla marcia, assai vivace*. Kerman suggests: 'The serious, and even agonising, expressive character of the A-minor Quartet was probably a factor in Beethoven's choice of the *Alla Marcia, assai vivace* to serve as a contrasting buffer zone between the *Heiliger Dankgesang* and the recitative finale.'[clxvii] Likewise Truscott: 'The intensity of feeling engendered by the *Adagio* is offset by the march that follows, a movement which also prepares for the mood of the finale.'[clxviii] Lam observes: 'As far back as [Piano Sonata] Op. 10, No. 3, Beethoven had encountered the problem of finding a sequel to a slow movement of exceptional gravity, and his solutions are as various as the pieces they follow.' He cites the manner in which, in the Piano Sonata, the 'tragic intensity' of the *Largo e mesto* is followed by the 'exquisitely pensive *Menuetto*'.[clxix] Radcliffe remarks: 'After the ethereal end of the [third] movement a sudden jerk down to earth seemed to be the only possible continuation.' Like Lam he also makes reference to compositional precedents to be found in the composer's writing for the keyboard: 'A rather similar situation occurs in the Piano Sonata in A major, Op. 101, where a particularly tender and intimate first movement is followed by a curiously angular and crabbed march.' He adds: 'In the A minor Quartet the decent is from an even loftier height and the march to which it leads is simpler and more aggressively earthy.'[clxx] The themes and rhythm of the *Alla marcia* borrow from those of the opening *Allegro*. It functions as a brief interlude in two repeated sections. It provides 'a decisive bounce, psychological relaxation and a simple and good-natured affirmation of vitality'.[clxxi]

Scott likens the short *Alla marcia* to a bridge that leads to the finale. She compares it with the bridge passage that opens the final movement of the Ninth Symphony.[clxxii] Simpson expresses similar thoughts: 'There is nothing more startling in music than the little *Alla marcia* ... It provokes protest, in recitatives closely related to those in the Ninth Symphony.'[clxxiii] Kerman likens the music to 'a miniscule dance movement' having the compressed dimensions of the bagatelles for piano with which Beethoven was becoming preoccupied at this period. He also argues: 'If the Trio of the second movement suggests a spiritualized country dance, so this *Alla marcia, assai vivace* suggests a parallel vision — a dandified march out of a Salzburg serenade or a stylish *opera buffa*.'[clxxiv] 'This is a special kind of Beethoven march, terse, full of unexpected twists and witticisms, and apt to be quite fierce.'[clxxv] Chua, however, has an altogether more serious take in the *Alla marcia*. He reminds us that at the period of the Napoleonic wars, the sound of marching in the streets of occupied Vienna were once prevalent and potentially threatening. In the context of the A minor Quartet he generalises: 'There is a peculiar narrative pattern of social estrangement. The individual and the institutional are alienated in this impasse of emotions, as prayer and passion are mixed with the aristocratic, the bucolic, and the military ... Beethoven snatches indifferent objects from the real world to invade the privacy of the quartet; the minuet, musette, and march deliberately mimic the social formalities of an ideal world, and perhaps the way they are used would have signified radical changes in society at the time.'[clxxvi]

We recall the letter Beethoven wrote to his nephew on 11 August 1825 in which he perceived the A minor Quartet to have *six* movements; the closing twenty-two bars of the *Alla marcia* were originally conceived as a separate movement, not merely as a transition to the final *Allegro Appassionato*. Cooper comments: 'These twenty-two bars could be regarded as a separate movement ... Thus, as in the Sonata, Op. 110, there is a deliberate ambiguity about whether short sections should be viewed as a single, compound movement.'[clxxvii] As finally composed, a few bars derived from the closing notes of the march lead to 'a sudden outburst of recitative' played by the first violin against a disturbing background of tremolo. Kerman, whose words we have just quoted, identifies three other works in which similar passages of this kind occur, namely, the Ninth Symphony, the Piano Sonatas in D minor, Op. 31, No. 2 and the already cited A-flat major, Op. 110. He comments how in these works and the A minor Quartet, the phrases are of a very similar kind that 'evoke vividly the atmosphere of opera and produce a feeling of suspense'. He posits: 'It is possible ... that the recitative in Op. 132 may have some connection with the fact that its finale was originally intended for the Ninth Symphony.'[clxxviii] Frank Dobbins expresses similar views and reminds us of Beethoven's originality: 'With the tremolos on the lower strings below the violent figures of the first violin, the varied and rapidly changing dynamics, the prominent silences, and to conclude, *Presto*, the solitary course of the first violin, these twenty-two bars ... were something new in the language of the string quartet.' He adds: 'These recitatives which Beethoven had already used for their expressive effect and transitional strength in his piano sonatas and the Ninth Symphony, find here a new outlet in the context of the string quartet.'[clxxix]

Stravinsky did not like this movement. He dismissed the *Alla marcia* protesting that it might have been composed thirty years earlier 'and shelved', being nothing less than 'a bombastic recitative incorporating a version of the violin paroxysm from the first movement'.[clxxx]

Invoking her lyric-theatre imagery, Rebecca Clarke likens the manner in which the first violin 'heralds the last movement' and compares it to an 'operatic recitative'.[clxxxi] She is referring to the 'passionate burst of recitative' given to the first violin that is heard above 'the shimmering tremolo accompaniment' of the other players.[clxxxii]

With passion spent, after a momentary pause the final movement opens without a break.

The fifth and final movement is an *Allegro appassionato*. As befitting the designation 'fast with passion' the music is: 'passionately beautiful ... with a haunting theme;'[clxxxiii] 'passionate and vehement';[clxxxiv] 'as all embracing and as simple in its formal outlines as any movement in these [Galitzin] quartets';[clxxxv] and 'possessed of instrumental texture [that] is as masterly as it is original — without simulating orchestral effects, Beethoven produces a depth and amplitude of symphonic grandeur'.[clxxxvi] Could this 'heartrendingly beautiful rondo' perhaps be 'a kind of translation of Mozart into a different sphere' as suggested by Robert Simpson? For him: '[The] pathos of the A major in the coda is very near to some of Mozart's last-minute transformations to the major, now informed with a kind of wild intensity, conveyed with high originality by switching the registers of viola and cello.'[clxxxvii] Could it be that the spirit of the *Allegro appassionato* is a sub-conscious transfiguration of Beethoven's own 'dancing, triumphant *Allegretto*' in the Piano Sonata in D minor, Op. 31, No. 2 — *The Tempest*?[clxxxviii] The classical rondo form was used sparingly by Beethoven in his later compositions; this, and the companion example in the finale of Op. 130, are rare examples. Remarking on Beethoven's adoption of this form Truscott enthuses: 'It is a full-scale sonata rondo with a huge coda, and yet it is one of the shortest movements in all the third period. This is principally because most of the movement is quickly accomplished without the slightest hurry.'[clxxxix]

One bar *poco adagio* — 'a little slowly' — leads to the *Allegro appassionato*. After two bars in which the plaintive second violin hovers above the sonorous base, the 'haunting theme' to which we have just referred is heard. De Marliave comments: '[The] melody that enters at the third bar reflects marvellously, by its quality at once impassioned, proud, appealing, the musician's bruised and weary spirit his unsatisfied longing for piece.' He considered it to be 'one of the most profoundly conceived melodies that Beethoven ever wrote'. Moreover he believed Beethoven develops the theme to such wonderful effect that it 'lifts the movement to place it amongst the finest quartet music in existence'.[cxc]

As with so many of Beethoven's melodies that seem to spring forth naturally from the instruments to enchant the ear, the composer's sketches reveal it underwent a number of transformations before arriving at its final form. A further complication in the evolution of the melody was that Beethoven was undecided whether to use it for the final movement of the Ninth Symphony — in what would have been a *finale instromentale*. Thayer narrates: 'Sketches for the finale [of the Ninth Symphony] show that Beethoven had made considerable progress with the setting of Schiller's *Ode* before he decided to incorporate it with the symphony.' In his sketchbook for July 1823 Beethoven wrote out a melody in D minor that he designated as being for a *finale instromentale*. This was subsequently transformed and recast in the key of A minor for the Quartet Op. 132. Thayer continues: 'That [the original melody] was intended for the finale of the Symphony is proved by the fact that it is surrounded with sketches for the Symphony in D minor and Beethoven recurred to it twice before the end of the year; there was no thought of the Quartet at the time.'[cxci] Lam gives the following summary account of the creation origins of the final movement melody: 'The noble sombre theme of the finale was ... sketched for the Ninth Symphony, and its presence here is further evidence of the fragmented construction of this Quartet, with its extensive quotations from earlier compositions in the second movement.' He places the earliest source for the D minor theme headed *finale instromentale* as 'just before June 1823'. By late 1823 he suggests Beethoven had by then decided on the choral finale to the Symphony so that when a year later he began work on the finale of Op. 132 'he noted a quite different theme, followed by a variant of the Ninth Symphony idea'.[cxcii]

De Marliave believed the pressing obligation Beethoven had to Galitzin to provide him with three string quartets may have had a bearing on the composer's actions. Discussing the progress he was then making with the A minor Quartet he states: 'There remained only the finale. But his illness had delayed him, and he was probably afraid lest he should not get the work finished in time for his noble patron in Russia; consequently he abandoned the scheme for the finale that he had started on, and took up an earlier study from the notebooks of 1822–3, intended originally for the Ninth Symphony. From this he evolved the *Allegro appassionato*, that *valse tragique* as it has been called.'[cxciii]

Notwithstanding the singular origins of the theme to the final movement, authorities are united in acknowledging how well suited is the A minor melody to the Quartet. Radcliffe comments: 'With all its sombre and passionate character, the tune in its eventual version is more suited to the intimate atmosphere of a string quartet than to a work of the monumental nature and dimensions of the Ninth Symphony.' The version intended for the Symphony he finds possessed of 'a very persistent rhythm' whereas in the final quartet version he considers 'the greater rhythmic flexibility gives the tune a far more sweeping and compelling character'.[cxciv] Matthews refers to the subject of the opening of the finale as being one 'of great beauty'.[cxcv] It is worked in a recitative-like manner revealing further affinities with the Ninth Symphony: 'Like the choral finale of the Ninth, the finale movement of Op. 132 is introduced by a passionate recitative-transition. A violin recitative is heard here above tremolo textures in the other strings, suggesting an almost operatic setting.'[cxcvi] Kerman is even more expressive: 'The finale of the Quartet in A minor, Op. 132, is led by an almost hysterical violin recitative, with tremolo and all the trimmings — the rawest that Beethoven ever conceived.'[cxcvii]

The movement's working-out suggested to de Marliave 'the interweaving of parts' in the *scherzo* of the composer's String Quartet Op. 59, No. 1. He personified the 'rugged burst of melody' as 'the outpouring of a liberated and jubilant spirit, growing in ardour as the cello takes up the melodic line ... in contrary movement with the first violin'.[cxcviii] The character of the movement similarly disposed Chua to look back at another of the composer's great compositions: 'Beethoven seems to be recalling something of his earlier "heroism" in the finale with off-beat *sforzandos* sometimes reminiscent of the syncopations in the first movement of the *Eroica*.'[cxcix] Of the movement's coda Truscott enthuses: 'One of the most magically radiant passages Beethoven ever wrote, the main theme developing a heartfelt happiness which breeds a scherzo-like dance of staccato quavers and supporting chords.'[cc] Matthews likens the manner of 'the ecstatic breaking-in of the major key over the minor', at the end of Op. 132, to the depiction of 'a triumph of the human spirit'. Doubtless recalling his own challenging days as a concert pianist, he adds: '[It] makes superhuman demands on the players comparable with the strenuous vocal climaxes in the Ninth.'[ci]

Marx considered the finale of the String Quartet in A minor, Op. 132 to be 'the wonderful psychological outcome of the artist's trials and triumphs, suffering and consolation, bringing new vitality of youth; ill health overcome, but the suffering it involved can never be forgotten, nor the old creative force be recaptured'.[ccii] Radcliffe takes leave of the Op. 132 Quartet with the tribute: 'The finale provides a magnificent climax to one of the most intimate and withdrawn of Beethoven's works.'[cciii] We give the last words to Becker: 'An indescribable sense of bliss, not ecstatic as in the Seventh Symphony, not humorous as in the Eighth, but passionate and perfect, dominates the close ... It is the mood of which Bettina von Arnim makes Beethoven speak when he declares that he has no fears for the future of his music, "for whoever really understands it must become free of all the misery which others bear about them".'

[i] Radcliffe, Philip, 1978, pp. 121–22.
[ii] Peter Clive, 2000, pp. 226–7.
[iii] Robin Wallace, 1986, pp. 58–8.
[iv] Cited in: Joseph de Marliave, 1925 (reprint 1961), pp. 328–9.
[v] See, for example: Margaret Notely, *With a Beethoven-like sublimity: Beethoven in the works of other composers* in: Glenn Stanley, editor *The Cambridge companion to Beethoven*, 2000, pp. 242–3.
[vi] Joseph Kerman, 1967, p. 262.
[vii] Arthur Shepherd, 1935, p. 62.
[viii] Daniel K. L. Chua, *The "Galitzin" quartets of Beethoven: Opp.127, 132, 130*, 1995, p. 105.
[ix] Sanya Shoilevska Henderson, *Alex North, film composer: a biography, with musical analyses of a Streetcar named desire, Spartacus, The misfits, Under the volcano, and Prizzi's honor*, 2003, p. 68.
[x] See: Beethoven House, Digital Archives, Document B 1408.
[xi] Richard Kramer in: Christoph Wolff and Robert Riggs, *The string quartets of Haydn, Mozart and Beethoven: studies of the autograph manuscripts: a conference at Isham Memorial Library*, March 15–17, 1979, pp. 234–5.
[xii] Barry Cooper, 2000, pp. 322–3.
[xiii] Douglas Porter Johnson, editor, 1985, pp. 306–7.
[xiv] See: Beethoven House, Digital Archives, Document, NE 47a.
[xv] Douglas Porter Johnson, editor, 1985, p. 308. See also: Nickolas Marston, *Biographical and musical source material* in: Barry Cooper, 1991, pp. 186–7 and Thayer-Forbes, 1967, pp. 957–8.

xvi Douglas Porter Johnson, editor, 1985, pp. 299–304.
xvii *Ibid*, pp. 424–5.
xviii *Ibid*, pp. 419–23. See also: Nicholas Marston, *Biographical and musical source material* in: Barry Cooper, *The Beethoven compendium: a guide to Beethoven's life and music*, 1991, pp. 186–7.
xix Beethoven House, Digital Archives, Document, H. C. Bodmer, HCB Bsk 19/67.
xx *Ibid*, H. C. Bodmer, HCB Mh 100.
xxi *Ibid*, H. C. Bodmer, HCB Mh 98.
xxii Beethoven House, Digital Archives, Document, Sammlung Wegeler, W 4.
xxiii Douglas Porter Johnson, editor, 1985, pp. 475–81. Score sketches are preserved in Artaria 213 MS, Staatsbibliothek Preussischer Kulturbesitz, Berlin, with related leaves in the archives of Koblenz, Stockholm, Vienna and London. See: William Kinderman editor, 2005, p. 328.
xxiv Richard Kramer in: Christoph Wolff and Robert Riggs, *The string quartets of Haydn, Mozart and Beethoven: studies of the autograph manuscripts: a conference at Isham Memorial Library*, March 15–17, 1979, pp. 234–5.
xxv William Kinderman editor, 2005, p. 328.
xxvi *Ibid*, pp. 283–4.
xxvii Marion Scott, 1940, p. 266.
xxviii Paul Bekker, 1925, p. 327.
xxix William Kinderman, 1997, pp. 283–4.
xxx *Ibid*.
xxxi Maynard Solomon, 1977, p. 322.
xxxii David Wyn Jones, *Beethoven and the Viennese legacy* in: Robin Stowell editor, *The Cambridge companion to the string quartet*, 2003, pp. 223–4.
xxxiii Daniel K. L. Chua, 1995, p. 108.
xxxiv Paul Bekker, 1925, p. 328.
xxxv Marion M. Scott, 1940, pp. 266–7.
xxxvi Harold Truscott, 1968, pp. 64–7.
xxxvii Basil Lam, 1975, pp. 84–5.
xxxviii Tully Potter in: Robin Stowell, editor *The Cambridge companion to the string quartet*, 2003, pp. 43–4.
xxxix Emily Anderson, editor and translator, 1961, Vol. 3, Letter No. 1292, pp. 1127–9.
xl Thayer-Forbes, 1967, pp. 937–39. Op. 127 was not in fact ready for the projected premier and the String Quartet Op. 95 had to be performed instead.
xli Theodore Albrecht, translator and editor, 1996, Vol. 3, Letter No.405, pp. 95–6.
xlii Emily Anderson, editor and translator, 1961, Vol. 3, Letter No. 1359, p. 1186.
xliii See: Beethoven House, Digital Archives, Document B 1408.
xliv Emily Anderson, editor and translator, 1961, Vol. 3, Letter No. 1371, pp. 1195–96.
xlv *Ibid*, Vol. 3, Letter No. 1372, p. 1197.
xlvi Thayer-Forbes, 1967, pp. 946–7.
xlvii Emily Anderson, editor and translator, 1961, Vol. 3, Letter No. 1209, pp. 1064–5.
xlviii Anton Schindler, 1860, English edition: Donald MacArdle, 1966, p. 300, p. 354 and endnote 230. See also our accompanying text *The Galitzin Quartets*. Neate made Beethoven's acquaintance on a visit to Vienna in 1815–16. On his return to England he took with him, on behalf of the (Royal) Philharmonic Society, the three Concert Overtures *Die Ruinen von Athen*, *König Stephan* and *Zur Namensfier* for which the composer received the fee of 75 guineas. Beethoven got on well with Neate and described him to friends

xlix Emily Anderson, Vol. 3, Letter No. 1378, p. 1201. For a facsimile reproduction of this letter see: Beethoven House, Digital Archives, Document H. C. Bodmer, HCB Br 179.
l Emily Anderson, editor and translator, 1961, Vol. 3, Letter No.1403, pp. 1222–3. For a facsimile reproduction of this letter, together with an audio commentary, see: Beethoven House, Digital Archives, Document H. C. Bodmer HCB BBr 213.
li Emily Anderson, editor and translator, 1961, Vol. 3, Letter No. 1402, pp. 1221–2.
lii Theodore Albrecht, translator and editor, 1996, Vol. 3 Letter No. 413, pp. 107–8.
liii Emily Anderson, editor and translator, 1961, Vol. 3, Letter No. 1406, pp. 1226–7.
liv *Ibid*, Letter No. 1421, pp. 1241–2. For facsimile reproduction of this letter see: Beethoven House Digital Archives, H. C. Bodmer, HCB BBr 22.
lv *Ibid*, Letter No. 1410, pp. 1231–2.
lvi Barry Cooper, 1990, p. 4.
lvii Emily Anderson, editor and translator, 1961, Vol. 3, Letter No. 1421, pp. 1241–2.
lviii *Ibid*, Letter No. 1424, pp. 1243–4.
lix *Ibid*, Letter No. 1415, pp. 1236–7.
lx *Ibid*, Letter No. 1416, pp. 1237–8.
lxi Ibid, Letter No. 1429, pp. 1246–7. For a facsimile reproduction of this letter, see: Beethoven House, Digital Archives, Document, H. C. Bodmer, HCB Br 21.
lxii Thayer-Forbes, 1967, pp. 960–1.
lxiii *Ibid*, pp. 961–3. See also: Beethoven House, Digital Archives, Document NE 51. A Beethoven conversation book survives that contains a record of the table talk from the evening of 9 September 1825, following the first rehearsal of the String Quartet Op. 132 in the Viennese *Zum Wilden Mann*. See: Beethoven House, Digital Archives, Document H. C. Bodmer, HCB Br 287.
lxiv Theodore Albrecht, translator and editor, 1996, Vol. 3 Letter No.417, pp. 114–5.
lxv Beethoven House, Digital Archives, Document NE 164. The text of the letter is included, written in French by another hand, and signed by Beethoven.
lxvi Thayer-Forbes, 1967, p. 968.
lxvii Theodore Albrecht, translator and editor, 1996, Vol. 3 Letter No. 419, pp. 116–18.
lxviii Anton Felix Schindler, *Beethoven as I knew him*, edited by Donald W. MacArdle and translated by Constance S. Jolly from the German edition of 1860, 1966, p. 306.
lxix Thayer-Forbes, 1967, p. 968.
lxx Theodore Albrecht, translator and editor, 1996, Vol. 3 Letter No. 425, pp. 129–30. See also: Thayer-Forbes, 1967, p. 978.
lxxi Anton Felix Schindler, *Beethoven as I knew him*, edited by Donald W. MacArdle and translated by Constance S. Jolly from the German edition of 1860, 1966, p. 302.
lxxii Peter Clive, 2001, pp. 135–7.
lxxiii For facsimile reproductions of various copies and editions of the A minor Quartet, Op. 132 see the Beethoven House Digital Archives.
lxxiv See Beethoven's correspondence as recorded in Emily Anderson, editor and translator, 1961, Vol. 3, Letters Nos. 1537–39.
lxxv Alan Tyson, 1963, pp. 128–9.

[lxxvi] Pamela J. Willets, 1970, pp. 27–31.
[lxxvii] Alan Tyson, 1963, pp. 128–9.
[lxxviii] Robert Winter, *Performing the Beethoven quartets in their first century* in: Robert Winter and Robert Martin editors, *The Beethoven quartet companion*, 1994, p. 42.
[lxxix] Philip Radcliffe, 1978, p. 181.
[lxxx] The words quoted have been adapted. For their precise formulation see: Robin Wallace, 1986, pp. 58–8.
[lxxxi] Marion M Scott, 1940, pp. 267–8.
[lxxxii] Paul Bekker, 1925, p. 329.
[lxxxiii] Joseph Kerman, 1967, p. 242.
[lxxxiv] Basil Lam, 1975, p. 85.
[lxxxv] Romain Rolland, 1917, p. 190.
[lxxxvi] Quoted in: Joseph de Marliave, 1925 (reprint 1961), p. 329. Martin Cooper had little time for Marx's interpretation, remarking: 'A.B. Marx tried to fit a sickroom programme to the first movement, imagining the slow opening bars as Beethoven stretching himself uncomfortably, and seeing bursts of physical irritation in the tempo and mood.' He conceded: 'This movement has, it is true, a number of unusual traits; but they are not to be explained by such naïve methods as these.' Martin Cooper, 1970, pp. 358– 359.
[lxxxvii] Harold Truscott, 1968, p. 68.
[lxxxviii] Martin Cooper, 1970, p. 359.
[lxxxix] See, for example, Stephen C. Rumph, 2004, p. 138.
[xc] David Wyn Jones, *Beethoven and the Viennese legacy*, in: Robin Stowell editor, *The Cambridge companion to the string quartet*, 2003, p. 224.
[xci] John Daverio, *Manner, tone, and tendency in Beethoven's chamber music for strings* in: Glenn Stanley editor, *The Cambridge companion to Beethoven*, 2000, pp. 147–64.
[xcii] Denis Matthews, 1985, p. 141.
[xciii] Quoted in: Arthur Shepherd, 1935, p. 64.
[xciv] Philip Radcliffe, 1978, pp. 109–10.
[xcv] Robert Simpson, *The chamber music for strings* in: Denis Arnold and Nigel Fortune editors, *The Beethoven companion*, 1973, pp. 267–8.
[xcvi] Misha Donat, *String Quartet in B-flat major, Op. 127: Notes to the BBC Radio Three Beethoven Experience*, Friday 10 June 2005, www.bbc.co.uk/radio3/Beethoven
[xcvii] Joseph de Marliave, 1925 (reprint 1961), pp. 229– 330. Beethoven's sketches reveal that finding the form of the *Allegro* caused Beethoven considerable difficulty. See: Philip Radcliffe, 1978, p. 110.
[xcviii] Arthur Shepherd, 1935, p. 64.
[xcix] Joseph de Marliave, 1925 (reprint 1961), p. 334.
[c] Joseph Kerman, 1967, p. 248.
[ci] Basil Lam, 1975, p. 87.
[cii] Paul Bekker, 1925, p. 329.
[ciii] Joseph Kerman, 1967, p. 249.
[civ] Quoted in: Joseph de Marliave, 1961, pp. 228–9.
[cv] See, for example, Philip Radcliffe, 1978, p. 184.
[cvi] *Ibid*, pp. 109–10.
[cvii] Igor Stravinsky, 1972, p. 258.
[cviii] Igor Stravinsky and Robert Craft, 1959, pp. 114–5.
[cix] Joseph de Marliave, 1925 (reprint 1961), p. 329.
[cx] Basil Lam, 1975, p, 89.
[cxi] Joseph Kerman, 1967, p. 250.
[cxii] Rolland, Romain, 1917, p. 190.
[cxiii] Harold Truscott, 1968, p. 75.

cxiv Misha Donat, *String Quartet in B-flat major, Op. 127: Notes to the BBC Radio Three Beethoven Experience*, Friday 10 June 2005. www.bbc.co.uk/radio3/Beethoven
cxv Marion M. Scott, 1940, p. 268.
cxvi Martin Cooper, 1970, p. 361.
cxvii Basil Lam, 1975, p, 89.
cxviii Philip Radcliffe, 1978, p. 113.
cxix Joseph Kerman, 1967, p. 253.
cxx Paul Bekker, 1925, p. 329.
cxxi Joseph Kerman, 1967, p. 250.
cxxii Daniel K. L. Chua, 1995, pp. 65–6.
cxxiii Thayer-Forbes, 1967, p. 957 and John Daverio, *Manner, tone, and tendency in Beethoven's chamber music for strings* in: Glenn Stanley editor, *The Cambridge companion to Beethoven*, 2000, pp. 147–64.
cxxiv Philip Radcliffe, 1978, pp. 114–15.
cxxv Michael Steinberg, *String Quartet, Op. 132*, in: Robert Winter and Robert Martin editors, *The Beethoven quartet companion*, 1994, p. 265.
cxxvi Joseph de Marliave, 1925 (reprint 1961), pp. 338–9
cxxvii Igor Stravinsky, 1972, p. 258.
cxxviii Denis Matthews, 1985, p. 141.
cxxix Daniel K. L. Chua, 1995, pp. 108–9.
cxxx Paul Bekker, 1925, pp. 329–30.
cxxxi Misha Donat, *String Quartet in B-flat major, Op. 127: Notes to the BBC Radio Three Beethoven Experience*, Friday 10 June 2005, www.bbc.co.uk/radio3/Beethoven
cxxxii Robert Simpson, *The chamber music for strings* in: Denis Arnold and Nigel Fortune editors, *The Beethoven companion*, 1973, p. 267.
cxxxiii Harold Truscott, 1968, p. 75.
cxxxiv C. Egerton Lowe, 1929, p. 32.
cxxxv As tentatively suggested by Philip Radcliffe, 1978, p. 114.
cxxxvi Basil Lam, 1975, pp. 90–1.
cxxxvii Martin Cooper, 1970, p. 361.
cxxxviii Misha Donat, *String Quartet in B-flat major, Op. 127: Notes to the BBC Radio Three Beethoven Experience*, Friday 10 June 2005, www.bbc.co.uk/radio3/Beethoven
cxxxix Basil Lam, 1975, p, 89.
cxl Joseph Kerman, 1967, p. 252. Kerman refers to the later 'lumbering bear-dance phrase'.
cxli Joseph de Marliave, 1925 (reprint 1961), pp. 340–1.
cxlii David Blum, 1986, pp. 95–6.
cxliii John Crabbe, 1982, p. 101.
cxliv Arthur Shepherd, 1935, p. 67.
cxlv Joseph Kerman, 1967, p. 253.
cxlvi Paul Bekker, 1925, p. 330.
cxlvii Martin Cooper, 1970, p. 362.
cxlviii Paul Bekker, 1925, p. 327.
cxlix Thayer-Forbes 1967 p. 957 and Barry Cooper, 2000, p. 328.
cl Arthur Shepherd, 1935, p. 64.
cli David Wyn Jones, *Beethoven and the Viennese legacy* in: Robin Stowell editor, *The Cambridge companion to the string quartet*, 2003, pp. 223–4. Beethoven's composition pupil the Archduke Rudolph owned a copy of Zarlino's treatise.
clii Basil Lam, 1975, p. 91.
cliii Denis Matthews, 1985, p. 141.
cliv Sieghard Brandenburg, *Historical background to the Heiliger Dankgesang*, in:

Alan Tyson, editor, *Beethoven studies 3*, 1982, p. 169.
[cv] Theodore Albrecht, translator and editor, 1996, Vol. 3 Letter No. 461, pp. 183–5. By way of evidence of Beethoven's receptivity to antiquarian influences, Albrecht cites the researches of Alan Tyson 1982, pp. 161–191 (especially p. 163) and Johnson-Tyson-Winter, pp. 315–7.
[cvi] Daniel K. L. Chua, 1995, p. 67.
[cvii] Martin Cooper, 1970, p. 362.
[cviii] Basil Lam, 1975, p. 93.
[cix] Arthur Shepherd, 1935, p. 68.
[cx] John Crabbe, 1982, p. 111.
[cxi] Barry Cooper, 2000, pp. 328–9.
[cxii] Harold Truscott, 1968, p. 77.
[cxiii] Marion M. Scott, 1940, p. 268.
[cxiv] Frank Dobbins, Liner notes to Vaudis Valois.
[cxv] Joseph de Marliave, 1925 (reprint 1961), pp. 344–6.
[cxvi] *Ibid.*
[cxvii] William Kinderman, 1997, p. 288.
[cxviii] Harold Truscott, 1968, p. 79.
[cxix] Basil Lam, 1975, p. 95.
[cxx] Philip Radcliffe, 1978, p. 119.
[cxxi] Frank Dobbins, *Liner notes*, Vaudis Valois.
[cxxii] Marion M. Scott, 1940, p. 268.
[cxxiii] Robert Simpson, *The chamber music for strings* in: Denis Arnold and Nigel Fortune editors, *The Beethoven companion*, 1973, p. 270.
[cxxiv] Joseph Kerman, 1967, pp. 261–2.
[cxxv] Robert Winter and Robert Martin editors, *The Beethoven quartet companion*, 1994, p. 272.
[cxxvi] Daniel K. L. Chua, 1995, p. 108.
[cxxvii] Barry Cooper, 2000, p. 329.
[cxxviii] Philip Radcliffe, 1978, p. 119.
[cxxix] Frank Dobbins, *Liner notes*, Vaudis Valois.
[cxxx] Igor Stravinsky, 1972, p. 258.
[cxxxi] Rebecca Clarke, *The Beethoven quartets as a player sees them* in: *Musical Times*. Special Issue, London: Vol. VIII, No. 2, 1927, pp. 184–90.
[cxxxii] Misha Donat, *String Quartet in B-flat major, Op. 127*: **Notes to the BBC Radio Three Beethoven Experience**, Friday 10 June 2005.
[cxxxiii] Marion M Scott, 1940, p. 269.
[cxxxiv] Frank Dobbins, *Liner notes*, Vaudis Valois.
[cxxxv] Harold Truscott, 1968, p. 80.
[cxxxvi] Basil Lam, 1975, p. 97.
[cxxxvii] Robert Simpson, *The chamber music for strings* in: Denis Arnold and Nigel Fortune editors, *The Beethoven companion*, 1973, p. 270.
[cxxxviii] As suggested by Maynard Solomon, 1977, p. 106.
[cxxxix] Harold Truscott, 1968, p. 80.
[cxc] Joseph de Marliave, 1925 (reprint 1961), p. 350–1.
[cxci] Thayer-Forbes, 1967, pp. 80-9–91. See also, amongst others, William Kinderman, 1997, p. 284 and Barry Cooper, 2000, p. 329.
[cxcii] Basil Lam, 1975, p. 96.
[cxciii] Joseph de Marliave, 1961, p. 211.
[cxciv] Philip Radcliffe, 1978, p. 121.
[cxcv] Denis Matthews, 1985, p. 142.
[cxcvi] William Kinderman, 1997, p. 284.
[cxcvii] Joseph Kerman, 1967, p. 200.
[cxcviii] Joseph de Marliave, 1925 (reprint 1961), p. 353.
[cxcix] Daniel K. L. Chua, 1995, p. 111.

STRING QUARTET IN B-FLAT MAJOR, OP. 130

'When the instruments of the north and south polar regions have to battle against enormous difficulties, when each of them ornaments the theme differently and they cut across one another in irregular progressions and innumerable dissonances, when the musicians, distrustful of themselves, fail to play with absolute precision, then, indeed, the confusion of Babel is complete; then we have a concert that only the Moroccans might enjoy. Perhaps so much would not have been written into the piece if the Master could hear his own works. Yet we must not denounce the work prematurely; there will come a time when what at first glance seems to us so turbid and confused will be perceived as clear and perfectly balanced.' Derived from the music correspondent writing in issue XXVIII of the *Allgemeine musikalische Zeitung*, 1826 and quoted in:

Anton Felix Schindler, *Beethoven as I knew him*, edited by Donald W. MacArdle and translated by Constance S. Jolly from the German edition of 1860, 1966, p. 307.

'Its youthful vitality, instinct with the enthusiasm of recovered strength, leaves little room for the melodies of a melancholy cast, but overflows in bursts of infectious humour. If one accepts the term *humour* in its broadest meaning, as the expression of imaginative freedom and the triumph of the mind over the sorrows and sordidness of the world, the Op. 130 Quartet can be said to be the most *humorous* of them all ... In the old revived joy of creation the Master is swept away by the force of his inspiration, in a flood of fresh melodies and big designs, and technical effects hitherto unknown in music.'

Joseph de Marliave, *Beethoven's Quartets*, 1925 (reprint 1961), p. 256

'With the Quartet in B flat, Beethoven had completed the three works of its kind which he had been commissioned to compose by Prince Galitzin. He had taken three years to perform the task, but in the end the patience of his patron had been nobly rewarded. Meanwhile the Prince had

> been privileged to shine in the musical circles of St. Petersburg as one who stood particularly close to the greatest of all living composers. During the delay, Prince Galitzin's conduct was in the highest degree honourable. In his letters he was most generous in his offers of assistance, practically giving Beethoven *carte blanch* to draw on his bankers in case of need.'

Elliot Forbes editor, *Thayer's life of Beethoven*, 1967, p. 977.

> '[A] mercurial, brilliant, paradoxical work, toying with the dissociation of its own sensibility and toying with the listener's limping powers of prediction. Force jostles with whimsy, prayer with effrontery, dangerous innocence with an even more dangerous sophistication. The Quartet in B flat is the most problematic of Beethoven's compositions, a fact that he himself was almost the first to acknowledge, with his deeply equivocal behaviour toward the finale ... but the heart of the problem lies in the balance, confrontation, or sequence of the movements.'

Joseph Kerman, *The Beethoven Quartets*, 1967, p. 304 and p. 319.

> 'This is the most radical of the quartets; most modern too ... the written-out violin *glissando* in the *Presto*, for example, would pass undetected as a contribution by Beethoven in a collage of last week's premières ... my assumption that the wide assortment of the pieces indicates a desire to

> enlarge the form and enrich the variety of the contents ...'.

Igor Stravinsky, *Themes and Conclusions*, 1972, p. 258.

> '[With] the *Grosse Fuge* [the String Quartet in B-flat major, Op. 130] is one of the greatest and most overwhelmingly impressive of Beethoven's compositions.'

Robert Simpson, *The Chamber Music for Strings* in: Denis Arnold and Nigel Fortune editors, *The Beethoven Companion*, 1973, p. 274.

> 'In its original form, with the final fugue, Op. 130 has inspired much speculative writing and industrious analysis; the existence of such commentaries is a kind of tribute to the greatness of the work, but at the same time suggests that special gifts are necessary to the hearer who hopes to understand it. Beethoven himself did not set out to write the "music of the future", and the last quartets were in fact played and admired in spite of their formidable difficulty.'

Basil Lam, *Beethoven String Quartets*, 1975. p. 99.

> 'In its original form with the *Grosse Fuge*, the Quartet in B-flat major, Op. 130 held a position among the quartets similar to that of Op. 106 among the piano sonatas, that of a towering colossus. No less remarkable than the size of the works as a whole was the disparity of size between the individual movements, ranging from the enormous

proportions of the finale to the extreme concision of the second and fifth movements.'

Philip Radcliffe, *Beethoven's String Quartets*, 1978, p. 123.

'The B flat Quartet takes the expansion a stage further to encompass six movements, but these can be understood as including two attempts at *scherzo* and slow movements: the first *scherzo* is in B-flat minor and major, followed by an *Andante* in D flat, but this strangely nonchalant piece is obviously not sufficient to function as a slow movement, and so there is another *scherzo*, in G and C, marked "Alla danza tedesca", followed by the *Cavatina* in E flat and then, in the original version, by the "Grosse Fuge", which makes all the preceding movements, despite their unusual number and great character, seem a collective preparation for this unparalleled challenge to the resources of chamber musicians and their audiences.'

Paul Griffiths, *The String Quartet*, 1983, p. 106.

'The great B-flat major Quartet contrasts with Beethoven's other quartets, seen as a whole, more a suite-like, free formation than a strict sonata. That is revealed by the great first movement and the colossal closing movement, the famous so-called *Grosse Fuge*.'

Wilhelm Furtwängler quoted in: Michael Tanner editor, *Notebooks, 1924–1954: Wilhelm Furtwängler*, 1989, p. 120.

'What can Ignaz Schuppanzigh and the colleagues with whom he gave the first performance have thought when they received the music? What, for that matter, must Galitzin's reaction have been? Whatever their individual peculiarities of detail, the E-flat Quartet and the A-minor would have looked familiar from the point of view of overall design, even with the "extra" march movement in the latter piece. But the B-flat? Here is a first movement of, generally, the sort and scale one would expect. But then the Quartet seems to go off into the world of divertimentos or suites, for what follows is an altogether strange miscellany of movements. And, to conclude, a fugue of outsize dimensions and outlandish difficulty ... The six-movement Op. 130 is inspired eccentricity *in excelsis.*'

Michael Steinberg, *The Late Quartets*, in: Robert Winter and Robert Martin editors, *The Beethoven Quartet Companion*, 1994, p. 218.

'[The] B-flat Quartet represents yet another scission of creative thought, exploring a space more abstract, more extreme and more enigmatic than Op. 132. But although there is undoubtedly a leap between the A minor and B-flat major Quartets, it is a leap in the same direction, towards a splintering of Classical decorum that would ultimately result in the impossibility of closure, since the *Grosse Fugue* and the new finale of 1826 negate each other in their attempt to finalize the work.'

Daniel K. L. Chua, *The "Galitzin" Quartets of Beethoven*. Opp.127, 132, 130, 1995. p. 163.

> 'The ... string quartet from 1825, the one in B-flat major, could be called a kind of "diary of the spirit" in which all shades of emotion pass before us, from defiant vexation with fate to a dance full of humour to a *Cavatina* lustrous with the tears of the composer's sufferings and pains.'

Anton Neumayr, *Music and Medicine*, 1994—1997, p. 284.

> 'Although the *Grosse Fuge* is widely preferred as the finale today, Beethoven clearly intended the new finale to replace it and the *Grosse Fuge* to be performed as a separate work.'

Barry Cooper, *Beethoven: The Master Musicians Series*, 2000, p. 345.

> 'Beethoven must have realized that the *Grosse Fuge* threatened to upset the balance of power in the B-flat major Quartet, dwarfing what had gone before — even the profoundly moving *Cavatina* that precedes it — through its sheer size and intensity. His replacement of the *Grosse Fuge* with a new finale demonstrates a genuine concern for proportion — and also for generic propriety.'

John Daverio, *Manner, Tone, and Tendency in Beethoven's Chamber Music for Strings* in: Glenn Stanley editor, *The Cambridge Companion to Beethoven*, 2000, pp. 147—64.

'The extreme simplicity of Beethoven's themes in the first two movements of the Quartet in B-flat major, Op. 130, and the tremendous complexity of the texture into which they are woven at first seems mysterious and tangible rather than astonishing. The boldness with which the slow introduction is blended in broad statement and counter-statement with the *Allegro* is directly impressive, as is the entry of the second subject with its dark harmony and tone; but the work needs familiarity before its vast mass of thought reveals itself to us in its true lucidity.' Donald Francis Tovey, *Beethoven*, originally published in *Encyclopaedia Britannica*, 1914, Vol. 3, pp. 317–22 and quoted in:

Michael Tilmouth editor, *Donald Francis Tovey: The Classics of Music: talks, essays, and other writings previously uncollected*, 2001.

'Whether the Quartet is performed with the original *Grosse Fuge* or with the substitute finale, it is possible to read the cycle as a compendium of contrasting movement types, sonata form, scherzo and trio, slow movement as variations, a German dance, a slow movement in ternary form, and a fugue or rondo; instead of choosing four from these movement types Beethoven provides them all.'

David Wyn Jones, *Beethoven and the Viennese Legacy*, in: Robin Stowell, editor, *The Cambridge Companion to the String Quartet*, 2003, pp. 224–5.

'The String Quartet No. 13 in B-flat major, Op. 130 is the third in the Galitzin set. The number traditionally assigned to it is based on the order of its publication; it is the fourteenth in order of composition. Beethoven composed the Quartet in 1825 and in March the following year it was premiered by the Schuppanzigh Quartet. Publication followed in 1827 bearing the dedication to its sponsor Prince Galitzin.

The B flat Quartet bears testimony to Beethoven exploring new ideas regarding the number of movements in a quartet and their coherence in a cyclical order of psychological events.[i] William Kinderman characterises the hallmarks of Beethoven's changing style as embracing: 'I, Departure from sonata form (first movement); II, Divergence toward the group of contrasted pieces analogous to the suite; III, Incorporation of the fugue; IV, Inclusion of the choral variation; and V, Reversion to Incorporation of the fugue.' He describes these as 'salient features' of Beethoven's last manner to which the B flat Quartet is the 'open sesame'.[ii] Writing of Beethoven's innovations in the Op. 130 Quartet and its successor the Op. 131 — that explores an even more expansive format — Joseph Kerman observes: 'The slow movements no longer feel central — for there are now two movements in each quartet — and in consequence the finales are treated with new complexity and emphasis.'[iii]

Beethoven was aware of the demands he was imposing on instrumentalists endeavouring to interpret his new work as is evident from the care he took in annotating the score with respect, for example, to 'the shifting key signatures, the expressive silences, and the dramatic instrumental solos'.[iv] Concerning performance practice, and Beethoven's expectations, Barry Cooper comments: 'The additional qualifying terms used by Beethoven enabled him to indicate a degree of flexibility and to demand a more precise interpretation than hitherto, regarding regulating sophisticated variations in speed.'[v] The late quartets also reveal a tendency for Beethoven's indications to performers to become more painstaking with respect to establishing the desired mood, tempo, volume and phrasing. Of Beethoven's need to take such precautions, Maynard Solomon maintains: 'With the Quartet in B-flat, Op. 130, Beethoven perhaps (almost certainly) had tried to carry his audience [and, we may add, performers] with him into realms which their training and sensibility would not permit them to enter.'[vi] Even Anton Schindler, Beethoven's most ardent admirer, was disposed to pronounce the B-flat Major Quartet 'the monster of all quartets' — *Monstrum aller Quartett-Muisk*.[vii]

In its original form the String Quartet in B-flat major, Op. 130 consisted of six movements having a performing time approaching fifty minutes — without parallel in the quartet repertoire of the period. The movements in questions are headed: *Adagio, man non troppo — Allegro; Presto; Andante con moto, ma non troppo Poco scherzoso; Alla danza tedesca: Allegro assai; Cavatina: Adagio molto espressivo; Grosse Fuge: Overtura — Allegro — Fuga*. Following the first performance, as we shall in due course relate, the unfavourable reactions of the audience and the cautious observation of the composition's future publisher, disposed Beethoven to replace the fugal ending with a lighter and shorter movement that he designated *Allegro*. Contemporary performance-practice favours restoration of the original multi-sectional *Great Fugue* despite it being Beethoven's lengthiest, and most taxing, chamber-music movement.

The violinist Ignaz Schuppanzigh will feature in our

narrative and therefore requires a few words of introduction. Since we have already encountered him in our preceding discussions of the Galitzin Quartets we confine the following remarks to a brief outline of some of the circumstances that make him such an important figure in Beethoven's development of the string-quartet ensemble. He was violinist to Beethoven's benefactor Prince Karl Lichnowsky from 1794 to 1799 when he regularly led quartet sessions. In the winter of 1804–5 he pioneered the concept of subscription concerts. In 1808 Beethoven's patron Count Razumovsky invited Schuppanzigh to assemble a quartet for him that subsequently premiered the *Razumovsky* Quartets, Op. 59. It was Schuppanzigh's Quartet that also gave the first performance in May 1814 of the composer's String Quartet, Op. 95. With the calamitous loss of Razumovsky's palace in a great fire – that deprived the Count of much of his fortune – Schuppanzigh was obliged to disbanded his Quartet and leave Vienna. After a period of concert touring he returned to Vienna in 1823 and was soon once more absorbed in the city's music life. As Tully Potter states 'the knowledge that this faithful servant was once again available was undoubtedly a stimulus to Beethoven, who always had performance in mind for even his most advanced music'.[viii]

A measure of Schuppanzigh's standing in Vienna's musical circle is that his Quartet gave the first public performance of Schubert's A minor Quartet (D. 804), in 1824, as well as private readings of his D minor Quartet (D. 810) alongside performances of his other chamber music. Of related interest is that Schuppanzigh's second violinist was Karl Holz. He was a close friend of Beethoven at the period when he was working on the Galitzin Quartets and, moreover, had temporarily supplanted Anton Schindler as the composer's amanuensis and secretary-assistant. Both

Schuppanzigh and Holtz will assume a sharper focus as our narrative proceeds.

When composing the B flat Quartet Cooper considers Beethoven had reached a crossroads 'but an unmarked crossroads, where nobody had ventured before'. He identifies the challenges Beethoven had to confront, namely: the overall balance of the quartet structure; the contrasts required between the movements; and 'the element of novelty by which his art would be advanced (his devotion to the advancement of his art was always an important consideration)'. Regarding the latter, we recall Beethoven was given to saying: 'I never repeat myself.' In his consideration of the challenges Beethoven sought to confront, Cooper poses the questions: 'Should the new Quartet have a four-movement structure, as in the case of the Op. 127? ... Should he experiment with five or more movements as with the newly composed Op. 132?' ... and, most notably, ... 'What kind of finale [should] round off the work effectively?'[ix] In his discussion of the structure of Op. 130, Igor Stravinsky is content to state: 'My assumption that the wide assortment of the pieces [movements] indicates [Beethoven's] desire to enlarge the form and enrich the variety of the contents.'[x]

Notwithstanding the boldness of conception of the six-movement B flat Quartet, Beethoven was in some ways looking back to the older multi-movement form of the classical suite and divertimento. As William Kinderman points out: '[The] feature that immediately attracts attention is the division into six movements, thus bringing it in general alliance with the older design of the suite or divertimento.'[xi] Likewise Denis Matthews: 'There were ... Classical precedents for six-movement works, and Op. 130 showed its remote allegiance to the divertimento by including two dance-type movements and two slow (or slowish) ones, though in the most contrasted styles imaginable.'[xii] To cite

Cooper once more: 'The six-movement structure ... [recalls] the eighteenth-century divertimento genre, which customarily used more than four movements and had already been explored in Beethoven's Serenade, Op. 8 and Septet, Op. 20.' He further draws attention to the role of the dance that was such a feature of the divertimento and which, in the form of the *Alla danza tedesca*, manifests itself so memorably in the B flat Quartet.[xiii] Harold Truscott takes a more detached view and questions why Beethoven shouldn't experiment with new structural forms? He asserts: 'There never was, in any living music known to Beethoven, a convention of classical sonata form, and certainly no convention governing the number of possible movement divisions into which such a work could be subdivided.'[xiv]

The remarks of David Wyn Jones, already cited in our opening quotations, are worthy of recall here: 'Whether the Quartet is performed with the original *Grosse Fuge* or with the substitute finale, it is possible to read the cycle as a compendium of contrasting movement types, sonata form, scherzo and trio, slow movement as variations, a German dance, a slow movement in ternary form, and a fugue or rondo; instead of choosing four from these movement types Beethoven provides them all.'[xv] Daniel Chua is more impassioned: 'This quartet represents Beethoven at his most extreme — even against the standard of Op. 132. If the sequence of movements in the A minor Quartet disintegrates within a symmetry of contrasts, then the series of movements of the B-flat major Quartet is in danger of falling apart altogether; the B-flat Quartet not only intensifies the collision of elements but also shuns a central focus in which its broken and dispersed structure can be symmetrically anchored.'[xvi] Chua's 'central focus' is a reference to the Quartet's inner movements, concerning which Truscott contends: 'The extreme formal simplicity of these four movements is, of course, calculated and the perfect foil to the formal complexity of the first movement and the original finale, the *Grosse Fugue*: and I would add that this still applies if the substitute finale is used.'[xvii]

The creation origins of the String Quartet Op. 130 can be traced through Beethoven's correspondence with the various publishers with whom he was conducting negotiations at this period. It is to these therefore that we now direct our attention.

We learn of the progress Beethoven claimed he was making with the composition of the B flat Quartet in a letter he wrote on 19 March 1825 to the Mainz publisher Bernhard Schotts. In this he reassured Schotts the first of the Galitzin Quartets, Op. 127 would be delivered 'in a few days', adding the other violin quartets Op. 132 and Op. 130 'are still being composed'.[xviii] The work's dedicatee Prince Galitzin was clearly under the impression Beethoven was indeed at work on the two remaining quartets that he had commissioned. In a letter of 29 April he took pleasure in remarking on the favourable reception in St. Petersburg of the E-flat major Quartet, Op. 127 and expressed equal pleasure on receiving the composer's reassurance that the remaining two Quartets Opp. 132 and 130 'will soon be finished'.[xix]

Although Beethoven had some financial security in the form of a number of bank shares — invested from the proceeds he had derived from a series of concerts he had given at the period of the Congress of Vienna (1814—15) — he resisted drawing on these since he regarded them as being his nephew Karl's inheritance. Consequently, he was typically in need of money. As a consequence he hoped to derive financial benefit from the sale of the Galitzin Quartets in England. With this in mind, in the summer of 1824 he wrote to his former piano pupil Ferdinand Ries in the hope his new quartets would be of interest to a London publisher. Ries appears to have had some initial success in this regard through the offices of fellow pianist and composer Charles Neate. Like Ries, he had a close association with the (Royal) Philharmonic Society, London. In the event, however, despite Neate's efforts he could not find sufficient support amongst the London publishers.[xx] Undeterred, Beethoven wrote to Neate once more on 25 May 1825 trusting that he could still offer the three Galitzin Quartets for sale in London; he requested a fee of £100 sterling. In this letter — written in French by another hand — Beethoven drew attention to the fact he had already handed over exclusive rights for the first Quartet (Op. 127) that, he proudly asserted, 'is cherished by the most celebrated artists in Vienna'. He asked Neate to inform him as soon as possible whether he wanted to accept his offer 'as other publishers were also interested in the quartets'. At this time Op. 127 had already been sold to Schotts although the engraver's model had not yet been delivered. Beethoven assured Neate he would ask for payment 'only when the other two Quartets, Op. 132 and Op. 130, were completed'.[xxi]

In a further attempt to find an outlet for his quartets, Beethoven wrote, sometime between 15–19 July, to the Berlin publisher Adolf Martin Schlesinger. He first expressed his pleasure on reading favourable reviews in the *Berliner Allgemeine musikalische Zeitung* of his Piano Sonatas Op. 110 and Op. 111. The music critic in question was Adolph Bernhard Marx who, we recall, was also editor of the influential *Berliner AmZ* that Schlesinger had founded the previous year. Beethoven thought highly of Marx, describing him as 'gifted', and enthused: 'I hope that he will continue to reveal more and more of what is noble and true in the sphere of art.' In response to Schlesinger's previous requests for compositions Beethoven informed him of the progress he was making with 'two grand violin quartets' for which the fee would be '80 ducats *for each work*' (Beethoven's emphasis) — the works in question being Op. 132 and Op. 130. He emphasised — in the manner of Beethoven the business-man: 'I must add that for some time now people everywhere have been clamouring for my works. Thus for each of these quartets I have already been offered the sum of 80 ducats. So if you would like to have them at this price, I will gladly give you preference.' Beethoven enticed Schlesinger with the prospect of being able to sell the quartets in Paris and London.[xxii] Meanwhile, in late July, Beethoven reassured Galitzin: 'The third Quartet ... is almost finished.'[xxiii] This was in fact not the case.

At this time Beethoven had formed a close friendship with Schuppanzigh's second violinist Karl Holz. A letter Beethoven wrote to Holz on 24 August 1825 provides evidence he was trying to make up his mind as to which publisher should bring out his new quartets. Addressed humorously to his 'Most excellent piece of mahogany' (a pun on Holtz's German name) he intimated he was telling his nephew to cease corresponding on his behalf, for the time-being, with the publishers Peters and Schlesinger (see later) since he was now waiting for a reply from the music dealer Artaria. From this letter it is evident Beethoven was indeed working on the third of the Galitzin Quartets, Op. 130 since he remarks 'the last Quartet is to have six movements'. He expressed the intention to have this completed 'by the end of the month'. Disabling illness though was once more a problem (see text to String Quartet, Op. 132); Beethoven complained of a sick stomach and the wish 'that someone could give him something for it'.[xxiv]

On the same day that Beethoven wrote to Holz he also wrote to his nephew Karl: 'I have already made up my mind. We will give this Quartet [Op. 132] to [Mathias] Artaria and the last one [Op. 130] to Peters.' He closed optimistically 'The third Quartet will be finished in ten, at most, twelve days'. [xxv] It will be helpful to explain here Beethoven's relationship with his nephew at this time. When Karl left school in 1823 he took on the duties of secretary to his uncle. For his part Beethoven regarded Karl as his adopted son and frequently addressed him as such. Whilst he was at work on the B flat Quartet, Beethoven spent the summer at Baden. Meanwhile, Karl lived in Vienna and consequently Beethoven relied upon him to manage his affairs there, including assisting him with his correspondence with publishers.

Moritz (Maurice) Schlesinger looked after the family publishing business in Paris. Eager to seek new works from Beethoven, early in September 1825 he paid a visit to discuss business affairs with the composer who was at this time, as remarked, seeking respite in the spa town Baden. Moritz's travelling companion was Karl Holtz that doubtless assisted him to gain access to the wary composer. Moritz had learned from his father Adolf, who managed the Berlin side of the firm's affairs, that Beethoven was seeking 80 ducats for new string quartets. Despite this being a considerable sum, the Schlesinger's were prepared to oblige the composer. Moritz considered Beethoven's quartets were masterpieces the equal of his other great works 'and would live as long'.[xxvi] Moritz's negotiations with Beethoven clearly went well since on 22 September he wrote in formal contractual terms: 'I the undersigned attest that I have acquired two Quartets as my property for one of which [Op. 132] I will immediately pay 80 ducats in gold here and now, and the other Herr Biedermann here in Vienna will take over on my behalf, and likewise will pay the fee of 80 ducats in gold upon delivery.' The inference is that Beethoven may have intended to sell Schlesinger the Quartet Op. 130, which was still unfinished. In the event Op. 130 went to Artaria and Schlesinger received Op. 135 as his second quartet.[xxvii]

At the same time that he was negotiating with Schlesinger, Beethoven sent copies of the parts for Op. 132 to Prince Galitzin. He politely asked his majesty to pay the money he owed him via the company Henikstein, stating 'at present his expenses were high'. He reassured the Prince the third Quartet would soon be finished — Op. 130 was still not completed. Beethoven once more expressed delight with the Prince's praise for the first Quartet, Op. 127, and now hoped the second one he had just sent would give equal pleasure.[xxviii]

To take our narrative forward it is necessary to reflect for a moment on Beethoven's putative association with the Leipzig-based music publisher Carl Peters. In 1814 he became owner of the *Bureau de musique* and subsequently was keen to have eminent composers such as Beethoven on his books.[xxix] For several years, however, he had held off from approaching the composer for fear of offending the Viennese publishers, a number of whom considered they had prior claims to the composer and his new works. On 18 May 1822, Peters found the courage to introduce himself and wrote to Beethoven explaining how long he had 'zealously endeavoured to issue [his] excellent works in good printings'. He stated that whatever the composer could send him would be welcome 'for I seek your association not from self interest, but rather from honour'.[xxx]

Beethoven replied to Peters on 5 June, apologising for the delay in giving his reply on the grounds he was occupied with the composition of his Mass (*Missa Solemnis*). Of significance in this letter is that Beethoven also makes reference to his preoccupation with his *Elegischer Gesang* ('Elegiac Song'), Op. 118, scored for string quartet and four mixed voices. This is considered to be significant by musicologists as evidence of Beethoven turning his mind (creative energies) to the medium of the string quartet. Concerning this genre of compositions, Beethoven informed Peters: 'For a quartet for two violins, viola and violincello ... you could have one very soon [for] 50 ducats.'[xxxi] Beethoven's words 'very soon' have been taken to infer that he already had such a composition in hand, although it is known he was disposed to offer publishers such reassurances even when the promised work existed only in sketch form. Ten days later Peters replied to Beethoven in a long letter in which he reaffirmed his awareness that such other publishers as Adolf Martin Schlesinger (in Berlin) and his son Moritz (in Paris), were also vying for Beethoven's attention. Nonetheless, he confirmed he was still enthusiastic to bring out his editions of the composer's works. He cites his interest in trios, concert overtures, songs with piano accompaniment, and solo pieces for piano. Regarding string quartets, though, his response was more qualified: 'Finally, I would very much like to have your new quartet [the one Beethoven claimed to have in hand] ... but 50 ducats might exceed my capabilities, for the highest that I have paid for a quartet before now was 150 florins, and I have to make that back before I make any profit.'[xxxii]

Beethoven's negotiations with Peters duly lapsed but in July 1825 he sought to revive Peters' interest in his new chamber compositions. On the 19th of the month he instructed his nephew Karl to see if Peters was interested in publishing 'a new *Grand String Quartet*' – Beethoven's own description and italics; he was a referring to the A minor String Quartet that was then available. Concerning payment, Karl explained that Beethoven proposed to draw on the 360 gulden that Peters had already generously deposited for such a purpose. Beethoven instructed Karl to inform Peters he was offering him '*the best that I have at present*' (Beethoven's emphasis). Notwithstanding, Karl added a little Beethovenian arm-twisting: 'Should you not be inclined to do this [publish the Quartet], my uncle must therefore turn it over to another publisher who has offered him the same amount for it.' As we have just seen, Beethoven was in fact negotiating at this time with Adolf Martin Schlesinger in Berlin and, shortly thereafter, with Schlesinger's son Moritz, in Paris.'[xxxiii]

Nothing appears to have come of these promptings such that on 25 November Beethoven, now relocated in Vienna, wrote himself to Peters. He inferred that if Peters should accept the A minor Quartet he could have a further one – the B-flat major Quartet. He pointed out to Peters that such was the regard for his works he could 'demand an even greater sum for a quartet'. He made it clear if his terms were not acceptable he would return the 360 gulden he had on deposit. Peters was quick to respond. Just five days later he sent Beethoven a cryptic note of just five lines requesting the return of his money.[xxxiv] Thereby terminated what initially had promised to be a fruitful collaboration between composer and publisher.

By November Beethoven had almost completed the Quartet in B-flat major and an entry in his Conversation Book reads '3-ième Quatuor. Pour deux Violins, Viola, et Violincello composé aux désirs de S. A. Monseigneur le Prince Nicolas Galitzin et dédié au meme ... par L. v. B'.[xxxv] Of related interest is that the sketchbooks reveal Beethoven was actively engaged at this time on the composition of his projected Tenth Symphony. The sources reveal some 250 bars of sketches for the first movement alongside ideas for the subsequent movements. The need to complete the B flat Quartet, in order to fulfil the obligations to Galitzin, meant Beethoven had to set the Symphony aside as a consequence of which it remained unfinished at the time of his death.xxxvi

Beethoven eventually sold the B flat Quartet in January 1826 not, as he had promised to Moritz Schlesinger, but to Matthias Artaria; he received his requested payment of 80 ducats.xxxvii xxxviii On 22 April Beethoven wrote to Schlesinger in Paris to explain his actions; these had come about, in part, due to some confusion. He writes: '[I] gave the Quartet [Op. 130] not to my brother but to Matthias Artaria ... so you will realize that nothing more can be done about this Quartet.' By way of compensation he adds: 'I inform you that another new quartet will be finished in two or three weeks at latest.' This is a reference to the String Quartet Op. 135. Anticipating Schlesinger's willingness to purchase this work he urged: 'Please arrange therefore that the sum of 80 Imperial and Royal gold ducats be paid to me immediately.' More generally he enthused: 'And let there be no delay, for quartets are now in demand everywhere; and it really seems that our age is taking a step forward.'xxxix

A year later Beethoven entered into a contract with the Austrian composer and music publisher Ignaz Pleyel; in 1815 he had established his publishing firm in Paris in partnership with his son Camille. Beethoven's Contract with Pleyel is dated 24 January 1827. It is written in French, by another hand, and signed by Beethoven. In translation it reads: 'I the undersigned Louis van Beethoven declare, in the presence of a notary, that I have sold, as entirely their property for the full extent of the kingdom of France, to Messieurs Ignace [sic] Pleyel & Elder Son in Paris, my three compositions as follows: Op. 130 being the third Quartet dedicated to Prince Nicolas de Galitzin; Op. 133. *Grosse Fugue* in B flat ... dedicated to Archduke Rudolph of Austria; [and] Op. 134. The same *Grosse Fugue* in B flat arranged for piano, four hands by myself.' As witness,

Beethoven enlisted Mathias Artaria who held the Viennese publication rights to these works. The Contract survives and is of particular interest insofar as it brings together, in a single document, several signatures that now belong to musicological history; not least is that of Beethoven whose wavering hand bears evidence of the onset of his final illness. [xl]

We consider next the creation origins of the String Quartet in B-flat Major, Op. 130 as it evolved through the medium of the composer's sketchbooks and draft scores.

Beethoven's sketches at the period of composition of the Galitzin Quartets are of three types: compilations of miscellaneous leaves — the so called pocket-sketchbooks that Beethoven could annotate in pencil when out on his strolls in the countryside; pre-bound sketchbooks — desk sketchbooks — with which he could work in ink when seated at his writing desk; and, unique to the latter part of his life, loose-leaf extended draft-score sketches. Autograph scores represented the culmination of the creative process. Beethoven appears to have worked intensively on the B flat Quartet in the summer and autumn of 1825. Although having the longest performing time of the Galitzin Quartets it was the most rapidly composed; perhaps Beethoven felt a sense of urgency to fulfil what had become a long drawn-out commission?

There are suggestions Beethoven 'extemporised', in a manner of speaking, allowing the Quartet to evolve as his imagination turned this way and that. The sketches reveal that having completed the first two movements he had only a general idea as to what was to follow, beyond the music having a slow-movement character. Similarly, he had not decided upon the number of movements the Quartet should have. As Cooper remarks: 'The Quartet was thus being created as a kind of narrative, rather than a canvas where the overall outline is clear from the start ... The later movements could be moulded to suit the earlier ones.'[xli] This touches upon a subject the American composer and teacher Roger Session raised in his lecture series presented in 1949 at the Julliard School of Music, New York City. His overall theme was 'The composer and the musical experience'. In Lecture three he proposed 'a composer's relation to his work is an organic one; that the conception and the composition of a piece of music are not a matter of set procedure, but a living piece of growth.' In relation to Beethoven he asserted: 'There are compositions ... without, strictly speaking, any "themes" at all ... In the first movements of Beethoven's Quartets, Op. 74 and Op. 130 ... the themes are obviously of secondary importance to the movement structure as a whole.'[xlii]

Robert Hatten gives the following summary-overview of the gestation of the music: 'After completing the weighty first movement, in B-flat major, and the short *Presto*, in B-flat minor, Beethoven abandoned several sketches for a slow movement in D flat, that would eventually become the *Cavatina*, and quickly wrote the *Andante*, also in D flat, in its place. The finale, originally conceived as a much lighter and shorter movement, gradually evolved into a fugue and then expanded into the monumental *Grosse Fuge*.' Hatten suggests Beethoven's awareness of what he calls 'the mammoth proportions' of the fugue led him to reconsider the middle cycle of movements and consequently added another dance slow-movement pair to help balance the design. For the dance movement Beethoven chose the *Alla danza tedesca* that he had originally conceived using as the fourth movement of the String Quartet Op. 132, transposing it from A to G major; the slow movement evolved from earlier sketches into the *Cavatina*, now in E-flat major.[xliii]

From May to September 1825 Beethoven made use of the so-called De Roda sketchbook. It derives its name from the Spanish collector Cecilio de Roda who owned it early in the twentieth century and from whose heirs it was acquired by the Beethovenhaus in 1962. The sketchbook's first owner was the publisher Artaria. It consists today of 40 miscellaneous leaves, the cover (added later) reads: 'Autograph e Louis van Beethoven. Livre d'esquisses des motifs du Quatour/en La Mineur et autre études/L'authenticié en est garantie par Artaria & Co. à Vienne/1847.' Op. 130 is represented as follows: first movement, folios 13v–21v passim; second movement, folios 21v–22r, 23r; third movement, folios 28v–34r passim; fourth movement, folios 34v–35r; fifth movement, folios 34v–39v passim. Ideas for the *Grosse Fuge* as finale appear at folios 35r–40v passim. The De Roda sketchbook also incorporates ideas for Op. 127 and Op. 132.[xliv]

From May or June to July Beethoven made use of a pocket sketchbook now preserved in the Central Glinka Museum for Music culture, Moscow. It is thought to have once been in the possession of Felix Mendelssohn. Its 25 leaves contain ideas for the first movement of Op. 130 at pp. 6–28 passim amidst sketches for the Quartet Op. 132 and the *Credo* of the *Missa Solemnis*.[xlv]

Between 1870 and 1895 the Department of Manuscripts of the British Museum acquired a number Beethoven documents including holographs of finished compositions, sketchbooks and sketch sheets. These include the so-called Egerton pocket sketchbook, MS 2795. This consists of 16 leaves that include sketches for movements I–III and V of Op. 130 as follows: first movement, folios 1r–3v, 5r–4, 15r; second movement, folios 4v, 8r–9v; third movement, folios 4v, 5v–7v; fifth movement, folios 7v–8r, 9v–10v, 11v, 12v, 13v–16v.

In 1911 the French collector of music memorabilia Charles Malherbe bequeathed a number of Beethoven's sketches from the period September-October 1825 to the Paris Conservatory. These were later acquired by the Bibliothèque Nationale and are now known as Ms 62 and Ms 66. They consist of some 29 and 2 leaves respectively. Although many of the sketches are for the last three movements of the Quartet Op. 135 they also include work on the new finale for Op. 130.

In 1846 Anton Schindler sold a number of pocket sketchbooks to the Berlin Royal Library, now the Berlin Staatsbibliothek Preussischer Kulturbesitz. So-called Autograph 9/5 dates from August-September and includes the following drafts for Op. 130: third movement, folios 1r–8v, 12r–v; fourth movement, folios 14r, 15r; fifth movement, folios 14v–17r, 19v–21v, 22v, 25v. Also making an appearance are ideas for Op. 133: folios 8v–26v passim. Autograph 9/2 dates from September-October and consists of 35 leaves. These are mainly devoted to the *Grosse Fuge*, Op. 133 but also include sketches for the opening of the *Cavatina* of Op. 130. Autograph 9/1 represents Beethoven's progress through the period October and November 1825. The 18 leaves of this sketchbook are primarily concerned with the *Grosse Fuge*, from folio 5v to the end with interruptions at folios 11r and 14r for late work on the *Cavatina*. From November 1825 into early 1826 Beethoven made use of the pocket sketchbook Autograph 9/1A. By now he had conceived ideas for the String Quartet Op. 131 but was still at work on the *Grosse Fuge* that appear at folios 1r–7v, 12r, 14r.

The Berlin Staatsbibliothek Preussischer Kulturbesitz possesses a number of sketchbooks that were purchased by Domenico Artaria at the *Nachlass* auction of Beethoven's effects in November 1827. One of these came into the possession of the collector Franz Kullak who later donated it to the Berlin Royal Library. It consists of 62 leaves that

Beethoven worked on between November 1825 and November of the following year. Studies for Op. 130 are represented as follows: third movement, folio 7r; fifth movement, folio 1r; and sixth movement (the new finale), folios 52r, 59r and 60v–62r.[xlvi]

In the archives of the Beethoven House, Bonn are two bifolium sketches – double format pages – that reveal the close connections between the Op. 132 and Op. 130 Quartets. The Beethoven House text to these sketches reads: 'The first page contains score sketches for the third movement *Heiliger Dankgesang* from the String Quartet Op. 132. The remaining three pages (2–4) contain drafts for a movement in A major, which was actually intended as the final movement for Op. 132. We know it today in G major as the fourth movement *Alla danza tedesca* in the Quartet Op. 130.' The author of these remarks observes that Anton Schindler drew attention to these connections in his 1860 Biography of the composer.[xlvii] A second bifolium contains sketches for the new finale that Beethoven was urged to compose for the B flat Quartet after he was persuaded the *Grosse Fuge* was too overpowering.

We have said Beethoven did not make extensive use of score sketches until he began work on the late string quartets – from about 1822 onwards. We quote the following from the Beethoven House Digital Archives: 'Depending on how advanced the work on a composition was, the score sketches like these sometimes give the impression of being autograph scores. In "normal" sketches ideas and melodic lines are shown in one, or at most two systems. However, in his score sketches Beethoven set out the instruments underneath each other. In doing so the aim was not only to find the horizontal melodic line, but also to have an overview of the harmony and structure of the movement.'[xlviii] Thirty leaves of score sheets for the B flat Quartet have survived from the original

seen the man before. At that time the Master's physical ear already was deaf to all tone. With confusion written on his face, with more than earthly enthusiasm in his eye, swinging his baton to and fro with violent motions, he stood in the midst of the playing musicians and did not hear a single note.' She further describes how Beethoven's best efforts served merely to throw singers and orchestra into confusion and to put them entirely off beat, Beethoven all the while being unaware of the ensuing circumstances but apparently content with the rehearsal, 'for he laid down his baton with a happy smile'. Schröder-Devrient recalls it fell to the lot of the violinist-conductor Michael Umlauf to tactfully suggest he should take charge of the actual performances. This he subsequently did, Beethoven apparently being consigned to having to sit behind Umlauf – 'lost in profound meditation'.[li]

In November 1822 Louis Schlösser made Beethoven's acquaintance. He was then a twenty-two year old musician residing in Vienna receiving instruction in composition from Salieri. Beethoven came to regard Schlösser 'as a young and talented artist' possessed of 'a cordial and friendly manner'. Years later Schlösser left an account of his first meeting with the composer. Although Beethoven scholars view Schlösser's recollections with some caution – he may have embroidered his accounts – if they are taken at face value they offer insights into the composer's living conditions and personal circumstances at the period when he was turning his mind to writing for the medium of the string quartet. Schlösser met Beethoven when he was then living in a relatively poor district of Vienna known as the *Wiedener* suburb. Schlösser describes Beethoven's apartment as being rather undecorated with a large, four-square oak table and various chairs presenting a somewhat untidy aspect. On the table lay books, pens, pencils, music-paper a metronome and an ear trum-

Artaria collections upon which Beethoven worked during his stay with his brother Johann in October-November 1826 on his estate at Gneixendorf. Six other such sheets derive from other origins. The various movements of Op. 130 are distributed throughout these sources.

Beethoven's Autograph Scores have become trophy items. That for the B-flat major String Quartet, Op. 130 has been dismembered and its various movements are now the cherished possession of various institutions: First movement: Biblioteka Jagiellońska, Kraków; Second movement: Library of Congress, Washington; Third Movement: Bibliothèque National, Paris; Fourth Movement: Moravian Museum, Institute of Music History, Brno; Fifth and Sixth Movements: Biblioteka, Jagiellońska, Kraków.[xlix]

We pause for a moment in our discussion of the creation origins of the B flat Quartet in order to make way for a selection of impressions of Beethoven left by his contemporaries from the period under consideration.

Gerhard von Breuning was the son of Beethoven's lifelong friend, Stephan von Breuning. Beethoven held a particular affection for Gerhard, whom he knew as a child, referring to him as 'Hosenknopf' – 'trouser button' – because he attached himself like a button to the composer's trousers. In the last two years of his life, Beethoven had rooms in the so-called *Schwarzspanierhause. Unlike many of Beethoven's other residences it has not survived being demolished in 1903–4.* Von Breuning is remembered in musicology today for his reflections on Beethoven in the title of which he adopted the name of *Schwarzspanierhause*. These were originally published in Vienna in 1874 under the title *Aus dem Schwarzspanierhause: Erinnerungen an L. van Beethoven aus meiner Jugendzeit*, known today in english translation as *Memories of Beethoven: From the house of the black-robed Spaniards*. This work has the authority of being one of only three book-length wri[tten] written by authors who knew Beethoven personally, other two being the *Biographische Notizen über Ludwig [van] Beethoven – Remembering Beethoven: the biographi[cal] notes of Franz Wegeler and Ferdinand Ries* – and Ant[on] Schindler's *Biographie von Ludwig van Beethoven [–] Beethoven as I new him.*

One day young Gerhard had been sent to call o[n] Beethoven and recalls: 'I found him at his desk, facing the open door to the piano room, writing one of the last Galitzin quartets [Op. 130]. He looked up and told me to wait a bit until he had put his idea on paper. I was quiet for a while and then went over to the Graf piano [which incorporated an added amplifying apparatus].' Gerhard tells how he began to strum the keys, all the while looking to see if Beethoven had any awareness of the sound. When he saw Beethoven was completely unaware he played louder but Beethoven merely kept on writing 'unconcerned until finally he was finished and came out with me'.[l]

Wilhelmine Schröder-Devrient was a young opera singer who, by all accounts, had a phenomenal voice – Beethoven once described it as being 'as big as the side of a house'! In 1821 she established her reputation in Vienna as a highly acclaimed dramatic artist in the role of Pamina in Mozart's *Die Zauberflöte*; she was just seventeen at the time. The following year she appeared to considerable acclaim as Agathe in Weber's *Der Freischütz* – earning warm praise from the composer himself. Later that year she took on the challenging role of Leonora in Beethoven's revised opera *Fidelio* that had not been performed for several years. Beethoven himself insisted on directing the dress rehearsal from which occasion Wilhelmine left the following account: 'Beethoven sat in the orchestra and waved his baton above the heads of us all, and I never ha[d]

Beethoven worked on between November 1825 and November of the following year. Studies for Op. 130 are represented as follows: third movement, folio 7r; fifth movement, folio 1r; and sixth movement (the new finale), folios 52r, 59r and 60v–62r.[xlvi]

In the archives of the Beethoven House, Bonn are two bifolium sketches – double format pages – that reveal the close connections between the Op. 132 and Op. 130 Quartets. The Beethoven House text to these sketches reads: 'The first page contains score sketches for the third movement *Heiliger Dankgesang* from the String Quartet Op. 132. The remaining three pages (2–4) contain drafts for a movement in A major, which was actually intended as the final movement for Op. 132. We know it today in G major as the fourth movement *Alla danza tedesca* in the Quartet Op. 130.' The author of these remarks observes that Anton Schindler drew attention to these connections in his 1860 Biography of the composer.[xlvii] A second bifolium contains sketches for the new finale that Beethoven was urged to compose for the B flat Quartet after he was persuaded the *Grosse Fuge* was too overpowering.

We have said Beethoven did not make extensive use of score sketches until he began work on the late string quartets – from about 1822 onwards. We quote the following from the Beethoven House Digital Archives: 'Depending on how advanced the work on a composition was, the score sketches like these sometimes give the impression of being autograph scores. In "normal" sketches ideas and melodic lines are shown in one, or at most two systems. However, in his score sketches Beethoven set out the instruments underneath each other. In doing so the aim was not only to find the horizontal melodic line, but also to have an overview of the harmony and structure of the movement.'[xlviii] Thirty leaves of score sheets for the B flat Quartet have survived from the original

Artaria collections upon which Beethoven worked during his stay with his brother Johann in October-November 1826 on his estate at Gneixendorf. Six other such sheets derive from other origins. The various movements of Op. 130 are distributed throughout these sources.

Beethoven's Autograph Scores have become trophy items. That for the B-flat major String Quartet, Op. 130 has been dismembered and its various movements are now the cherished possession of various institutions: First movement: Biblioteka Jagiellońska, Kraków; Second movement: Library of Congress, Washington; Third Movement: Bibliothèque National, Paris; Fourth Movement: Moravian Museum, Institute of Music History, Brno; Fifth and Sixth Movements: Biblioteka, Jagiellońska, Kraków.[xlix]

We pause for a moment in our discussion of the creation origins of the B flat Quartet in order to make way for a selection of impressions of Beethoven left by his contemporaries from the period under consideration.

Gerhard von Breuning was the son of Beethoven's lifelong friend, Stephan von Breuning. Beethoven held a particular affection for Gerhard, whom he knew as a child, referring to him as 'Hosenknopf' – 'trouser button' – because he attached himself like a button to the composer's trousers. In the last two years of his life, Beethoven had rooms in the so-called *Schwarzspanierhause*. *Unlike many of Beethoven's other residences it has not survived being demolished in 1903–4.* Von Breuning is remembered in musicology today for his reflections on Beethoven in the title of which he adopted the name of *Schwarzspanierhause*. These were originally published in Vienna in 1874 under the title *Aus dem Schwarzspanierhause: Erinnerungen an L. van Beethoven aus meiner Jugendzeit*, known today in english translation as *Memories of Beethoven: From the house of the black-robed Spaniards*. This work has the authority of being one of only three book-length writings written by authors who knew Beethoven personally, the other two being the *Biographische Notizen über Ludwig van Beethoven – Remembering Beethoven: the biographical notes of Franz Wegeler and Ferdinand Ries* – and Anton Schindler's *Biographie von Ludwig van Beethoven – Beethoven as I new him.*

One day young Gerhard had been sent to call on Beethoven and recalls: 'I found him at his desk, facing the open door to the piano room, writing one of the last Galitzin quartets [Op. 130]. He looked up and told me to wait a bit until he had put his idea on paper. I was quiet for a while and then went over to the Graf piano [which incorporated an added amplifying apparatus].' Gerhard tells how he began to strum the keys, all the while looking to see if Beethoven had any awareness of the sound. When he saw Beethoven was completely unaware he played louder but Beethoven merely kept on writing 'unconcerned until finally he was finished and came out with me'.

Wilhelmine Schröder-Devrient was a young opera singer who, by all accounts, had a phenomenal voice – Beethoven once described it as being 'as big as the side of a house'! In 1821 she established her reputation in Vienna as a highly acclaimed dramatic artist in the role of Pamina in Mozart's *Die Zauberflöte*; she was just seventeen at the time. The following year she appeared to considerable acclaim as Agathe in Weber's *Der Freischütz* – earning warm praise from the composer himself. Later that year she took on the challenging role of Leonora in Beethoven's revised opera *Fidelio* that had not been performed for several years. Beethoven himself insisted on directing the dress rehearsal from which occasion Wilhelmine left the following account: 'Beethoven sat in the orchestra and waved his baton above the heads of us all, and I never had seen the man before. At that time the Master's physical ear already was deaf to all tone. With confusion written on his face, with more than earthly enthusiasm in his eye, swinging his baton to and fro with violent motions, he stood in the midst of the playing musicians and did not hear a single note.' She further describes how Beethoven's best efforts served merely to throw singers and orchestra into confusion and to put them entirely off beat, Beethoven all the while being unaware of the ensuing circumstances but apparently content with the rehearsal, 'for he laid down his baton with a happy smile'. Schröder-Devrient recalls it fell to the lot of the violinist-conductor Michael Umlauf to tactfully suggest he should take charge of the actual performances. This he subsequently did, Beethoven apparently being consigned to having to sit behind Umlauf — 'lost in profound meditation'[li]

In November 1822 Louis Schlösser made Beethoven's acquaintance. He was then a twenty-two year old musician residing in Vienna receiving instruction in composition from Salieri. Beethoven came to regard Schlösser 'as a young and talented artist' possessed of 'a cordial and friendly manner'. Years later Schlösser left an account of his first meeting with the composer. Although Beethoven scholars view Schlösser's recollections with some caution — he may have embroidered his accounts — if they are taken at face value they offer insights into the composer's living conditions and personal circumstances at the period when he was turning his mind to writing for the medium of the string quartet. Schlösser met Beethoven when he was then living in a relatively poor district of Vienna known as the *Wiedener* suburb. Schlösser describes Beethoven's apartment as being rather undecorated with a large, four-square oak table and various chairs presenting a somewhat untidy aspect. On the table lay books, pens, pencils, music-paper a metronome and an ear trumpet. In another room Schlösser noticed the Broadwood piano Beethoven had received a few years previously as a personal gift from the English piano maker John Broadwood. On its music rack rested a volume from the complete works of Handel that he had also received as a gift in recognition of his admiration for his works; towards the end of his life, Handel displaced Mozart as Beethoven's most respected composer. On entering the apartment, Schlösser found Beethoven preoccupied at his writing desk and he had to stamp with his feet to secure his attention. He writes of the composer's 'characteristic head' with its 'surrounding mane of heavy hair ... the furrowed brow of a thinker ... profoundly serious eyes ... [and] ... the amiably smiling expression'. Schlösser attempted to convers with the composer using his ear trumpet but Beethoven laid it aside complaining 'it agitated his nerves too greatly'. Conversation between the two continued by Schlösser writing his thoughts on paper — as by then had become Beethoven's custom. Schlösser records he left the composer feeling 'the day felt like a beautiful dream'.

On a subsequent occasion Beethoven favoured Schlösser with thoughts concerning his working method. He described his ideas as coming to him 'uninvited, directly or indirectly, such that he could almost grasp them in his hands ... when in the open woods ... during his promenades ... in the silence of the night ... tones ... that take shape for me as notes'. In composing he described how he made many changes, rejecting until he was satisfied adding: 'I am conscious of what I want, the basic idea never leaves me ... It rises, grows upward, and I hear and see the pictures as a whole take shape and stand forth before me as though cast in a single piece, so that all that is left to me is the work of writing it down.'[lii]

With these impressions of Beethoven in our mind, we

turn now to the circumstance of the first performance of the B-flat major Quartet.

From Thayer we learn 'there was a good deal of talk' at the start of 1826 concerning the performance of Beethoven's new string quartets. Ignaz Schuppanzigh's Quartet was then participating in the evening *Concerts spirituels* and in the string-quartet concerts that took place in the home of Ignaz Dembscher — a government official and keen music-lover. Having inherited a fortune he had the means to support music-making usually under the direction of the violinist Joseph Mayseder, with Dembscher himself playing the cello. On 6 March 1826 Beethoven's String Quartet Op. 127 was performed at Dembscher's where rehearsals of the String Quartet Op. 132 also took place.[liii]

The first performance of the B-flat major Quartet was on 21 March 1826. Schindler states: 'Every lover of quartets in Vienna was present to witness the first playing of this newest creation about which many strange things had already been said.'[liv] Beethoven himself was not present. According to Thayer he was feeling unwell and 'Schuppanzigh and his fellows [members of his Quartet] had taken the String Quartet Op. 130 in hand'.[lv] The second and fourth movements were so well received they had to be repeated. However the challenge, to both performers and audience, proved to be the concluding fugue. Cooper comments: '[The] finale, a massive fugue of 741 bars, was inevitably bewildering; for Beethoven, following his principle that difficulty and greatness are closely connected, seems to have set out to make the movement extremely taxing both to performers and listeners to comprehend.'[lvi] It disposed the music correspondent of the Leipzig *Allgemeine musikalische Zeitung* to write: 'But the critic does not dare to interpret the meaning behind the fugal finale: for him it was incomprehensible, like Chinese. When the instruments in the regions of the South and North Poles have to battle with immense difficulties, when one plays different motifs and the musical lines cross each other per transitum irregularem in a host of dissonances, when the players mistrust themselves, are not able to play properly in tune, I declare the Babylon-like confusion is then complete; then there is a concert which can only be enjoyed by the Moroccans.'[lvii] Anton Schindler, Beethoven's most ardent admirer, was disposed to remark: 'The reader may picture to himself from the words of this generally accurate reporter of public opinion the mood of the departing audience, for never has an instrumental work opposed such sharp contrasts to one another as this Quartet: the listener, after the most delighted enjoyment of clear skies above, is suddenly either shrouded in mysterious darkness or confronted with the utmost solemnity as if the composer intended to make a game of his emotions.'[lviii]

In more restrained manner, Thayer records the performers 'found the concluding fugue extremely troublesome' what he describes as 'a crux'. He continues: 'Some of Beethoven's friends argued that it had not been understood and that the objections would vanish with repeated hearings; others, plainly a majority, asked that a new movement be written to take its place.' Beethoven's brother Johann told the composer, exaggerating perhaps by way of encouragement, 'the whole city was delighted with the work'.[lix] At the close of the performance, Karl Holz wasted no time in searching out Beethoven who, as remarked, had not been present at the concert; he was waiting for a report of the unfolding events in a nearby tavern. Holtz drew attention to the warm reception of the *Presto* and *Alla danza tedesca* and how they had been encored. Beethoven appears to have been unimpressed, dismissing these movements as 'mere delicacies'. 'Why not the Fugue?' he snapped. When

Holtz conveyed the audience's response, it provoked Beethoven to the rejoinder: 'Cattle! Asses!'[lx]

Beethoven sent Prince Galitzin copies of the parts of the B flat Quartet sometime in January 1826 accompanied by a letter in French; the parts having been made by the composer's copyist Wenzel Rampl. The Prince also received a dedication copy of the Quartet as it was originally conceived with the majestic fugal ending.[lxi] The score of the Quartet was prepared later in August and was published the following year by Mathias Artaria in Vienna and Moritz Schlesinger in Paris. The Title page announced: 'Troisième / QUATOUR / pour deux Violons, Alto & Violoncelle, / des Quatuors / COMPOSÉ / et Dédié à Son Altelse Monseigneur le Prince / Nicolas de Galitzin / Lieutenant-Colonel de la Garde de S. m. Impériale de toutes les Russies, / PAR / L. VAN BEETHOVEN. / Qeuvre 130 Proprieté de l'Editeur / VIENNE / chez Math. Artaria.' [List number of Score 870, of Parts 871.][lxii]

The Schuppanzigh Quartet performed the Op. 130 for the second time on 22 April 1827 incorporating the composer's revised finale; Beethoven's death on 26 March deprived him of receiving any account of the work's reception. According to Schindler: 'The audience was happy to be persuaded that now the whole work was more comprehensible.' In its original form, however, the work continued to pose a challenge, as Schindler recalled in 1860 when he published his *Beethoven as I knew Him*: 'It is strange indeed that quartet players today are no longer more confident in their approach to this fearsome work than in 1827, and that all the quartet groups, even the Paris Quartet of Maurin and Chevillard, have always been most reluctant to attack this monster.' This assessment may though not be strictly accurate on Schindler's part as his editor Donald MacArdle points out: 'The Maurin-Chevillard Quartet can hardly be accused of avoiding the Quartet Op. 130. The *Société des Grands Derniers Quatuors de Beethoven* [J.P. Maurin, J.P. Sabtier, Louis Mas, Alexandre Chevillard] presented its first cycle (the last five quartets and the *Grosse Fuge*) in Paris between December 1852 and March 1853. They opened their first tour of the Rhineland on 7 December at Frankfurt with Op. 130; during their second tour through Germany in 1856 they performed Op. 130 five times, and later that season they performed it at least once in Paris. Before 1856 there had never been more than five performances of Op. 130 in any one year by all the quartets that were active in Europe.'[lxiii]

When he had assimilated the B flat Quartet, Holtz said to Beethoven it was the greatest of his quartets, to which he responded: 'Each in its way. Art demands of us that we shall not stand still. You will find a new manner of voice-treatment' [part-writing] and, thank God, there is less lack of fancy [pleasure in conventional music] than ever before.' These words disposed Marion Scott to enthuse: 'This is an admirable summary of a composition almost terrifying in its vitality and grandeur.'[lxiv]

An indication of the cautious progress the reception of the Op. 130 Quartet was making in France is conveyed in an account of a performance of the work in April 1849. The celebrated music critic Henri Blanchard, writing in the *Revue et Gazette musicales de Paris*, stated: 'The first movement is remarkable for the elaboration of strange harmonies, the long delay in the resolution of discords, and a consistent avoidance of the perfect cadence in concluding melodic phrases. It seems to point to an exhausted imaginative power, which is using every possible technical conceit and device of composition in default of fresh inspiration.' The work's other movements also failed to move the critic: 'The Fifth and Sixth movements especially (the *Cavatina* and the *Finale*) are full of these interrupted resolutions ...'. He did concede though 'they were lightened by flashes of brilliant melodic writing'. He reserved his scorn for the final movement: 'Beethoven's worn-out imagination in the finale ... makes one think of a tired swallow imprisoned in a fast-shut room, beating its wings wearily against the closed window.'[lxv]

An entry from the diary of Cosima Wagner sheds further light on the reception of the Op. 130 String Quartet and its demanding original fugal ending. On 15 February 1871 she wrote: 'Around four o'clock our musicians arrive; we start on the so-called *Grosse Fuge*, respectfully acknowledged that it can be interpreted correctly only by the greatest virtuosos and only after long study.' However, the attempt failed and the performance was abandoned. Instead the ensemble played through the Op. 130 Quartet with Beethoven's revised ending. This disposed Cosima to suggest to Wagner that the *scherzo* reminded her of Haydn and the finale of Mozart. To this he responded: "Yes, it is like with children, when we suddenly see unfulfilled volitions planted by Nature in our ancestors putting in an appearance, thus bringing to light the wonderful resemblances between succeeding generations; it is like that here."[lxvi] We offer other estimations of the B-flat major String Quartet, Op. 130 in connection with the work's individual movements to which we now direct our attention.

When Beethoven was planning the first movement of Op. 130, designated *Adagio ma non troppo – Allegro*, he wrote in his De Roda sketchbook 'last quartet with a serious and weighty introduction'.[lxvii] The Quartet does in fact open on a scale grander in conception than the slow introductions to the companion Galitzin Quartets Op. 127 and Op. 132. 'The first four bars, question and answer, seem to propound the subject for the whole vast work.'[lxviii] In Kinderman's words: 'One guiding factor in his labours was surely the thematic motto heard at the outset of the entire Quartet, in the *Adagio* tempo, which prefigures musical events in the work as a whole.'[lix] Stephen Rumph finds the manner in which the *Allegro* theme opens in double counterpoint has affinities with the opening of the Quartet Op. 127.[lx] Philip Radcliffe considers the movement's broad construction and economically wrought treatment look back to the composer's last piano sonata: 'It has some of the same feeling of intense concentration that Beethoven had achieved, on a smaller scale and in a more tragic mood, in the first movement of the Piano Sonata in C minor, Op. 111.'[lxi] On the occasion in 2005 when all of Beethoven's works were broadcast by the BBC, Alison Bullock wrote in her accompanying programme notes: 'The Quartet opens with a gentle adagio, mysterious at first but then opening out into a warm exchange of themes. When the *Allegro* breaks the atmosphere with its fast, furious semi-quavers, we hardly expect the slow introductory music to return, but that is exactly what happens shortly afterwards.'[lxii]

Commentators question if the movement is in strict sonata form[lxiii] or more-or-less sonata form with perhaps a hint in the introduction of a version of the Quartet's later fugue subject.[lxiv] Beethoven's craftsmanship here is much admired: '[The] themes are woven with exceptional clearness into their context and the movement needs a patient approach for its full beauty and profundity to be appreciated.'[lxv] '[The] first movement is an astonishing amalgam of slow introduction and a main allegro, the integration of the former continuing right through into the coda.'[lxvi] 'The development is one of the wonders of music in its sheer simplicity and the complexity which is always part of utter tranquillity. Beethoven here takes us step by step through his thought processes.'[lxvii] 'The brief development brings together, with relaxed casualness as it appears, the essential of all the main themes ... In this *dance of the blessed spirits* [italics added] the cadence figure murmurs as tirelessly as the brook in the *Pastoral* Symphony, while cello and violin pursue a dialogue of blissful levity.'[lxxviii] Basil Lam, whom we have just quoted, also considers the slow introduction to the first movement brings back the 'serene objectivity' of the Quartet Op. 127 after the intensity of Quartet Op. 132.[lxxix] Others remark on the movement's 'compact energy'[lxxx] and its 'spacious breadth'.[lxxxi] And to quote Bullock once more: '[It] is the juxtaposition of the two opening ideas, slow and fast, that form perhaps the most essential aspect of this movement.'[lxxxii] To Kinderman's ear the persistent alternation of slow and fast tempi imparts to the movement 'a capricious aspect'.[lxxxiii] The movement ends in a manner characteristic of Beethoven with 'a hushed *pianissimo* being swept aside at the last moment by a loud chord'.[lxxxiv]

The second movement — *Presto* — is a scherzo, although it is not described as such by the composer. Bullock is in no doubt: 'A minute but fully formed scherzo follows, quiet and playful.' [lxxxv] De Marliave elaborates: 'Although this movement is not so named, it is in reality a scherzo of the most robust type. Its brevity, its striking rhythm, and its concise four-and eight-bar form make it one of the most popular movements among the later quartets ... The combination of different elements invests it with a fantastic fairy charm, a sort of wild dance of elves.'[lxxxvi] Paul Bekker similarly finds the *Presto* '[possessed of] fantasy, sometimes dark, sometimes sunny.'[lxxxvii] Martin Cooper asks: 'In contrast to the opening, spacious, and sunny movement, is the *Presto* which follows a whispering, half-sinister scherzo in B-flat minor?[lxxxviii]

True to the spirit of a scherzo: '[it] is exceedingly deft in style and concise in form.'[lxxxix] Radcliffe pays tribute to Beethoven's skill in allowing art to conceal art: 'The whole movement is a masterpiece of imaginative understatement: its liveliness and rhythmic energy make a quick and ready appeal, but behind these are half-shades that are all the more impressive for being no more.' Radcliffe also believes the second movement of the Piano Sonata in A-flat major, Op. 110 and passages from the Bagatelle in B minor from Op. 126, foreshadow, to some extent, the mood of the *Presto* with the reservation that in these works it is more aggressive, whereas in the *Presto* 'it is more veiled and mysterious'.[xc] Lam goes back further in his conjectures bearing on precedents to be found in Beethoven's music that anticipate the *Presto* in the Op. 130 Quartet. He suggests it is necessary to look back to the F minor *Allegretto* of the Piano Sonata Op. 10, No. 1 that for him 'has the same quiet strength with, however, an undertone of pathos that could not survive for a moment the un-emphatic impact of the later piece'.[xci] Its *alla breve* tempo marking, 'with a minimum beat', ensures the movement 'passes in a flash [such that] one just has time to admire the interplay of the middle parts'.[xcii] Cooper asserts in the *Presto* Beethoven takes compression 'almost to the point of absurdity, with most of the sections consisting of four-bar phrases'.[xciii] Radcliffe considers the spirit of the *Presto* benefits from the contrast it has with its neighbouring movements: 'Apart from its intrinsic qualities, this movement is particularly effective in its context, coming between one of the largest and most elaborate of Beethoven's first movements on one side and a delightfully leisurely and discursive slow movement on the other.'[xciv]

The three middle-movement companions to the *Presto* are relatively short. The *Presto*, however, is the shortest but, notwithstanding, is not without complexity and corresponding technical difficulty: 'As always when Beethoven is being profound, the movement is based on the simplest possible idea — a section of falling scales answered by a rise.'[xcv] Radcliffe's observations are relevant here: '[The] *Presto* ... makes so quick and ready appeal that it may on first hearing seem slighter than it really is. Beethoven's immense capacity for building on a large scale has sometimes blinded his admirers to his equally great gift for saying much in a small space. In this movement, engagingly clear and simple in its themes, he has produced a fascinating miniature, with curious undercurrents of mystery and boisterousness.'[xcvi] The Trio in the movement is a showpiece for the first violin with its 'explosive chromatics',[xcvii] 'slow-motion glissando scales ... playful ornaments, octave leaps and trills' all of which 'add to the tension'.[xcviii] Little wonder the *Presto* was so heartily encored at the Quartet's first performance.

Commentators are fulsome in their praise for Beethoven here in the *Presto*, pronouncing it to be 'a masterpiece of pianissimo sound'[xcix] and 'a miraculous little movement'.[c] We give the last words in this context to the German Musicologist Michael Steinberg: 'It is a marvel of gentle humour, this movement *poco scherzoso* is exactly right, and in its moments of tenderness Beethoven pleads for *cantabile* and *dolce*. It is exceptionally rich in texture as well. Its exquisite, beautifully "heard" sounds — heard by a composer who in the literal, physical sense had heard nothing for ten years — are a feature that is exceptionally lovely and almost unbearably moving.' Steinberg continues: 'One's first reaction on hearing the music is to marvel that Beethoven created it at all.' He elaborates: 'But then you are confronted with the near incomprehensible miracle of the deaf Beethoven. Not only did his musical thought become more steadily, incredibly richer with the years, so did his fantasy for the physical details of sound. Not only did he compose more beautiful music for the string quartet and the piano the older he got;

the more beautifully, imaginatively, and effectively he composed string quartet and piano music.'[ci]

The third movement is headed *Andante con moto, ma non troppo* and takes the form of 'a long, wonderfully wrought *andante* in D flat, the texture presenting a tissue of melodies as smooth-pacing as Palestrina, as infinitely varied as Bach'.[cii] Its tempo is neither slow nor fast enabling it to move 'with a luxurious sense of time limitlessly available'.[ciii] Romain Rolland was one the earliest commenters to declare the *Andante* to be 'really a scherzo treated like an *andante* in form'.[civ] Cooper makes the same observation and elaborates: '[This movement] resembles a slow scherzo rather than a conventional slow movement, and the detailed filigree writing, closely woven texture and rococo richness of ornaments recall the second variation in the *Adagio* [in] Op. 127.'[cv] The character of the third movement disposed Lam to reflect on Beethoven's slow movements more generally, pointing out that after the Second Symphony they assume a new 'depth and variety' and 'a high seriousness whether elegiac, contemplative or lyrical'. Here, in the Op. 130, he likens the feeling of the music to a divertimento of which the tone is set by the two introductory bars that in a sketch Beethoven actually marked *Preludio*.[cvi] In the score these two bars are marked *poco scherzoso* – 'a little playfully-jokingly' – to which Radcliffe assigns them a feeling of playfulness rather than solemnity. He justifies this on the grounds that they keep the hearer in doubt 'until the last half-beat of the second bar, whether the music is in B-flat minor, the key of the preceding movement, or D-flat major; they also anticipate the main theme'.[cvii] For Bullock the *poco scherzando* expression mark is confirmation the *Andante* 'is not a slow movement proper'. She finds it in some ways comparable in spirit to the second movements of the Seventh and Eighth Symphonies – 'slightly ambiguous in mood and characterised by extreme rhythmic precision and imaginatively varied textures'.[cviii] In the estimation of Denis Matthews, the humour is more restrained than in what he describes as the first of the slow movements but, nonetheless, is 'packed with scherzando elements and full of mercurial textures'.[cix]

Robert Schumann described the third movement, in its remote key of D-flat major, as an *intermezzo*. Nicolas Slonimsky concurred, remarking: 'Harmonically, melodically, rhythmically, it is extraordinary, anticipating as it does the future development of Romantic music. There is drama in the uncertainty of key, in the shimmering use of tremolo, in the abrupt ending.'[cx] Notwithstanding these endearing features, Kinderman makes the case that the third movement 'is not easy going on first hearing'. He considers it to be 'a very elusive movement by reason of its closely woven texture and the variation-like unfolding of the melodic lines and their accompanying arabesques'. He calls to mind Wilhelm von Lenz, writing in his pioneering *Beethoven et ses trois styles*, that this is 'not so much a quartet as a discourse between four instruments'.[cxi] Paul Bekker considered the third movement to be possessed of 'fantasy' that is 'sometimes dark' and 'sometimes sunny'.[cxii] Rebecca Clarke, writing on the occasion of Beethoven's Death Centenary, found the composer evoking the sounds of nature: 'If ever Beethoven wrote music near to the sounds of nature it seems to me he has done it here; the innumerable gentle little phrases, so inconspicuous but so essential a part of the whole, the ever-changing moods, and the deep half-unconscious feeling pervading it all, make this movement unique in chamber music.'[cxiii] Joseph de Marliave regarded the *Andante* of the Op. 130 Quartet to be 'its most deeply inspired' by reason of 'its depth of fantasy, its whimsical blending of conflicting melodies, from gayest to the gravest, its ethereal yet firmly coherent construction built upon unified themes growing one out of another and making the movement a unique example of thematic variation'.[cxiv] For once Stravinsky was not curmudgeonly in his praise: 'If the *Cavatina* is the most tormented movement in the [late] quartets, then the *Andante* must be one of the most insouciant — in the manner of the *Allegretto* of the Eighth Symphony.'[cxv] Robert Hatten was content to describe the *Andante* as 'an unusual movement' whose expressive meaning 'can best be understood in terms of its relationship to the other movements in the Quartet ... and its many rhetorical shifts in level of discourse'.[cxvi]

The Andante has been much admired for its construction and musicological craftsmanship. 'A masterpiece of the 'finest jeweller's work (durchbrochene Arbeit) of the subtlest and most highly polished kind.'[cxvii] 'There is absolutely no end to what can be found in it, every smallest mark having such significance, and every note containing so much meaning.'[cxviii] 'The accompaniment, a fantastic delicacy, transforms the classical quartet into an instrument unknown to the sublunar inventiveness and scientific precision in the imagining of unheard sonorities.'[cxix] 'As for the main body of the movement, it offers such a spontaneous flow of musical notions, so perfectly disposed and so brilliantly scored, such an enchantment of intelligence and warmth and airy poise, that analytical formulations seem somehow helplessly beside the point ... The piece is also one of [Beethoven's] most imaginative in texture, polishing like an intricate cluster of diamonds the obbligato openwork that he had come upon earlier, in Variation 2 of the slow movement of Op. 127 and in the Neue Kraft sections of Op. 132.'[cxx] Truscott describes the music as 'an outpouring of harmonic counterpoint in a quasi-sonata style' for the reason 'it really never leaves a lyrical exploration of D-flat major, and no second key is ever established'.[cxxi] The movement ends 'with two highly exhilarating bars which have something of the exuberance of the Andante sections of the third movement of Op. 132, but in a more playful and light-hearted mood'.[cxxii]

Alla danza tedesca is how Beethoven designates the fourth movement. He had already used a version of this expression in the *presto* of the first movement of the Piano Sonata Op. 79, which is headed *presto alla tedesca*, and a few years earlier he incorporated a French variant of the terminology – *à l'Allemande* – in the set of Bagatelles of Op. 119. Steinberg elucidates: '*Alla danza tedesca* – in the manner of a German dance – is the sort of piece Mozart called a *treutsche*. It is quick, very quick – *Allegro assai*. It is also amiable, up to a point ... In humorous emulation of a wheeling hurdy-gurdy.'[cxxiii] Here in the Op. 130 String Quartet, Beethoven's meaning may be freely interpreted to indicate 'in the German style'.[cxxiv]

Barry Cooper reminds us of the fact that Beethoven wrote a considerable amount of music for dancing that captures the light and popular style of his early period with its 'strong but regular rhythms and simple harmonies'. He also remarks how this 'occasionally infiltrates his more serious music'. He cites, by way of illustration, the finale of the *Eroica* Symphony and the fourth movement of the String Quartet, Op. 130.[cxxv] In similar vein Radcliffe comments: 'In Beethoven's day the gulf between serious and popular music was far smaller than it is now, and even in as late a work as Op. 130 it was possible for him to introduce a movement described as a *alla danza tedesca* without the element of irony.'[cxxvi] Robert Simpson declares the spirit of the music here to be a 'masterpiece of German dance of quiet humour'.[cxxvii] Similarly, de Marliave describes it as 'a triumph of whimsical humour ... in the popular vein of the German dance form' whose motifs 'recall the unaffected simplicity of Haydn'.^{cxxviii} As the movement progresses, in Steinberg's words 'it covers a lot of harmonic territory' that for him also calls to mind the music of Haydn. He cites as a possible model the drinking chorus at the end of *Autumn* in Haydn's *The Seasons* with its 'unbuttoned rustic good humour'.^{cxxix}

Bearing in mind Beethoven initially planned the B-flat major Quartet to have the *Grosse Fuge* as its finale, Lam perceives the function of the fourth movement as acting as a necessary 'tonal division' placed in the centre of the Quartet. He imaginatively describes this as being 'like some geological fault in a range of hills'.^{cxxx} The movement is in effect the Quartet's second *scherzo*, as remarked, in the style of a German Ländler 'its air of rusticity enhanced by the pairing of instruments in octaves'.^{cxxxi} In Kinderman's estimation the incorporation of the *Alla danza tedesca*, as the fourth of the sixth movements of Op. 130, 'marked a decisive development in the genesis of the A minor and B-flat major quartets'. He reasons: 'To judge from the sketches, Beethoven may have remained undecided for several months about what movement would follow the great slow movement of Op. 132, the *Heiliger Dankgesang*.' We recall Beethoven composed this whilst residing at his summer lodgings at Baden in the summer of 1825, following his sustained period of illness beginning in mid-April. We let Kinderman continue the narrative: 'By July, Op. 132 was finished in the autograph, in a version with the *Alla danza tedesca* as fourth movement. Only in August did Beethoven settle on a six-movement plan for the following Quartet in B flat, in which the *Alla danza tedesca* found its new home.'^{cxxxii} Schindler gives expression to these thoughts in his *Biography* of the composer: 'Let me note in passing that the fourth movement, *Alla danza tedesca*, now in G major, was written in A major, and we still have the original manuscript.

It appears to have been composed as an integral part of another quartet, not improbably the A minor, the immediate predecessor of the B-flat major.'[cxxxiii]

For Kerman, the fascination of the fourth movement 'lies not in melody, shape, or texture ... but in details of the rhythmic figuration and dynamics'.[cxxxiv] Bekker is more succinct considering the *Alla danza tedesca* to be possessed of 'unclouded happiness'.[cxxxv]

In heading the fifth movement *Cavatina*, with the instruction to players for the music to be performed *Adagio molto espressivo*, Beethoven was intent to convey the piece is imbued with intense emotional feeling – 'its most eloquent witness'.[cxxxvi] It is cast in the manner of an operatic aria for four instruments – 'one of the noblest tunes ever conceived'.[cxxxvii] Beethoven had given expression to such feeling before in Florestan's *Andante* in his Opera *Fidelio*. Kerman finds a comparable level of feeling in Tamino's air *Dies Bildnis ist bezaubernd schön* in Mozart's *The Magic Flute*. He also cites Weber's contemporary use of the term *cavatina* in Agathe's soliloquy in *Der Freischütz*.[cxxxviii]

As typical of Beethoven, the surviving sketches provide a record of the movement's compositional evolution. Their extent bear testimony that its gestation was protracted. In 1825 Beethoven worked on an aria-like theme in the key of D flat and explored its potential until well into the following August. The theme was subsequently transposed to E flat and expanded into 'the broad, expansive melodic line' with which we are now familiar.[cxxxix] The sketches also reveal the music underwent 'several changes of key or metre' before being finished off only after the early sketches for the projected *Grosse Fuge* finale.[cxl] A further indication of the level of feeling Beethoven sought to enshrine in the movement is that within its sixty or so bars he indents some fifty-eight expression marks.[cxli]

The movement opens solemnly 'plunging the listener immediately into a highly-charged emotional atmosphere', one that is so possessed of chromatic alterations as to 'emphasize the pathos of what would otherwise by no more than another example of Beethoven's familiar hymn-like adagios'.[cxlii] A feeling of 'intense religious fervour' is felt.[cxliii] The French composer Arthur Honegger relates an interesting circumstance that suggests Beethoven's profound deafness and, thereby, his acute awareness of his own heartbeat, may have had a bearing on the rhythmic pulse he established for the *Cavatina*. Honegger recalls how by chance he found an old number of the journal *Die Musik* containing an article by the clinician Dr. J. Niemack that was devoted to Beethoven's loss of hearing. Niemack singled out for discussion the *Cavatina* from Op. 130 where the first violin declaims what Honegger describes as 'a strangely broken rhythm' — the melodic line that Beethoven marked 'anguished' (see later). Niemack asked: "Let a cardiologist hear this passage and ask if he knows the rhythm?" Niemack likened it to the sound of the human heart. As remarked, given that Beethoven's deafness had rendered him more sensitive to the sound of his heartbeats, Niemack suggested musicologists "might take this into consideration when evaluating the passage in question".[cxliv] Chua believes the music bears testimony to other considerations personal to the composer. He considers the *Cavatina* can be listened to with the same respect with which one reads an intimate letter. He justifies this on the grounds: 'Beethoven brought into the Quartet the privacy and purity of domestic life — the very life that he himself longed for, and the space which chamber music was increasingly confined to'. Chua reasons that it is therefore not so fanciful 'for some commentators to regard this movement as a window into Beethoven's innermost emotions, almost too private to be disclosed'. He concludes: 'It is a fleeting autobiographical intrusion — a sudden need to speak in prose within song.'[cxlv] Scott avers: 'It was one of his supreme inspirations; it must speak to each man according to his understanding.'[cxlvi]

Amidst these plaudits a dissentient point of view must be allowed its place. Whilst Igor Stravinsky acknowledged the B-flat major String Quartet, Op. 130 to be 'the most radical' of the late Quartets and 'the most modern sounding', he distanced himself from the adulation bestowed on the *Cavatina* by others: 'I do not find its melodic-harmonic substance especially distinguished, and the treatment attenuates it ... the piece is handicapped in the first place ... by offering too extreme a contrast to the preceding *Andante*.'[cxlvii] In his rebuttal, Kerman responded: 'Beethoven's wish, in transcribing for quartet an unwritten opera song, must have been to make the most immediate kind of emotional overture. In the eyes of his essential public, then or now, I do not think it can be said that he failed.'[cxlviii]

Authorities comment on the inherent simplicity of Beethoven's construction and the relative brevity of the *Cavatina*; it has a performing time of just over six minutes compared with some fifteen minutes for the slow movements of the String Quartets Op. 127 and Op. 132. Notwithstanding, the compressed timescale — the movement extends for a mere sixty-six bars — Steinberg draws attention to the 'direct emotional force' of the music and its 'complex texture'. As regards melody, he likens the role of the first violin to that of the principal singer in an opera. However, in acknowledgement of Beethoven's compositional resourcefulness, he adds 'at no point, were the song to break off, could we foretell its continuation, for all that whatever does come always sounds like the inevitable way'.[cxlix] Kerman also likens the role of the first violin to that of a singer 'while the other instruments play the orchestra'.[d] 'The tune grows by natural extensions and repetitions which do not sound contrived but are part of the general flow and shape of the melodic line.'[cli] Barry Cooper considers the *Cavatina* to be unique in Beethoven's quartet writing in the manner in which he 'maintains a single texture so consistently ... the melody so skilfully crafted and thoroughly sketched, with subtle irregularities of phrase structure'. He also likens the violin writing to that suited to a solo singer that he observes 'even keeps within the range of the mezzo-soprano voice' and which, at its most anguished, 'is interspersed with little rests or sighs, as if the singer is gasping for breath'.[clii]

We recall how important Carl Holtz had become at this period in Beethoven's life and it is from him we learn how much the *Cavatina* meant to the composer. He alleges Beethoven confided in him how he had composed the music 'in tears of melancholy' and confessed 'his own music never had such an effect on him before, and that even thinking back to that piece cost him fresh tears'.[cliii] A measure of the extent the movement meant to Beethoven, and his absorption in it, is indicated by his incorporation of the expression mark *Beklemmt* – 'agonized ... heavy at the heart, oppressed' (*Dictionary of Music and Musicians*). This occurs in the middle section of the movement 'where it modulates into C flat and where the choked and broken accents of the first violin fully bear out the expression'. Commenting on this, Maynard Solomon, from whom we have just quoted, movingly adds: 'In the penultimate movement of the B-flat major String Quartet, [Beethoven] openly permitted himself to acknowledge music's power to represent depths of suffering and fear. The ... section of the *Cavatina*, marked by Beethoven *Beklemmt*, plunges into darkness, melancholia, and dread and carrying an almost tangibly oppressive physicality, Beethoven poses the most difficult questions – how to endure pain of this intensity, how to awaken from a burdensome nightmare, how to breathe freely again.'[cliv] In this same spirit, Lam considered the Cavatina 'speaks with the accents of King Lear'.[clv]

Radcliffe considers the overall impression created by the *Cavatina* has similarities to the first movement of the Piano Sonata Op. 101 in its 'unbroken continuity' and of hardly any 'conscious formal landmarks'. He also endorses the view of Vincent d'Indy that when the movement adopts 'subtle variations of melody' it reveals affinities with the *Adagio* of the Ninth Symphony: 'Not only is there the same feeling of what might be called *serene intensity* [italics added] but also a similarity in the cadences and in the way in which they are echoed.'[clvi] Lam also considered the *cavatina*-like theme in the slow movement of the Ninth Symphony and the *Arioso dolente* passage in the Piano Sonata Op. 110 represent 'a kind of personal utterance'. He makes the generalisation: '[The] greatest masters do not yearn, and the whole of this most moving of *Adagios* is characterised by a noble restraint looking back to the world of Bach rather than forward to the emotional excesses of self-enjoying Romantic sorrow.' He emphasises: 'Beethoven's griefs were real and devastating and are not fit subjects for public discussion.'[clvii] In the same spirit Matthews regarded the *Cavatina* as being 'an even more personal, confiding and consoling document' than the *Lydian Hymn* of the String Quartet Op. 132.[clviii] To cite Barry Cooper once more, he believes the *Cavatina's* 'deeply anguished lyricism' belongs to the same highly emotional sound world of the slow movement of the *Hammerklavier* Piano Sonata that Beethoven marked *Appassionato e con molto sentiment*.[clix] In his admiration for this serene music, Simpson was of the opinion that in the *Cavatina* Beethoven had achieved 'the impossible' by surpassing the feeling embodied in the slow movement of the Violin Sonata, No. 10 in G major, Op. 96 and that of the Piano Trio in B-flat major, Op. 97.[clx]

An anecdote from the *Autobiography* of Bruno Walter bears testimony to the capacity the *Cavatina* has to reach out to our innermost feelings. Walter once attended a quartet recital led by the celebrated violinist Joseph Joachim. He writes: 'He was an aged man, and his hand and intonation were no longer reliable. But his simplicity, greatness, and ultimate maturity made a deep indelible impression on me. His sublime absorption at singing phrases, as for instance at the *Cavatina* of Beethoven's B-flat major Quartet, touched my very soul.' It clearly made a lasting impression since he confided: 'It has been a model to me throughout my life.'[clxi] Writing on the occasion when the BBC performed all of Beethoven's compositions within a single week, Alison Bullock, in her contribution to the programmes devoted to the composer's string quartets, stated: 'The *Cavatina* is one of Beethoven's greatest slow movements, a deeply-felt work of internalised emotion. Whether it is an expression of sorrow or joy may be up to the listener to decide.'[clxii] We give the final words to Phillip Radcliffe: Of the overwhelming depth of the *Cavatina* there have never been two opinions, but ... writers have reacted to it in different ways; some have felt it to be a profoundly tragic piece of music, while others have stressed its religious fervour. Perhaps, in the long run, the most satisfying description can be found in the simple words of d'Indy: "A masterpiece of melody".'[clxiii]

Beethoven originally concluded the B-flat major String Quartet, Op. 130 with an extended fugal movement, often performed today as a separate work as Op. 133 with the designation *Grosse Fuge* or *Great Fugue*. We concern ourselves here with the so-called 'revised finale', a rondo set in *allegro* time. First, however, we recall the circumstances that gave rise to Beethoven providing the Quartet's alternative ending.

We have seen that first performance of Op. 132 took place on 21 March 1826 with its original fugal ending. Thayer writes: 'The doubts about the effectiveness of the fugue, felt by Beethoven's friends, found an echo in the opinion of the critics.[clxiv] Even Anton Schindler, Beethoven's most ardent admirer, felt disposed to respond: 'This composition seems to be an anachronism. It should belong to that grey future when the relationship of notes will be determined by mathematical computation. Unquestionably such combinations must be regarded as the extreme limit of speculative intellect, and its effect will always remain one of Babelic confusion. We cannot speak here of darkness in contrast to light.'[clxv]

Despite the fact that the engraved proofs for the Quartet containing the fugal ending were well advanced,[clxvi] Matthias Artaria, who had secured the publication rights for the composition, had doubts about its potential commercial success; we recall he had paid 80 ducats for the work — a considerable sum. He was also apprehensive about the technical difficulties and abstruseness presented by the fugue and felt that a substitute finale, of a lighter kind, was required. Artaria, fearful of incurring Beethoven's wrath at the very idea of requesting that Beethoven should modify his work in such a manner, asked Carl Holz to mediate on his behalf. According to Holtz's account: '[Artaria] charged me with the terrible and difficult mission of convincing Beethoven to compose a new finale, which would be more accessible to the listeners as well as the instrumentalists.' Holtz duly found the courage to suggest to Beethoven that his fugue so departed from the ordinary, and surpassed anything of its kind in the companion quartets in originality, that it should be published as a separate work and thereby would merit its own designation with a separate opus.[clxvii] As an incentive, Holtz held out the prospect that Artaria was prepared to offer the composer a supplementary honorarium for a new finale. Perhaps to his surprise, and relief, Holtz relates that Beethoven said he would reflect on the proposal. Evidently he quickly did so and sent a letter to Holtz giving his consent.[clxviii]

When Artaria made his request for a new finale, Beethoven was already at work on the String Quartet in F major, Op. 135. Thereafter he set about work on the requested replacement finale with his customary diligence — it would in fact be his last completed work. Writing of Beethoven's readiness to comply with Artaria's request, Barry Cooper observes: 'Naturally [Beethoven] expected to be paid extra for the new movement, but the decision to write it must have been made on aesthetic grounds: he would never have compromised his artistic integrity for the sake of a few ducats; nor would he have composed a simpler movement merely because of perceived technical difficulties, or to placate a few friends.'[clxix] Griffiths expresses similar thoughts with a touch of his typical imagery: 'The alternative finale ... is no mere concession on Beethoven's part to the anxiety of his publisher, the weakness of his executants and the puzzlement of the public: rather it makes possible for the work to present a quite different face, the six movements now to be understood as equal planets in the same solar system, not as five satellites around a massive finale.'[clxx] Of Beethoven's obligingness to contribute a new movement Kerman states: 'His decision has been deplored; even his motives have been questioned. But Beethoven must have understood that the world he had pronounced unready for Mozart's Quartet in A major, K. 464, was hardly ready for the *Grosse Fuge*, even twenty years later — even after twenty years of Beethoven.'[clxxi] In Beethoven's defence, Simpson proposes: '[It] is possible the thought of providing another ending to the Quartet, totally different, was something of a challenge to his imagination ... A humorous ending to this compendious Quartet is, as he proved, not impossible or inapt, but there can be no doubt that such a conclusion cannot integrate the whole as comprehensively as the fugue; vast issues may be hinted at, or dismissed, by a joke, but they cannot be exhausted.' That said, Simpson concludes: '[We] must not decry this marvellous and by no means small movement; it was the last thing Beethoven wrote and in its way just as much a triumph over adversity as the *Grosse Fuge* itself.'[clxxii]

Beethoven worked on the new finale whilst he as residing at the house of his younger brother Johann; he stayed with him from September to December 1826. At this time Tobias Haslinger, an art and music dealer and occasional composer, rendered many services to his distinguished friend, in effect acting as his intermediary. With the new movement finished, Beethoven wrote to Haslinger on 11 November: 'Now I have a request to make. A small parcel for Herr Matthias Artaria is being sent to your address. As soon as the parcel arrives, please let him know that the parcel is with you. But you must give it to him only against a payment of 15 gold ducats ... I have written to him on the same lines.'[clxxiii] Artaria was prompt in his response and duly sent the requested 15 ducats to Beethoven on 25 November.[clxxiv] De Marliave recounts these circumstances in his characteristic fulsome manner: 'It was during the days of suffering at Gneixendorf that Beethoven conceived the movement in its final form, radiant with gaiety and wit.'[clxxv] Thayer records that in December, Ignaz Schuppanzigh's Quartet gave a private performance of the piece and later informed Beethoven how the company 'thought it exquisite (*köstlich*) and that Artaria was overjoyed when he heard it'.[clxxvi]

The revised final movement is shorter than the fugal

ending being some 493 bars long compared with the original 741. That said, the finale *Allegro* is not a slight piece; it has a performing time approaching that of the opening movement. Beethoven composed the alternative finale after he had written the C sharp minor Quartet, Op. 131 and the F major Quartet, Op. 135. He was therefore even more experienced in writing for the genre of the string quartet, of extending its boundaries, and of exploring its possibilities. With this in mind, some regard the closing *Allegro* as having more of connection with the F major Quartet, that is of being part of a *new* phase of creative development — that Beethoven did not live to realise — rather than being the culmination of his so-called third period.'[clxxvii]

De Marliave likens the two opening viola bars to 'a guitar-like accompaniment' that draw an immediate response from the first violin waiting to declaim the principal theme 'like a ripple of laughter'.[clxxviii] The character of the music is thereby established, although with typical Beethovenian cunning. He exploits the same G with which the *Grosse Fuge* opens but, as Cooper observes, 'it is much lighter in texture ... smaller in scale and optimistic in character'.[clxxix] John Daverio is convinced Beethoven's exploitation of G is no mere fleeting reminiscence of the discarded original ending: 'Beethoven's last completed movement includes many echoes of its earlier counterpart; the opening Gs in the viola ironically recall the emphatic initial gesture of the *Grosse Fuge*.' He elaborates his musicological analysis: '[The movement's] finely wrought *obbligato* textures answer to the gritty counterpoint of the original finale; the A-flat major episode prefacing its development corresponds to the first stages of the *Allegro molto con brio* of the *Grosse Fuge*; and finally, the closing phrases of the episode (mm. 132–40) brings a motivic relative of the four-note cell that runs through the *Grosse Fuge* and many of the other late quartets.'[clxxx] Kinderman describes the movement as 'gay and exuberant' and 'a final challenge to the grim *Intruder*' – a poignant reminder that this was the last composition that came from Beethoven's pen.[clxxxi] Rebecca Clarke's words have particular relevance here: '[In] the last months of his life [he] wrote a new last movement so full of buoyancy and humour that it is difficult to believe it could have been written by a man already stricken with a fatal illness.'[clxxxii]

Electra Yourke suggests the replacement finale to the B-flat major Quartet could well have a lower opus number, as with the *Alla danza tedesca* movement. She perceives perceives the music as being 'a rustic dance in 2/4 time'.[clxxxiii] In this respect she is not alone. In his *Biography* of the composer, Anton Schindler writes: 'Those diligent folk who pride themselves on their ability to distinguish Beethoven's various styles would surely come to grief over this movement if the time and conditions of its composition were known, for is not this finale similar in style and clarity to many of the quartet movements of an earlier period?' However, Schindler acknowledges that in the late quartets 'one meets ... the deepest depths of obscurity right next to the brightest light of clarity'.[clxxxiv] Solomon, discussing Beethoven's work on the F-major Quartet Op. 135 and the new finale for the B-flat major Quartet Op. 130 remarks, 'they reflect a tranquil and confident return to a happier, Haydnesque play world'. More reflectively he gives expression to one of his characteristic philosophical generalisations: 'In the substitute finale Beethoven moves directly from the torment-ridden *Cavatina* to a pastoral celebration of life's simple gifts. The return to nature is achieved without much struggle. Paradise is gained (or regained) by a quick stroke ... Whereas the *Grosse Fuge* is learned and encyclopaedic, the rondo is a Haydnesque romp, illustrating that healing can be effected either by way of wisdom or by way of innocence. Both are authentic versions of the dialectic of suffering and healing that is central to Beethoven's creative project.'[clxxxv]

Yourke identifies the concluding music of the B-flat major Quartet to be typical of his first style, 'imaginative, brilliant, with episodic ideas constantly brought into play'. In her estimation: 'In his third period, Beethoven had not relinquished the youthfulness, vigour, and simplicity of the first'.[clxxxvi] This reversion by Beethoven to his earlier style of composition has disposed some commentators to the view that the alternative movement is more easy-going and technically less demanding than the *Grosse Fuge* it replaced. Truscott, for one, rejects this reading of the music for reasons that it also poses considerable technical challenges to the performer. He maintains: 'It is superficially easier to listen to and understand than the fugue, but only superficially. It is quite as subtle as its opposite number, and I believe it to be even more so.' Truscott even confers on this smaller-scale movement the status of being 'the most complex tonal design in the whole of the late quartets'.[clxxxvii] Radcliffe accepts that beside what he describes as 'the Olympian striving and monumental structure of the *Grosse Fuge*' the revised finale may seem insignificant'. But he too defends the piece: 'The second finale has not the lyrical grace of the last movement of Op. 127 nor the passionate sweep of that of Op. 132, and on first acquaintance at least it may leave a rather impersonal impression. But, as in the decidedly similar finale to the *Archduke Trio*, a superficially flippant exterior conceals much that is highly characteristic and imaginative and with all its sonority it is superbly written for its medium.'[clxxxviii]

We take leave of the String Quartet in B-flat major, Op. 130 with a selection of reflections on its final movement and Beethoven's achievement.

'It was to contain the very consummation of Beethoven's genius, for the Master's inspiration rises triumphant above the plane of bodily anguish; knowing nothing of sorrow and suffering, this new finale breathes an unclouded serenity and joy from the first to the last bar.'

Joseph de Marliave, *Beethoven's Quartets,* 1925 (reprint 1961), p. 257.

'We are faced then with a dilemma. On the one hand the *Grosse Fuge*, coming at the end of the Quartet, almost annihilates not only the listener, but his experience of what has gone before. On the one hand the new finale seems to have been written by a composer so different from the man who wrote the foregoing movements that it leaves sense of inconsequence and almost of deprivation ... As a replacement for the Cyclopean masonry of the *Grosse Fuge* the effect [of the revised movement] is as incongruous as that of a Baroque chapel attached to a Romanesque cathedral'.

Martin Cooper, *Beethoven: the last decade*, 1817–1827, 1970, p. 390.

'There are no "Inevitable" solutions of the problems of order and sequence in even the greatest compositions. To praise a work for its *inevitability* [italics added] is to express enthusiasm for its combination of beauty and power, but the composer's free will is never compromised and he is bound only by his own discrimination ... Op. 130

must be considered as a work planned to end with a vast fugue, but the existence of the second finale is proof that Beethoven regarded a different conclusion as aesthetically valid.'

Basil Lam, *Beethoven String Quartets*, 1975, p. 107.

'Beethoven must have originally believed that he had accomplished [a too powerful effect] in the enormous coda of the *Fugue*, with its dance-like *Siegessymphonie* and its feeling of sunshine after storm. Evidently, however, the reverberation of pain and strife had not yet sufficiently died away, let alone been fully dissipated. And so he may have decided that the work required a catharsis, a return to normality, an epilogue in full daylight, a simple descent to earth, a reversion to Classicism such as we find in the [new] *Allegro finale*.'

Maynard Solomon, *Beethoven*, 1977, p. 323.

'[So] far as dimensions are concerned there can be no suggestion of its being inadequate as a finale to Op. 130. But the ultimate choice between this movement and the *Grosse Fuge* is bound to depend not only on the intrinsic merits of the two compositions, but the more elusive question: is the sublime *Cavatina* best followed by the high spirits of the one or the extreme complexity of the other?'

Philip Radcliffe, *Beethoven's String Quartets*, 1978, p. 136.

'This movement was the last piece that Beethoven completed, and it is music of consummate grace,

> robust humour, warmth, and, in all modesty, fullness of invention.'

Michael Steinberg, *The Late Quartets*, in: Robert Winter and Robert Martin editors, *The Beethoven Quartet Companion*, 1994, p. 244.

> 'Which of the two finales is a better movement, or a better conclusion to Op. 130, is a matter on which critics will no doubt continue to disagree. But now that the *Grosse Fuge* can be seen as something of an intrusion into the Quartet, rather than the germ from which the work sprang, Beethoven's decision to replace it with a different movement, more in line with the others and with the finale he had intended while writing them, must seem entirely justified.'

Barry Cooper, *Beethoven and the Creative Process*, 1990, p. 214.

> 'Beethoven must have realized that the *Grosse Fugue* threatened to upset the balance of power in the B-flat major Quartet, dwarfing what had gone before — even the profoundly moving *Cavatina* that precedes it — through its sheer size and intensity. His replacement of the *Grosse Fuge* with a new finale demonstrates a genuine concern for proportion — and also for generic propriety.'

John Daverio, *Manner, Tone, and Tendency in Beethoven's Chamber Music for Strings* in: Glenn Stanley editor, *The Cambridge Companion to Beethoven*, 2000, pp. 162–3.

---

[i] See, for example, Joseph Kerman, 1967, pp. 322–3. Kerman writes: 'That something new was in the wind ... may so be indicated by a slightly earlier composition ... The Six Bagatelles for Piano, Op. 126 of 1824, show signs of cyclic unification on some level.'

[ii] William Kinderman editor, 2005, p. 51.

iii Joseph Kerman, 1967, p. 303.
iv Electra Slonimsky Yourke, editor, *Nicolas Slonimsky: Writings on music*, 4 Vols. 2003–2005, p. 164.
v Barry Cooper, 1991, p. 283.
vi Maynard Solomon, 1977, pp. 319–20. Solomon considered the B flat Quartet to be 'the most enigmatic' of the late quartets (p. 322).
vii Anton Felix Schindler, *Beethoven as I knew him*, edited by Donald W. MacArdle and translated by Constance S. Jolly from the German edition of 1860, 1966, p. 307.
viii Tully Potter, in: Robin Stowell editor, *The Cambridge companion to the string quartet*, 2003, pp. 43–4.
ix Barry Cooper, 1990, p. 197.
x Igor Stravinsky, 1972, p. 259.
xi William Kinderman, editor, 2005, p. 53–4.
xii Denis Matthews, 1985, p. 142.
xiii Barry Cooper, 2000, p. 331.
xiv Harold Truscott, 1968, p. 83.
xv David Wyn Jones, *Beethoven and the Viennese legacy*, in: Robin Stowell, editor *The Cambridge companion to the string quartet*, 2003, pp. 224–5.
xvi Daniel K. L. Chua, 1995, p. 163.
xvii Harold Truscott, 1968, p. 93.
xviii Emily Anderson, editor and translator, 1961, Vol. 3, Letter No. 1354, pp. 1180–1.
xix Theodore Albrecht, editor and editor, 1996, Vol. 3, Letter No. 405, pp. 95–6. Beethoven's letter to Galitzin, bearing news of the progress he was making with the String Quartets Opp. 132 and 130, is now thought to be lost.
xx Anton Schindler, 1860, English edition: Donald MacArdle, 1966, p. 300, p. 354 and endnote 230. See also our accompanying text *The Galitzin Quartets*. Neate made Beethoven's acquaintance on a visit to Vienna in 1815–16. On his return to England he took with him, on behalf of the (Royal) Philharmonic Society, the three Concert Overtures *Die Ruinen von Athen, König Stephan* and *Zur Namensfier* for which the composer received the fee of 75 guineas. Beethoven got on well with Neate and described him to friends as 'an excellent musician and a charming man'.
xxi Emily Anderson, editor and translator, 1961, Vol. 3, Letter No. 1378, p. 1201. For a facsimile reproduction of this letter see: Beethoven House, Digital Archives, Document H. C. Bodmer, HCB Br 179.
xxii Emily Anderson, editor and translator, Vol. 3, Letter No.1403, pp. 1222–3. For a facsimile reproduction of this letter, together with an audio commentary, see: Beethoven House, Digital Archives, Document H. C. Bodmer HCB BBr 213.
xxiii Emily Anderson, editor and translator, 1961, Vol. 3, Letter No. 1405, pp. 1224–6.
xxiv *Ibid*, Vol. 3, Letter No. 1415, pp. 1236–7.
xxv *Ibid*, Vol. 3, Letter No. 1416, pp. 1237– 8. For a facsimile reproduction of this letter see: Beethoven House, Digital Archives, Document BH 29. For a discussion of related contextual matters, see also: Elliot Forbes, editor, Thayer's life of Beethoven, 1967, 2000, p. 970.
xxvi Barry Cooper, 2000, pp. 334–5.
xxvii Theodore Albrecht, editor and translator, 1996, Vol. 3 Letter No.417, pp.

[xvii] 114–5.
[xviii] Beethoven House, Digital Archives, Document NE 164. The text of the letter is written in French by another hand, and signed by Beethoven.
[xix] For an account of Carl Peters and his negotiations with Beethoven see Peter Clive, 2001, p. 260.
[xx] Theodore Albrecht, editor and translator, 1996, Vol. 2, Letter No. 286, pp. 204–6.
[xxi] Emily Anderson, editor and translator, Vol. 2, Letter No. 1079, pp. 947–50, 1961.
[xxii] Theodore Albrecht, editor and translator, 1996, Vol. 2 Letter No. 290, pp. 211–14.
[xxiii] *Ibid*, 1996, Vol. 3 Letter No. 413, pp. 107–8.
[xxiv] *Ibid*, 1996, Vol. 3 Letter No. 420, pp. 118–9. See also the audio letter, text and facsimile in Beethoven House, Digital Archives, Library Document H. C. Bodmer, HCB BBr 42.
[xxv] Elliot Forbes, editor, *Thayer's life of Beethoven*, 1967, Chapter XXXVIII.
[xxvi] Barry Cooper, 2000, pp. 337–8.
[xxvii] *Ibid*, See also: Elliot Forbes editor, *Thayer's life of Beethoven*, 1967, p. 970.
[xxviii] The first of the Galitzin Quartets, Op. 127, appeared in June 1826. The third of the Quartets, Op. 130 in B flat, did not appear until May 1827. The fact that it did appear before the second Quartet, Op. 132 in A minor, which Schlesinger did not publish until September 1827, accounts for its having received the earlier opus number.
[xxix] Emily Anderson, editor and translator, 1961, Vol. 3, Letter No. 1481, pp. 1283–4.
[xl] Theodore Albrecht, editor and translator, 1996, Vol. 3 Letter No. 458, pp. 176–7. For a facsimile reproduction of this letter see: Beethoven House, Digital Archives, H. C. Bodmer, HCB Br 289.
[xli] Barry Cooper, 2000, p. 330.
[xlii] Edward T. Cone, editor, *Roger Sessions on music: collected essays*, 1979, pp. 52–3.
[xliii] Robert Hatten, *Plenitude as fulfilment*, in: William Kinderman editor' *The string quartets of Beethoven*, 2005, p. 215.
[xliv] For a facsimile reproduction of the De Roda sketchbook see: Beethoven House, Digital Archives, Library Document, NE 47a
[xlv] For a facsimile reproduction of a bifolium for the Moscow sketchbook, see: Beethoven House, Digital Archives, H. C.Bodmer, HCB BSk 19/67.
[xlvi] With acknowledgment to: Douglas Porter Johnson, editor, 1985, pp. 471–4 and William Kinderman editor, 2005, p. 327.
[xlvii] Beethoven House, Digital Archives, Library Document, Sammlung Wegeler, W 4.
[xlviii] Beethoven House, Digital Archives, Library Document, BH 113.
[xlix] In addition to the sources identified in the main text, the following have also been consulted: Douglas Porter Johnson, editor, *The Beethoven sketchbooks: history, reconstruction, inventory*, 1985, p. 73, p. 313, pp. 309–10, pp. 424–5, 426–9, pp. 430–1, 436–7, pp. 453–7, and pp. 453–7; Richard Kramer, in: Christoph Wolff and Robert Riggs, *The string quartets of Haydn, Mozart and Beethoven: studies of the autograph manuscripts: a conference at Isham Memorial Library, March 15–17*, 1979, pp. 234–5;

Barry Cooper, *Planning the later movements: Stages in the creative process*, in: *Beethoven and the creative process*, 1990; *The Beethoven compendium: a guide to Beethoven's life and music*, 1991; and *Beethoven: The master musicians series*, 2000. Joseph Kerman, *The Beethoven quartets*, 1967 and Joseph Kerman Beethoven Sketchbooks in the British Museum, *Proceedings of the Royal Musical Association*, 93rd Sess. (1966 - 1967), pp. 77–96; William Kinderman editor, *The string quartets of Beethoven*, 2005, pp. 328–9.

[i] Gerhard von Breuning, *Memories of Beethoven: from the house of the black-robed Spaniards*, 1874, reprinted and edited by Maynard Solomon, 1992, p. 72.

[ii] Derived from Oscar George Theodore Sonneck, 1927, pp. 129–30. See also: Peter Clive, 2001, pp. 325–6 and p. 374.

[iii] Derived from Oscar George Theodore Sonneck, *Beethoven: impressions of contemporaries*, 1927, pp. 132–48.

[iiii] Peter Clive, 2001, pp. 86–7 and pp. 231–2.

[iv] Anton Felix Schindler, *Beethoven as I knew him*, edited by Donald W. MacArdle and translated by Constance S. Jolly from the German edition of 1860, 1966, p. 307.

[v] Elliot Forbes editor, *Thayer's life of Beethoven*, 1967, pp. 975–6.

[vi] Barry Cooper, 2000, p. 337.

[vii] Beethoven House, Digital Archives, Library Documents, H. C. Bodmer, HCB Mh 104.

[viii] Anton Felix Schindler, *Beethoven as I knew him*, edited by Donald W. MacArdle and translated by Constance S. Jolly from the German edition of 1860, 1966, p. 307.

[ix] Elliot Forbes editor, *Thayer's life of Beethoven*, 1967, pp. 975–6.

[x] This anecdote is recalled by many commentators. See, for example, Maynard Solomon, 1977, pp. 322–3.

[xi] Beethoven House, Digital Archives, Library Document, BH 90.

[xii] Beethoven House, Digital Archives, Library Document, C 130/10. See the same source for facsimile representations of other early editions.

[xiii] Anton Felix Schindler, *Beethoven as I knew him*, edited by Donald W. MacArdle and translated by Constance S. Jolly from the German edition of 1860, 1966, pp. 355–6 and endnote 240.

[xiv] Marion M. Scott, 1940, 269.

[xv] Quoted in Joseph de Marliave, 1925 (reprint 1961), pp. 230–1.

[xvi] Gregor-Dellin and Dietrich Mack, editors, *Cosima Wagner's diaries: Vol. 1, 1869 - 1877*, pp. 337–8.

[xvii] William Kinderman, 1997, p. 295.

[xviii] Martin Cooper, 1970, p. 371.

[xix] William Kinderman, 1997, p. 295.

[xx] Stephen C. Rumph, 2004, p. 141.

[xxi] Philip Radcliffe, 1978, pp. 123–4.

[xxii] Alison Bullock, *Notes to the BBC Radio Three Beethoven experience*, Friday 10 June 2005, www.bbc.co.uk/radio3/Beethoven

[xxiii] Electra Slonimsky Yourke editor, *Nicolas Slonimsky: writings on music*, 4 Vols. 2003–2005, p. 164.

[xxiv] Marion Scott, 1940, p. 269.

[xxv] Philip Radcliffe, 1978, pp. 126–7.

[xxvi] Denis Matthews, 1985, p. 142.

lxxvii Harold Truscott, 1968, p. 86.
lxxviii Basil Lam, 1975. p. 102.
lxxix *Ibid*, p. 99.
lxxx Paul Bekker, 1925, p. 332.
lxxxi Barry Cooper, 2000, p. 330.
lxxxii Alison Bullock, *Notes to the BBC Radio Three Beethoven experience*, Friday 10 June 2005, www.bbc.co.uk/radio3/Beethoven
lxxxiii William Kinderman, editor, 2005, p. 53—4.
lxxxiv Philip Radcliffe, 1978, p. 126.
lxxxv Alison Bullock, *Notes to the BBC Radio Three Beethoven experience*, Friday 10 June 2005, www.bbc.co.uk/radio3/Beethoven
lxxxvi Joseph de Marliave, 1925 (reprint 1961), p. 267.
lxxxvii Paul Bekker, 1925, p. 332.
lxxxviii Martin Cooper, 1970, pp. 374—5.
lxxxix William Kinderman, editor, 2005, p. 53—4.
xc Philip Radcliffe, 1978, p. 127.
xci Basil Lam, 1975, pp. 103—4.
xcii Denis Matthews, 1985, p. 142.
xciii Barry Cooper, 2000, p. 330.
xciv Philip Radcliffe, 1978, p. 127.
xcv Harold Truscott, 1968, p. 88.
xcvi Philip Radcliffe, 1978, p. 127.
xcvii Denis Matthews, 1985, p. 142.
xcviii Martin Cooper, 1970, pp. 374—5.
xcix Robert Simpson, *The chamber music for strings* in: Denis Arnold and Nigel Fortune, editors, *The Beethoven companion*, 1973, p. 299.
c Marion M. Scott, 1940, pp. 269.
ci Michael Steinberg, *The late quartets*, in: Robert Winter and Robert Martin, editors, *The Beethoven quartet companion*, 1994, p. 233.
cii Marion M. Scott, 1940, p. 270.
ciii Michael Steinberg, *The late quartets*, in: Robert Winter and Robert Martin, editors, *The Beethoven quartet companion*, 1994, pp. 212—3.
civ Romain Rolland, 1917, p. 189.
cv Martin Cooper, 1970, p. 375.
cvi Basil Lam, 1975, p. 104.
cvii Philip Radcliffe, 1978, p. 128.
cviii Alison Bullock, *Notes to the BBC Radio Three Beethoven experience*, Friday 10 June 2005, www.bbc.co.uk/radio3/Beethoven
cix Denis Matthews, 1985, pp. 142—3.
cx Electra Slonimsky Yourke, editor, *Nicolas Slonimsky: writings on music*, 4 Vols. 2003—2005, p. 164.
cxi William Kinderman, editor, 2005, p. 53—4.
cxii Paul Bekker, 1925, p. 332.
cxiii Rebecca Clarke, *The Beethoven quartets as a player sees them* in: *Musical Times*, Special Issue, London: Vol. VIII, No. 2, 1927, pp. 184—90.
cxiv Joseph de Marliave, 1925 (reprint1961), p. 272.
cxv Igor Stravinsky, 1972, p. 259.
cxvi Robert Hatten, *Plenitude as fulfilment*, in: William Kinderman editor, *The string quartets of Beethoven*, 2005, p. 214.
cxvii Robert Simpson, *The chamber music for strings* in: Denis Arnold and Nigel Fortune, editors, *The Beethoven companion*, 1973, p. 299.
cxviii Rebecca Clarke, *The Beethoven quartets as a player sees them* in: *Musical*
cxix Basil Lam, 1975, pp. 104—5.

  Times, Special Issue, London: Vol. VIII, No. 2, 1927, pp. 184–90.
[xxx] Joseph Kerman, 1967, pp. 316–7.
[xxxi] Harold Truscott, 1968, p. 90.
[xxxii] Philip Radcliffe, 1978, p. 129.
[xxxiii] Michael Steinberg, *The late quartets*, in: Robert Winter and Robert Martin, editors, *The Beethoven quartet companion*, 1994, p. 234.
[xxxiv] As suggested, by amongst others, William Kinderman, editor, 2005, p. 53–4.
[xxxv] Barry Cooper, 2000, p. 33.
[xxxvi] Philip Radcliffe, 1978, p. 130.
[xxxvii] Robert Simpson, *The chamber music for strings* in: Denis Arnold and Nigel Fortune, editors, *The Beethoven companion*, 1973, p. 299.
[xxxviii] Joseph de Marliave, 1925 (reprint1961), p. 281.
[xxxix] Michael Steinberg, *The late quartets*, in: Robert Winter and Robert Martin, editors, *The Beethoven quartet companion*, 1994, p. 234.
[xxxx] Basil Lam, 1975, p. 106.
[xxxxi] Alison Bullock, *Notes to the BBC Radio Three Beethoven experience*, Friday 10 June 2005, www.bbc.co.uk/radio3/Beethoven
[xxxxii] William Kinderman, 1997, pp. 283–4.
[xxxxiii] Anton Felix Schindler, *Beethoven as I knew him*, edited by Donald W. MacArdle and translated by Constance S. Jolly from the German edition of 1860, 1966, p. 308.
[xxxxiv] Joseph Kerman, 1967, p. 318.
[xxxxv] Paul Bekker, 1925, p. 332.
[xxxxvi] Joseph Kerman, 1967, pp. 196–8.
[xxxxvii] Harold Truscott, 1968, p. 92.
[xxxxviii] Joseph Kerman, 1967, pp. 196–8.
[xxxxix] *Ibid.*
[cl] Barry Cooper, 1990, p. 152 and 2000, p. 331.
[cli] With acknowledgement to Neville Cardus, 1957, p. 277.
[clii] Martin Cooper, 1970, p. 379.
[cliii] Paul Bekker, 1925, p. 332.
[cliv] Arthur Honegger quoted in: John L. Holmes, *Composers on composers*, 1990, pp. 468–9. Honegger's text was originally published in *Je suis compositeur*, 1951.
[clv] Daniel K. L. Chua, 1995, p. 196.
[clvi] Marion M. Scott, 1940, p. 270.
[clvii] Igor Stravinsky, 1972, pp. 258–9.
[clviii] Joseph Kerman, 1967, c1966, p. 199.
[clix] Michael Steinberg, *The late quartets*, in: Robert Winter and Robert Martin, editors, *The Beethoven quartet companion*, 1994, p. 234.
[cl] Joseph Kerman, 1967, p. 196.
[cli] Harold Truscott, 1968, p. 93.
[clii] Barry Cooper, 2000, p, 331.
[cliii] Several authorities relate this anecdote. Holtz's words here are derived from H. C. Robbins Landon, 1970, p. 190.
[cliv] Maynard Solomon, 2003, p. 240.
[clv] Basil Lam, 1975, p. 106.
[clvi] Philip Radcliffe, 1978, p. 132.
[clvii] Basil Lam, 1975, p. 106.
[clviii] Denis Matthews, 1985, p. 144.
[clix] Barry Cooper, 2000, pp. 261–2.
[clx] Robert Simpson, *The chamber music for strings* in: Denis Arnold and Nigel

clxi Fortune, editors, *The Beethoven companion*, 1973, p. 299.
clxii Bruno Walter, 1948, p. 28.
clxiii Alison Bullock, *Notes to the BBC Radio Three Beethoven experience*, Friday 10 June 2005, www.bbc.co.uk/radio3/Beethoven
clxiii Philip Radcliffe, 1978, pp. 133–4.
clxiv Thayer-Forbes, pp. 975–6.
clxv Anton Felix Schindler, *Beethoven as I knew him*, edited by Donald W. MacArdle and translated by Constance S. Jolly from the German edition of 1860, 1966, p. 307.
clxvi Cooper gives a comprehensive account of the circumstances leading to the composition of the revised finale, see: Barry Cooper, 2000, pp. 344–5.
clxvii Maynard Solomon, 1977. Originally derived from Thayer-Dieters-Riemann, Vol. V, p. 298.
clxviii This letter has not survived.
clxix Barry Cooper, 2000, pp. 344–5.
clxx Paul Griffiths, 1983, p. 106.
clxxi Joseph Kerman, *Beethoven Quartet Audiences* in: Robert Winter and Robert Martin, editors, *The Beethoven quartet companion*, 1994, p. 21.
clxxii Robert Simpson, *The chamber music for strings* in: Denis Arnold and Nigel Fortune, editors, *The Beethoven companion*, 1973, p. 270.
clxxiii Emily Anderson, editor and translator, 1961, Vol. 3, Letter No. 1539, pp.1319–40. For an audio version of this letter with accompanying text see: Beethoven House, Digital Archives, Library Document, H. C. Bodmer, HCB Br 149.
clxxiv *Ibid*, footnote 3.
clxxv Joseph de Marliave, 1925 (reprint1961), p. 214.
clxxvi Thayer-Forbes, 1967, p. 1010.
clxxvii Harold Truscott, 1968, p. 134.
clxxviii Joseph de Marliave, 1925 (reprint1961), p. 287.
clxxix Barry Cooper, Beethoven, 2000, p. 346.
clxxx John Daverio, *Manner, tone, and tendency in Beethoven's chamber music for strings* in: Glenn Stanley editor, *The Cambridge companion to Beethoven*, 2000, pp. 147–64.
clxxxi William Kinderman, editor, 2005, p. 53–4.
clxxxii Rebecca Clarke, *The Beethoven quartets as a player sees them* in: *Musical Times*, Special Issue, Vol. VIII, No. 2, 1927, pp. 184–90.
clxxxiii Electra Slonimsky Yourke, editor, *Nicolas Slonimsky: Writings on music*, 4 Vols. 2003–2005, p. 164.
clxxxiv Anton Felix Schindler, *Beethoven as I knew him*, edited by Donald W. MacArdle and translated by Constance S. Jolly from the German edition of 1860, 1966, p. 308.
clxxxv Maynard Solomon, 1977, p. 241 and p. 283.
clxxxvi Electra Slonimsky Yourke editor, *Nicolas Slonimsky: Writings on music*, 4 Vols. 2003–2005, p. 164–5.
clxxxvii Harold Truscott, 1968, p. 134.
clxxxviii Philip Radcliffe, 1978, p. 136.

BIBLIOGRAPHY

The author has individually consulted all the publications listed in this bibliography and can confirm that each makes reference, in some way or other, to Beethoven and his works. It will be evident from their titles which of these are publications devoted exclusively to the composer. Others that make only passing reference to Beethoven and his compositions, nevertheless unfailingly bear testimony to his genius and humanity. The diversity of the titles listed testifies to the centrality of Beethoven to western culture and beyond; the mere survey of these should be of itself a rewarding experience for a lover of so-called classical music. The entries are confined to book publications, reflecting the scope of the author's researches. The cut-off date for this was 2007; no works after this date are listed, notwithstanding the author is mindful that Beethoven musicology, and related publication, continue to be a major field of endeavour.

Abraham, Gerald. *Beethoven's second-period quartets.* London: Oxford University Press: Humphrey Milford, 1944.

Abraham, Gerald. *Essays on Russian and East European music.* Oxford: Clarendon Press: New York: Oxford University Press, 1985.

Abraham, Gerald, Editor. *The age of Beethoven, 1790-1830.* London: Oxford University Press, 1982.

Abraham, Gerald. *The tradition of Western music.* London: Oxford University Press, 1974.

Abse, Dannie and Joan. *The Music lover's literary companion.* London: Robson Books, 1988.

Adorno, Theodor W., Translator. *Alban Berg: master of the smallest link.* Cambridge: Cambridge University Press, 1991.

Adorno, Theodor W. *Beethoven: the philosophy of music; fragments and texts.* Cambridge: Polity Press, 1998.

Albrecht, Daniel, Editor. *Modernism and music: an anthology of sources.* Chicago; London: University of Chicago Press, 2004.

Albrecht, Theodore, Translator and Editor. *Letters to Beethoven and other correspondence.* Lincoln, New England: University of Nebraska Press, 3 vols., 1996.

Allsobrook, David Ian. *Liszt: my travelling circus life.* London: Macmillan, 1991.

Anderson, Christopher, Editor and Translator. *Selected writings of Max Reger.* New York; London: Routledge, 2006.

Anderson, Emily, Editor and Translator. *The letters of Beethoven.* London: Macmillan, 3 vols.,1961.

Anderson, Martin, Editor. *Klemperer on music: shavings from a musician's workbench.* London: Toccata Press, 1986.

Antheil, George. *Bad boy of music.* London; New York: Hurst & Blackett Ltd., 1945.

Appleby, David P. *Heitor Villa-Lobos: a bio-bibliography.* New York: Greenwood Press, 1988.

Aprahamian, Felix, Editor. *Essays on music: an anthology from The Listener.* London, Cassell, 1967.

Armero, Gonzalo and Jorge de Persia. *Manuel de Falla : his life & works.* London: Omnibus Press, 1999.

Arnold, Ben, Editor. *The Liszt companion.* Westport, Connecticut; London: Greenwood Press, 2002.

Arnold, Denis and Nigel Fortune, Editors. *The Beethoven companion.* London: Faber and Faber, 1973.

Ashbrook, William. *Donizetti.* London: Cassell, 1965.

Auner, Joseph Henry. *A Schoenberg reader: documents of a life.* New Haven Connecticut; London: Yale University Press, 2003.

Avins, Styra, Editor. *Johannes Brahms: life and letters.* Oxford: Oxford University Press, 1997.

Azoury, Pierre H. *Chopin through his contemporaries: friends, lovers, and rivals.* Westport, Connecticut: Greenwood Press, 1999.

Badura-Skoda, Paul. *Carl Czerny: On the Proper Performance of all Beethoven's Works for the Piano.* Universal Edition: A. G. Wien, 1970.

Bailey, Cyril. *Hugh Percy Allen.* London: Oxford University

Press, 1948.

Bailey, Kathryn. *The life of Webern.* Cambridge: Cambridge University Press, 1998.

Barenboim, Daniel. *A life in music.* London: Weidenfeld & Nicolson, 1991.

Barlow, Michael. *Whom the gods love: the life and music of George Butterworth.* London: Toccata Press, 1997.

Barrett-Ayres, Reginald. *Joseph Haydn and the string quartet.* New York: Schirmer Books, 1974.

Bartos, Frantisek. *Bedrich Smetana: Letters and reminiscences.* Prague: Artia, 1953.

Barzun, Jacques. *Pleasures of music: an anthology of writing about music and musicians.* London: Cassell, 1977.

Bauer-Lechner, Natalie. *Recollections of Gustav Mahler.* London: Faber Music, 1980.

Bazhanov, N. Nikolai. *Rakhmaninov.* Moscow: Raduga, 1983.

Beaumont, Antony, Editor. *Ferruccio Busoni: Selected letters.* London: Faber and Faber, 1987.

Beaumont, Antony, Editor. *Gustav Mahler, letters to his wife.* London: Faber and Faber, 2004.

Beecham, Thomas. *A mingled chime: an autobiography.* New York: Da Capo Press, 1976.

Bekker, Paul. *Beethoven.* London: J. M. Dent & Sons, 1925.

Bellasis, Edward. *Cherubini: memorials illustrative of his life.* London: Burns and Oates, 1874.

Bennett, James R. Sterndale. *The life of William Sterndale Bennett.* Cambridge: University Press, 1907.

Benser, Caroline Cepin. *Egon Wellesz (1885–1974): chronicle of twentieth-century musician.* New York: P. Lang, 1985.

Berlioz, Hector. *Evenings in the orchestra.* Harmondsworth: Penguin Books, 1963.

Berlioz, Hector. *The musical madhouse (Les grotesques de la musique).* Rochester, New York: University of Rochester Press, 2003.

Bernard, Jonathan W., Editor. *Elliott Carter: collected essays and lectures, 1937-1995.* Rochester, New York; Woodbridge: University of Rochester Press, 1998.

Bernstein, Leonard. *The joy of music.* New York: Simon and Schuster, 1959.

Bertensson, Sergei. *Sergei Rachmaninoff: a lifetime in music.* London: G. Allen & Unwin, 1965.

Biancolli, Louis. *The Flagstad manuscript.* New York: Putnam, 1952.

Bickley, Nora, Editor. *Letters from and to Joseph Joachim.* London: Macmillan, 1914.

Bie, Oskar. *A history of the pianoforte and pianoforte players.* New York: Da Capo Press, 1966.

Blaukopf, Herta. *Mahler's unknown letters.* London: Gollancz, 1986.

Blaukopf, Kurt and Herta. *Mahler: his life, work and world.* London: Thames and Hudson, 1991.

Bliss, Arthur. *As I remember.* London: Thames Publishing, 1989.

Block, Adrienne Fried. *Amy Beach, passionate Victorian: the life and work of an American composer, 1867–1944.* New York: Oxford University Press, 1998.

Bloch, Ernst. *Essays on the philoso-*

phy of music. Cambridge: Cambridge University Press, 1985.

Blocker, Robert. *The Robert Shaw reader*. New Haven; London: Yale University Press, 2004.

Blom, Eric. *A musical postbag*. London: J. M. Dent, 1945.

Blom, Eric. *Beethoven's pianoforte sonatas discussed*. London: J. M. Dent, 1938.

Blom, Eric. *Classics major and minor: with some other musical ruminations*. London: J. M. Dent, 1958.

Blum, David. *The art of quartet playing: the Guarneri Quartet in conversation with David Blum*. London: Gollancz, 1986.

Blume, Friedrich. *Classic and Romantic music: a comprehensive survey*. London: Faber and Faber, 1972.

Boden, Anthony. *The Parrys of the Golden Vale: background to genius*. London: Thames Publishing, 1998.

Bonavia, Ferruccio. *Musicians on music*. London: Routledge & Kegan Paul, 1956.

Bonds, Mark Evan *After Beethoven: imperatives of originality in the symphony*. Cambridge, Massachusetts; London: Harvard University Press, 1996.

Bonis, Ferenc, Editor. *The selected writings of Zoltán Kodály*. London; New York: Boosey & Hawkes, 1974.

Bookspan, Martin. *André Previn: a biography*. London: Hamilton, 1981.

Boros, James and Richard Toop, Editors. *Brian Ferneyhough: Collected writings*. Amsterdam: Harwood Academic, 1995.

Boulez, Pierre. *Stocktakings from an apprenticeship*. Oxford: Clarendon Press, 1991.

Boult, Adrian. *Boult on music: words from a lifetime's communication*. London: Toccata Press, 1983.

Boult, Adrian. *My own trumpet*. London, Hamish Hamilton, 1973.

Boult, Adrian with Jerrold Northrop Moore. *Music and friends: seven decades of letters to Adrian Boult from Elgar, Vaughan Williams, Holst, Bruno Walter, Yehudi Menuhin and other friends*. London: Hamish Hamilton, 1979.

Bovet, Marie Anne de. *Charles Gounod: his life and his works*. London: S. Low, Marston, Searle & Rivington, Ltd., 1891.

Bowen, Catherine Drinker. *Beloved friend: the story of Tchaikowsky and Nadejda von Meck*. London: Hutchinson & Co., 1937.

Bowen, Meirion, Editor. *Gerhard on music: selected writings*. Brookfield, Vermont: Ashgate, 2000.

Bowen, Meirion. *Michael Tippett*. London: Robson Books, 1982.

Bowen, Meirion, Editor. *Music of the angels: essays and sketchbooks of Michael Tippett*. London: Eulenburg, 1980.

Bowen, Meirion, Editor. *Tippett on music*. Oxford: Clarendon Press, 1995.

Bowers, Faubion. *Scriabin: a biography*. Mineola: Dover; London: Constable, 1996.

Boyden, Matthew. *Richard Strauss*. London: Weidenfeld & Nicolson, 1999.

Bozarth, George S., Editor. *Brahms studies: analytical and historical perspectives; papers delivered at the International Brahms Conference, Washington, DC, 5-8 May 1983*. Oxford: Clarendon Press, 1990.

Brand, Juliane, Christopher Hailey and Donald Harris, Editors. *The Berg-Schoenberg correspondence: selected letters*. Basingstoke: Macmillan, 1987.

Brandenbugh, Sieghard, Editor. *Haydn, Mozart, & Beethoven: studies in the music of the classical period: essays in honor of Alan Tyson*. Oxford: Clarendon Press, 1998.

Braunstein, Joseph. *Musica Æterna, program notes for 1961–1971*. New York: Musica Æterna, 1972.

Braunstein, Joseph. *Musica Æterna, program notes for 1971–1976*. New York: Musica Æterna, 1978.

Brendel, Alfred. *Alfred Brendel on music: collected essays*. Chicago, Iliinois: A Cappella Books, 2001.

Brendel, Alfred. *The veil of order: Alfred Brendel in conversation with Martin Meyer*. London: Faber and Faber, 2002.

Breuning, Gerhard von. *Memories of Beethoven: from the house of the black-robed Spaniards*. Cambridge: Cambridge University Press, 1992.

Briscoe, James R., Editor. (Brief Description): *Debussy in performance*. New Haven: Yale University Press, 1999.

Brott, Alexander Betty Nygaard King. *Alexander Brott: my lives in music*. Oakville, Ontario; Niagara Falls, New York: Mosaic Press, 2005.

Brown, Alfred Peter. *The symphonic repertoire. Vol. 2, The first golden age of the Viennese symphony: Haydn, Mozart, Beethoven, and Schubert*. Bloomington, Indiana: Indiana University Press, 2002.

Brown, Maurice John Edwin. *Schubert: a critical biography*. London: Macmillan; New York: St. Martin's Press, 1958.

Broyles, Michael. *Beethoven: the emergence and evolution of Beethoven's heroic style*. New York: Excelsior Music Publishing Co., 1987.

Brubaker, Bruce and Jane Gottlieb, Editors. *Pianist, scholar, connoisseur: essays in honor of Jacob Lateiner*. Stuyvesant, N.Y., Pendragon Press, 2000.

Buch, Esteban. *Beethoven's Ninth: a political history*. Chicago; London: University of Chicago Press, 2003.

Burk, John N., Editor. *Letters of Richard Wagner: the Burrell collection*. London: Gollancz, 1951.

Burnham, Scott G. *Beethoven hero*. Princeton, New Jersey: Princeton University Press, 1995.

Burnham, Scott G and Michael P. Steinberg, Editors. *Beethoven and his world*. Princeton, New Jersey; Oxford: Princeton University Press, 2000.

Burton, William Westbrook, Editor. *Conversations about Bernstein*. New York; Oxford: Oxford University Press, 1995.

Busch, Fritz. *Pages from a musician's life*. London: Hogarth Press, 1953.

Busch, Hans, Editor. *Verdi's Aida: the history of an opera in letters and documents*. Minneapolis:

University of Minnesota Press, 1978.

Busch, Hans, Editor. *Verdi's Falstaff in letters and contemporary reviews.* Bloomington: Indiana University Press, 1997.

Busch, Marie, Translator. *Memoirs of Eugenie Schumann.* London: W. Heinemann, 1927.

Bush, Alan Dudley. *In my eighth decade and other essays.* London: Kahn & Averill, 1980.

Busoni, Ferruccio. *Letters to his wife.* Translated by Rosamond Ley. New York: Da Capo Press, 1975.

Byron, Reginald. *Music, culture, & experience: selected papers of John Blacking.* Chicago: University of Chicago Press, 1995.

Cairns, David. *Responses: musical essays and reviews.* New York: Da Capo Press, 1980.

Cardus, Neville. *Talking of music.* London: Collins, 1957.

Carley, Lionel. *Delius: a life in letters.* London: Scolar Press in association with the Delius Trust, 1988.

Carley, Lionel. *Grieg and Delius: a chronicle of their friendship in letters.* London: Marion Boyars, 1993.

Carner, Mosco. *Major and minor.* London: Duckworth, 1980

Carner, Mosco. *Puccini: a critical biography.* London: Duckworth, 1958.

Carroll, Brendan G. *The last prodigy: a biography of Erich Wolfgang Korngold.* Portland, Oregon: Amadeus Press, 1997.

Carse, Adam von Ahn. *The life of Jullien: adventurer, showman-conductor and establisher of the Promenade Concerts in England, together with a history of those concerts up to 1895.* Cambridge England: Heffer, 1951.

Carse, Adam von Ahn. *The orchestra from Beethoven to Berlioz: a history of the orchestra in the first half of the 19th century, and of the development of orchestral baton-conducting.* Cambridge: W. Heffer, 1948.

Casals, Pablo. *Joys and sorrows: reflections by Pablo Casals as told to Albert E. Kahn.* London: Macdonald, 1970.

Casals, Pablo. *The memoirs of Pablo Casals as told to Thomas Dozier.* London: Life en Español, 1959.

Chappell, Paul. *Dr. S. S. Wesley, 1810–1876: portrait of a Victorian musician.* Great Wakering: Mayhew-McCrimmon, 1977.

Chasins, Abram. *Leopold Stokowski, a profile.* New York: Hawthorn Books, 1979.

Charlton, Davi, Editor and Martyn Clarke Translator. *E.T.A. Hoffmann's musical writings: Kreisleriana, The Poet and the Composer.* Cambridge: Cambridge University Press, 1989.

Chávez, Carlos. *Musical thought.* Cambridge: Harvard University Press, 1961.

Chesterman, Robert, Editor. *Conversations with conductors: Bruno Walter, Sir Adrian Boult, Leonard Bernstein, Ernest Ansermet, Otto Klemperer, Leopold Stokowski.* Totowa, New Jersey: Rowman and Littlefield, 1976.

Chissell, Joan. *Clara Schumann: a dedicated spirit; a study of her life and work.* London: Hamilton, 1983.

Chua, Daniel K. L. *The "Galitzin" quartets of Beethoven: Opp.127, 132, 130.* Princeton: Princeton

University Press, 1995.

Citron, Marcia, Editor. *The letters of Fanny Hensel to Felix Mendelssohn*. Stuyvesant, New York: Pendragon Press, 1987.

Clark, Walter Aaron. *Enrique Granados: poet of the piano*. Oxford, England; New York, N.Y.: Oxford University Press, 2006.

Clark, Walter Aaron. *Isaac Albéniz: portrait of a romantic*. Oxford; New York: Oxford University Press, 1999.

Clive, Peter. *Beethoven and his world*. Oxford University Press, 2001.

Closson, Ernest. *History of the piano*. Translated by Delano Ames and edited by Robin Golding. London: Paul Elek, 1947.

Cockshoot, John V. *The fugue in Beethoven's piano music*. London: Routledge & Kegan Paul, 1959.

Coe, Richard N, Translator. *Life of Rossini by Stendhal*. London: Calder & Boyars, 1970.

Coleman, Alexander, Editor. *Diversions & animadversions: essays from The new criterion*. New Brunswick, New Jersey; London: Transaction Publishers, 2005.

Colerick, George. *From the Italian girl to Cabaret: musical humour, parody and burlesque*. London: Juventus, 1998.

Coleridge, A. D. *Life of Moscheles, with selections from his diaries and correspondence by his wife*. London: Hurst & Blackett, 1873.

Colles, Henry Cope. *Essays and lectures*. London: Humphrey Milford, Oxford University Press, 1945.

Cone, Edward T., Editor. *Roger Sessions on music: collected essays*. Princeton, New Jersey: Princeton University Press, 1979.

Cone, Edward T. *The composer's voice*. Berkeley; London: University of California Press, 1974.

Cook, Susan and Judy S. Tsou, Editors. *Cecilia reclaimed: feminist perspectives on gender and music*. Urbana: University of Illinois Press, 1994.

Cooper, Barry. *Beethoven*. The master musicians series. Oxford: Oxford University Press, 2000.

Cooper, Barry. *Beethoven and the creative process*. Oxford: Clarendon Press, 1990.

Cooper, Barry. *Beethoven's folksong settings: chronology, sources, style*. Cambridge: Cambridge University Press, 1991.

Cooper, Barry. *The Beethoven compendium: a guide to Beethoven's life and music*. London: Thames and Hudson, 1991.

Cooper, Martin. *Beethoven: the last decade, 1817–1827*. London: Oxford University Press, 1970.

Cooper, Martin. *Judgements of value: selected writings on music*. Oxford; New York: Oxford University Press, 1988.

Cooper, Martin. *Ideas and music*. London: Barrie and Rockliff, 1965.

Cooper, Victoria L. *The house of Novello: the practice and policy of a Victorian music publisher, 1829–1866*. Aldershot, Hants: Ashgate, 2003.

Coover, James. *Music at auction: Puttick and Simpson (of London), 1794–1971: being an annotated, chronological list of sales of musical materials*. Warren, Michigan: Harmonie Park Press, 1988.

Copland, Aaron. *Copland on music.* London: Deutsch, 1961.

Corredor, J. Ma. *Conversations with Casals.* London: Hutchinson, 1956.

Cott, Jonathan. *Stockhausen: conversations with the composer.* London: Picador, 1974.

Cottrell, Stephen. *Professional music making in London: ethnography and experience.* Aldershot: Ashgate, 2004.

Cowell, Henry. *Charles Ives and his music.* New York: Oxford University Press, 1955.

Cowling, Elizabeth. *The cello.* London: Batsford, 1983.

Crabbe, John. *Beethoven's empire of the mind.* Newbury: Lovell Baines, 1982.

Craft, Robert. *An improbable life: memoirs.* Nashville: Vanderbilt University Press, 2002.

Craft, Robert, Editor. *Stravinsky: selected correspondence.* London: Faber and Faber, 3 Vols. 1982–1985.

Craw, Howard Allen. *A biography and thematic catalog of the works of J. L. Dussek: 1760–1812.* Ann Arbor: Michigan, 1965.

Crawford, Richard, R. Allen Lott and Carol J. Oja, Editors. *A Celebration of American music: words and music in honor of H. Wiley Hitchcock.* Ann Arbor: University of Michigan Press, 1990.

Craxton, Harold and Tovey, Donald Francis. *Beethoven: Sonatas for Pianoforte.* London: The Associated Board, [1931].

Crichton, Ronald: Editor. *The memoirs of Ethel Smyth.* New York: Viking, 1987.

Crist, Stephen A. and Roberta M. Marvin, Editors. *Historical musicology: sources, methods, interpretations.* Rochester, New York: University of Rochester Press, 2004.

Crofton, Ian and Donald Fraser, Editors. *A dictionary of musical quotations.* London: Croom Helm, 1985.

Crompton, Louis, Editor. *Shaw, Bernard: The great composers: reviews and bombardments.* Berkeley; London: University of California Press, 1978.

Csicserry-Ronay, Elizabeth, Translator and Editor. *Hector Berlioz: The art of music and other essays: (A travers chants).* Bloomington: Indiana University Press, 1994.

Curtiss, Mina Kirstein. *Bizet and his world.* London: Secker & Warburg, 1959.

Cuyler, Louise Elvira. *The symphony.* New York: Harcourt Brace Jovanovich, 1973.

Dahlhaus, Carl. *Ludwig van Beethoven: approaches to his music.* Oxford: Clarendon Press, 1991.

Dahlhaus, Carl. *Nineteenth-century music.* Translated by J. Bradford Robinson. Berkeley; London: University of California Press, 1989.

Daniels, Robin. *Conversations with Cardus.* London: Gollancz, 1976.

Daniels, Robin. Conversations with Menuhin. London: Macdonald General Books, 1979.

Day, James. *Vaughan Williams.* London: Dent, 1961.

Davies, Peter Maxwell. *Studies from two decades.* Selected and introduced by Stephen Pruslin.

London: Boosey & Hawkes, 1979.

Dean, Winton. *Georges Bizet: his life and work*. London: J.M. Dent, 1965.

Deas, Stewart. *In defence of Hanslick*. London: Williams and Norgate, 1940.

Debussy, Claude. *Debussy on music*. London: Secker & Warburg, 1977.

Delbanco, Nicholas. *The Beaux Arts Trio*. London: Gollancz, 1985.

Demény, Janos, Editor. *Béla Bartók: letters*. London: Faber and Faber, 1971.

Dent, Edward Joseph. *Selected essays*. Edited by Hugh Taylor. Cambridge; New York: Cambridge University Press, 1979.

Deutsch, Otto Erich. *Mozart: a documentary biography*. London: Adam & Charles Black, 1965.

Deutsch, Otto Erich. *Schubert: a documentary biography*. London: J.M. Dent, 1946

Deutsch, Otto Erich. *Schubert: memoirs by his friends*. London: Adam & Charles Black, 1958.

Dibble, Jeremy. *C. Hubert H. Parry: his life and music*. Oxford: Clarendon Press, 1992.

Dibble, Jeremy. *Charles Villiers Stanford: man and musician*. Oxford: Oxford University Press, 2002.

Donakowski, Conrad L. *A muse for the masses: ritual and music in an age of democratic revolution, 1770–1870*. Chicago: University of Chicago Press, 1977.

Dower, Catherine. *Alfred Einstein on music: selected music criticisms*. New York: Greenwood Press, 1991.

Downs, Philip G. *Classical music: the era of Haydn, Mozart, and Beethoven*. New York: W.W. Norton, 1992.

Drabkin, William. *Beethoven: Missa Solemnis*. Cambridge: Cambridge University Press, 1991.

Dreyfus, Kay. *The farthest north of humanness: letters of Percy Grainger, 1901–1914*. South Melbourne; Basingstoke: Macmillan, 1985.

Dubal, David, Editor. *Remembering Horowitz: 125 pianists recall a legend*. New York: Schirmer Books, 1993.

Dubal, David. *The world of the concert pianist*. London: Victor Gollancz, 1985.

Dvorák, Otakar. *Antonín Dvorák, my father*. Spillville, Iowa: Czech Historical Research Center, 1993.

Dyson, George. *The progress of music*. London: Oxford University Press, Humphrey Milford, 1932.

Eastaugh, Kenneth. *Havergal Brian: the making of a composer*. London: Harrap, 1976.

Edwards, Allen. *Flawed words and stubborn sounds: a conversation with Elliott Carter*. New York: Norton & Company, 1971.

Edwards, Frederick George. *Musical haunts in London*. London: J. Curwen & Sons, 1895.

Ehrlich, Cyril. *First philharmonic: a history of the Royal Philharmonic Society*. Oxford: Clarendon Press, 1995.

Einstein, Alfred. *A short history of music*. London: Cassell and Company Ltd., 1948.

Einstein, Alfred. *Essays on music*. London: Faber and Faber, 1958.

Einstein, Alfred. *Mozart: his character, his work*. London: Cassell and Company Ltd., 1946.

Einstein, Alfred. *Music in the Romantic era*. London: J.M. Dent Ltd., 1947.

Ekman, Karl. *Jean Sibelius, his life and personality*. New York: Tudor Publishing. Co., 1945.

Elgar, Edward. *A future for English music: and other lectures*, Edited by Percy M. Young. London: Dobson, 1968.

Elkin, Robert. *Queen's Hall, 1893–1941*. London: Rider, 1944.

Ella, John. *Musical sketches, abroad and at home: with original music by Mozart, Czerny, Graun, etc., vocal cadenzas and other musical illustrations*. London: Ridgway, Vol. 1., 1869.

Ellis, William Ashton. *The family letters of Richard Wagner*. Edited and translated by William Ashton Ellis and enlarged with introduction and notes by John Deathridge. Basingstoke: Macmillan, 1991.

Ellis, William Ashton. *Richard Wagner's prose works: Vol. 1, The art-work of the future*. Edited and translated by William Ashton Ellis. London: Kegan Paul, Trench, Trübner, 1895.

Ellis, William Ashton. *Richard Wagner's prose works: Vol. 2, Opera and drama*. Edited and translated by William Ashton Ellis. London: Kegan Paul, Trench, Trübner, 1900.

Ellis, William Ashton. *Richard Wagner's prose works: Vol. 3, The theatre*. Edited and translated by William Ashton Ellis. London: Kegan Paul, Trench, Trübner, 1907.

Ellis, William Ashton. *Richard Wagner's prose works: Vol. 4, Art and politics*. Edited and translated by William Ashton Ellis. London: Kegan Paul, Trench, Trübner, 1895.

Ellis, William Ashton. *Richard Wagner's prose works: Vol. 5, Actors and singers*. Edited and translated by William Ashton Ellis. London: Kegan Paul, Trench, Trübner, 1896.

Ellis, William Ashton. *Richard Wagner's prose works: Vol. 6, Religion and art*. Edited and translated by William Ashton Ellis. London: Kegan Paul, Trench, Trübner, 1897.

Ellis, William Ashton. *Richard Wagner's prose works: Vol. 7, In Paris and Dresden*. Edited and translated by William Ashton Ellis. London: Kegan Paul, Trench, Trübner, 1898.

Ellis, William Ashton. *Richard Wagner's prose works: Vol. 8, Posthumous*. Edited and translated by William Ashton Ellis. London: Kegan Paul, Trench, Trübner, 1899.

Elterlein, Ernst von. *Beethoven's pianoforte sonatas: explained for the lovers of the musical art*. London: W. Reeves, 1898.

Engel, Carl. *Musical myths and facts*. London: Novello, Ewer & Co.; New York: J.L. Peters, 1876.

Eosze, László. *Zoltán Kodály: his life and work*. London: Collet's, 1962.

Etter, Brian K. *From classicism to modernism: Western musical culture and the metaphysics of order*. Aldershot: Ashgate, 2001.

Ewen, David. *From Bach to Stravinsky: the history of music by its foremost critics*. New York, Greenwood Press, 1968.

Ewen, David. *Romain Rolland's Essays on music*. New York: Dover Publications, 1959.

Fay, Amy. *Music-study in Germany: from the home correspondence of Amy Fay*. New York: Dover Publications, 1965.

Fenby, Eric. *Delius as I knew him*. London: Quality Press, 1936.

Ferguson, Donald Nivison. *Masterworks of the orchestral repertoire: a guide for listeners*. Minneapolis: University of Minnesota Press, 1954.

Fétis, François-Joseph. *Curiosités historiques de la musique: complément nécessaire de la Musique mise à la portée de tout le monde*. Paris: Janet et Cotelle, 1830.

Fifield, Christopher. *Max Bruch: his life and works*. London: Gollancz, 1988.

Fifield, Christopher. *True artist and true friend: a biography of Hans Richter*. Oxford: Clarendon Press, 1993.

Finson, Jon and R. Larry Todd, Editors. *Mendelssohn and Schumann: essays on their music and its context*. Durham, N.C.: Duke University Press, 1984.

Fischer, Edwin. *Beethoven's pianoforte sonatas: a guide for students & amateurs*. London: Faber and Faber, 1959.

Fischer, Edwin. *Reflections on music*. London: Williams and Norgate, 1951.

Fischer, Hans Conrad and Erich Kock. *Ludwig van Beethoven: a study in text and pictures*. London: Macmillan; New York, St. Martin's Press, 1972.

Fischmann, Zdenka E. *Janác̆ek-Newmarch correspondence. 1st limited and numbered edition*. Rockville, MD: Kabel Publishers, 1986.

Fitzlyon, April. *Maria Malibran: diva of the romantic age*. London: Souvenir Press, 1987.

FitzLyon, April. *The price of genius: a life of Pauline Viardot*. London: John Calder, 1964.

Forbes, Elliot, Editor. *Thayer's life of Beethoven*. Princeton, New Jersey: Princeton University Press, 1967.

Foreman, Lewis. *Bax: a composer and his times*. London: Scolar Press, 1983.

Foreman, Lewis, Editor. *Farewell, my youth, and other writings by Arnold Bax*. Aldershot: Scolar Press, 1992.

Foster, Myles Birket. *History of the Philharmonic Society of London, 1813–1912: a record of a hundred years' work in the cause of music*. London: Bodley Head, 1912.

Foulds, John. *Music today: its heritage from the past, and legacy to the future*. London: I. Nicholson and Watson, limited, 1934.

Frank, Mortimer H. *Arturo Toscanini: the NBC years*. Portland, Oregon: Amadeus Press, 2002.

Fraser, Andrew Alastair. *Essays on music*. London: Oxford University Press, H. Milford, 1930.

Frohlich, Martha. *Beethoven's Appassionata' sonata*. Oxford: Clarendon Press, 1991.

Gal, Hans. *The golden age of Vienna*. London: Max Parrish & Co. Limited, 1948.

Gal, Hans. *The musician's world: great composers in their letters*. London: Thames and Hudson,

1965.

Galatopoulos, Stelios. *Bellini: life, times, music.* London: Sanctuary, 2002.

Garden, Edward and Nigel Gottrei, Editors. *'To my best friend': correspondence between Tchaikovsky and Nadezhda von Meck, 1876–1878.* Oxford: Clarendon Press, 1993.

Geck, Martin. Beethoven. London: Haus, 2003.

Gerig, Reginald. *Famous pianists & their technique.* Washington: R. B. Luce, 1974.

Gilliam, Bryan. *The life of Richard Strauss.* Cambridge: Cambridge University Press, 1999.

Gilliam, Bryan, Editor. *Richard Strauss and his world.* Princeton, New Jersey: Princeton University Press, 1992.

Gillies, Malcolm and Bruce Clunies Ross, Editors. *Grainger on music.* Oxford; New York: Oxford University Press, 1999.

Gillies, Malcolm and David Pear, Editors. *The all-round man: selected letters of Percy Grainger, 1914–1961.* Oxford: Clarendon Press, 1994.

Gillies, Malcolm, Editor. *The Bartók companion.* London: Faber and Faber, 1993.

Gillmor, Alan M. *Erik Satie.* Basingstoke: Macmillan Press, 1988.

Glehn, M. E. *Goethe and Mendelssohn : (1821–1831).* London: Macmillan, 1874.

Glowacki, John, Editor. *Paul A. Pisk: Essays in his honor.* Austin, Texas: University of Texas, 1966

Gollancz, Victor. *Journey towards music: a memoir.* London: Victor Gollancz Ltd., 1964.

Good, Edwin Marshall. *Giraffes, black dragons, and other pianos: a technological history from Cristofori to the modern concert grand.* Stanford, California: Stanford University Press, 1982.

Gordon, David. *Musical visitors to Britain.* London: Routledge, 2005.

Gordon, Stewart. *A history of keyboard literature: music for the piano and its forerunners.* Schirmer Books: New York: London : Prentice Hall International, 1996.

Gorrell, Lorraine. *The nineteenth-century German lied.* Portland, Oregon: Amadeus Press, 1993.

Goss, Glenda D. *Jean Sibelius: the Hämeenlinna letters: scenes from a musical life, 1875–1895.* Esbo, Finland: Schildts, 1997.

Goss, Madeleine. *Bolero: the life of Maurice Ravel.* New York: Tudor, 1945.

Gotch, Rosamund Brunel, Editor. *Mendelssohn and his friends in Kensington: letters from Fanny and Sophy Horsley, written 1833–36.* London: Oxford University Press, 1938.

Gounod, Charles. *Charles Gounod; autobiographical reminiscences: with family letters and notes on music; from the French.* London: William Heinemann, 1896.

Grabs, Manfred, Editor. *Hanns Eisler: a rebel in music; selected writings.* Berlin: Seven Seas Publishers, 1978.

Grace, Harvey. *A musician at large.* London: Oxford University Press, H. Milford, 1928.

(La) Grange, Henry-Louis de. *Gustav Mahler.* Oxford: Oxford University Press, 1995.

Graves, Charles L. *Hubert Parry: his life and works.* London: Macmillan, 1926.

Graves, Charles L. *Post-Victorian music: with other studies and sketches.* London: Macmillan and Co., limited, 1911.

Graves, Charles L. *The life & letters of Sir George Grove, Hon. D.C.L. (Durham), Hon. LL.D. (Glasgow), formerly director of the Royal college of music.* London: Macmillan and Co., Ltd.; New York: The Macmillan Co., 1903.

Gray, Cecil. *Musical chairs, or, between two stools: being the life and memoirs of Cecil Gray.* London: Home & Van Thal, 1948.

Gregor-Dellin and Dietrich Mack, Editors. *Cosima Wagner's diaries.: Vol. 1, 1869 - 1877.* London: Collins, 1978-1980.

Griffiths, Paul. *Modern music: the avant-garde since 1945.* London: J. M. Dent & Sons Ltd., 1981.

Griffiths, Paul. *Olivier Messiaen and the music of time.* London: Faber and Faber, 1985.

Griffiths, Paul. *Peter Maxwell Davies.* London: Robson Books, 1988.

Griffiths, Paul. *The sea on fire: Jean Barraqué.* Rochester, New York: Woodbridge: University of Rochester Press, 2003.

Griffiths, Paul. *The string quartet.* London: Thames and Hudson, 1983.

Grout, Donald Jay and Claude V. Palisca, Editors. *A history of Western music.* London: J. M. Dent, 1988.

Grove, George. *Beethoven and his nine symphonies.* London: Novello, Ewer, 1896.

Grover, Ralph Scott. *Ernest Chausson: the man and his music.* London: The Athlone Press, 1980.

Grover, Ralph Scott. *The music of Edmund Rubbra.* Aldershot: Scolar Press, 1993.

Grun, Bernard. *Alban Berg: letters to his wife.* Edited and translated by Bernard Grun. London: Faber and Faber, 1971.

Gutman, David. *Prokofiev.* London: Omnibus Press, 1990.

Hadow, William Henry. *Collected essays.* London: H. Milford at the Oxford University Press, 1928.

Hadow, William Henry. *Beethoven's Op. 18 Quartets.* London: H. Milford at the Oxford University Press, 1926.

Haggin, Bernard H. *Music observed.* New York: Oxford University Press, 1964.

Hailey, Christopher. *Franz Schreker, 1878-1934: a cultural biography.* Cambridge: Cambridge University Press, 1993.

Hall, Michael. *Leaving home: a conducted tour of twentieth-century music with Simon Rattle.* London: Faber and Faber, 1996.

Hall, Patricia and Friedemann Sallis, Editors. (Brief Description): *A handbook to twentieth-century musical sketches.* Cambridge: Cambridge University Press, 2004.

Hallé, C. E. *Life and letters of Sir Charles Hallé: being an autobiography (1819-1860) with correspondence and diaries.* London: Smith, Elder & Co., 1896.

Halstead, Jill. *The woman composer: creativity and the gendered poli-*

tics of musical composition. Aldershot: Ashgate, 1997.

Hamburger, Michael, Editor and Translator. *Beethoven letters, journals, and conversations.* New York: Thames and Hudson, 1951.

Hammelmann, Hanns A. and Ewald Osers. *The correspondence between Richard Strauss and Hugo von Hofmannsthal.* London: Collins, 1961.

Hanson, Lawrence and Elisabeth Hanson. *Tchaikovsky: the man behind the music.* New York: Dodd, Mead & Co, 1967.

Harding, James. *Massenet.* London: J. M. Dent & Sons Ltd., 1970.

Harding, James. *Saint-Saëns and his circle.* London: Chapman & Hall, 1965.

Harding, Rosamond E. M. *Origins of musical time and expression.* London: Oxford University Press, 1938.

Harman, Alec with Anthony Milner and Wilfrid Mellers. *Man and his music: the story of musical experience in the West.* London: Barrie & Jenkins, 1988.

Harper, Nancy Lee. *Manuel de Falla: his life and music.* Lanham, Maryland; London: The Scarecrow Press, 2005.

Hartmann, Arthur. *'Claude Debussy as I knew him' and other writings of Arthur Hartmann.* Edited by Samuel Hsu, Sidney Grolnic, and Mark Peters. Rochester, New York; Woodbridge: University of Rochester Press, 2003.

Haugen, Einar and Camilla Cai. *Ole Bull: Norway's romantic musician and cosmopolitan patriot.* Madison: The University of Wisconsin Press, 1993.

Headington, Christopher. *The Bodley Head history of Western music.* London: The Bodley Head, 1974.

Heartz, Daniel. *Music in European capitals: the galant style, 1720–1780.* New York; London: W. W. Norton, 2003.

Hedley, Arthur, Editor. *Selected correspondence of Fryderyk Chopin: abridged from Fryderyk Chopin's correspondence.* London: Heinemann, 1962.

Heiles, Anne Mischakoff. *Mischa Mischakoff: journeys of a concertmaster.* Sterling Heights, Michigan: Harmonie Park Press, 2006.

Henderson, Sanya Shoilevska. *Alex North, film composer: a biography, with musical analyses of a Streetcar named desire, Spartacus, The misfits, Under the volcano, and Prizzi's honor.* Jefferson, N.C.; London: McFarland, 2003.

Henschel, George. *Personal recollections of Johannes Brahms: some of his letters to and pages from a journal kept by George Henschel.* Boston: R G. Badger, 1907.

Henze, Hans Werner. *Bohemian fifths: an autobiography.* London: Faber and Faber, 1998.

Henze, Hans Werner. *Music and politics: collected writings 1953–81.* London: Faber and Faber, 1982.

Herbert, May, Translator. *Early letters of Robert Schumann.* London: George Bell and Sons, 1888.

Heyman, Barbara B. *Samuel Barber: the composer and his music.* New York: Oxford University

Press, 1992.

Heyworth, Peter. *Otto Klemperer, his life and times.* Cambridge: Cambridge University Press, 2 Vols. 1983–1996.

Hildebrandt, Dieter. *Pianoforte: a social history of the piano.* London: Hutchinson, 1988.

Hill, Peter. *The Messiaen companion.* London: Faber and Faber, 1995.

Hill, Peter and Nigel Simeone. Messiaen. New Haven Connecticut; London: Yale University Press, 2005.

Hiller, Ferdinand. *Mendelssohn: Letters and recollections.* New York: Vienna House, 1972.

Hines, Robert Stephan. *The orchestral composer's point of view: essays on twentieth-century music by those who wrote it.* Norman: University of Oklahoma Press, 1970.

Ho, Allan B. *Shostakovich reconsidered.* London: Toccata Press, 1998.

Hodeir, André. *Since Debussy: a view of contemporary music.* New York: Da Capo Press, 1975.

Holmes, Edward. *The life of Mozart: including his correspondence.* London: Chapman and Hall, 1845.

Holmes, John L. *Composers on composers.* New York: Greenwood Press, 1990.

Hopkins, Antony. *The concertgoer's companion.* London: J.M. Dent & Sons Ltd., 1984.

Hopkins, Antony. *The seven concertos of Beethoven.* Aldershot: Scolar Press, 1996.

Holt, Richard. *Nicolas Medtner (1879–1951): a tribute to his art and personality.* London: D. Dobson, 1955.

Honegger, Arthur. *I am a composer.* London: Faber and Faber, 1966.

Hoover, Kathleen and John Cage. *Virgil Thomson: his life and music.* New York; London: T. Yoseloff, 1959.

Horgan, Paul. *Encounters with Stravinsky: a personal record.* London: The Bodley Head, 1972.

Horowitz, Joseph. *Conversations with Arrau.* London: Collins, 1982.

Horowitz, Joseph. Understanding Toscanini. London: Faber and Faber, 1987.

Horwood, Wally. *Adolphe Sax, 1814–1894: his life and legacy.* Bramley: Bramley Books, 1980.

Howie, Crawford. *Anton Bruckner: a documentary biography.* Lewiston, N.Y.; Lampeter: Edwin Mellen Press, 2002.

Hueffer, Francis. *Correspondence of Wagner and Liszt.* New York: Greenwood Press, 2 Vols. 1969.

Hughes, Spike. *The Toscanini legacy: a critical study of Arturo Toscanini's performances of Beethoven, Verdi, and other composers.* London: Putnam, 1959.

Hullah, Annette. *Theodor Leschetizky.* London and New York: J. Land & Co., 1906.

Le Huray, Peter and James Day, Editors. *Music and aesthetics in the eighteenth and early-nineteenth centuries.* Cambridge: Cambridge University Press, 1988.

D'Indy, Vincent. *César Franck.* New York: Dover Publications, 1965.

Jacobs, Arthur. *Arthur Sullivan: A Victorian musician.* Aldershot: Scolar Press, 1992.

Jahn, Otto. *Life of Mozart.* London: Novello, Ewer & Co., 1882.

Jefferson, Alan. *Sir Thomas Beecham: a centenary tribute.* London: World Records Ltd., 1979.

Jezic, Diane. *The musical migration and Ernst Toch.* Ames: Iowa State University Press, 1989.

Johnson, Douglas Porter, Editor. *The Beethoven sketchbooks: history, reconstruction, inventory.* Oxford: Clarendon, 1985.

Johnson, Stephen. *Bruckner remembered.* London: Faber and Faber, 1998.

Jones, David, Wyn. *Beethoven: Pastoral symphony.* Cambridge: Cambridge University Press, 1995.

Jones, David Wyn. *The life of Beethoven.* Cambridge: Cambridge University Press, 1998.

Jones, David Wyn. *The symphony in Beethoven's Vienna.* Cambridge: Cambridge University Press, 2006.

Jones, J. Barrie, Editor. *Gabriel Fauré: a life in letters.* London: Batsford, 1989.

Jones, Peter Ward, Editor and Translator. *The Mendelssohns on honeymoon: the 1837 diary of Felix and Cécile Mendelssohn Bartholdy, together with letters to their families.* Oxford: Clarendon Press, 1997.

Jones, Timothy. *Beethoven, the Moonlight and other sonatas, Op. 27 and Op. 31.* Cambridge; New York, N.Y.: Cambridge University Press, 1999.

Kalischer, A. C., Editor. *Beethoven's letters: a critical edition.* London: J. M. Dent, 1909.

Kárpáti, János. *Bartók's chamber music.* Stuyvesant, New York: Pendragon Press, 1994.

Keefe, Simon P. *The Cambridge companion to the concerto.* Cambridge, New York, N.Y.: Cambridge University Press, 2005.

Keller, Hans. *The great Haydn quartets: their interpretation.* London: J. M. Dent, 1986.

Keller, Hans, Editor. *The memoirs of Carl Flesch.* New York: Macmillan, 1958.

Keller, Hans, and Christopher Wintle. *Beethoven's string quartets in F minor, Op. 95 and C minor, Op. 131: two studies.* Nottingham: Department of Music, University of Nottingham, 1995.

Kelly, Thomas Forrest. *First nights at the opera: five musical premiers.* New Haven: Yale University Press, 2004.

Kennedy, Michael. *Adrian Boult.* London: Hamish Hamilton, 1987.

Kennedy, Michael. *Barbirolli, conductor laureate: the authorised biography.* London: Hart-Davis, MacGibbon, 1973.

Kennedy, Michael, Editor. *The autobiography of Charles Hallé; with correspondence and diaries.* London: Paul Elek, 1972.

Kennedy, Michael. *Hallé tradition: a century of music.* Manchester: Manchester University Press, 1960.

Kennedy, Michael. *The works of Ralph Vaughan Williams.* London: Oxford University Press, 1964.

Kemp, Ian. *Tippett: the composer and his music.* London; New York: Eulenburg Books, 1984.

Kerman, Joseph. *The Beethoven quartets.* London: Oxford University Press, 1967, c1966.

Kerman, Joseph. *Write all these down: essays on music.* Berkeley, California; London: University of California Press, 1994.

Kildea, Paul, Editor. *Britten on music.* Oxford: Oxford University Press, 2003.

Kinderman, William. *Beethoven.* Oxford: Oxford University Press, 1997.

Kinderman, William. *Beethoven's Diabelli variations.* Oxford: Clarendon Press; New York: Oxford University Press, 1987.

Kinderman, William, Editor. *The string quartets of Beethoven.* Urbana, Ilinois: University of Illinois Press, 2005.

King, Alec Hyatt. *Musical pursuits: selected essays.* London: British Library, 1987.

Kirby, F. E. *Music for piano: a short history.* Amadeus Press: Portland, 1995.

Kirkpatrick, John, Editor. *Charles E. Ives: Memos.* New York: W.W. Norton, 1972.

Knapp, Raymond. *Brahms and the challenge of the symphony.* Stuyvesant, N.Y.: Pendragon Press, c.1997.

Knight, Frida. *Cambridge music: from the Middle Ages to modern times.* Cambridge, England.: New York: Oleander Press, 1980.

Knight, Max, Translator. *A confidential matter: the letters of Richard Strauss and Stefan Zweig, 1931–1935.* Berkeley; London: University of California Press, 1977.

Kok, Alexander. *A voice in the dark: the philharmonia years.* Ampleforth: Emerson Edition, 2002.

Kopelson, Kevin. *Beethoven's kiss: pianism, perversion, and the mastery of desire.* Stanford, California: Stanford University Press, 1996.

Kostelanetz, Richard, Editor. *Aaron Copland: a reader; selected writings 1923–1972.* New York; London: Routledge, 2003.

Kostelanetz, Richard. *Conversing with Cage.* New York; London: Routledge, 2003.

Kostelanetz, Richard. *On innovative musicians.* New York: Limelight Editions, 1989.

Kostelanetz, Richard, Editor. *Virgil Thomson: a reader ; selected writings, 1924–1984.* New York; London: Routledge, 2002.

Kowalke, Kim H. *Kurt Weill in Europe.* Ann Arbor, Michigan: UMI Research Press, 1979.

Krehbiel, Henry Edward. *The pianoforte and its music.* New York: Cooper Square Publishers, 1971.

Kruseman, Philip, Editor. *Beethoven's own words.* London: Hinrichsen Edition, 1948.

Kurtz, Michael. *Stockhausen: a biography.* London: Faber and Faber, 1992.

Lam, Basil. *Beethoven string quartets.* Seattle: University of Washington Press, 1975.

Lambert, Constant. *Music ho!: a study of music in decline.* London: Faber and Faber, Ltd. 1934.

Landon, H. C. Robbins. *Beethoven: a documentary study.* London: Thames and Hudson, 1970.

Landon, H. C. Robbins. *Beethoven: his life, work and world.* London: Thames and Hudson,

1992.

Landon, H. C. Robbins. *Essays on the Viennese classical style: Gluck, Haydn, Mozart, Beethoven*. London: Barrie & Rockliff The Cresset Press, 1970.

Landon, H. C. Robbins. *Haydn: chronicle and works/Haydn, the late years, 1801–1809*. Bloomington: Indiana University Press, 1977.

Landon, H. C. Robbins. *Haydn: his life and music*. London: Thames and Hudson, 1988.

Landon, H. C. Robbins. *Haydn in England, 1791–1795*. London: Thames and Hudson, 1976.

Landon, H. C. Robbins. *Haydn: the years of 'The creation', 1796–800*. London: Thames and Hudson, 1977.

Landon, H. C. Robbins. *Mozart: the golden years, 1781–1791*. New York: Schirmer Books, 1989.

Landon, H. C. Robbins. *1791, Mozart's last year*. London: Thames and Hudson, 1988.

Landon, H. C. Robbins *The collected correspondence and London notebooks of Joseph Haydn*. London: Barrie and Rockliff, 1959.

Landon, H. C. Robbins: Editor. *The Mozart companion*. London: Faber, 1956.

Landowska, Wanda. *Music of the past*. London: Geoffrey Bles, 1926.

Lang, Paul Henry. *Musicology and performance*. New Haven: Yale University Press, 1997.

Lang, Paul Henry. *The creative world of Beethoven*. New York: W. W. Norton 1971.

Laurence, Dan H., Editor. *Shaw's music: the complete musical criticism in three volumes*. London: Max Reinhardt, the Bodley Head, 1981.

Lawford-Hinrichsen, Irene. *Music publishing and patronage: C. F. Peters, 1800 to the Holocaust*. Kenton: Edition Press, 2000.

Layton, Robert, Editor. *A guide to the concerto*. Oxford: Oxford University Press, 1996.

Layton, Robert, Editor. *A guide to the symphony*. Oxford: Oxford University Press, 1995.

Lebrecht, Norman. *The maestro myth: great conductors in pursuit of power*. London: Simon & Schuster, 1991.

Lee, Ernest Markham. *The story of the symphony*. London: Scott Publishing Co., 1916.

Leibowitz, Herbert A., Editor. *Musical impressions: selections from Paul Rosenfeld's criticism*. London: G. Allen & Unwin, 1970.

Lenrow, Elbert, Editor and Translator. *The letters of Richard Wagner to Anton Pusinelli*. New York: Vienna House, 1972.

Leonard, Maurice. *Kathleen: the life of Kathleen Ferrier: 1912–1953*. London: Hutchinson, 1988.

Lesure, François and Roger Nichols, Editors. *Debussy, letters*. London: Faber and Faber, 1987.

Letellier, Robert Ignatius, Editor and Translator. *The diaries of Giacomo Meyerbeer*. Madison: Fairleigh Dickinson University Press; London: Associated University Presses, 4 Vols., 1999–2004.

Levas, Santeri. *Sibelius: a personal portrait*. London: J. M. Dent, 1972.

Levy, Alan Howard. *Edward Mac-

Dowell, an American master. Lanham, Md. & London: Scarecrow Press, 1998.

Levy, David Benjamin. *Beethoven: the Ninth Symphony.* New Haven, Connecticut; London: Yale University Press, 2003.

Leyda, Jay and Sergi Bertensson. *The Musorgsky reader: a life of Modeste Petrovich Musorgsky in letters and documents.* New York: W.W. Norton, 1947.

Lewis, Thomas P., Editor. *Raymond Leppard on music: an anthology of critical and personal writings.* White Plains, N.Y.: Pro/Am Music Resources, 1993.

Liébert, Georges. *Nietzsche and music.* Chicago: University of Chicago Press, 2004.

Liszt, Franz. *An artist's journey: lettres d'un bachelier ès musique, 1835-1841.* Chicago: University of Chicago Press, 1989.

Litzmann, Berthold, Editor. *Clara Schumann: an artist's life, based on material found in diaries and letters.* London: Macmillan; Leipzig: Breitkopf & Härtel, 2 Vols. 1913.

Litzmann, Berthold, Editor. *Letters of Clara Schumann and Johannes Brahms, 1853-1896.* New York, Vienna House. 2 Vols. 1971.

Lloyd, Stephen. *William Walton: muse of fire.* Woodbridge, Suffolk: The Boydell Press, 2001.

Locke, Ralph P. and Cyrilla Barr, Editors. *Cultivating music in America: women patrons and activists since 1860.* Berkeley: University of California Press, 1997.

Lockspeiser, Edward. *Debussy: his life and mind.* London: Cassell. 2 Vols. 1962-1965.

Lockspeiser, Edward. *The literary clef: an anthology of letters and writings by French composers.* London: J. Calder. 1958.

Lockwood, Lewis, Editor. *Beethoven essays: studies in honor of Elliot Forbes.* Cambridge, Massachusetts: Harvard University Department of Music: Distributed by Harvard University Press, 1984.

Lockwood, Lewis and Mark Kroll, Editors. *The Beethoven violin sonatas: history, criticism, performance.* Urbana: University of Illinois Press, 2004.

Loft, Abram. *Violin and keyboard: the duo repertoire.* New York: Grossman Publishers. 2 Vols. 1973.

Longyear, Rey Morgan. *Nineteenth-century romanticism in music.* Englewood Cliffs: Prentice-Hall, 1969.

Lowe, C. Egerton. *Beethoven's pianoforte sonatas: hints on their rendering, form, etc., with appendices on definition of sonata, music forms, ornaments, pianoforte pedals, and how to discover keys.* London: Novello, 1929.

Macdonald, Hugh, Editor. *Berlioz: Selected letters.* London: Faber and Faber, 1995.

Macdonald, Malcolm, Editor. *Havergal Brian on music: selections from his journalism: Volume One, British music.* London: Toccata Press, 1986.

MacDonald, Malcolm. *Varèse: astronomer in sound.* London: Kahn & Averill, 2003.

MacDowell, Edward. *Critical and historical essays: lectures deliv-*

ered at Columbia University. Edited by W. J. Baltzell. London: Elkin; Boston: A.P. Schmidt, 1912.

MacFarren, Walter. Memories: an autobiography. London: Walter Scott Publishing Co.,1905.

Mackenzie, Alexander Campbell. *A musician's narrative.* London: Cassell and company, Ltd, 1927.

McCarthy, Margaret William, Editor. *More letters of Amy Fay: the American years, 1879–1916.* Detroit: Information Coordinators, 1986.

McClary, Susan. *Feminine endings: music, gender, and sexuality.* Minneapolis: University of Minnesota Press, 1991.

McClatchie, Stephen, Editor and Translator. *The Mahler family letters.* Oxford: Oxford University Press, 2006.

McVeigh, Simon. *Concert life in London from Mozart to Haydn.* Cambridge: Cambridge University Press, 1993.

Mahler, Alma. *Gustav Mahler: memories and letters.* Enlarged edition revised and edited and with and introduction by Donald Mitchell. London: John Murray, 1968.

Mai, François Martin. *Diagnosing genius: the life and death of Beethoven.* Montreal; London: McGill-Queen's University Press, 2007.

Del Mar, Norman. *Orchestral variations: confusion and error in the orchestral repertoire.* London: Eulenburg, 1981.

Del Mar, Norman. *Richard Strauss: a critical commentary on his life and works.* London: Barrie & Jenkins. 3 Vols. 1978.

(La) Mara [pseudonym]. *Letters of Franz Liszt.* London: H. Grevel & Co., 2 Vols. 1894.

Marek, George Richard. *Puccini.* London: Cassell & Co., 1952.

Marek, George Richard. *Toscanini.* London: Vision, 1976.

(De) Marliave, Joseph. *Beethoven's quartets.* New York: Dover Publications (reprint), 1961.

Martin, George Whitney. *Verdi: his music, life and times.* London: Macmillan, 1965.

Martner, Knud, Editor. *Selected letters of Gustav Mahler.* London; Boston: Faber and Faber, 1979.

Martyn, Barrie. *Nicolas Medtner: his life and music.* Aldershot: Scolar Press, 1995.

Martyn, Barrie. *Rachmaninoff: composer, pianist, conductor.* Aldershot: Scolar, 1990.

Massenet, Jules. *My recollections.* Westport, Connecticut: Greenwood Press.1970.

Matheopoulos, Helena. *Maestro: encounters with conductors of today.* London: Hutchinson, 1982.

Matthews, Denis. *Beethoven.* London: J. M. Dent, 1985.

Matthews, Denis. *Beethoven piano sonatas.* London: British Broadcasting Corporation, 1967.

Matthews, Dennis. *In pursuit of music.* London: Victor Gollancz Ltd., 1968.

Matthews, Denis. *Keyboard music.* Newton Abbot: London David & Charles, 1972.

Mellers, Wilfrid Howard. *Caliban reborn: renewal in twentieth-century music.* London: Victor Gollancz, 1967.

Mellers, Wilfrid Howard. *The sonata

principle (from c. 1750). London: Rockliff, 1957.

Mendelssohn Bartholdy. *Letters from Italy and Switzerland*. London: Longman, Green, Longman, and Roberts, 1862.

Mendelssohn Bartholdy, Paul. *Letters of Felix Mendelssohn Bartholdy, from 1833 to 1847*. London: Longman, Green, Longman, Roberts, & Green, 1864.

Menuhin, Yehudi and Curtis W. Davis. *The music of man*. London: Macdonald and Jane's, 1979.

Menuhin, Yehudi. *Theme and variations*. London: Heinemann Educational Books Ltd., 1972.

Menuhin, Yehudi. *Unfinished journey*. London: Macdonald and Jane's, 1977.

Messian, Olivier. *Music and color: conversations with Claude Samuel*. Portland, Oregon: Amadeus, 1994.

Miall, Antony. *Musical bumps*. London: J.M. Dent & Sons Ltd, 1981.

Michotte, Edmond. *Richard Wagner's visit to Rossini (Paris 1860): and, An evening at Rossini's in Beau-Sejour (Passy), 1858*. Chicago; London: University of Chicago Press, 1982.

Mies, Paul. *Beethoven's sketches: an analysis of his style based on a study of his sketchbooks.*

New York: Johnson Reprint, 1969.

Milhaud, Darius. *My happy life*. London: Boyars, 1995.

Miller, Mina. *The Nielsen companion*. London: Faber and Faber, 1994.

Milsom, David. *Theory and practice in late nineteenth-century violin performance: an examination of style in performance, 1850–1900*. Aldershot: Ashgate, 2003.

Mitchell, Donald, Editor. *Letters from a life: the selected letters and diaries of Benjamin Britten 1913–1976*. London: Faber and Faber. 3 Vols., 1991.

Mitchell, Donald and Hans Keller, Editors. *Music survey: new series 1949–1952*. London: Faber Music in association with Faber & Faber, 1981.

Mitchell, Jon C. *A comprehensive biography of composer Gustav Holst, with correspondence and diary excerpts: including his American years*. Lewiston, New York: Edwin Mellen Press, 2001.

Moldenhauer, Hans. *Anton von Webern: a chronicle of his life and work*. London: Victor Gollancz, 1978.

Monrad-Johansen. Edvard Grieg. New York: Tudor Publishing Co., 1945.

Moore, Gerald. *Am I too loud?: memoirs of an accompanist*. London: Hamish Hamilton, 1962.

Moore, Gerald. *Farewell recital: further memoirs*. Harmondsworth: Penguin Books, 1979.

Moore, Gerald. *Furthermoore: interludes in an accompanist's life*. London: Hamish Hamilton, 1983.

Moore, Jerrold Northrop. *Edward Elgar: a creative life*. Oxford: Oxford University Press, 1984.

Moore, Jerrold Northrop. *Elgar, Edward. The windflower letters: correspondence with Alice Caroline Stuart Wortley and her family*. Oxford: Clarendon Press; New York: Oxford Uni-

versity Press, 1989.
Moore, Jerrold Northrop. *Elgar, Edward. Edward Elgar: letters of a lifetime.* Oxford: Clarendon Press; New York: Oxford University Press, 1990.
Moore, Jerrold Northrop. *Elgar, Edward. Elgar and his publishers: letters of a creative life.* Oxford: Clarendon, 1987.
Moreux, Serge. *Béla Bartók.* London: Harvill Press, 1953.
Morgan, Kenneth. *Fritz Reiner, maestro and martinet.* Urbana: University of Illinois Press, 2005.
Cone, Edward T., Editor. *Music, a view from Delft: selected essays.* Chicago: University of Chicago Press, 1989.
Morgan, Robert P. *Twentieth-century music: a history of musical style in modern Europe and America.* New York: Norton, 1991.
Morgenstern, Sam., Editor. *Composers on music: an anthology of composers' writings.* London: Faber & Faber, 1956.
Morrow, Mary Sue. *Concert life in Haydn's Vienna: aspects of a developing musical and social institution.* Stuyvesant, New York: Pendragon Press, 1989.
Moscheles, Felix, Editor and Translator. *Letters from Felix Mendelssohn-Bartholdy to Ignaz and Charlotte Moscheles.* London: Trübner and Co., 1888.
Mudge, Richard B., Translator. *Glinka, Mikhail Ivanovich: Memoirs.* Norman: University of Oklahoma Press, 1963.
Munch, Charles. *I am a conductor.* New York: Oxford University Press, 1955.
Mundy, Simon. *Bernard Haitink: a working life.* London: Robson Books, 1987.
Musgrave, Michael. *The musical life of the Crystal Palace.* Cambridge: Cambridge University Press, 1995.
Music & Letters. *Beethoven: special number.* London: Music & Letters, 1927.
Musical Times. *Special Issue.* John A. Fuller-Maitland London: Vol. VIII, No. 2, 1927.
Myers, Rollo H., Editor. *Twentieth-century music.* London: Calder and Boyars, 1960.
National Gallery (Great Britain). *Music performed at the National Gallery concerts, 10th October 1939 to 10th April 1946.* London: Privately printed, 1948.
Nattiez, Jean-Jacques, Editor. *Orientations: collected writings – Pierre Boulez.* London: Faber and Faber, 1986.
Nauhaus, Gerd, Editor. *The marriage diaries of Robert & Clara Schumann.* London: Robson Books, 1994.
Nectoux, Jean Michel. *Gabriel Fauré: a musical life.* Translated by Roger Nichols. Cambridge: Cambridge University Press, 1991.
Nettl, Paul. *Beethoven handbook.* Westport, Connecticut: Greenwood Press, 1975.
Neumayr, Anton. *Music and medicine.* Bloomington, Illinois: Medi-Ed Press, 1994–1997
Newbould, Brian. *Schubert and the symphony: a new perspective.* Surbiton: Toccata Press, 1992.
Newlin, Dika. *Schoenberg remembered: diaries and recollections (1938–76).* New York: Pendragon Press, 1980.
Newman, Ernest. *From the world of*

Newman, Ernest. *music: essays from 'The Sunday Times'.* London: J. Calder, 1956.

Newman, Ernest. *Hugo Wolf.* New York: Dover Publications, 1966.

Newman, Ernest, Annotated and Translated. *Memoirs of Hector Berlioz from 1803 to 1865, comprising his travels in Germany, Italy, Russia, and England.* New York: Knopf, 1932.

Newman, Ernest. *More essays from the world of music: essays from the 'Sunday Times'.* London: John Calder, 1958.

Newman, Ernest. *Musical studies.* London; New York: John Lane, 1910.

Newman, Ernest. *Testament of music: essays and papers.* London: Putnam, 1962.

Newman, Richard. *Alma Rosé: Vienna to Auschwitz.* Portland, Oregon: Amadeus Press, 2000.

Newman, William S. *The sonata in the classic era.* Chapel Hill: University of North Carolina Press 1963.

Newman, William S. *The sonata in the Classic era.* New York; London: W.W. Norton, 1983.

Newmarch, Rosa Harriet. *Henry J. Wood.* London & New York: John Lane, 1904.

Nicholas, Jeremy. *Godowsky: the pianists' pianist; a biography of Leopold Godowsky.* Hexham: Appian Publications & Recordings, 1989.

Nichols, Roger. *Debussy remembered.* London: Faber and Faber, 1992.

Nichols, Roger. *Mendelssohn remembered.* London: Faber and Faber, 1997.

Nichols, Roger. *Ravel remembered.* London: Faber and Faber, 1987.

Niecks, Frederick. *Robert Schumann.* London: J. M. Dent, 1925.

Nielsen, Carl. *Living music.* Copenhagen, Wilhelm Hansen, 1968.

Nielsen, Carl. *My childhood.* Copenhagen, Wilhelm Hansen, 1972.

Nikolska, Irina. *Conversations with Witold Lutoslawski, (1987–92).* Stockholm: Melos, 1994.

Nohl, Ludwig. *Beethoven depicted by his contemporaries.* London: Reeves, 1880.

De Nora, Tia. *Beethoven and the construction of genius: musical politics in Vienna, 1792–1803.* Berkeley: University of California Press, 1997.

Norton, Spencer, Editor and Translator. *Music in my time: the memoirs of Alfredo Casella.* Norman: University of Oklahoma Press, 1955.

Nottebohm, Gustav. *Two Beethoven sketchbooks: a description with musical extracts.* London: Gollancz, 1979.

Oakeley, Edward Murray. *The life of Sir Herbert Stanley Oakeley.* London: George Allen, 1904.

Lucas, Brenda and Michael Kerr. *Virtuoso: the story of John Ogdon.* London: H. Hamilton, 1981.

Oliver, Michael, Editor. *Settling the score: a journey through the music of the twentieth century.* London: Faber and Faber, 1999.

Olleson, Philip. *Samuel Wesley: the man and his music.* Woodbridge: Boydell Press, 2003.

Olleson, Philip, Editor. *The letters of Samuel Wesley: professional and social correspondence, 1797–1837.* Oxford; New York: Oxford University Press, 2001.

Olmstead, Andrea. *Conversations with Roger Sessions.* Boston: Northeastern University Press, 1987.

Orenstein, Arbie, Editor. *A Ravel reader: correspondence, articles, interviews.* New York: Columbia University Press, 1990.

Orenstein, Arbie. *Ravel: man and musician.* New York: Columbia University Press, 1975.

Orledge, Robert. *Charles Koechlin (1867–1950): his life and works.* New York: Harwood Academic Publishers, 1989.

Orledge, Robert. *Gabriel Fauré.* London: Eulenburg Books, 1979.

Orledge, Robert. *Satie remembered.* London: Faber and Faber, 1995.

Orledge, Robert. *Satie the composer.* Cambridge: Cambridge University Press, 1990.

Orlova, Alexandra. *Glinka's life in music: a chronicle.* Ann Arbor: UMI Research Press, 1988.

Orlova, Alexandra. *Musorgsky's days and works: a biography in documents.* Ann Arbor: UMI Research Press, 1983.

Orlova, Alexandra. *Tchaikovsky: a self-portrait.* Oxford: Oxford University Press, 1990.

Osborne, Charles, Editor and Translator. *Letters of Giuseppe Verdi.* London: Victor Gollancz, 1971.

Osmond-Smith David, Editor and Translator. *Luciano Berio: Two interviews with Rossana Dalmonte and Bálint András Varga.* New York; London: Boyars, 1985.

Ouellette, Fernand. *Edgard Varèse.* London: Calder & Boyars, 1973.

Paderewski, Ignacy Jan and Mary Lawton. *The Paderewski memoirs.* London: Collins, 1939.

Page, Tim: Editor. *The Glenn Gould reader.* London: Faber and Faber, 1987.

Page, Tim. *Music from the road: views and reviews, 1978–1992.* New York; Oxford: Oxford University Press, 1992.

Page, Tim and Vanessa Weeks, Editors. *Selected letters of Virgil Thomson.* New York: Summit Books, 1988.

Page, Tim. *Tim Page on music: views and reviews.* Portland, Oregon: Amadeus Press, 2002.

Palmer, Christopher. *Herbert Howells, (1892–1983): a celebration.* London: Thames, 1996.

Palmer, Christopher, Editor. *Sergei Prokofiev: Soviet diary 1927 and other writings.* London: Faber and Faber, 1991.

Palmer, Fiona M. *Domenico Dragonetti in England (1794–1846): the career of a double bass virtuoso.* Oxford: Clarendon, 1997.

Palmieri, Robert, Editor. *Encyclopedia of the piano.* New York: Garland, 1996.

Panufnik, Andrzej. *Composing myself.* London: Methuen, 1987.

Parsons, James, Editor. *The Cambridge companion to the Lied.* Cambridge: Cambridge University Press, 2004.

Paynter, John, Editor. *Between old worlds and new: occasional writings on music by Wilfrid Mellers.* London: Cygnus Arts, 1997.

Pestelli, Giorgio. *The age of Mozart and Beethoven.* Cambridge: Cambridge University Press, 1984.

Peyser, Joan. *Bernstein: a biography: revised & updated.* New York: Billboard Books, 1998.

Phillips-Matz, Mary Jane. *Verdi: a biography.* Oxford: Oxford University Press, 1993.

Piggott, Patrick. *The life and music of John Field, 1782–1837: creator of the nocturne.* London: Faber and Faber, 1973.

Plantinga, Leon. *Beethoven's concertos: history, style, performance.* New York: Norton, 1999.

Plantinga, Leon. *Clementi: his life and music.* London: Oxford University Press, 1977.

Plantinga, Leon. *Romantic music: a history of musical style in nineteenth-century Europe.* New York; London: Norton, 1984.

Plaskin, Glenn. *Horowitz: a biography of Vladimir Horowitz.* London: Macdonald, 1983.

Pleasants, Henry, Editor and Translator. *Hanslick, Eduard: Music criticisms, 1846–99.* Baltimore: Penguin Books, 1963.

Pleasants, Henry, Editor and Translator. *Hanslick's music criticisms.* New York: Dover Publications, 1988.

Pleasants, Henry, Editor and Translator. *The music criticism of Hugo Wolf.* New York: Holmes & Meier Publishers, 1978.

Pleasants, Henry, Editor and Translator. *The musical journeys of Louis Spohr.* Norman: University of Oklahoma Press, 1961.

Pollack, Howard. *Aaron Copland: the life and work of an uncommon man.* New York: Henry Holt, 1999.

Poulenc, Francis. *My friends and myself.* London: Dennis Dobson, 1978.

Powell, Richard, Mrs. *Edward Elgar: memories of a variation.* Aldershot, Hants, England: Scolar Press; Brookfield, Vermont, USA: Ashgate Publishing. Co., 1994.

Poznansky, Alexander, Editor. *Tchaikovsky through others' eyes.* Bloomington: Indiana University Press, 1999.

Praeger, Ferdinand. *Wagner as I knew him.* London; New York: Longmans, Green, 1892.

Previn, Andre. *Antony Hopkins. Music face to face.* London, Hamish Hamilton, 1971.

Prieberg, Fred K. *Trial of strength: Wilhelm Furtwängler and the Third Reich.* London: Quartet, 1991.

Procter-Gregg, Humphrey. *Beecham remembered.* London: Duckworth, 1976.

Prokofiev, Sergey. *Prokofiev by Prokofiev: a composer's memoir.* London: Macdonald and Jane's, 1979.

Rachmaninoff, Sergei. *Rachmaninoff's recollections told to Oskar von Riesemann.* London: George Allen & Unwin, 1934.

Radcliffe, Philip. *Beethoven's string quartets.* Cambridge: Cambridge University Press, 1978.

Radcliffe, Philip. *Piano Music in: The Age of Beethoven, The New Oxford History of Music, Vol. VIII.* Gerald Abraham, (Editor), 1988, p. 340.

Ratner, Leonard G. *Romantic music: sound and syntax.* New York: Schirmer Books, 1992.

Raynor, Henry. *A social history of music: from the middle ages to Beethoven.* London: Barrie & Jenkins, 1972.

Rees, Brian. *Camille Saint-Saëns: a life.* London: Chatto & Windus, 1999.

Reich, Willi, Editor. *Anton Webern: The path to the new music.* London; Bryn Mawr: Theodore Presser in association with Universal Edition, 1963.

Reid, Charles. *John Barbirolli: a biography.* London, Hamish Hamilton, 1971.

Reid, Charles. *Malcolm Sargent: a biography.* London: Hamilton, 1968.

Rennert, Jonathan. *William Crotch (1775–1847): composer, artist, teacher.* Lavenham: Terence Dalton, 1975.

Rice, John A. *Antonio Salieri and Viennese Opera.* Chicago, Illinois: University of Chicago Press, 1998.

Rice, John A. *Empress Marie Therese and music at the Viennese court, 1792–1807.* Cambridge: Cambridge University Press, 2003.

Richards, Fiona. *The Music of John Ireland.* Aldershot: Ashgate, 2000.

Rigby, Charles. *Sir Charles Hallé: a portrait for today.* Manchester: Dolphin Press, 1952.

Ringer, Alexander, Editor. *The early Romantic era: between Revolutions; 1789 and 1848.* Basingstoke: Macmillan, 1990.

Roberts, John P.L. and Ghyslaine Guertin, Editors. *Glenn Gould: Selected letters.* Toronto; Oxford: Oxford University Press, 1992.

Robertson, Alec. *More than music.* London: Collins, 1961.

Robinson, Harlow, Editor and Translator. *Selected letters of Sergei Prokofiev.* Boston: Northeastern University Press, 1998.

Robinson, Harlow. *Sergei Prokofiev: a biography.* London: Hale, 1987.

Robinson, Paul A. *Ludwig van Beethoven, Fidelio.* Cambridge: Cambridge University Press, 1996.

Robinson, Suzanne, Editor. *Michael Tippett: music and literature.* Aldershot: Ashgate, 2002.

Rochberg, George. *The aesthetics of survival: a composer's view of twentieth-century music.* Ann Arbor, Michigan: University of Michigan Press, 2004.

Rodmell, Paul. *Charles Villiers Stanford.* Aldershot: Ashgate, 2002.

Roeder, Michael Thomas. *A history of the concerto.* Portland, Oregon: Amadeus Press, 1994.

Rohr, Deborah Adams. *The careers of British musicians, 1750–1850: a profession of artisans.* Cambridge: Cambridge University Press, 2001.

Rolland, Romain. *Goethe and Beethoven.* New York; London: Blom, 1968.

Rolland, Romain. *Beethoven and Handel.* London: Waverley Book Co., 1917.

Rolland, Romain. *Beethoven the creator.* Garden City, New York: Garden City Pub., 1937.

Roscow, Gregory, Editor. *Bliss on music: selected writings of Arthur Bliss, 1920–1975.* Oxford: Oxford University Press, 1991.

Rosen, Charles. *Beethoven's piano sonatas: a short companion.* New Haven, Connecticut: London: Yale University Press, 2002.

Rosen, Charles. *Critical entertainments: music old and new.* Cambridge, Massachusetts; London: Harvard University Press, 2000.

Rosen, Charles. *The classical style: Haydn, Mozart, Beethoven.* London: Faber and Faber, 1976.

Rosen, Charles. *The romantic generation.* Cambridge, Massachusetts: Harvard University Press, 1995.

Rosenthal, Albi. *Obiter scripta: essays, lectures, articles, interviews and reviews on music, and other subjects.* Oxford: Offox Press; Lanham: Scarecrow Press, 2000.

Rostal, Max. *Beethoven: the sonatas for piano and violin; thoughts on their interpretation.* London: Toccata Press, 1985.

Rostropovich, Mstislav and Galina Vishnevskaya. *Russia, music, and liberty.* Portland, Oregan: Amadeus Press, 1995.

Rubinstein, Arthur. *My many years.* London: Jonathan Cape, 1980.

Rubinstein, Arthur. *My young years.* London: Jonathan Cape, 1973.

Rumph, Stephen C. *Beethoven after Napoleon: political romanticism in the late works.* Berkeley; London: University of California Press, 2004.

Rye, Matthew Rye. *Notes to the BBC Radio Three Beethoven Experience, Friday 10 June 2005,* www.bbc.co.uk/radio3/Beethoven.

Sachs, Harvey. *Toscanini.* London: Weidenfeld and Nicholson, 1978.

Sachs, Joel. *Kapellmeister Hummel in England and France.* Detroit: Information Coordinators, 1977.

Saffle, Michael, Editor. *Liszt and his world: proceedings of the International Liszt Conference held at Virginia Polytechnic Institute and State University, 20–23 May 1993.* Stuyvesant, New York: Pendragon Press, 1998.

Safránek, Milos. *Bohuslav Martinu, his life and works.* London: Allan Wingate, 1962.

Saint-Saëns, Camille. *Outspoken essays on music.* Westport, Connecticut: Greenwood Press, 1970.

Saussine, Renée de. *Paganini.* Westport, Connecticut: Greenwood Press, 1976.

Sayers, W. C. Berwick. *Samuel Coleridge-Taylor, musician: his life and letters.* London; New York: Cassell and Co., 1915.

Schaarwächter, Jürgen. *HB: aspects of Havergal Brian.* Aldershot: Ashgate, 1997.

Schafer, R. Murray. *E.T.A. Hoffmann and music.* Toronto: University of Toronto Press, 1975.

Schafer, R. Murray, Editor. *Ezra Pound and music: the complete criticism.* London: Faber and Faber, 1978.

Schat, Peter. *The tone clock.* Chur, Switzerland; Langhorne, Pa.: Harwood Academic Publishers, 1993.

Schenk, Erich. *Mozart and his times.* Edited and Translated by Richard and Clara Winstin. London: Secker & Warburg, 1960.

Schindler, Anton Felix. *Beethoven as I knew him.* Edited by Donald W. MacArdle and Translated by Constance S. Jolly from the German edition of 1860 London: Faber and Faber, 1966.

Schlosser, Johann. *Beethoven: the first biography, 1827.* Edited by Barry Cooper. Portland, Oregon: Amadeus Press, 1996.

Schnabel, Artur. *My life and music.*

London: Longmans, 1961.

Schnittke, Alfred. *A Schnittke reader*. Bloomington: Indiana University Press, 2002.

Scholes, Percy Alfred. *Crotchets: a few short musical notes*. London: John Lane, 1924.

Schonberg, Harold C. *The great pianists*. London: Victor Gollancz, 1964.

Schrade, Leo. *Beethoven in France: the growth of an idea*. New Haven; London: Yale University Press, H. Milford, Oxford University Press, 1942.

Schrade, Leo. *Tragedy in the art of music*. Cambridge, Massachusetts: Harvard University Press, 1964.

Schuh, Willi. *Richard Strauss: a chronicle of the early years 1864–1898*. Cambridge: Cambridge University Press, 1982.

Schuh, Willi, Editor. *Richard Strauss: Recollections and reflections*. London; New York: Boosey & Hawkes, 1953.

Schuller, Gunther. *Musings: the musical worlds of Gunther Schuller*. New York: Oxford University Press, 1986.

Schumann, Robert. *Music and musicians: essays and criticisms*. London: William Reeves, 1877.

Schuttenhelm, Editor. *Selected letters of Michael Tippett*. London: Faber and Faber, 2005.

Schwartz, Elliott. *Music since 1945: issues, materials, and literature*. New York: Schirmer Books, 1993.

Scott, Marion M. *Beethoven: (The master musicians)*. London: Dent, 1940.

Scott-Sutherland, Colin. *Arnold Bax*. London: J. M. Dent, 1973.

Searle, Muriel V. *John Ireland: the man and his music*. Tunbridge Wells: Midas Books, 1979.

Secrest, Meryle. *Leonard Bernstein: a life*. London: Bloomsbury, 1995.

Seeger, Charles. *Studies in musicology II, 1929–1979*. Edited by Anne M. Pescatello. Berkeley; London: University of California Press, 1994.

Selden-Goth, Gisela, Editor. *Felix Mendelssohn: letters*. London: Paul Elek Publishers Ltd, 1946.

Senner, Wayne M., Robin Wallace and William Meredith, Editors. *The critical reception of Beethoven's compositions by his German contemporaries*. Lincoln: University of Nebraska Press, in association with the American Beethoven Society and the Ira F. Brilliant Center for Beethoven Studies, San José State University, 1999.

Seroff, Victor I. *Rachmaninoff*. London: Cassell & Company, 1951.

Sessions, Roger. *Questions about music*. Cambridge, Massachusetts: Harvard University Press, 1970.

Sessions, Roger. *The musical experience of composer, performer, listener*. New York: Atheneum, 1966, 1950.

Seyfried, Ignaz von. *Louis van Beethoven's Studies in thorough-bass, counterpoint and the art of scientific composition*. Leipzig; New-York: Schuberth and Company, 1853.

Sharma, Bhesham R. *Music and culture in the age of mechanical reproduction*. New York: Peter Lang, 2000.

Shaw, Bernard. *How to become a musical critic.* London: R. Hart Davis, 1960.

Shaw, Bernard. *London music in 1888–89 as heard by Corno di Bassetto (later known as Bernard Shaw): with some further autobiographical particulars.* London: Constable and Company, 1937.

Shaw, Bernard. *Music in London, 1890–1894.* London: Constable and Company Limited, 3 Vols., 1932.

Shedlock, John South. *Beethoven's pianoforte sonatas: the origin and respective values of various readings.* London: Augener Ltd., 1918.

Shedlock, John South. *The pianoforte sonata: its origin and development.* London: Methuen, 1895.

Shepherd, Arthur. *The string quartets of Ludwig van Beethoven.* Cleveland: H. Carr, The Printing Press, 1935.

Sheppard, Leslie and Herbert R. Axelrod. *Paganini: containing a portfolio of drawings by Vido Polikarpus.* Neptune City, New Jersey: Paganiniana Publications, 1979.

Short, Michael. *Gustav Holst: the man and his music.* Oxford: Oxford University Press, 1990.

Shostakovich, Dmitry. *Dmitry Shostakovich: about himself and his times.* Moscow: Progress Publishers, 1981.

Simpson, John Palgrave. *Carl Maria von Weber: the life of an artist, from the German of his son Baron, Max Maria von Weber.* London: Chapman and Hall, 1865.

Simpson, Robert. *Beethoven symphonies.* London: British Broadcasting Corporation, 1970.

Sipe, Thomas. *Beethoven: Eroica symphony.* Cambridge: Cambridge University Press, 1998.

Sitwell, Sacheverell. *Mozart.* Edinburgh: Peter Davies Limited, 1932.

Skelton, Geoffrey. *Paul Hindemith: the man behind the music; a biography.* London: Victor Gollancz, 1975.

Smallman, Basil. *The piano trio: its history, technique, and repertoire.* Oxford: Clarendon Press; Oxford; New York: Oxford University Press, 1990.

Smidak, Emil. *Isaak-Ignaz Moscheles: the life of the composer and his encounters with Beethoven, Liszt, Chopin, and Mendelssohn.* Aldershot, Hampshire, England: Scolar Press; Brookfield, Vermont, USA: Gower Publishing Co., 1989.

Smith, Barry. *Peter Warlock: the life of Philip Heseltine.* Oxford: Oxford University Press, 1994.

Smith, Joan Allen. *Schoenberg and his circle: a Viennese portrait.* New York: Schirmer Books, London: Collier Macmillan, 1986.

Smith, Richard Langham, Editor. *Debussy on music: the critical writings of the great French composer Claude Debussy.* London: Secker & Warburg, 1977.

Smith, Ronald. *Alkan.* London: Kahn and Averill, 1976.

Snowman, Daniel. *The Amadeus Quartet: the men and the music.* London: Robson Books, 1981.

Solomon, Maynard. *Beethoven.* New York: Schirmer, 1977.

Solomon, Maynard. *Beethoven*

essays. Cambridge, Massachusetts; London: Harvard University Press, 1988.

Solomon, Maynard. *Late Beethoven: music, thought, imagination.* Berkeley; London: University of California Press, 2003.

Solomon, Maynard. *Mozart: a life.* London: Hutchinson, 1995.

Sonneck, Oscar George Theodore. *Beethoven: impressions of contemporaries.* London: Oxford University Press, 1927.

Spalding, Albert. *Rise to follow: an autobiography.* London: Frederick Muller Ltd., 1946.

Spohr, Louis. *Louis Spohr's autobiography.* London: Longman, Green, Longman, Roberts, & Green, 1865.

Stafford, William. *Mozart myths: a critical reassessment.* Stanford, California: Stanford University Press, 1991.

Stanford, Charles Villiers. *Interludes: records and reflections.* London: John Murray, 1922.

Stanley, Glenn, Editor. *The Cambridge companion to Beethoven.* Cambridge; New York: Cambridge University Press, 2000

Stedman, Preston. *The symphony.* Englewood Cliffs, New Jersey; London: Prentice-Hall, 1979.

Stedron, Bohumír, Editor and Translator. *Leos Janácek: letters and reminiscences.* Prague: Artia, 1955.

Stein, Erwin, Editor. *Arnold Schoenberg: letters.* London: Faber and Faber, 1964.

Stein, Erwin. *Orpheus in new guises.* London: Rockliff, 1953.

Stein, Jack Madison. *Poem and music in the German lied from Gluck to Hugo Wolf.* Cambridge, Massachusetts: Harvard University Press, 1971.

Stein, Leonard, Editor. *Style and idea: selected writings of Arnold Schoenberg.* London: Faber and Faber, 1975.

Steinberg, Michael P. *Listening to reason: culture, subjectivity, and nineteenth-century music.* Princeton, New Jersey: Princeton University Press, 2004.

Steinberg, Michael. *The concerto: a listener's guide.* New York: Oxford University Press, 1998.

Steinberg, Michael. *The symphony: a listener's guide.* Oxford; New York: Oxford University Press, 1995.

Sternfeld, Frederick William. *Goethe and music: a list of parodies and Goethe's relationship to music; a list of references.* New York: Da Capo Press, 1979.

Stivender, David. *Mascagni: an autobiography compiled, edited and translated from original sources.* New York: Pro/Am Music Resources; London: Kahn & Averill, 1988.

Stone, Else and Kurt Stone, Editors. *The writings of Elliott Carter: an American composer looks at modern music.* Bloomington: Indiana University Press, 1977.

Stowell, Robin. *Beethoven: violin concerto.* Cambridge: Cambridge University Press, 1998.

Stowell, Robin: Editor. *The Cambridge companion to the cello.* Cambridge: Cambridge University Press, 1999.

Stowell, Robin: Editor. *The Cambridge companion to the string quartet.* Cambridge: Cambridge University Press, 2003.

Stratton, Stephen Samuel. *Men-

delssohn. London: J.M. Dent & Co.; New York: E.P. Dutton & Co., 1901.

Straus, Joseph N. *Remaking the past: musical modernism and the influence of the tonal tradition*. Cambridge, Massachusetts: Harvard University Press, 1990.

Stravinsky, Igor. *An autobiography*. London: Calder and Boyars, 1975.

Stravinsky, Igor. *Themes and conclusions*. London: Faber and Faber, 1972.

Stravinsky, Igor and Robert Craft. *Conversations with Igor Stravinsky*. London: Faber and Faber, 1959.

Stravinsky, Igor and Robert Craft. *Dialogues and a diary*. London: Faber and Faber 1968.

Stravinsky, Igor and Robert Craft. *Memories and commentaries*. London: Faber and Faber, 2002.

Strunk, Oliver. *Source readings in music history, 4: The Classic era*. London: Faber and Faber 1981.

Sullivan, Blair, Editor. *The echo of music: essays in honor of Marie Louise Göllner*. Warren, Michigan: Harmonie Park Press, 2004.

Sullivan, Jack, Editor. *Words on music: from Addison to Barzun*. Athens: Ohio University Press, 1990.

Symonette, Lys and Kim H. Kowalke, Editors and Translators. *Speak low (when you speak love): the letters of Kurt Weill and Lotte Lenya*. London: Hamish Hamilton, 1996.

Swalin, Benjamin F. *The violin concerto: a study in German romanticism*. New York, Da Capo Press, 1973.

Szigeti, Joseph. *With strings attached: reminiscences and reflections*. London: Cassell & Co. Ltd, 1949.

Tanner, Michael, Editor. *Notebooks, 1924–1954: Wilhelm Furtwängler*. London: Quartet Books, 1989.

Taylor, Robert, Editor. *Furtwängler on music: essays and addresses*. Aldershot: Scolar, 1991.

Taylor, Ronald. *Kurt Weill: composer in a divided world*. London: Simon & Schuster, 1991.

Tchaikovsky, Peter Ilich. *Letters to his family: an autobiography*. Translated by Galina von Meck. London: Dennis Dobson, 1981.

Tertis, Lionel. *My viola and I: a complete autobiography; with, 'Beauty of tone in string playing', and other essays*. London: Paul Elek, 1974.

Thayer, Alexander Wheelock. *Salieri: rival of Mozart*. Edited by Theodore Albrecht. Kansas City, Missouri: Philharmonia of Greater Kansas City, 1989.

Thomas, Michael Tilson. *Viva voce: conversations with Edward Seckerson*. London: Faber and Faber 1994.

Thomson, Andrew. *Vincent d'Indy and his world*. Oxford: Clarendon Press, 1996.

Thomson, Virgil. *The musical scene*. New York: Greenwood Press, 1968.

Thomson, Virgil. *Virgil Thomson*. London: Weidenfeld & Nicolson, 1967.

Tillard, Françoise. *Fanny Mendelssohn*. Amadeus Press: Portland, 1996.

Tilmouth, Michael, Editor. *Donald Francis Tovey: The classics of music: talks, essays, and other writings previously uncollected.* Oxford: Oxford University Press, 2001

Tippett, Michael. *Moving into Aquarius.* London: Routledge and Kegan Paul, 1959.

Tippett, Michael. *Those twentieth century blues: an autobiography.* London: Hutchinson, 1991.

Todd, R. Larry, Editor. *Nineteenth-century piano music.* New York; London: Routledge, 2004.

Todd, R. Larry, Editor. *Schumann and his world.* Princeton: Princeton University Press, 1994.

Tommasini, Anthony. *Virgil Thomson: composer on the aisle.* New York: W.W. Norton, 1997.

Tortelier, Paul. *A self-portrait: in conversation with David Blum.* London: Heinemann, 1984.

Tovey, Donald Francis. *A Companion to Beethoven's Pianoforte Sonatas.* Revised by Barry Cooper. London: The Associated Board, [1931], 1998.

Tovey, Donald Francis. *Beethoven.* London: Oxford University Press, 1944.

Tovey, Donald Francis. *Essays and lectures on music.* London: Oxford University Press, 1949.

Tovey, Donald Francis. *Essays in musical analysis.* London: Oxford University Press, H. Milford, 7 Vols., 1935–41.

Tovey, Donald Francis. *The forms of music: musical articles from The Encyclopaedia Britannica.* London: Oxford University Press, 1944.

Toye, Francis. *Giuseppe Verdi: his life and works.* London: William Heinemann Ltd., 1931.

Truscott, Harold. *Beethoven's late string quartets.* London: Dobson, 1968.

Tyler, William R. *The letters of Franz Liszt to Olga von Meyendorff, 1871–1886, in the Mildred Bliss Collection at Dumbarton Oaks.* Translated by William R. Tyler. Washington: Dumbarton Oaks, Trustees for Harvard University; Cambridge, Massachusetts: distributed by Harvard University Press, 1979.

Tyrrell, John. *Janácek: years of a life. Vol. 1, (1854–1914) The lonely blackbird.* London: Faber and Faber, 2006.

Tyrrell, John, Editor and Translator. *My life with Janácek: the memoirs of Zdenka Janácková.* London: Faber and Faber, 1998.

Tyson, Alan, Editor. *Beethoven studies 2.* Cambridge: Cambridge University Press, 1977.

Tyson, Alan, Editor. *Beethoven studies 3.* Cambridge: Cambridge University Press, 1982.

Tyson, Alan. *Mozart: studies of the autograph scores.* Cambridge, Massachusetts; London: Harvard University Press, 1987.

Tyson, Alan. *The authentic English editions of Beethoven.* London: Faber and Faber, 1963.

Underwood, J. A., Editor. *Gabriel Fauré: his life through his letters.* London: Marion Boyars, 1984.

Vechten, Carl van, Editor. *Nikolay, Rimsky-Korsakov: My musical life.* London: Martin Secker & Warburg Ltd., 1942.

Vinton, John. *Essays after a dictionary: music and culture at the close of Western civilization.* Lewisburg: Bucknell University Press, 1977.

Volkov, Solomon, Editor. *Testimony: the memoirs of Dmitri Shostakovich. London: Faber and Faber, 1981.

Volta, Ornella, Editor. *A mammal's notebook: collected writings of Erik Satie.* London: Atlas Press, 1996.

Wagner, Richard. Beethoven: *With [a] supplement from the philosophical works of A. Schopenhauer.* Translated by E. Dannreuther. London: Reeves, 1893.

Wagner, Richard. *My life.* London: Constable and Company Ltd., 1911.

Walden, Valerie. *One hundred years of violoncello: a history of technique and performance practice, 1740–1840.* Cambridge: Cambridge University Press, 1998.

Walker, Alan. *Franz Liszt. Volume 1, The virtuoso years: 1811–1847.* New York: Alfred A. Knopf, 1983.

Walker, Alan. *Franz Liszt. Volume 2, The Weimar years: 1848–1861.* London: Faber and Faber, 1989.

Walker, Alan. *Franz Liszt. Volume 3, The final years, 1861–1886.* London: Faber and Faber, 1997.

Walker, Bettina. *My musical experiences.* London: Richard Bentley and Son, 1890.

Walker, Ernest. *Free thought and the musician, and other essays.* London; New York: Oxford University Press, 1946.

Walker, Frank. *Hugo Wolf: a biography.* London: J. M. Dent, 1951.

Walker, Frank. *The man Verdi.* London: Dent, 1962.

Wallace, Grace, [Lady Wallace]. *Beethoven's letters (1790–1826): from the collection of Dr. Ludwig Nohl. Also his letters to the Archduke Rudolph, Cardinal-Archbishop of Olmutz, K.W., from the collection of Dr. Ludwig Ritter Von Kolchel.* London: Longmans, Green, 2 Vols., 1866.

Wallace, Robin. *Beethoven's critics: aesthetic dilemmas and resolutions during the composer's lifetime.* Cambridge; New York: Cambridge University Press, 1986.

Walter, Bruno. *Theme and variations: an autobiography.* London: H. Hamilton, 1948.

Warrack, John Hamilton. *Writings on music.* Cambridge: Cambridge University Press, 1981.

Wasielewski, Wilhelm Joseph von. *Life of Robert Schumann: with letters, 1833–1852.* London: William Reeves, 1878.

Watkins, Glenn. *Proof through the night: music and the Great War.* Berkeley: University of California Press, 2003.

Watkins, Glenn. *Pyramids at the Louvre: music, culture, and collage from Stravinsky to the postmodernists.* Cambridge, Massachusetts; London: Belknap Press of Harvard University Press, 1994.

Watkins, Glenn. *Soundings: music in the twentieth century.* New York: Schirmer Books London: Collier Macmillan, 1988.

Watson, Derek. *Liszt.* London: J. M. Dent, 1989.

Weaver, William, Editor. *The Verdi-Boito correspondence.* Chicago; London: University of Chicago Press, 1994.

Wegeler, Franz. *Remembering Beethoven: the biographical*

notes of Franz Wegeler and Ferdinand Ries. London: Andre Deutsch, 1988.

Weingartner, Felix. *Buffets and rewards: a musician's reminiscences.* London: Hutchinson & Co., 1937.

Weinstock, Herbert. *Rossini: a biography.* New York: Limelight, 1987.

Weiss, Piero and Richard Taruskin. *Music in the Western World: a history in documents.* New York: Schirmer; London: Collier Macmillan, 1984.

Weissweiler, Eva *The complete correspondence of Clara and Robert Schumann.* New York: Peter Lang, 2 Vols., 1994.

Whittaker, William Gillies. *Collected essays.* London: Oxford University Press, 1940.

Whittall, Arnold. *Exploring twentieth-century music: tradition and innovation.* Cambridge; New York: Cambridge University Press, 2003.

Whittall, Arnold. *Music since the First World War.* London: J. M. Dent, 1977.

Whitton, Kenneth S. *Lieder: an introduction to German song.* London: Julia MacRae, 1984.

Wightman, Alistair, Editor. *Szymanowski on music: selected writings of Karol Szymanowski.* London: Toccata Press, 1999.

Wilhelm, Kurt. *Richard Strauss: an intimate portrait.* London: Thames and Hudson, 1999.

Will, Richard James. *The characteristic symphony in the age of Haydn and Beethoven.* Cambridge: Cambridge University Press, 2002.

Willetts, Pamela J. *Beethoven and England: an account of sources in the British Museum.* London: British Museum, 1970.

Williams, Adrian, Editor and Translator. *Liszt, Franz: Selected letters.* Oxford: Clarendon Press, 1998.

Williams, Adrian. *Portrait of Liszt: by himself and his contemporaries.* Oxford: Clarendon Press, 1990.

Williams, Ralph Vaughan. *Heirs and rebels: letters written to each other and occasional writings on music.* London; New York: Oxford University Press, 1959.

Williams, Ralph Vaughan. *Some thoughts on Beethoven's Choral symphony: with writings on other musical subjects.* London; Oxford University Press, 1953.

Williams, Ralph Vaughan. *The making of music.* Ithaca, New York: Cornell University Press, 1955.

Williams, Ursula Vaughan. *R.V.W.: a biography of Ralph Vaughan Williams.* London: Oxford University Press, 1964.

Wilson, Conrad. *Notes on Beethoven: 20 crucial works.* Edinburgh: Saint Andrew Press, 2003.

Wilson, Elizabeth. *Shostakovich: a life remembered.* Princeton, New Jersey: Princeton University Press, 1994.

Winter, Robert, Editor. *Beethoven, performers, and critics: the International Beethoven Congress, Detroit, 1977.* Detroit: Wayne State University Press, 1980.

Winter, Robert. *Compositional origins of Beethoven's opus 131.* Ann Arbor, Michigan: UMI Research Press, 1982.

Winter, Robert and Robert Martin,

Editors. *The Beethoven quartet companion.* Berkeley: University of California Press, 1994.

Wolf, Eugene K. and Edward H. Roesner, Editors. *Studies in musical sources and style: essays in honor of Jan LaRue.* Madison, Wisconsin: A-R Editions, 1990.

Wolff, Christoph and Robert Riggs. *The string quartets of Haydn, Mozart and Beethoven: studies of the autograph manuscripts: a conference at Isham Memorial Library, March 15–17, 1979.* Cambridge, Massachusetts: Department of Music, Harvard University, 1980.

Wolff, Konrad. *Masters of the keyboard: individual style elements in the piano music of Bach, Haydn, Mozart, Beethoven, Schubert, Chopin, and Brahms.* Bloomington: Indiana University Press, 1990.

Wörner, Karl Heinrich. *Stockhausen: life and work.* London: Faber, 1973.

Wright, Donald, Editor. *Cardus on music: a centenary collection.* London: Hamish Hamilton, 1988.

Wyndham, Henry Saxe. *August Manns and the Saturday concerts: a memoir and a retrospect.* London and Felling-on-Tyne, New York, The Walter Scott Publishing Co., Ltd., 1909.

Yastrebtsev, V.V. Edited and Translated by Florence Jonas. *Reminiscences of Rimsky-Korsakov.* New York: Columbia University Press, 1985.

Yates, Peter. *Twentieth century music: its evolution from the end of the harmonic era into the present era of sound.* London: Allen & Unwin Ltd., 1968.

Young, Percy M. *Beethoven: a Victorian tribute based on the papers of Sir George Smart.* London: D. Dobson, 1976.

Young, Percy M. *George Grove, 1820–1900: a biography.* London: Macmillan, 1980.

Young, Percy M. *Letters of Edward Elgar and other writings.* London: Geoffrey Bles, 1956.

Young, Percy M., Editor. *Letters to Nimrod: Edward Elgar to August Jaeger, 1897–1908.* London: Dennis Dobson, 1965.

Young, Percy M. *The concert tradition: from the middle ages to the twentieth century.* London: Routledge and Kegan Paul, 1965.

Young, Rob, Editor. *(Brief Description): Undercurrents: the hidden wiring of modern music.* London; New York, N.Y.: Continuum, 2002.

Yourke, Electra Slonimsky, Editor. *Nicolas Slonimsky: writings on music.* New York, N.Y.; London: Routledge, 4 Vols. 2003-2005.

Slonimsky, Nicolas. *The great composers and their works.* Edited by Electra Slonimsky Yourke. New York: Schirmer Books, 2 Vols. 2000.

Ysaÿe, Antoine. *Ysaÿe: his life, work and influence.* London: W. Heinemann, 1947.

Zamoyski, Adam. *Paderewski.* London: Collins, 1982.

Zegers, Mirjam, Editor. *Louis Andriessen: The art of stealing time.* Todmorden: Arc Music, 2002.

Zemanova, Mirka, Editor. *Janácek's uncollected essays on music.* London: Marion Boyars, 1989.

INDEX

Index to: String Quartets Op. 59, Nos. 1-3; String Quartet, Op. 74; and String Quartet, Op. 95. Incorporating a Beethoven time-line of significant musical and related events.

The order adopted for the listing of the individual entries in this index, for each of the string quartets under consideration, is chronological — according to the sequential unfolding of events under discussion. Thereby, the reader is provided with both a guide to the contents discussed in the main text and a timeline of the principal events bearing on Beethoven's life and work.

THE GALITZIN QUARTETS PP. 1-59

Beethoven's return to quartet writing
Final public performance as pianist
Deafness, implications of
Mälzel's ear trumpets
Beethoven portraits
Cipriani Potter, impressions of
Beethoven
Philharmonic Society of Laibach
Beethoven's evolving musical language
Beethoven and variation form
Extension of quartet medium
Karl Holz, impressions of

Beethoven
Gioacchino Rossini, meeting with Beethoven
Sir John Russell, impressions of Beethoven
Christian Schubart, musical theory
Wilhelm von Lenz, musical theory
Ignaz Schuppanzigh, role in quartet playing
Friedrich Reichardt, impressions of Schuppanzigh
Public interest in string quartet medium
Carl Peters, role in Beethoven's affairs
Adolf Martin Schlesinger, role in Beethoven's affairs
Peters' negotiations with Beethoven
Antonio Pacini, request for string quartet
Nicholas (Nikolai) Galitzin request for string quartets
Beethoven's response to Galitzin
Beethoven's business negotiations with Galitzin
Charles Neate, Beethoven's English negotiations with
Galitzin's protracted negotiations with Beethoven
Missa Solemnis, reception of in Russia
Georg Friedrich Waldmüller, Beethoven's portrait
Anton Neumayr, Beethoven's illnesses
1824, Beethoven honoured
Galitzin, protracted negotiations with
Op. 127, work on
Dr. Johann Malfatti, Beethoven's physician
Dr. Jacob von Staudenheim, Beethoven's physician
Carl Peters, negotiations with
Beethoven's sketches, significance of
Landsberg 11 sketchbook
Score sketches
De Roda Sketchbook
Kullak Sketchbook
Charles Neate, negotiations with
Beethoven's plans to visit London
Philharmonic Society (London), putative negotiations with
Karl Holz, recollections of Beethoven
Moritz (Maurice) Schlesinger, negotiations with
Muzio Clementi, English publication
Gesellschaft der Musikfreunde, Beethoven honoured
Recurrent illness
Mathias Artaria, negotiations with
Galitzin, strained relationship with
Schwarzspanierhaus, Beethoven's final residence
Stephan von Breuning, recollections of
Johann Andreas Stumpff, recollections of
Dr. Andreas Wawruch, Beethoven's physician
Anton Schindler, recollections of
Philharmonic Society, gift of £100
Louis Spohr, recollections of
Franz Schubert, views on contemporary music
Carl Maria von Weber, recollections of
Count Franz von Brunsvik, study of late quartets
Beethoven's views on his string quartets
Early reception of Galitzin Quartets

STRING QUARTET OP. 127 PP. 95-144

Phase of prodigious creative energy
Expansion of musical style
Growing interest in string-quartet genre
Rise of professional string quartet
Ludwig Rellstab
Emergent romanticism

Wilhelm von Lenz
Berliner Allgemeine musikalische Zeitung
Joseph de Marliave
William Kinderman
Paul Griffiths
(Sir) Julius Benedict
Carl Maria Weber
Allgemeine musikalische Zeitung
Early interpretations of Beethoven
Nineteenth-century performances
Hugo Wolf
Donald Tovey
Ezra Pound
Marion Scott
Views of: Igor Stravinsky, Basil Lam, Dennis Matthews
Sketch origins
Quartet-score sketches
Douglas Porter Johnson
Landsberg 8 Bundle 2 (8/2)
Artaria 205 Bundle 4 (205/4)
Grasnick 4
Autograph 11/2
De Roda
Beethoven's 'new method of working'
Stuttgart: *Morgenblatt für gebildete Stände*
Dr. Wilhelm Christian Müller
Sir John Russell
Joseph Carl Stieler, Beethoven's likeness
Gioacchino Rossini, meeting with Beethoven
Carl F. Peters, negotiations with
Nikolay Galitzin, commission for three string quartets
Beethoven's response to Galitzin
Ferdinand Ries
Missa Solemnis
Emperor Louis XVIII, honour of gold medal
Fellow musicians, admiration of
Schott's and Sons, request for compositions
Protracted negotiations with Galitzin
Baden and Beethoven's illness: Dr. Malfatti and Dr. Jacob von Staudenheim
Schuppanzigh String Quartet
New technical challenges
First performance of Op. 127
Joseph Böhm, recollections of
Reception of Op. 130: *Allgemeine musikalische Zeitung, Revue et Gazette musicales de*, Cosima Wagner et al
Musicological estimation

STRING QUARTET, OP. 132 PP. 154-218

Key of A minor
Adolf Bernhard Marx, views of
Mendelsohn, influence on
Romain Rolland, views of
1825, creation origins
Sketchbook sources
Interrelationships between late quartets
Changing thoughts on number of movements
Emotional intensity, heightened expression of
Thematic connections
Ignaz Schuppanzigh, role of
Galitzin, negotiations with
Illness, impairment to progress
Charles Neate, London negotiations with
Adolf Martin Schlesinger, negotiations with
Karl van Beethoven, assistance to Beethoven
Karl Holtz, assistance to Beethoven
Negotiations with publishers
Rehearsals, impressions of
Performance, impressions of
Beethoven's negotiations with Galitzin and publishers
Gesellschaft der Musikfreunde, public performance

AmZ, review
Op. 132 sent to Galitzin
Title Page
English edition
Early reception
Adolf Bernhard Marx, views of
Quartet movements, discussion of
Summative remarks

STRING QUARTET, OP. 130 PP. 224-283

Further expansion of quartet concept
New demands on instrumentalists
Ignaz Schuppanzigh, role of
Quartet structure
Beethoven's negotiations with publishers
Charles Neate, London negotiations
Karl Holz, role of
Adolf and Maurice Schlesinger, publishers
Completion of Op. 130
Ignaz Pleyel, French (Paris) negotiations with
Sketchbook sources for Op. 130
Gerhard von Breuning, recollections of
Wilhelmine Schröder-Devrient, recollections of
Louis Schlösser, recollections of
21 March 1826, first performance
Reception of
Challenge of fugal ending
Galitzin receives Op. 130
Title page
22 April 1827, performance with revised finale
Beethoven's personal estimation of his quartets
Nineteenth-century reception
Quartet movements, discussion of
Summative remarks

ABOUT THE AUTHOR

Terence M. Russell graduated with first class honours in architecture and was a nominee for the coveted Silver Medal of the Royal Institute of British Architects. He is a Fellow of the Royal Incorporation of Architects in Scotland (retired), was formerly Reader in the School of Arts, Culture and Environment at the University of Edinburgh, a Fellow of the British Higher Education Academy, and Senior Assessor to the Scottish Higher Education Funding Council. Alongside his professional work in the field of architecture — embracing practice, teaching and research — he has maintained a lifetime's interest in the music and musicology of Beethoven. He has an equal admiration for the work of Franz Schubert and was for many years an active member of the Schubert Institute, UK. His book writings in the field of architecture include the following:

The Built Environment: A Subject Index, Gregg Publishing (1989):
- Vol. 1: Town planning and urbanism, architecture, gardens and landscape design
- Vol. 2: Environmental technology, constructional engineering, building and materials
- Vol. 3: Decorative art and industrial design, international exhibitions and collections, recreational and performing arts
- Vol. 4: Public health, municipal services, community welfare

Architecture in the Encyclopédie of Diderot and D'Alemebert: The Letterpress Articles and Selected Engravings, Scolar Press (1993)

The Encyclopaedic Dictionary in the Eighteenth Century: Architecture, Arts and Crafts, Scolar Press (1997):
- Vol. 1: John Harris, Lexicon Technicum
- Vol. 2: Ephraim Chambers, Cyclopaedia
- Vol. 3: The Builder's Dictionary
- Vol. 4: Samuel Johnson, A Dictionary of the English Language
- Vol. 5: A Society of Gentlemen, Encyclopaedia Britannica

Gardens and Landscapes in the Encyclopédie of Diderot and D'Alemebert: The Letterpress Articles and Selected Engravings, 2 Vols., Ashgate (1999)

The Napoleonic Survey of Egypt: The Monuments and Customs of Egypt, 2 Vols., Ashgate (2001)

The Discovery of Egypt: Vivant Denon's Travels with Napoleon's Army, History Press (2005)

www.ingramcontent.com/pod-product-compliance
Lightning Source LLC
Chambersburg PA
CBHW011956090526
44590CB00023B/3746